Java™ Security

THE JAVA™ SERIES

Java™ Security

Scott Oaks

O'REILLY™

Cambridge • *Köln* • *Paris* • *Sebastopol* • *Tokyo*

SHROFF PUBLISHERS & DISTRIBUTORS PVT. LTD.
Mumbai   **Calcutta**

Java ™Security
by Scott Oaks

Copyright © 1998 O'Reilly & Associates, Inc. All rights reserved. ISBN: 1-56592-403-7
Originally published by O'Reilly & Associates, Inc., 101 Morris Street, Sebastopol, CA 95472, USA

Editor: Mike Loukides

Production Editor: Jane Ellin

Printing History:

May 1998:	First Edition.
February 1999:	Minor corrections.

First Indian Reprint: April 2000

ISBN: 81-7366-108-1

Published by **Shroff Publishers and Distributors Pvt. Ltd.**, Room No. 8/9, Patel Building, First Floor, 8/16, M.K. Amin Marg, Fort, Mumbai 400 001, Tel: (91 22) 263 1572, 264 1488, Fax: (91 22) 262 3551, e-mail: spd@vsnl.com. Printed at Rose Fine Arts, Kurla, Mumbai

Table of Contents

Preface

When I first mentioned to a colleague of mine that I was writing a book on Java™ security, he immediately starting asking me questions about firewalls and Internet DMZs. Another colleague overheard us and started asking about electronic commerce, which piqued the interest of a third colleague who wanted to hear all about virtual private networks. All this was interesting, but what I really wanted to talk about was how a Java applet could be allowed to read a file.

Such is the danger of anything with the word "security" in its title: security is a broad topic, and everyone has his or her own notion of what security means. Complicating this issue is the fact that Java security and network security (including Internet security) are complementary and sometimes overlapping topics: you can send encrypted data over the network with Java, or you can set up a virtual private network that encrypts all your network traffic and remove the need for encryption within your Java programs.

This is a book about security from the perspective of a Java program. In this book, we discuss the basic platform features of Java that provide security—the class loader, the bytecode verifier, the security manager—and we discuss recent additions to Java that enhance this security model—digital signatures, security providers, and the access controller. The ideas in this book are meant to provide an understanding of the architecture of Java's security model and how that model can be used (both programmatically and administratively).

Who Should Read This Book?

This book is intended primarily for programmers who want to write secure Java applications. Much of the book is focused on various APIs within Java that provide security; we discuss both how those APIs are used by standard Java-enabled browsers and how they can be used in your own Java applications. From a programming perspective, this latter case is the most interesting: Java-enabled browsers have each adopted particular security models, but there's not much a programmer or administrator can do to alter those models. However, this is beginning to change, as technologies like Sun Microsystems' Java Plug-in bring Sun's basic security model to popular browsers.

For the end user or system administrator who is interested in Java security, this book will provide knowledge of the facilities provided by the basic Java platform and how those facilities are used by Java-enabled browsers and by Java applications. We do not delve into the specific security features of any Java-enabled browser, although we do point out along the way which security features of Java are subject to change by the companies that provide Java-enabled browsers. Hence, end users and system administrators can read this book (and skip over many of the programming examples) to gain an understanding of the fundamental security features of the Java platform, and they can understand from each of its parts how the security feature might be administrated (especially for Java applications). This is particularly true for end users and administrators who are interested in assessing the risk of using Java: we give full details of the implementation of Java's security model not only so that you can program within that model (and adjust it if necessary), but also so that you have a deep understanding of how it works and can assess for yourself whether or not Java meets your definition of security.

From a programming perspective, we assume that developers who read this book have a good knowledge of how to program in Java, and in particular how to write Java applications. When we discuss advanced security features and cryptographic algorithms, we do so assuming that the programmer is primarily interested in using the API to perform certain tasks. Hence, we explain at a rudimentary level what a digital signature is and how it is created and used, but we do not explain the cryptographic theory behind a digital signature or prove that a digital signature is secure. For developers who are sufficiently versed in these matters, we also show how the APIs may be extended to support new types of cryptographic algorithms, but again we leave the mathematics and rigorous definitions of cryptography for another book.

Versions Used in This Book

JDK 1.2 FCS has recently been renamed Java 2. We continue to use the older name because it's more familiar and because it's used in the actual code.

Writing a book on Java security has been a challenge for a number of reasons, not the least of which is that the security APIs have been radically changing over the past year. Java 1.1 introduced many of the APIs we'll be discussing in this book, including the notion of a security provider that supplies an implementation of the security package. Java 1.2 introduced significant changes to the security package as well as a new fundamental security object called the "access controller," which takes on much of the responsibility that has resided with the security manager since Java 1.0.

For the most part, we assume that developers using this book will be using the Java 2 platform, and our primary focus will be on the Java Development Kit (JDK) from Sun Microsystems. However, for developers using 1.1, we will provide full details of what's available in 1.1, and what has changed in Java 2; in some cases, this information has changed so radically that the information is relegated to an appendix. Complicating all of this is that while overall there are few differences between the 1.2 beta releases of the JDK and the Java 2 platform, many of those important differences occur in the Security APIs. Unlike the first printing of this book, which focused on the 1.2 beta 3 release, this printing covers the API as it exists only in the Java 2 platform.

For the most part, we do not track changes between 1.0 and 1.1 in this book.

Most of the examples used in this book are available via ftp from the O'Reilly web site, *www.oreilly.com*. A few of the examples have been withheld from the online distribution because of U.S. restrictions on the export of cryptography.

Conventions Used in This Book

Constant width font is used for:

- Code examples
- Class, variable, and method names within the text

Italicized font is used for:

- Filenames
- Host and domain names
- URLs

When a new method or class is introduced, its definition will appear beginning with italicized text like this:

public void checkAccess(Thread t)
    Check whether the current thread is allowed to modify the state of the parameter thread.

In addition, one of the following symbols may appear next to a definition:

   ★ Indicates that the method/class is available only in 1.2.
   ☆ Indicates that the method/class has been deprecated in 1.2.

There are some examples of commands scattered through the book, especially in sections and appendices that deal with administration. By convention, all examples are shown as they would be executed on a Unix system, e.g.:

```
piccolo% keytool -export -alias sdo -file /tmp/sdo.cer
Enter keystore password:  ******
Certificate stored in file </tmp/sdo.cer>
```

In these examples, the text typed by the user or administrator is always shown in bold font; the remaining text is output from the command (the string `piccolo%` indicates a command prompt). On other systems, the names of the files would have to be changed to conform to that system (e.g., *C:\sdo.cer* for a Windows system). However, note that while Windows systems often use a forward-slash (/) for command-line options, Java tools (even on those systems) universally use a hyphen (-) to indicate command-line options. In these examples, then, only the filenames are different between platforms.

Organization of This Book

This book is organized in a bottom-up fashion: we begin with the very low-level aspects of Java security and then proceed to the more advanced features.

Chapter 1, *Java Application Security*

   This chapter gives an overview of the security model (the Java sandbox) used in Java applications and sets the stage for the rest of the book.

Chapter 2, *Java Language Security*

   This chapter discusses the memory protections built into the Java language, how those protections provide a measure of security, and how they are enforced by the bytecode verifier.

Chapter 3, *Java Class Loaders*

   This chapter discusses the class loader, which is the class that reads in Java class files and turns them into classes. From a security perspective, the class loader is important in determining where classes originated and whether or not they were digitally signed (and if so, by whom), so the topic of class loaders appears throughout this book.

Chapter 4, *The Security Manager Class*

This chapter discusses the security manager, which is the primary interface to application-level security in Java. The security manager is responsible for arbitrating access to all local resources: files, the network, printers, etc.

Chapter 5, *The Access Controller*

The access controller is the basis for security manager implementations in Java 1.2. This chapter discusses how to use the access controller to achieve fine-grained levels of security in your application.

Chapter 6, *Implementing Security Policies*

This chapter ties together the information on the security manager and the access controller and shows how to implement one or both to achieve a desired security policy in your application.

Chapter 7, *Introduction to Cryptography*

This chapter provides an overview to the cryptographic algorithms of the Java security package. It provides a background for the remaining chapters in the book.

Chapter 8, *Security Providers*

This chapter discusses the architecture of the Java security package, and how that architecture may be used to extend or supplant the default cryptographic algorithms that come with the JDK.

Chapter 9, *Message Digests*

This chapter discusses message digests: how to create them, how to use them, and how to implement them.

Chapter 10, *Keys and Certificates*

This chapter discusses the APIs available to model cryptographic keys and certificates, and how those keys and certificates may be electronically transmitted.

Chapter 11, *Key Management*

This chapter discusses how keys can be managed within a Java program: how and where they may be stored and how they can be retrieved and validated.

Chapter 12, *Digital Signatures*

This chapter discusses how to create, use, and implement digital signatures. This chapter also contains a discussion of signed classes.

Chapter 13, *Encryption*

This chapter discusses the Java Cryptography Extension, which allows developers to encrypt and decrypt arbitrary streams of traffic.

Appendix A, *Security Tools*

This appendix discusses the administrative tools that come with Java that enable end users and administrators to work with the Java security model: keytool, jarsigner, and policytool.

Appendix B, *Identity-Based Key Management*

Key management in Java 1.1 was radically different than the systems we explored in the main text. This appendix discusses how key management was handled in Java 1.1; it uses classes that are still present (but are deprecated) in 1.2.

Appendix C, *Security Resources*

This appendix discusses how to keep up–to–date with information about Java's security implementation, including a discussion of Java security bugs and general resources for further information.

Appendix D, *Quick Reference*

This appendix is a simple reference guide to the classes that are discussed in this book.

Acknowledgments

I am grateful to the many people who have helped me with this book along the way; this book is as much a reflection of their support as anything else. I offer my heartfelt thanks to Mike Loukides for stewarding me through the editorial process.

Various drafts of this book were foisted upon my colleagues Mark Bordas, Charles Francois, David Plotkin, and Henry Wong; I am indebted to each of them for their feedback and support, and to Wendy Talmont for all her support. In addition, I was extremely fortunate to receive technical assistance from a highly talented group of individuals: to Jim Farley, Li Gong, Jon Meyer, Michael Norman, and especially to David Hopwood, I offer my deepest thanks for all your input. Finally, I must thank Roland Schemers for handling my last-minute barrage of questions with patience and insight.

The staff at O'Reilly & Associates was enormously helpful in producing this book, including Jane Ellin, the Production Editor; Robert Romano, who created the figures; Seth Maislin, who wrote the index; Hanna Dyer, the cover designer;

Nancy Priest, the interior designer; Mike Sierra for Tools support; and Claire Cloutier LeBlanc, Nancy Wolfe Kotary, and Sheryl Avruch for quality control.

Finally, I must offer my thanks to James for all his patience and support, and for putting up with my continual state of distraction during phases of this process.

Feedback for the Author

I welcome any comments on the text that you might have; despite the contributions of the people I've just listed, any errors or omissions in the text are my responsibility. Please send notice of these errors or any other feedback to *scott.oaks@sun.com.*

1

Java Application Security

When Java was first released by Sun Microsystems, it attracted the attention of programmers throughout the world. These developers were attracted to Java for different reasons: some were drawn to Java because of its cross-platform capabilities, some because of its ease of programming (especially compared to object-oriented languages like C++), some because of its robustness and memory management, some because of Java's security, and some for still other reasons.

Just as different developers came to Java with different expectations, so too did they bring different expectations as to what was meant by the ubiquitous phrase "Java is secure." Security means different things to different people, and many developers who had certain expectations about the word "security" were surprised to find that their expectations were not necessarily shared by the designers of Java.

This book discusses the features of Java that make it secure. In this book, we'll discuss why Java is said to be secure, what that security means (and doesn't mean), and—most importantly—how to use the security features of the Java platform within your own programs. This last point is actually the focus of this book: while some of Java's security features are automatically a part of all Java programs, many of them are not. In this book, we'll learn about all those features, and how to utilize them in our own Java applications.

What Is Security?

The first thing that we must do to facilitate our discussion of Java security is to discuss just what Java's security goals are. The term "security" is somewhat vague unless it is discussed in some context; different expectations of the term "security" might lead us to expect that Java programs would be:

- *Safe from malevolent programs*: Programs should not be allowed to harm a user's computing environment. This includes Trojan horses as well as harmful programs that can replicate themselves—computer viruses.

- *Non-intrusive*: Programs should be prevented from discovering private information on the host computer or the host computer's network.

- *Authenticated*: The identity of parties involved in the program should be verified.

- *Encrypted*: Data that the program sends and receives should be encrypted.

- *Audited*: Potentially sensitive operations should always be logged.

- *Well-defined*: A well-defined security specification would be followed.

- *Verified*: Rules of operation should be set and verified.

- *Well-behaved*: Programs should be prevented from consuming too many system resources.

- *C2 or B1 certified*: Programs should have certification from the U.S. government that certain security procedures are included.

In fact, while all of these features could be part of a secure system, only the first two were within the province of Java's 1.0 default security model. Other items in the list have been introduced in later versions of Java: authentication was added in 1.1, encryption is available as an extension to 1.2,* and auditing can be added to any Java program by providing an auditing security manager. Still others of these items will be added in the future. But the basic premise remains that Java security was originally and fundamentally designed to protect the information on a computer from being accessed or modified (including a modification that would introduce a virus) while still allowing the Java program to run on that computer.

The point driving this notion of security is the new distribution model for Java programs. One of the driving forces behind Java, of course, is its ability to download programs over a network and run those programs on another machine within the context of a Java-enabled browser (or within the context of other Java applications). Coupled with the widespread growth of Internet use—and the public-access nature of the Internet—Java's ability to bring programs to a user on an as-needed, just-in-time basis has been a strong reason for its rapid deployment and acceptance.

---

* 1.2 is now Java 2.

The nature of the Internet created a new and largely unprecedented requirement for programs to be free of viruses and Trojan horses. Computer users had always been used to purchasing shrink-wrapped software. Many soon began downloading software via ftp or other means and then running that software on their machines. But widespread downloading also led to a pervasive problem of malevolent attributes both in free and (ironically) in commercial software (a problem which continues unabated). The introduction of Java into this equation had the potential to multiply this problem by orders of magnitude, as computer users now download programs automatically and frequently.

For Java to succeed, it needed to circumvent the virus/trojan horse problems that plagued other models of software distribution. Hence, the early work on Java focused on just that issue: Java programs are considered safe because they cannot install, run, or propagate viruses, and because the program itself cannot perform any action that is harmful to the user's computing environment. And in this context, safety means security. This is not to say that the other issues in the above list are not important—each has its place and its importance (in fact, we'll spend a great deal of time in this book on the third and fourth topics in that list). But the issues of protecting information and preventing viruses were considered most important; hence, features to provide that level of security were the first to be adopted. Like all parts of Java, its security model is evolving (and has evolved through its various releases); many of the notions about security in our list will eventually make their way into Java.

One of the primary goals of this book, then, is to explain Java's security model and its evolution through releases. In the final analysis, whether or not Java is secure is a subjective judgment that individual users will have to make based on their own requirements. If all you want from Java is freedom from viruses, any release of Java should meet your needs. If you need to introduce authentication or encryption into your program, you'll need to use a 1.1 or later release of Java. If you have a requirement that all operations be audited, you'll need to build that auditing into your applications. If you really need conformance with a U.S. government-approved definition of security, Java is not the platform for you. We take a very pragmatic view of security in this book: the issue is not whether a system that lacks a particular feature qualifies as "secure" according to someone's definition of security. The issue is whether Java possesses the features that meet your needs.

When Java security is discussed, the discussion typically centers around Java's applet-based security model—the security model that is embodied by Java-enabled browsers. This model is designed for the Internet. For many users, this is not necessarily the most appropriate model: it is somewhat restrictive, and the security concerns on a private, corporate network are not the same as those on the Internet.

In this book, we take a different tack: the goal of this book is to show how to use the security model and how to write your own secure Java applications. While some of the information we present will be applicable to a browser environment, the security of any particular browser is ultimately up to the provider of the browser. Some browsers allow us to change the security policy the browser uses, but many do not. Hence, reading about the security manager in this book may help you understand how a particular browser works (and why it works that way), but that won't necessarily allow you to change the security model provided by that browser.

The Java Sandbox

Discussions of Java's security model often center around the idea of a sandbox model. The idea behind this model is that when you allow a program to be hosted on your computer, you want to provide an environment where the program can play (i.e., run), but you want to confine the program's play area within certain bounds. You may decide to give the program certain toys to play with (i.e., you may decide to let it have access to certain system resources), but in general, you want to make sure that the program is confined to its sandbox.

This analogy works better when you consider it from the view of a close relative rather than from the view of a parent. If you're a parent, you probably consider the purpose of a sandbox to be to provide a safe environment for your child to play in. When my niece Rachel visits me, however, I consider the purpose of a sandbox not (only) to be to protect her, but also to protect my grandmother's china *from* her. I love my niece, but I can't give her leave to run through my house; I enjoy running the latest cool applet on the Internet, but I can't give it leave to run through my filesystem.

The Java sandbox is responsible for protecting a number of resources, and it does so at a number of levels. Consider the resources of a typical machine as shown in Figure 1-1. The user's machine has access to many things:

- Internally, it has access to its local memory (the computer's RAM).

- Externally, it has access to its filesystem and to other machines on the local network.

- For running applets, it also has access to a web server, which may be on its local (private) net, or may be on the Internet.

- Data flows through this entire model, from the user's machine through the network and (possibly) to disk.

Each of these resources needs to be protected, and those protections form the basis of Java's security model.

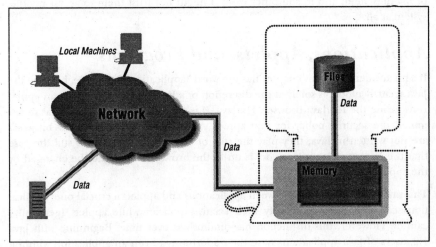

Figure 1-1. A machine has access to many resources

We can imagine a number of different-sized sandboxes in which a Java program might run:

- A sandbox in which the program has access to the CPU, the screen, keyboard, and mouse, and to its own memory. This is the minimal sandbox—it contains just enough resources for a program to run.

- A sandbox in which the program has access to the CPU and its own memory as well as access to the web server from which it was loaded. This is often thought of as the default state for the sandbox.

- A sandbox in which the program has access to the CPU, its memory, its web server, and to a set of program-specific resources (local files, local machines, etc.). A word-processing program, for example, might have access to the *docs* directory on the local filesystem, but not to any other files.

- An open sandbox, in which the program has access to whatever resources the host machine normally has access to.

The sandbox, then, is not a one-size-fits-all model. Expanding the boundaries of the sandbox is always based on the notion of trust: when my one-year-old niece comes to visit, there's very little in the sandbox for her to play with, but when my six-year-old godchild comes to visit, I trust that I might give her more things to play with. In the hands of some visitors, a toy with small removable parts would be dangerous, but when I trust the recipient, it's perfectly reasonable to include that item in the sandbox. And so it is with Java programs: in some cases, I might trust them to access my filesystem; in other cases, I might trust them to access only part of my filesystem; and in still other cases, I might not trust them to access my filesystem at all.

Applications, Applets, and Programs

It's no accident that this chapter has the word "application" in its title, because the Java security model is solely at the discretion of a Java application. When an applet runs inside the HotJava browser, HotJava™ is the Java application that has determined the security policy for that applet. And although other popular browsers are not written in Java, they play the role of a Java application: it is still the case that the choice of security model is up to the browser and cannot be changed by the applet.

This makes the distinction between applications and applets a crucial one: applications can establish and modify their security policies while applets (generally) cannot. However, this distinction has diminished over time. Beginning with Java 1.2, users of Java applications have the opportunity to run an application within a sandbox that the user or system administrator has constructed. In the next section, we'll see how the same functionality can be achieved with Java 1.1 as well. Under these scenarios, the Java security model for applications is solely at the discretion of the user or system administrator.

This is a major change of perception for many users and developers of Java, who are used to considering the security differences between applets and applications as a significant differentiator between the two types of programs. There will, of course, always be particular programming differences between applets and applications: an applet extends the `java.applet.Applet` class and is written as a series of callbacks, while an application can be any class that has a static method called `main()`. When this programming distinction is important, we'll use the terms "applet" and "application" as appropriate. But we'll typically use the term "program" to refer to the Java code that we're running.

Anatomy of a Java Application

The anatomy of a typical Java application is shown in Figure 1-2. Each of the features of the Java platform that appears in a rectangle plays a role in the development of the Java sandbox. In particular, the elements of the Java sandbox are comprised of:

The bytecode verifier

The bytecode verifier ensures that Java class files follow the rules of the Java language. In terms of resources, the bytecode verifier helps enforce memory protections for all Java programs. As the figure implies, not all files are subject to bytecode verification.

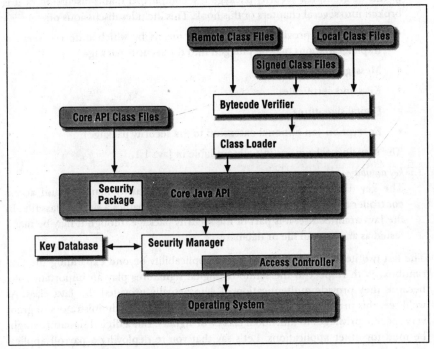

Figure 1-2. Anatomy of a Java application

The class loader

One or more class loaders load classes that are not found on the CLASSPATH. In 1.2, class loaders are responsible for loading classes that are found on the CLASSPATH as well.

The access controller

In Java 1.2, the access controller allows (or prevents) most access from the core API to the operating system.

The security manager

The security manager is the primary interface between the core API and the operating system; it has the ultimate responsibility for allowing or preventing access to all system resources. In 1.2, the security manager uses the access controller for most (but not all) of those decisions; in 1.0 and 1.1, the security manager is solely responsible for those decisions.

The security package

The security package (that is, classes in the java.security package) forms the basis for authenticating signed Java classes. Although it is only a small box in this diagram, the security package is a complex API, and discussion of it is broken into several chapters of this book. This includes discussions of:

- The security provider interface—the means by which different security implementations may be plugged into the security package
- Message digests
- Keys and certificates
- Digital signatures
- Encryption (an optional extension to the security package)

The security package was initially available in Java 1.1.

The key database

The key database is a set of keys used by the security manager and access controller to verify the digital signature that accompanies a signed class file. In the Java architecture, it is part of the security package, though it may be manifested as an external file or database.

The last two items in this list have broad applicability beyond expanding the Java sandbox. With respect to the sandbox, digital signatures play an important role, because they provide authentication of who actually provided the Java class. As we'll see, this provides the ability for end users and system administrators to grant very specific privileges to individual classes or signers. But a digital signature might be used for other applications. Let's say that you're deploying a payroll application throughout a large corporation. When an employee sends a request to view his payroll information, you really want to make sure that the request came from that employee rather than from someone else in the corporation. Often, this type of application is secured by a simple password, but a more secure system could require a digitially signed request before it sent out the payroll information.

We'll discuss security concerns in both these contexts in this book. In particular, two different examples will form the theme of the examples that are developed through this book:

- A browser-type program (called JavaRunner) that we'll use to explore the sandbox aspects of Java's security model
- The payroll application of a large company (XYZ Corporation) that we'll use to explore how the features of Java's security model can be used for purposes other than the sandbox (e.g., to sign a payroll request)

We'll develop a full implementation of the first of these examples; while we won't provide a complete payroll application, we will provide a number of examples of the security features required for such an application.

Running a Java Application

The parameters of the Java sandbox that we've outlined are possible elements of a Java application, but they are not required elements of an application. The remainder of this book will show us how and when those elements can be introduced into a Java application. First, however, we're going to discuss the techniques by which Java applications can be run.

There are two techniques that we'll introduce in this section: the JavaRunner technique and the Launcher technique. While both allow you to run an application securely, the examples in this chapter do not provide any security. We'll fill in the security pieces bit by bit, while we flesh out the security story. At that point, we'll show how to run Java applications securely.*

Typically, we're used to running Java applications simply by specifying on the command line the name of a class that contains a main() method. Consider this application that reads the file specified by a command-line argument:

```
public class Cat {
    public static void main(String args[]) {
        try {
            String s;
            FileReader fr = new FileReader(args[0]);
            BufferedReader br = new BufferedReader(fr);
            while ((s = br.readLine()) != null)
                System.out.println(s);
        } catch (Exception e) {
            System.out.println(e);
        }
    }
}
```

This is a regular Java application; if we wanted to run it and print out the contents of the password file on a Unix system, we could run the command:

```
piccolo% java Cat /etc/passwd
root:x:0:1:0000-Admin(0000):/:/usr/bin/csh
daemon:x:1:1:0000-Admin(0000):/:
bin:x:2:2:0000-Admin(0000):/usr/bin:
...
```

From a security point of view, this is a very rudimentary program. It contains none of the elements of the sandbox that we just listed; it has the default (wide-open) sandbox given by default to every Java application. This application can perform any operation it wants.

---

* See, for example, the end of Chapter 6.

Security and the Operating System

The security policy imposed by Java is augmented by the security features of the operating system on which Java is running. A Java application with a wide-open security policy may attempt to read the password file, but if the user running the application does not normally have permission to read the password file, the Java application will not succeed.

The actual security policy that is in effect for a Java application will be the intersection of the security policy built into the application and the security policy of the operating system when the application is run. For the purposes of this book, we ignore the security features that the operating system may provide.

There are two ways in which we can add security features to this application. One way is to add to the application a class loader, a security manager, use of the access controller, and so on. This additional programming would set the bounds of the sandbox for this particular application.

The other route we can take is to run this application under the auspices of another application that we'll call JavaRunner. This is completely analogous to the way in which we typically run applets: appletviewer is a Java application that runs applets, and JavaRunner is a Java application that runs other applications. Java-Runner is responsible for establishing the parameters of the Java sandbox (that is, it ensures that appropriate class loaders, a security manager, and the like are all in place) before it invokes the target application, just as appletviewer establishes the parameters of the Java sandbox before it invokes the target applet.

This technique removes the difference (in terms of security) between an applet and an application: both types of programs are now subject to the Java sandbox. There are a number of circumstances in which this is useful:

- If you download (or purchase) Java applications and want them to run in a sandbox.

- If you want to ensure that your internally developed applications all run in the desired sandbox (without having to include that code in every application).

- If you have a corporate or campus network and need to distribute Java applications under a new security model. Perhaps the new model will:

  — Give different security permissions to programs downloaded from within the corporate firewall than those from outside the corporate firewall (without requiring internal classes to be signed)

— Authenticate users on the corporate network before allowing sensitive payroll data to be sent (even over the corporate network)

— Encrypt that payroll data, so internal spies can't decipher it

— Allow the user greater discretion over the resources granted to a particular program

Although the JavaRunner program is designed to run other applications, there is no reason why it cannot be modified to run applets as well. Such a modification would require some extra code to parse the HTML containing the applet tag and set up an instance of the AppletStub and AppletContext classes for the applet itself. We're not showing the code to do that only because it's not really relevant to the discussion of Java security—but the JavaRunner could easily be extended to become an appletviewer (or, with an appropriate Java bean that interprets HTML, a full-fledged browser). The advantage, of course, is that as author of the browser you would have full control over the security model the browser employs.

Outline of the JavaRunner Application

Here's the basic implementation of the JavaRunner application:

```
public class JavaRunner implements Runnable {
    final static int numArgs = 1;
    private Object args[];
    private String className;

    JavaRunner(String className, Object args[]) {
        this.className = className;
        this.args = args;
    }

    void invokeMain(Class clazz) {
        Class argList[] = new Class[] { String[].class };
        Method mainMethod = null;
        try {
            mainMethod = clazz.getMethod("main", argList);
        } catch (NoSuchMethodException nsme) {
            System.out.println("No main method in " + clazz.getName());
            System.exit(-1);
        }

        try {
            mainMethod.invoke(null, args);
        } catch (Exception e) {
            Throwable t;
            if (e instanceof InvocationTargetException)
                t = ((InvocationTargetException) e)
                                .getTargetException();
```

```
            else t = e;
        System.out.println("Procedure exited with exception " + t);
        t.printStackTrace();
    }
}

public void run() {
    Class target = null;
    try {
        target = Class.forName(className);
        invokeMain(target);
    } catch (ClassNotFoundException cnfe) {
        System.out.println("Can't load " + className);
    }
}

static Object[] getArgs(String args[]) {
    String passArgs[] = new String[args.length - numArgs];
    for (int i = numArgs; i < args.length; i++)
        passArgs[i - numArgs] = args[i];

    Object wrapArgs[] = new Object[1];
    wrapArgs[0] = passArgs;
    return wrapArgs;
}

public static void main(String args[]) {
    if (args.length < 1) {
        System.err.println("usage:  JavaRunner classfile");
        System.exit(-1);
    }
    ThreadGroup tg = new ThreadGroup("JavaRunner Threadgroup");
    Thread t = new Thread(tg,
            new JavaRunner(args[0], getArgs(args)));
    t.start();
    try {
        t.join();
    } catch (InterruptedException ie) {
        System.out.println("Thread was interrupted");
    }
}
}
```

This is a fully functional (if not full-featured) version of the JavaRunner program; we can use it to run our Cat application like this:

```
piccolo% java JavaRunner Cat /etc/passwd
root:x:0:1:0000-Admin(0000):/:/usr/bin/csh
daemon:x:1:1:0000-Admin(0000):/:
bin:x:2:2:0000-Admin(0000):/usr/bin:
...
```

This will give us exactly the same results as when we ran the program by hand. The invokeMain() method will use the Java reflection API to find the static main() method of the Cat class and then construct an appropriate argument list to pass to that method. Note that the use of the reflection API introduces a dependency on Java 1.1 for this program. You can write a similar program under Java 1.0, but not without using the native (C) interface to Java.

Note also that we construct a new thread group and thread, and run the main() method under control of that thread. The primary reason we do that will become clear in Chapter 6 when we discuss thread security policies. But there's no reason why you couldn't expand this example to run multiple targets simultaneously, in which case each target should have its own thread and thread group anyway.

We've cheated a little bit here by using the forName() method of the Class class to find our target application class—we'll hear more about that in Chapter 3 when we discuss class loaders. For now, it will suffice to know that this will load our target class (assuming that the target class is found on the CLASSPATH). In addition, we still haven't done anything to set up a security manager or to enable the access controller. As a result, the sandbox for an application run under this program is non-existent: the bytecodes will not be verified, and there will be no restriction on any actions that the application may perform. But this is the example that we'll expand upon during the rest of this book as we add security features to it.

Don't think that the only function of a program like this is to run Java applications (or even Java applets). Consider the Java web server—it must dynamically invoke servlets for different web requests as those requests come in. An RMI server might operate similarly, perhaps even loading the code to perform its operations from a client machine. Although we stick with this example throughout the book, the need for security in server applications parallels the need for security in end-user applications.

Built-in Java Application Security

Beginning in Java 1.2, the Java platform itself comes with a security model built into applications it runs. This model is based upon information in the user's CLASSPATH. Setting the CLASSPATH is the same operation in Java 1.1 and Java 1.2, but in Java 1.2, classes that are found on the CLASSPATH may optionally be subject to a security model. This allows you to run the application code in a user- or administrator-defined sandbox: in particular, it uses the access controller of Java 1.2 to provide the same security environment for the target application as a Java-enabled browser provides for an applet.

The successful use of this facility depends upon the class loader that the built-in application runner will use, as well as depending upon the environment set up by the access controller and security manager. We'll examine how these facilities interact with this method of running applications in the next few chapters. For now, we'll just outline how this method operates.

As always, Java applications are run on the command line as follows:

```
piccolo% java Cat /etc/passwd
root:x:0:1:0000-Admin(0000):/:/usr/bin/csh
daemon:x:1:1:0000-Admin(0000):/:
bin:x:2:2:0000-Admin(0000):/usr/bin:
...
```

This example loads the *Cat.class* file from the user's CLASSPATH and runs the application with the single argument */etc/passwd.* As always, when an application is run in this manner, the sandbox in which the application runs is unlimited: the application can perform any activity it wants to.

There is a very important difference between running these examples in Java 1.1 and running them in 1.2: in 1.2, classes that are loaded from the CLASSPATH will be loaded by a class loader. The addition of the class loader to the CLASSPATH allows us to build a sandbox for the application. However, none of these examples actually builds a sandbox yet. In order to build a sandbox for these examples, we must specify the -Djava.security.manager flag on the command line. This flag enables a security manager and access controller to be installed; we'll discuss the details of this option in Chapter 6.

The -Djava.security.manager flag is only available in Java 1.2. Without it, Java applications in 1.2 behave exactly as they do in 1.1: they have a wide-open sandbox.

For historical reasons (and because it makes describing this facility easier), we'll refer to the ability to run applications with an optional argument to specify a sandbox as the Launcher. Given that the Launcher is a standard part of Java, you might ask why we're going to the trouble of implementing our own JavaRunner. One reason is simply to make our discussion clearer: it is easiest to understand the architecture of Java's security policy in the context of JavaRunner. Other reasons have to do with certain limitations that we'll discover about the Launcher:

- The Launcher comes only with Java 1.2 and later releases; if you're still using 1.1, you'll have to use the JavaRunner program.

- The Launcher can only run classes from the CLASSPATH—it cannot load classes from the network or from another location. However, simply because the program in question is an application does not mean we won't want to load its classes from a server—but we'll need JavaRunner to do that.

Secure Applications in 1.2 and 1.2 beta 2

In releases of 1.2 up through beta 2, running a secure application requires use of a special class: the Launcher class (sun.misc.Launcher). To run an application under control of the Launcher, you would execute this command:

```
piccolo% java sun.misc.Launcher Cat /etc/passwd
```

In 1.2 beta, classes that are loaded from the CLASSPATH are not subject to the sandbox. In order to load those classes through a class loader and subject them to the sandbox, you must specify an alternate classpath for the classes that make up the application:

```
piccolo% java -Djava.app.class.path=/classes sun.misc.Launcher \
Cat /etc/passwd
```

If the Cat class is found in */classes*, it will be subject to the sandbox. If it is found in the CLASSPATH, it will not.

Beginning in 1.2 beta 3, the Launcher class was incorporated into the virtual machine itself, but the syntax to use it changed in the last few beta releases. In FCS, the correct syntax is:

```
piccolo% java -Djava.security.manager Cat /etc/passwd
```

- The security manager used by the Launcher does not have all the features we might desire. While most of its features are configurable through the access controller (also a feature of Java 1.2), there are certain advanced policies that we cannot configure in that way. These features can only be achieved with some programming on our part.

Hence, both the Launcher and JavaRunner are useful mechanisms for running Java applications; which one you use depends on your particular requirements.

Summary

Security is a multifaceted feature of the Java platform. There are a number of facilities within Java that allow you to write a Java application that implements a particular security policy, and this book will focus on each of those facilities in turn. Java-enabled browsers (including those like HotJava that are written in Java) are the ultimate proof of these features: these browsers have used the features of the Java platform to allow users to download and run code on their local systems without fear of viruses or other corruption.

But the security features of Java need not be limited to the protections afforded to Java applets running in a browser: they can be applied as necessary to your own Java applications. This is done most easily by incorporating those features into a framework designed to run Java applications within a specified sandbox. The ability to define and modify that framework is one of the primary examples of this book. In addition, the security package allows us to create applications that use generic security features—such as digital signatures—for many purposes aside from expanding the Java sandbox. This other use of the security package will also be a constant theme throughout this book.

In the next chapter, we'll look into the security features of the Java language itself—the first set of security features that are available to any Java application.

2

Java Language
Security

The first components of the Java sandbox that we will examine are those components that are built into the Java language itself. These components primarily protect memory resources on the user's machine, although they have some benefit to the Java API as well. Hence, they are primarily concerned with guaranteeing the integrity of the memory of the machine that is hosting a program: in a nutshell, the security features within the Java language want to ensure that a program will be unable to discern or modify sensitive information that may reside in the memory of a user's machine. In terms of applets, these protections also mean that applets will be unable to determine information about each other; each applet is given, in essence, its own memory space in which to operate.

In this chapter, we'll look at the features of the Java language that provide this type of security. We'll also look at how these features are enforced, including a look at Java's bytecode verifier. With a few exceptions, the information in this chapter is largely informational; because the features we are going to discuss are immutable within the Java language, there are fewer programming considerations than we'll find in later chapters. However, the information we'll present here is crucial in understanding the entire Java security story; it is very helpful in ensuring that your Java environment is secure and in assessing the security risks that Java deployment might pose. The security of the Java environment is dependent on the security of each of its pieces, and the Java language forms the first fundamental piece of that security.

As we discuss the language features in this chapter, keep in mind that we're only dealing with the Java language itself—as is the common thread of this book, all security features we're going to discuss do not apply when the language in question is not Java. If you use Java's native interface to run arbitrary C code, that C code will be able to do pretty much anything it wants to do, even when it violates the precepts we're outlining in this chapter.

Java Language Security Constructs

In this chapter, we're going to be concerned primarily with how Java operates on things that are in memory on a particular machine. Within a Java program, every entity—that is, every object reference and every primitive data element—has an access level associated with it. To review, this access level may be:

- private: The entity can only be accessed by code that is contained within the class that defines the entity.

- Default (or package): The entity can be accessed by code that is contained within the class that defines the entity, or by a class that is contained in the same package as the class that defines the entity.

- protected: The entity can only be accessed by code that is contained within the class that defines the entity, by classes within the same package as the defining class, or by a subclass of the defining class.

- public: The entity can be accessed by code in any class.

The notion of assigning data entities an access level is certainly not exclusive to Java; it's a hallmark of many object-oriented languages. Since the Java language borrows heavily from C++, it's not surprising that it would borrow the basic notion of these access levels from C++ as well (although there are slight differences between the meanings of these access modifiers in Java and in C++).

As a result of this borrowing, the use of these access modifiers is generally thought of in terms of the advantage such modifiers bring to program design: one of the hallmarks of object-oriented design is that it permits data hiding and data encapsulation. This encapsulation ensures that objects may only be operated upon through the interface the object provides to the world, instead of being operated upon by directly manipulating the object's data elements. These and other design-related advantages are indeed important in developing large, robust, object-oriented systems. But in Java, these advantages are only part of the story.

In a language like C++, if I create a CreditCard object that encapsulates my mother's maiden name and my account number, I would probably decide that those entities should be private to the object and provide the appropriate methods to operate on those entities. But nothing in C++ prevents me from cheating and accessing those entities through a variety of back-door operations. The C++ compiler is likely to complain if I write code that attempts to access a private variable of another class, but the C++ runtime isn't going to care if I convert a pointer to that class into an arbitrary memory pointer and start scanning through memory until I find a location that contains a string with 16 digits—a possible account number. In C++ systems, no one typically worried about such occurrences because all parts of the system were presumed to originate from the same place: it's my program, and if I want to work around my data model to get access to that data, so be it.*

Things change with Java. I might be surfing to play some cool game applet on *www.EvilSite.org*, and then I might go shopping at *www.Acme.com*. When my Java wallet applet runs, I'd hate for the applet that is still running from *www.EvilSite.org* to be able to access the private CreditCard object that's contained in my Java wallet—and while it's necessary for *www.Acme.com* to know that I have a valid CreditCard object, I don't necessarily feel comfortable telling them my mother's maiden name. Because I'm now in the midst of a dynamic system with active programs from multiple sites, I need to make sure that the data entities are accessed by only those objects that are supposed to have access to them. It's obvious that I want protection from *EvilSite.org*, whom I don't want to know about the CreditCard object contained in my Java wallet. But I also want to be protected from *Acme.com*, a site I feel relatively comfortable about, but who should not be granted access to all the data elements of an object that it must use.

This is only one example of why the Java platform must provide memory integrity—that is, it must ensure that entities in memory are accessed only when they are allowed to be, and that these entities cannot be somehow corrupted. To that end, Java always enforces the following rules:

Access methods are strictly adhered to.

In Java, you cannot be allowed to treat a private entity as anything but private: the intentions of the programmer must always be respected. Object serialization involves an exception to this rule; we'll give more details about that a little bit later.

Programs cannot access arbitrary memory locations.

This is easy to ensure, as Java does not have the notion of a pointer. For example, casting between an int and an Object is strictly illegal in Java.

Entities that are declared as final must not be changed.

Final variables in Java are considered constants; they are immutable once they are initialized. Consider the havoc that could ensue if the final modifier were not respected:

- A public final variable could be changed, drastically altering the behavior of a program. If a rogue applet swapped the values of the variables EAST and WEST in the GridBagConstraints class, for example, any new applets would be laid out incorrectly (and probably incomprehensibly). That's a rather benign example of what could potentially be a dramatic security flaw.

---

* In a large project with multiple programmers, there's a strong argument that such an attitude on the part of an individual programmer is not to be dismissed so lightly, but we'll let that pass.

- A subclass could override a final method, altering the behavior of a class. One of the features of the Java API is that threads are not allowed to raise their priority above a certain maximum priority (typically, the priority of the thread group to which the thread belongs). This feature is enforced by the setPriority() method of the Thread class, which is a final method; allowing that method to be overridden would defeat the security mechanisms.

  This feature is used for virtually all of Java's security checks: performing an operation requires calling a final method in a Java class; only that final method can trap into the operating system to execute the operation. That final method is responsible for making sure the operation does not proceed if it would violate the security policy in place.

- A subclass could be created from a final class, with similar results. In Java, strings are considered as constants—their value may not be changed once the string has been created. If the String class could be subclassed, this rule could not be enforced.

Variables may not be used before they are initialized.

If a program were able to read the value of an uninitialized variable, the effect would be the same as if it were able to read random memory locations. A Java class wishing to exploit this defect might then declare a huge uninitialized section of variables in an attempt to snoop the memory contents of the user's machine. To prevent this type of attack, all local variables in Java must be initialized before they are used, and all instance variables in Java are automatically initialized to a default value.

Array bounds must be checked on all array accesses.

Like the access modifiers that started this discussion, bounds checking is generally thought of in terms other than security: the prime benefit to bounds checking is that it leads to fewer bugs and more robust programs. But it has security benefits as well: if an array of integers happens to reside in memory next to a string (which, in memory, is an array of characters), writing past the end of the array of integers would change the value of the string. The effect of this is generally a bug, but it could be exploited as a security hole as well: if the string held the destination account number for an electronic funds transfer, we could change the destination account number by willfully writing past the end of the array of integers.*

---

* This type of attack is not as far-fetched as it might seem; an early version of Netscape Navigator suffered from just this type of security hole. When long URLs were typed into the Goto field, the Netscape C code that read the string overwrote the bounds of the array where the characters were to be stored and clobbered a key location in memory, which allowed a security breach.

Objects cannot be arbitrarily cast into other objects.

Given the class fragment:

```
public class CreditCard {
    private String acctNo;
}
```

and the rogue class:

```
public class CreditCardSnoop {
    public String acctNo;
}
```

then the following code cannot be allowed to execute:

```
CreditCard cc = Wallet.getCreditCard();
CreditCardSnoop snoop = (CreditCardSnoop) cc;
System.out.println("Ha!  Your account number is " + snoop.acctNo);
```

Hence, Java does not allow arbitrary casting between objects; an object can only be cast to one of its superclasses or its subclasses (if, in the latter case, the object actually is an instance of that subclass). Note that the Java virtual machine is much stricter about this rule than the Java compiler is. In the example above, the compiler would complain about an illegal cast. We could satisfy the compiler by changing the code as follows:

```
Object cc = Wallet.getCreditCard();
CreditCardSnoop snoop = (CreditCardSnoop) cc;
```

Only the virtual machine will know if the returned object actually is of type CreditCard or not. In this case, then, the virtual machine is responsible for throwing a ClassCastException when the snoop variable is assigned to thwart the attack.

These are the techniques by which the Java language ensures that memory locations are read and written only when such access should normally be allowed. This restriction protects the user's machine from the outside: if I download an applet onto my machine, I don't want that applet accessing the private variables of my CreditCard class. However, if that applet has a private variable within it, nothing prevents me (depending on my operating system) from using a program outside of the browser to scan the memory on my system and figure out somehow what value that particular variable has. Similarly, nothing prevents me from having another program outside the browser change the value of a particular variable that is held in memory on my machine.

If you're an applet developer and are worried about this type of problem, you're pretty much on your own to come up with a solution to it. This might be particularly troublesome if you had, say, a variable somewhere in your applet that held a Boolean value indicating whether or not the user was licensed for a particular operation; a very clever user can go outside the browser and manipulate the machine's memory so that the integrity of your licensing scheme is violated. This problem is not new to Java, but it's not solved by Java either.

Object Serialization and Memory Integrity

There is one general exception to the rules about public, private, and protected access in Java. Object serialization is a feature of Java that allows an object to be written as a series of bytes; when those bytes are read someplace else, a new object is created that has the same state as the original object. Object serialization has two main purposes: it's used extensively in the RMI API to allow clients and servers to exchange objects, and it's used whenever you need to save a particular object to disk and want to recreate the object at some later point in time.

The murky issue here is just what constitutes an object's state. In the case of our CreditCard object, the account number is pretty basic to creating that object, but it's a variable that needs to be private for the reasons we've been discussing. In order for object serialization to work, it must have access to those private variables so it can correctly save and restore the object's state. That's why the object serialization API can access and save all private variables of an object (as well as its default, protected, and public variables). Similarly, the object serialization API is able to store those values back into the private data members when the object is actually reconstituted.

Depending on your perspective, this is a good thing or a bad thing. From a security perspective, it can be a bad thing: if the CreditCard object is saved to disk, something else can come along and read all that information from the disk file. Worse yet, the file could be edited in such a way that the object will be recreated in a completely different state than it originally had, with potentially damaging results.

In theory, this is the same problem we just discussed about influences outside the browser being able to read and write the private data of objects that are held in memory (which may help to explain why object serialization works this way by default). In practice, however, it's much easier to change the data in a binary file than to figure out how to access and change the value of an object in memory. Hence, object serialization has two additional mechanisms associated with it that make it more secure.

The first of these is that object serialization can only occur on objects that implement the java.io.Serializable interface (or its subclass, the java.io.Externalizable interface). The Serializable interface requires no methods, so it can be thought of simply as a flag to the virtual machine that says: "Hey, virtual machine—I've thought about the security aspects of this class, and it's okay if you serialize it by writing out all its data." By default, an object is not serializable, lest its internal private state be violated.

The second of these mechanisms is that object serialization respects the transient keyword associated with a variable: if our account number in the

CreditCard class were declared as private transient, then object serialization would not be allowed to read or write that particular variable. This lets us design classes that can be stored and reconstituted without showing their private data to the world.

Of course, a CreditCard object without an account number is worthless; what we really need is something that can save and reconstitute the transient data in such a way that the data can't be compromised. This can be achieved by having our class implement the writeObject() and readObject() methods. The writeObject() method is responsible for writing out all data in the class, it typically uses the defaultWriteObject() method to write out all non-transient data, and then it writes the transient data out in any format it desires. Similarly, the readObject() method uses the defaultReadObject() method to read the data and then must restore the corresponding transient data. It's your decision how to save and reconstitute the transient data so that its integrity is preserved, but this will mean that you'll want to use one of the encryption APIs we'll discuss in Chapter 13.

Storing and reconstituting the transient data can also be achieved by implementing the Externalizable interface and implementing the writeExternal() and the readExternal() methods of that interface. The difference in this case is that these two methods are now responsible for saving and reconstituting the entire state of the object—no data can be stored or reconstituted by any default methods.

Using either of these techniques, you have the ability to protect any sensitive data contained in your objects, even if you choose to share those objects over the network or save those objects to some sort of persistent storage.

Enforcement of the Java Language Rules

The list of rules we outlined above are fine in theory, but they must be enforced somehow. We've always been taught that overwriting the end of an array in C code is a bad thing, but I somehow still manage to do it accidentally all the time. There are also those who willfully attempt to overwrite the ends of arrays in an attempt to breach the security of a system. Without mechanisms to enforce these memory rules, they become simply guidelines and provide no sort of security at all.

This necessary enforcement happens at three different times in the development and deployment of a Java program: at compile time, at link time (that is, when a class is loaded into the virtual machine), and at runtime. Not all rules can be checked at each of these points, but certain checks are necessary at each point in order to ensure the memory security that we're after. As we'll see, enforcement of these rules (which is really the construction of this part of the Java sandbox) varies depending on the origin of the class in question.

Compiler Enforcement

The Java compiler is the first thing that is tasked with the job of enforcing Java's language rules. In particular, the compiler is responsible for enforcing all of the rules we outlined above except for the last two: the compiler cannot enforce array bound checking nor can it enforce all cases of illegal object casts.

The compiler does enforce certain cases of illegal object casts—namely, casts between objects that are known to be unrelated, such as the following code:

```
Vector v = new Vector();
String s = (String) v;
```

But the validity of a cast between an object of type X to type Y where Y is a subclass of X cannot be known at compile time, so the compiler must let such a construct pass.

The Bytecode Verifier

Okay, the compiler has produced a Java program for us, and we're about to run the Java bytecode of that program. But if the program came from an unknown source, how do we know that the bytecodes we've received are actually legal?

Bytecode Verification of Other Languages

Throughout this section, we're discussing the bytecode verifier as if it were tied to the Java language. This is somewhat imprecise: the bytecode verifier is actually independent of the original source language of the program. If we had a C++ compiler that generated Java bytecodes from C++ source, the bytecode verifier would still be able to verify (or not) the bytecodes.

However, the verification of the bytecodes would still depend upon the semantics of the Java language, and not the semantics of C++; just because the bytecodes in question originated from C++ code is no reason that they should suddenly be allowed to cast an arbitrary memory location into an object.

For this reason, I prefer to think of the bytecodes in terms of the Java language itself. There are tools to produce Java bytecodes from other languages (like Scheme), but in general, producing Java bytecodes from another language severely limits the constructs that can be written in that other language.

This brings us to the need for the bytecode verifier—the second link in the chain of responsibility of enforcing the rules of the Java language. Normally when the need for the bytecode verifier is discussed, it's in terms of an evil compiler—that is, a compiler that someone has written in such a way that the code produced by the compiler is not legal Java code. The theory is that code from such a compiler could be constructed in order to create and exploit a security hole by ignoring a rule in the Java language. Such an attack might seem to be difficult to achieve, in that it would require some detailed knowledge of the Java compiler.

It turns out that the evil compiler issue is a red herring—it doesn't really matter whether such an attack is likely or not, because it's trivial to create non-conforming Java code with any standard Java compiler. Assume that we have these classes:

```
public class CreditCard {
    public String acctNo = "0001 0002 0003 0004";
}

public class Test {
    public static void main(String args[]) {
        CreditCard cc = new CreditCard();
        System.out.println("Your account number is " + cc.acctNo);
    }
}
```

If we run this code, we'll create a CreditCard object and print out its account number. Now say that we realize the account number should really have been private, so we go back and change the definition of acctNo to be private and recompile only the CreditCard class. We then have two class files, and the Test class file contains Java code that illegally accesses the private instance variable acctNo of the CreditCard class.

The above example shows an innocent mistake, but a malicious programmer could use just this technique to produce illegal Java bytecodes. In order to modify the contents of a string, for example, all we need to do is:

1. Copy the java.lang.String source file into our CLASSPATH.

2. In the copy of the file, modify the definition of value—the private array that holds the actual characters of the string—to be public.

3. Compile this modified class, and replace the *String.class* file in the JDK.

4. Compile some new code against this modified version of the String class. The new code could include something like this:

```
public class CorruptString {
    public static void modifyString(String src, String dst) {
        for (int i = 0; i < src.length; i++) {
```

```
              if (i == dst.length)
                  return;
              src.value[i] = dst.value[i];
          }
      }
}
```

Now any time you want to modify a string in place, simply call this `modi-fyString()` method with the string you want to corrupt (`src`) and the new string you want it to have (`dst`).

5. Remove the modified version of the `String` class.

Now the `CorruptString` class can be referenced by a Java program, which can use it to attempt to corrupt any string that it has a reference to. Even though the program will run with the original version of the `String` class, the `CorruptString` class will be able to access the private value array within the `String` class—unless the bytecode verifier rejects the `CorruptString` class.

Inside the bytecode verifier

The bytecode verifier is an internal part of the Java virtual machine and has no interface: programmers cannot access it and users cannot interact with it. The verifier automatically examines most bytecodes as they are built into class objects by the class loader of the virtual machine (see Figure 2-1). We'll give just a brief overview of how the bytecode verifier actually works.

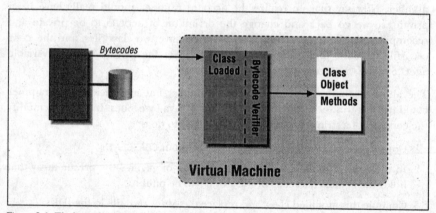

Figure 2-1. The bytecode verifier

The verifier is often referred to as a mini-theorem prover (a term first used in several documents from Sun). This sounds somewhat more impressive than it is; it's not a generic, all-purpose theorem prover by any means. Instead, it's a piece of code that can prove one (and only one) thing—that a given series of (Java) byte-codes represents a legal set of (Java) instructions.

Specifically, the bytecode verifier can prove the following:

- The class file has the correct format. The full definition of the class file for-mat may be found in the Java virtual machine specification; the bytecode veri-fier is responsible for making sure that the class file has the right length, the correct magic numbers in the correct places, and so on.

- Final classes are not subclassed, and final methods are not overridden.

- Every class (except for java.lang.Object) has a single superclass.

- There is no illegal data conversion of primitive data types (e.g., int to Object).

- No illegal data conversion of objects occurs. Because the casting of a super-class to its subclass may be a valid operation (depending on the actual type of the object being cast), the verifier cannot ensure that such casting is not attempted—it can only ensure that before each such attempt is made, the legality of the cast is tested.

- There are no operand stack overflows or underflows.

  In Java, there are two stacks for each thread. One stack holds a series of method frames, where each method frame holds the local variables and other storage for a particular method invocation. This stack is known as the data stack and is what we normally think of as the stack within a traditional program. The bytecode verifier cannot prevent overflow of this stack—an infi-nitely recursive method call will cause this stack to overflow. However, each method invocation requires a second stack (which itself is allocated on the data stack) that is referred to as the operand stack; the operand stack holds the values that the Java bytecodes operate on. This secondary stack is the stack that the bytecode verifier can ensure will not overflow or underflow.

Hence, when the bytecode verifier has completed its task, we know that the code in question follows many of the constraints of the Java language—including most of the rules that the compiler was also responsible for ensuring. The remaining rules are verified during the actual running of the program.

Delayed bytecode verification

When we began this section, we said that the bytecode verifier is responsible for *examining* all the bytecodes of the class—we explicitly did not say that the verifier is responsible for *verifying* all the bytecodes. This is because the bytecode verifier may delay some of the checks it is responsible for, as long as those checks are performed before the code is actually executed. In typical verifier implementa-tions, the bytecode verifier does not immediately test to see if all field and method accesses are legal according to the access modifiers associated with that field or method.

This is driven by a desire to be efficient—our Test class may reference the acctNo field of our CreditCard class, but it may do so only if a particular branch in the code is taken. In the following code, there's no need to verify that the access to acctNo is legal unless an IllegalArgumentException has been generated:

```
CreditCard cc = getCreditCard();
try {
    Wallet.makePurchase(cc);
} catch (IllegalArgumentException iae) {
    System.out.println("Can't process for account " + cc.acctNo);
}
```

Hence, the bytecode verifier delays all tests for field and method access until the code is actually executed. The process by which this happens is implementation independent; one technique that is often used is to ensure during verification that all accesses test the validity of the field access. If the access is valid, the standard bytecodes are then replaced during execution with a special bytecode indicating that the test has been performed and access to the field in question no longer needs to be tested. On the other hand, if the validity test fails, the virtual machine throws an IllegalAccessException.

This gives us the best of both worlds—verification of the access is performed during the actual running of the program (after traditional bytecode verification has occurred), but the verification is still only performed once (unlike the runtime verification we'll examine later).

Controlling bytecode verification

Bytecode verification seems like a great thing: not only can it help to prevent malicious attacks from violating rules of the Java language, it can also help detect simple programmer errors—such as when we changed the access modifier of acctNo in our CreditCard class, but forgot to recompile our Test class.

Nonetheless, bytecode verification is not used on all classes. Like many security-related features of Java, bytecode verification only applies to certain classes. In Java 1.1 and earlier, classes that are loaded from the CLASSPATH are deemed to be trusted and are not subject to bytecode verification, whereas classes that are loaded from another location (e.g., a file- or HTTP-based URL) are not deemed to be trusted and must be verified. In Java 1.2,* this policy has changed and all classes

---

* 1.2 is now Java 2.

except those in the core Java API are verified. This difference really reflects the class loader that is used to load the class, as we'll see in the next chapter.

In typical usage, this is a workable policy. Browsers always ensure that the code imported to run an applet is verified, and Java applications are typically not verified. Of course, this may or may not be the perfect solution:

• If a remote site can talk an end user into installing a local class into the browser's CLASSPATH, the local class will not be verified and may violate the rules we've discussed here. In 1.2, this is much harder, since the class must be added to the JAR file containing the core API classes.

• You may implicitly rely upon the verifier to help you keep files in sync so that when one is changed, other files are verified against it.

As a user, you (theoretically) have limited control over the verifier—though such control depends on the browser you are using. If you are running a Java application, you can run java with the -verify option, which will verify all classes. Similarly, if you are using a browser written in Java—including the applet-viewer—you can arrange for the java command to run with the -noverify option, which turns verification off for all classes. Occasionally, a browser not written in Java will allow the user to disable bytecode verification as well—e.g., Internet Explorer™ 3.0 for the Mac had this capability, although it was present only because the bytecode verifier could not run in certain limited memory configurations.

However, although these options to the virtual machine are well-documented, they are not implemented on all platforms. One way to ensure that application code is run through the bytecode verifier is to use the final version of the JavaRunner program (once we add a class loader to it in the next chapter) or the Launcher in Java 1.2.

Runtime Enforcement

Like the compiler, the bytecode verifier cannot completely guarantee that the bytecodes follow all of the rules we outlined earlier in this chapter: it can only ensure that the first four of them are followed. The virtual machine must still take responsibility for ultimately determining that the Java bytecodes provide the security we expect them to.

The remaining security protections of the Java language must be enforced at runtime by the virtual machine.

Array bounds checking

In theory, the bytecode verifier can detect certain cases of array bounds checking, but in general, this check must take place at runtime. Consider the following code:

```
void initArray(int a[], int nItems) {
    for (int i = 0; i < nItems; i++) {
        a[i] = 0;
    }
}
```

Since nItems and a are parameters, the bytecode verifier has no way of determining whether this code is legal. Hence, array bounds checking is always done at runtime. Failure to meet this rule results in an ArrayIndexOutOfBoundsException.

Object casting

The verifier can and will detect the legality of certain types of casts, specifically, whenever unrelated classes are cast to each other. The virtual machine must monitor when a superclass is cast into a subclass and test that cast's validity; failure to execute a legal cast results in a ClassCastException. This holds for casts involving interfaces as well, since objects that are defined as an interface type (rather than a class type) are considered by the verifier to be of type Object.

Summary

Because the notion of security in Java is pervasive, its implementation is equally pervasive. In this chapter, we've explored the security mechanisms that are built into the Java language itself. Essentially, at this level the security mechanisms are concerned with establishing a set of rules for the Java language that creates an environment where an object's view of memory is well-known and well-defined, so that a developer can ensure that items in memory cannot be accidentally or intentionally read, corrupted, or otherwise misused. We also took a brief look at Java's bytecode verifier, including why it is necessary, and why you should turn it on, even for Java applications.

It's important to keep in mind that the purpose of these security constraints is to protect the user's machine from a malicious piece of code and not to protect a piece of code from a malicious user. Java does not (and could not) prevent a user from acting on memory from outside the browser (with possibly harmful results).

3

Java Class Loaders

In this chapter, we're going to explore Java's class loading mechanism—the mechanism by which files containing Java bytecodes are read into the Java virtual machine and converted into class definitions. The operation of Java programs depends on the class loader; given Java's desire to ensure security throughout its architecture, it should come as no surprise that class loaders are also a very important piece of the Java security story. The class loader normally works in conjunction with the security manager and access controller to provide the bulk of the protections associated with the Java sandbox.

The class loader is important in Java's security model because initially, only the class loader knows certain information about classes that have been loaded into the virtual machine. Only the class loader knows where a particular class originated, and only the class loader knows whether or not a particular class was signed (although the class loader arranges for the Class object itself to carry its signature with it). Hence, one of the keys to writing a secure Java application is to understand the role of the class loader and to write (or at least use) a secure class loader.

We'll address both those points in this chapter. We begin with an overview of how the class loader functions, and the features that its basic functions add to the overall security of the Java platform. We'll then look into writing our own class loader, the motivation for which will vary depending on the release of Java you're using and the type of application you are running.

As with the other elements of the Java sandbox, the ability to create and use a class loader is limited to Java applications. Java applets use the class loader provided for them by the browser in which they are running, and they are generally prohibited from creating their own class loader.

Security and the Class Loader

There are two instances where the class loader plays an important role in the Java security model: it must coordinate with Java's security manager or access controller, and it must enforce certain rules about the namespace used by Java classes.

Class Loaders and Security Enforcement

The class loader must coordinate with the security manager and access controller of the virtual machine in order to determine the security policy for a Java program. We'll explore this in more detail in the next few chapters when we discuss these various security mechanisms; for now, we'll just consider the motivation for the following connection.

As we know, a Java applet cannot (normally) read a file when the applet is being run in a browser such as HotJava.* The HotJava browser itself, however, can read files, even while it is also running applets. Both the browser and the applets are using the same classes to (attempt to) read a file, so clearly there must be something that allows the java.io classes to determine that one case should fail while the other case should succeed. That differentiation is the by-product of the class loader: the class loader allows the security manager to find out particular information about the class, which allows the security manager to apply the correct security policy depending on the context of the request. When we discuss the security manager, we'll discuss the specific mechanics by which this can be achieved. For now, it is only important to keep in mind that the class loader is the piece of the Java architecture that is able to make this distinction. Since it loaded the class, it knows if the class came from the network (i.e., the class is part of the applet and should not be trusted) or if the class came from the local filesystem (i.e., the class is part of the browser and should be trusted). It also knows if the class was delivered with a digital signature, and the exact location from which the class was loaded. All these pieces of information may be used by the security manager and access controller to establish a security policy.

Class Loaders and Namespaces

The second place where the class loader provides security in Java is more subtle and has to do with Java's namespace rules. Recall that the full name of a Java class is qualified by the name of the package to which the class belongs; there is no standard class called String in the Java API, but there is the class

---

* This is true of all Java-enabled browsers, of course, but the point is clearer when we consider the Hot-Java browser since that browser is written in Java.

java.lang.String. On the other hand, a class does not need to belong to a package, in which case its full name is just the name of the class. It's often said that these classes are in the default package, but that's slightly misleading: as it turns out, there is a different default package for each class loader in use by the virtual machine.

Consider what happens if you surf to a page at *www.sun.com* and load an applet that uses a class called Car (with no package name); after that, you surf to a page at *www.ora.com* and load a different applet that uses a class called Car (also with no package name). Clearly, these are two different classes, but they have the same fully qualified name—how can the virtual machine distinguish between these two classes?

The answer to that question lies in the internal workings of the class loader. When a class is loaded by a class loader, it is stored in a reference internal to that class loader. A class loader in Java is simply an object whose type is some class that extends the ClassLoader class. When the virtual machine needs access to a particular class, it asks the appropriate class loader. For example, when the virtual machine is executing the code from *sun.com* and needs access to the Car class, it asks the class loader that loaded the applet (r1 in Figure 3-1) to provide that class.

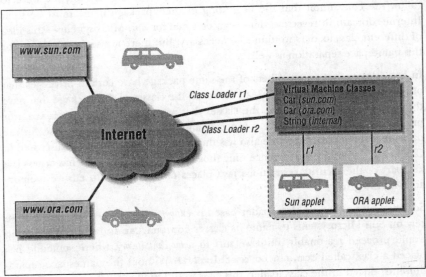

Figure 3-1. Different instances of the class loaders help to disambiguate class names

In order for this scheme to work, the Car class from *www.ora.com* must be loaded using a different class loader than that which loaded the Car class from *www.sun.com*. That way, when the virtual machine asks the class loader r2 for the definition of the Car class, it will get back (correctly) the definition from *ora.com*. The class loader does not need to be a different class; as this example implies, it must merely be a different *instance* of the class. Hence, applets that have a different CODEBASE (even if they originate on the same host) are always loaded by different instances of the browser's class loader. Applets on the same page with the same CODEBASE, however, may use the same class loader so that they may share class files (as well as sharing other information). Some browsers also allow applets on different pages to be loaded by the same class loader as long as those applets have the same CODEBASE, which is generally a more efficient and useful implementation.

This differentiation between class files loaded from different class loaders occurs no matter what packages are involved. Don't be confused by the fact that there were no explicit package names given in our example. A large computer company might define a class named com.sun.Car, a large oil company might also define a class called com.sun.Car, and the two classes need to be considered as distinct classes—which they will be if (and only if) they are loaded by different instances of the class loader.

So far we've given a logical reason why the class loader is involved in the namespace resolution of Java classes. You might think that if everyone were to follow the convention that the beginning of their package name must be their Internet domain in reverse order—e.g., com.sun for Sun Microsystems—this idea of different class loaders wouldn't be necessary. But there are security reasons for this namespace separation as well.

In Java, classes that are members of the same package have certain privileges that other classes do not have—they can access all the classes of the package that have the default protection (that is, the classes that are neither public, private, nor protected). Additionally, they can access any instance variable of classes in the package if the instance variable also has the default protection. As we discussed in Chapter 2, the ability to reference only those items to which a class has access is a key part of the security restrictions Java places on a program to ensure memory and API integrity.

So let's assume that no class loader based package separation exists, and that we rely on Sun Microsystems to name its classes com.sun.Car and so on. Everything would proceed reasonably, until we surf to *www.EvilSite.org*, where someone has placed a class called com.sun.DoSomethingEvil. Without the namespace separation introduced by the class loader, this class would suddenly have access to all the default protected classes and default protected variables of every class that had been downloaded from Sun. Worse, that site could supply a class called com.sun.Car with a much different implementation than Sun's—such that when the user (metaphorically, of course) applied the car's brakes, the new implementation sped up instead. Clearly, this is not a desirable situation.

Note too that with a badly written class loader, the hackers at *EvilSite.org* have the potential to supply new classes to override the core classes of the Java API. When the class loader that loaded the applet from *EvilSite* is asked to provide the java.lang.String class, it must provide the expected version of that class and not some version from *EvilSite.org*. In practice, this is not a problem, because the class loader is written to find and return the core class first.

Without enforcement of the namespace separation that we've just outlined, there is no way to ensure that the hackers at *EvilSite.org* have not forged a class into the com.sun package. The only way to prevent such forgeries would be to require that every class be a signed class which authenticated that it did in fact come from sun.com (or wherever its package name indicates that it should have come from). Authenticated classes certainly have their place in Java's security model, but it would be unmanageable to require that every site sign and authenticate every class on its site.

Hence, the separation of classes based on the class loader that loaded them—and the convention that applets on different pages are loaded by different class loaders—has its benefits for Java security as well as solving a messy logistical problem. We'll now look into the details of how the class loader actually works.

Anatomy of a Class Loader

When the Java virtual machine needs access to a particular class, it is up to a class loader to provide the class. The class loader goes through the following steps to load and define a class:

1. If the class loader has already loaded this class, it should find the previously defined class object and return that object immediately.

2. The security manager is consulted to see if this program is allowed to access the class in question. If it is not, a security exception is thrown. This step may be considered optional.

3. Otherwise, an internal class loader is consulted to attempt to load the class from the CLASSPATH. If that succeeds, the class loader returns. This ensures that classes within the Java API will not be superseded by classes loaded from the network (or other location).

   The way this is done varies between 1.1 and 1.2.* In 1.1, there is a single method (the findSystemClass() method) that handles this step. In 1.2, a

---

* 1.2 is now Java 2.

class loader must delegate to another class loader to find classes that are on the CLASSPATH and call the findSystemClass() method to find classes that are in the core API.

4. The security manager is consulted to see if this program is allowed to create the class in question. If it is not, a security exception is thrown. This step may be considered optional.

5. The class file is read into an array of bytes. The mechanism by which the class loader reads the file and creates the byte array will vary depending on the class loader (which, after all, is one of the points of having different class loaders).

6. The byte codes are run through the bytecode verifier.

7. A Class object is constructed from the bytecodes. In the process, the methods defining the class are created. In Java 1.1 and later, this process also ensures that the name in the class file matches the name that the class loader thought it was asked to load.

8. Before the class can be used, it must be resolved—which is to say that any classes that it immediately references must also be found by this class loader. The set of classes that are immediately referenced contains any classes that the class extends as well as any classes used by the static initializers of the class. Note that classes that are used only as instance variables, method parameters, or local variables are not normally loaded in this phase: they are loaded when the class actually references them (although certain compiler optimizations may require that these classes be loaded when the class is resolved).

Step 5 of this process varies depending on the policy of the particular class loader—the data for the class may be read from the network or the filesystem (or from any other location, such as a database). The other steps of this process will remain fixed for a well-defined class loader.

There are a number of class loaders that are used in Java programs, described in the following sections.

The Internal Class Loader

All Java programs must have the capability of loading certain classes—the Java API classes and any others located in the user's CLASSPATH. Some of these classes are bootstrapped into the virtual machine. The first thing the virtual machine typically does is load the Java API class files (the *rt.jar* file) for future use.

The internal class loader uses the native operating system's file access methods to open and read the class files into byte arrays. When one of these classes contains a reference to another class, the internal class loader is again consulted to load the referenced class.

Unlike other class loaders we'll explore, the internal class loader cannot be overridden. Most of the internal class loader, in fact, is written in native code so that it can be accessed directly by the virtual machine (a requirement for the virtual machine to be able to bootstrap the API classes).

The internal class loader is often referred to as the default class loader or the primordial class loader. Due to some details of the Class class, we often speak of classes that are loaded by the internal class loader as having no class loader at all (and as a result, the internal class loader is sometimes called the null class loader).

There is a significant change in the use of the primordial class loader between Java 1.1 and 1.2. In 1.1, the primordial class loader was used to load all classes on the CLASSPATH. In 1.2, the primordial class loader is used only to load the Java API class files; the virtual machine constructs an instance of the URLClassLoader class to load the classes from the CLASSPATH.

The Applet Class Loader

An applet needs the ability to load classes via HTTP from the network. Hence, applet class loaders typically use the URL class to read in the data for a class file from the applet's CODEBASE host.

There is no standard applet class loader in the Java API—each Java browser is responsible for implementing its own class loader. In practice, the class loaders of various browsers are indistinguishable (and are usually based on the reference class loader implemented in Sun's appletviewer), but a Java programmer cannot simply instantiate an applet class loader in a platform-independent way.*

The RMI Class Loader

Beginning with JDK 1.1, the Java API includes an RMI class loader that can be used by any application. Despite its name, the RMI class loader needn't be used in an RMI application, and it is not truly a class loader—that is, it does not extend the ClassLoader class. In function, the RMIClassLoader class (java.rmi.server.RMIClassLoader) is very similar to the applet class loader—it uses the HTTP protocol to load the desired class file from a remote machine and then defines the class from the data in that file.

The RMI class loader cannot be instantiated directly; you must use one of its static methods to load a class. Once an initial class is loaded by the RMI class loader, any classes it references will also be loaded by the RMI class loader. In addition, the

---

* If you want, you can figure out which class in the JDK on your system is the applet class loader, instantiate an instance of that class, and use it, but all virtual machines will not necessarily have that class available.

RMI class loader can only load classes from the URL specified by the
java.rmi.server.codebase property, so it is not a generic solution to all applications where a class loader might be used.

If you are loading individual, unsigned classes (i.e., classes that are not in a JAR
file) from a single URL (i.e., a single directory, whether a file-based or an HTTP-
based URL), using the RMI class loader is the simplest option for Java 1.1 applications. For Java 1.2 applications, you can use the RMI class loader for this purpose,
or you can use the URL class loader; the URL class loader will offer you more
flexibility.

The Secure Class Loader

Beginning with Java 1.2, the Java API includes a class loader in the java.security
package called SecureClassLoader. This class has a protected constructor, so its
real use is to provide the basis for the development of other class loaders. The
distinguishing feature of the secure class loader is that it associates a protection
domain with each class that it loads. Protection domains form the basis of the
operation of the access controller; we'll see more about them in Chapter 5. For
now, just accept the fact that if you want to use the access controller to establish
your security policy, you'll need to use a class loader that extends the Secure-
ClassLoader class.

The URL Class Loader

Also beginning with Java 1.2, the Java API includes a general-purpose class loader
that can load classes from a set of URLs: the URLClassLoader class
(java.net.URLClassLoader). This class is public and fully implemented, so for
1.2-based applications, it provides a truly useful, general purpose class loader:

public class URLClassLoader extends SecureClassLoader ★
  Load classes from a set of URLs. A URL in this set may be a directory-based
  URL, in which case the class loader will attempt to locate individual class files
  under that directory. A URL in this set may also be a JAR file, in which case
  the JAR file will be loaded, and the class loader will attempt to find a class in
  the JAR file.

An instance of the URLClassLoader class is created via one of these constructors:

public URLClassLoader(URL urls[]) ★
public URLClassLoader(URL urls[], ClassLoader parent) ★
  Construct a class loader based on the given array of URLs. This class loader
  attempts to find a class by searching each URL in the order in which it appears
  in the array.

The second of these constructors constructs a URL class loader that uses the 1.2-based delegation model for loading classes (which we discuss at the end of this chapter). In that case, the parent class loader will be asked to load the class first; if it fails, this URL class loader proceeds to load the class. This is the preferred constructor to use.

An instance of the URLClassLoader class may also be obtained via one of these methods:

public static URLClassLoader newInstance(URL[] urls) ★
public static URLClassLoader newInstance(URL[] urls, ClassLoader parent) ★

Create and return a URL class loader. The difference between these methods and constructing a URL class loader directly is that the class loader returned from these methods will call the security manager's checkPackageAccess() method before it attempts to define a class; this is the optional step 2 referred to earlier. In 1.2, only class loaders obtained this way will perform that optional step (unless you write your own class loader to perform that step).

We can construct a URL class loader like this:

```
URL urls[] = new URL[2];
urls[0] = new URL("http://piccolo.East/~sdo/");
urls[1] = new URL("file:/home/classes/LocalClasses.jar");
URLClassLoader ucl = new URLClassLoader(urls, parent);
```

When we use this class loader to load the class com.sdo.Car, the class loader first attempts to load it via the URL *http://piccolo.East/~sdo/com/sdo/Car.class*; if that fails, it looks for the class in the *LocalClasses.jar* file.

It should come as no surprise that this class is the basis for running the Launcher. In that case, the array of URLs is created based on the list of URLs that make up the CLASSPATH (but not including the core Java API classes).

Choosing the Right Class Loader

With all these class loaders to choose from, which is the better choice: an existing class loader or your own custom class loader? The answer depends upon your needs. It is better not to write your own class loader if an existing one can fit your needs, but that's not always possible. Here are some guidelines:

1. Start by trying to use an instance of the URLClassLoader class. This class can load classes from multiple sites, using file-based and HTTP-based URLs. It can process individual class files and JAR files (including signed JAR files, which will become important later in our discussion). This class is the basis of the Launcher, although with the Launcher itself, you're limited to file-based URLs.

When would you not use the URL class loader? Here are some possible cases:

— When you want to load classes other than via HTTP or the file system. You may have classes that are held in a database, or you may want to define the bytecodes for a class programmatically.   .

— When you want to load classes from different hosts and you have *a priori* knowledge of which class is on which host. The URL class loader will search for classes in its list of URLs sequentially; prior knowledge may allow you to load classes more efficiently.*

2. If you're on a 1.1-based system and only need to load classes from a single site, use the RMI class loader. Remember that you will have to define as a property the location where those classes are found.

3. Otherwise, you'll need to provide a custom class loader.

Loading Classes

We'll now explore the details of how a class loader actually loads classes. There is a single method of the ClassLoader class (and all its subclasses) that accomplishes this:

public Class loadClass(String name)

Load and resolve the named class. A ClassNotFoundException is thrown if the class cannot be found.

This is the simplest way to use a class loader directly: it simply requires that the class loader be instantiated and then be used via the loadClass() method. Once the Class object has been constructed, there are three ways in which a method in the class can be executed:

• A static method of the class can be executed using the native method interface of the Java virtual machine. This is the technique the Java virtual machine uses to execute the main() method of a Java application once the initial class has been loaded, but this is not generally a technique used by Java applications.

• An object of the class can be constructed using the newInstance() method of the Class class, but only if the class has an accessible constructor that requires no arguments. Once the object has been constructed, methods with well-known signatures can be executed on the object. This is the technique that a program like appletviewer uses: it loads the initial class of the applet, con-

---

* In 1.2, the URLClassLoader class fails to handle multiple HTTP-based URLs correctly. It is hoped that this will be fixed someday; if it is not and you need to load classes from multiple web servers, you will need to use your own class loader—see the information about the MultiLoader class in the section "Loading from Multiple Sites" later in this chapter.

structs an instance of the applet (which calls the applet's no-argument constructor), and then calls the applet's init() method (among other methods).

- Starting with JDK 1.1, the reflection API can be used to call a static method on the class, or to construct instances of the object and execute methods on that object. The reflection API allows more flexibility than the second choice, since it allows arguments to be passed to the constructor of the object. This is the technique that is used by our JavaRunner program.

The second case is more commonly implemented, if only because it's simpler (and it is applicable in all versions of Java). But consider the following modifications to our JavaRunner program:

```java
public class JavaRunner implements Runnable {
    final static int numArgs = 2;
    ClassLoader cl;
    String className;
    Object args[];

    JavaRunner(ClassLoader cl, String className, Object args[]) {
        this.cl = cl;
        this.className = className;
        this.args = args;
    }

    void invokeMain(Class clazz) {
        .. unchanged ..
    }

    public void run() {
        Class target = null;
        try {
            target = cl.loadClass(className);
            invokeMain(target);
        } catch (ClassNotFoundException cnfe) {
            System.out.println("Can't load " + className);
        }
    }

    static Object[] getArgs(String args[]) {
        .. unchanged ..
    }

    public static void main(String args[])
                        throws ClassNotFoundException {
        Class self = Class.forName("JavaRunner");
        JavaRunnerLoader jrl =
            new JavaRunnerLoader(args[0], self.getClassLoader());
```

```
ThreadGroup tg = new ThreadGroup("JavaRunner Threadgroup");
Thread t = new Thread(tg,
        new JavaRunner(jrl, args[1], getArgs(args)));
t.start();
try {
    t.join();
} catch (InterruptedException ie) {
    System.out.println("Thread was interrupted");
}
    }
}
```

We've replaced the forName() method that we used in our example in Chapter 1 with the highlighted code here: now we construct a class loader (an instance of the JavaRunnerLoader class, the definition of which we'll see in just a bit) and are now using the loadClass() method to find our target class.

In Java 1.2, constructing the class loader requires that we find the class loader that loaded our class and pass that to the constructor of the JavaRunnerLoader class. In 1.1, we would not use the self instance variable.

We've also changed the arguments required to run this program, which is why we've changed the definition of numArgs. Previously, we required the name of the class and any arguments the class requires. Now we require an additional argument: the name of the URL from which to load all the classes. Hence, if our Cat class was on the web server named *piccolo*, we could run our JavaRunner example like this:

```
piccolo% java JavaRunner http://piccolo/ Cat /etc/passwd
root:x:0:1:0000-Admin(0000):/:/usr/bin/csh
daemon:x:1:1:0000-Admin(0000):/:
bin:x:2:2:0000-Admin(0000):/usr/bin:
...
```

Note the difference between this implementation and the one we showed in Chapter 1. In this case, the Cat class is loaded from the JavaRunner class loader, and any classes the Cat class needs are dynamically loaded from that class loader. In Chapter 1, what happened was a product of the release of Java. In 1.1, the Cat class was loaded from the primordial class loader; any classes it required were loaded from the primordial class loader as well. In 1.2, the Cat class was loaded from an instance of the URLClassLoader class, and any classes it required were loaded from that class loader as well.

The practical result is that the security manager and access controller will give different permissions to the Cat class depending on which class loader loaded it: the permissions that are assigned to a class may be different depending upon whether the class was loaded from the URL class loader, the JavaRunner class loader, or the primordial class loader. Exactly how those permissions differ depends upon the internal implementation of the class loader as well as the security manager and access controller that are in effect. In a nutshell, these differences will be based upon where the class loader found the class, and whether or not that class was signed.

Implementing a Class Loader

Part of the security implications of a class loader depend upon its internal implementation. When you implement a class loader, you have two basic choices: you can extend the ClassLoader class, or you can extend the SecureClassLoader class. The second choice is preferred, but it is not an option for Java 1.1. If you're programming in 1.2, you may choose to use the URL class loader rather than implementing your own, but the information in this section will help you understand the security features of the URL class loader. In this section, then, we'll look at how to implement both default and secure class loaders.

Implementing the ClassLoader Class

Aside from the primordial class loader, all Java class loaders must extend the ClassLoader class (java.lang.ClassLoader). Since the ClassLoader class is abstract, it is necessary to subclass it to create a class loader.

Protected methods in the ClassLoader class

In order to implement a class loader, we start with this method:

protected abstract Class loadClass(String name, boolean resolve) ☆
protected Class loadClass(String name, boolean resolve) ★

Using the rules of the class loader, find the class with the given name and, if indicated by the resolve variable, ensure that the class is resolved. If the class is not found, this method should throw a ClassNotFoundException. This method is abstract in 1.1, but not in 1.2. In 1.2, you typically do not override this method.

The loadClass() method is passed a fully qualified class name (e.g., java.lang.String or com.xyz.XYZPayrollApplet), and it is expected to return a class object that represents the target class. If the class is not a system class, the loadClass() method is responsible for loading the bytes that define the class (e.g., from the network).

There are five final methods (listed below) in the ClassLoader class that a class loader can use to help it achieve its task.

protected final Class defineClass(String name, byte data[], int offset, int length)
protected final Class defineClass(String name, byte data[], int offset, int length, Protection-
    Domain pd) ★

Create a `Class` object from an array of bytecodes. The `defineClass()` method runs the data through the bytecode verifier and then creates the `Class` object. This method also ensures that the name in the class file is the same as the name of the argument—that is, that the bytes actually define the desired class. We'll look at protection domains in Chapter 5; if you use the signature without one, a default (system) domain will be provided for the class.

protected final Class findSystemClass(String name)

Attempt to find the named class by using the internal class loader to search the user's `CLASSPATH`. If the system class is not found, a `ClassNotFoundException` is generated. In 1.2, this method searches only the classes in the Java API.

protected final Class findLoadedClass(String name)

Find the class object for a class previously loaded by this class loader. If the class is not found, a null reference is returned.

Finding Previously Loaded Classes

According to the Java specification, a class loader is required to cache the classes that it has previously loaded, so that when it is asked to load a particular class, it is not supposed to re-read the class file. Not only is this more efficient, it allows a simpler internal implementation of many methods, including the `resolveClass()` method.

The Java specification hedges this somewhat by stating that this requirement may change in the future, when the classes will be cached by the virtual machine itself. Hence, the `ClassLoader` class in JDK 1.0 did not do any caching, and it was up to concrete implementations of class loaders to perform this caching.

Beginning with JDK 1.1, however, caching within the class loader was considered important enough that the base `ClassLoader` class now performs this caching automatically: a class is put into the cache of the class loader in the `defineClass()` method and may be retrieved from the cache with the `findLoadedClass()` method. Since these methods are final, and since the cache itself is a private instance variable of the `ClassLoader` class, this permits a class loader to be written without any knowledge of whether the class loader or the virtual machine is doing the caching.

protected final void resolveClass(Class c)

For a given class, resolve all the immediately needed class references for the class; this will result in recursively calling the class loader to ask it to load the referenced class.

The loadClass() method is responsible for implementing the eight steps of the class definition list given above. Typically, implementation of this method looks like this:

```
protected Class loadClass(String name, boolean resolve) {
    Class c;
    SecurityManager sm = System.getSecurityManager();

    // Step 1 -- Check for a previously loaded class
    c = findLoadedClass(name);
    if (c != null)
        return c;

    // Step 2 -- Check to make sure that we can access this class
    if (sm != null) {
        int i = name.lastIndexOf('.');
        if (i >= 0)
            sm.checkPackageAccess(name.substring(0, i));
    }

    // Step 3 -- Check for system class first
    try {
        // In 1.2 only, defer to another class loader if available
        if (parent != null)
            c = parent.loadClass(name, resolve);
        else

            // Call this method in both 1.1 and 1.2
            c = findSystemClass(name);

        if (c != null)
            return c;
    } catch (ClassNotFoundException cnfe) {
        // Not a system class, simply continue
    }

    // Step 4 -- Check to make sure that we can define this class
    if (sm != null) {
        int i = name.lastIndexOf('.');
        if (i >= 0)
            sm.checkPackageDefinition(name.substring(0, i));
    }

    // Step 5 -- Read in the class file
```

```
    byte data[] = lookupData(name);

    // Step 6 and 7 -- Define the class from the data; this also
    //      passes the data through the bytecode verifier
    c = defineClass(name, data, 0, data.length);

    // Step 8 -- Resolve the internal references of the class
    if (resolve)
        resolveClass(c);

    return c;
}
```

For most of the class loaders we're interested in, this skeleton of a class loader is sufficient, and all we need to change is the definition of the lookupData() method (as well as the constructor of the class, which might need various initialization parameters).

This method might be used to implement a 1.1-based class loader, where the loadClass() method is abstract. In 1.2, however, it is easier to use the existing loadClass() method and override only the existing findClass() method:

protected Class findClass(String name) ★

Load the given class according to the internal rules of the class loader. This method should assume that it is responsible for implementing only steps 5, 6, and 7 in our list: that is, it should read the data and call the defineClass() method, but it needn't look for an existing implementation of the class or check to see if it is a system class. If the class cannot be found, this method should return null (which is what the default implementation of this method returns in all cases).

We'll use this method in our example of a secure class loader. If you must implement a 1.1-based class loader, you can use the code from that example to implement a lookupData() method that could be used by the above implementation of the loadClass() method.

From a security point of view, the loadClass() method is important because it codifies several aspects of how Java handles security. One example of this is that the order in which the loadClass() method looks for classes is significant. Much of the security within Java itself depends on classes in the Java API doing the correct thing—e.g., the java.lang.String class is final and holds the array of characters representing the string in a private instance variable; this allows strings to be considered constants, which is important to several aspects of Java security. When a class loader is asked to find the java.lang.String class, it is very important that it return the class from the Java API rather than returning a class (possibly having different and insecure semantics) it loaded from a different location.

Hence, it is important that the class loader call the findSystemClass() method immediately after it attempts (and fails) to find the class in its internal cache (via the findLoadedClass() method). By codifying this behavior in the loadClass() method, the ClassLoader class ensures that the class loader will have the correct behavior to enforce the overall security of the virtual machine. This is why the loadClass() method is no longer abstract in 1.2. This method really should be made final now, but that would break compatibility with previously written class loaders.

Secure Class Loaders and the defineClass() Method

When a class is defined by a secure class loader, one of the parameters that it must specify is a CodeSource object or a ProtectionDomain object. A Code-Source object encapsulates certain information about the class—where it was loaded from and whether or not it was signed (and if so, by whom); a ProtectionDomain object encapsulates information about the specific permissions that have been granted to the class.

We're deferring discussion of these classes until Chapter 5, when we can discuss them in their proper context.

Violating security by returning the incorrect class would have required the cooperation of the class loader. This might have happened accidentally, if the author of the class loader did not provide a correct implementation. It might also have happened maliciously, if the author of the class loader intentionally wrote an incorrect implementation. The new implementation solves the first problem, but not the second: the author of the class loader can still override the loadClass() method directly to do whatever he wants. In general, you have to trust the author of your class loader anyway, so the new implementation enhances security mostly by assisting developers in writing more robust programs.

Implementing the SecureClassLoader Class

Starting with JDK 1.2, there is an extension of the ClassLoader class that any Java developer can use as the superclass of her own class loader: the SecureClass-Loader class (java.security.SecureClassLoader).

In terms of security, the benefit of the SecureClassLoader class comes because it is fully integrated with the notion of protection domains that was introduced in 1.2. We'll discuss this integration more fully in Chapter 5, when we have an understanding of what a protection domain is.

Protected methods of the SecureClassLoader class

The SecureClassLoader class provides this new method:

protected final Class defineClass(String name, byte[] buf, int offset, int length,
  CodeSource cs) ★

Define a class that is associated with the given code source. If the code source is null, this method is the equivalent of the. defineClass() method in the base ClassLoader class. We'll defer showing an example of this method to Chapter 5, when we discuss code source objects.

As our first example of a class loader, we'll use the same paradigm for loading classes that a Java-enabled browser uses, namely an HTTP connection to a web server:

```
public class JavaRunnerLoader extends SecureClassLoader {
    protected URL urlBase;
    public boolean printLoadMessages = true;

    public JavaRunnerLoader(String base, ClassLoader parent) {
        super(parent);
        try {
            if (!(base.endsWith("/")))
                base = base + "/";
            urlBase = new URL(base);
        } catch (Exception e) {
            throw new IllegalArgumentException(base);
        }
    }

    byte[] getClassBytes(InputStream is) {
        ByteArrayOutputStream baos = new ByteArrayOutputStream();
        BufferedInputStream bis = new BufferedInputStream(is);
        boolean eof = false;
        while (!eof) {
            try {
                int i = bis.read();
                if (i == -1)
                    eof = true;
                else baos.write(i);
            } catch (IOException e) {
                return null;
            }
        }
        return baos.toByteArray();
    }

    protected Class findClass(String name) {
        String urlName = name.replace('.', '/');
```

```
        byte buf[];
        Class cl;

        SecurityManager sm = System.getSecurityManager();
        if (sm != null) {
            int i = name.lastIndexOf('.');
            if (i >= 0)
                sm.checkPackageDefinition(name.substring(0, i));
        }
        try {
            URL url = new URL(urlBase, urlName + ".class");
            if (printLoadMessages)
                System.out.println("Loading " + url);
            InputStream is = url.openConnection().getInputStream();
            buf = getClassBytes(is);
            cl = defineClass(name, buf, 0, buf.length, null);
            return cl;
        } catch (Exception e) {
            System.out.println("Can't load " + name + ": " + e);
            return null;
        }
    }
}
```

The key decision in using this class loader is where the classes are located—that is, the URL that needs to be passed to the constructor. If we were using this class loader in a browser, that URL would be the applet's CODEBASE; for an application, this location is up to the application to decide, using whatever means it deems appropriate (in the JavaRunner application, we used a command-line argument for that purpose). Note that the URL that is passed to the constructor must be a directory; in order to compose that directory into a URL later in the findClass() method, the name must end with a slash.

The logic of the findClass() method itself is simple: we need to convert the class name (e.g., com.XYZ.HRApplet) to a URL, which we can do by replacing the package-separating periods with slashes. Once the URL has been created, we simply obtain an input stream to the URL, read the bytes from that stream, and pass the bytes to the defineClass() method.

Note that the findClass() method encompasses most of the logic that is necessary for the lookupData() method we'd need if we were writing a 1.1-based class loader. The only difference for a 1.1-based class loader is that we would not need to call the defineClass() method, as that is called in our 1.1-based implementation of the loadClass() method.

The implementation we've just shown is the basis for the implementation of the URLClassLoader class. The basic difference between the two is that our implementation operates on a single URL, while the URLClassLoader class operates on an array of URLs. The URLClassLoader class can also read JAR files while our present implementation can only read individual class files; we'll remedy both those situations in the next section.

Implementing Security Policies in the Class Loader

When we discussed the algorithm used to load classes, we mentioned that you could test to see if the class loader was allowed to access or define the package that the class belonged to. You might, for example, want to test whether the program should be allowed to access classes in the sun package, or define classes in the java package.

It is up to the author of the class loader to put these checks into the class loader—even in 1.2. In 1.2, if you want to make the check for package access, you can do that by calling the checkPackageAccess() method of the security manager in the same way that we called the checkPackageDefinition() method, but that will only prevent you from accessing classes that aren't found by the system class loader. Alternately in 1.2, you can use the newInstance() method of the URLClassLoader class, which makes such a check; or you can override the load-Class() method itself to provide such a check, as we showed earlier. In 1.1, of course, you have to write the loadClass() method from scratch, so you can call the security manager or not, as you deem appropriate.

In the case of defining a class in a package, the necessary code in a 1.2-based class loader must be inserted into the findClass() method as we did in our example class loader. Note that class loaders that are created by calling the constructor of the URLClassLoader class do not make such a call; they allow you to define a class in any package whatsoever.

For the Launcher (and any applications built on the URLClassLoader class), then, the default security model does not perform either of these checks. This is unfortunate: if a program is allowed to define a class in the java package, then that class will have access to all the package-protected classes and variables within that package, which carries with it some risk. The reason this model is the default has to do with the way in which the access controller defines permissions; we'll explore it more in depth when we write our own security manager in Chapter 6.

Extensions to the Class Loader

When we implemented a class loader above, we had a fully operational class loader that paralleled the first class loaders that were used by Java's appletviewer or by a Java-enabled browser. However, there are other extensions to the class loader that are often useful.

> ### Class Loaders and Other Protocols
>
> Long before HTTP and the Web became popular, IP networks like the Internet had dozens of other protocols upon which a class loader could be based—FTP, NFS, RCP, and others. It's possible to write a class loader based on any of these protocols, although it's not as easy as using HTTP. The standard Java URL class will handle all the low-level details of the HTTP protocol for us, whereas we'd have to write the low-level details of the ftp (or whichever) protocol ourselves. We won't show an example of any of these protocols, since the concepts are all the same.
>
> One advantage these protocols have is that they typically offer some level of user authentication: FTP requires a password, NFS requires appropriate credentials to be sent, etc. Hence, some of these protocols might seem well-suited to an implementation where security is a concern—except that this level of authentication is often no stronger than simply putting the classes to be downloaded on a web server that requires a password to get into a particular directory.

Loading from Multiple Sites

We started with a complete class loader suitable for use in appletviewer-type programs where the classes are to be loaded from the network. This is good as far as it goes, but let's delve a little more into the security issues that surround that class loader.

In the world of Java-enabled browsers, an applet can retrieve classes from only one site—the CODEBASE specified in the applet's HTML tag. There are other reasons why an applet can only make a network connection to its CODEBASE (which we'll discuss in Chapter 4), but one of the reasons is contained in the discussion we outlined above: because classes loaded by the same class loader are considered to be in the same package, and an applet that loaded classes from multiple sites could run the risk of classes from different sites interfering with each other.

In an ideal world, however, a Java program may want to load classes from several locations on the network. Consider the deployment outlined in Figure 3-2 for XYZ Corporation: XYZ Corporation employs a network support group to manage its departmental servers, and within each department, there are programmers who are responsible for deploying the department's applications on those servers.

When the corporate network support group develops some useful JavaBeans™ components, everyone in the corporation is encouraged to use them in their

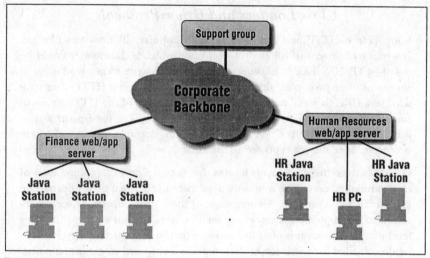

Figure 3-2. A distributed deployment

departmentally developed applications. This gives the applications a certain consistency between departments as well as promoting reuse of the efforts of the network support group. But as it stands now, the support group must distribute the Java Bean class files to each department so that these beans can be used by programs that are hosted on each departmental server.

Of course, there are technologies outside of Java that can manage distribution, but this is just a variation of the same application distribution problem that Java was originally hailed for solving. Unfortunately, the single-host-based class loader employed by standard Java-enabled browsers doesn't address this situation.

One improvement that we might make is to allow our class loader to load classes from multiple hosts on the network. There's some overhead involved here: when a program running on a machine on the HR network needs to load a class, does it check for the class on the HR server first or on the support group server first? Either way, there will be a number of lookups that check the wrong server first, which is somewhat inefficient. Judicious use of package names could help: if the support group beans were all placed in a single package, the class loader could be smart enough to contact the support group server only when asked to load classes from that package.

Remember that this intelligence about package names solves a logistical problem as well. Say that the support group writes a Java bean called Check that provides a nice graphical representation of a checkbox; this graphical representation is part of the look-and-feel on which XYZ Corporation wants to standardize. Now the HR group wants to create a payroll application, so they create a Check class representing the financial instrument that is used to pay their employees. Now when an HR applet wants to instantiate a Check object, what is it referring to—a GUI class or a financial instrument?

Solving this problem in the intranet world is straightforward—it's easy for the support and HR groups to coordinate their namespace so that the class loader won't see these collisions (e.g., by having the support group use names in a particular package, which again could make the class loader more efficient). In the case of the freewheeling Internet, this type of coordination is not possible: there can be no guarantee that two unrelated sites won't use classes that are in the same package. So the multiple-site class loader is only appropriate for intranet use.

There are various ways in which the multiple-site class loader could be implemented—for this example, we'll assume that any classes that are in the com.XYZ.support package should be loaded from the network support group's server (which we'll hardcode into the class loader, though we would normally configure this to be a property). Any other classes should come from the server that initialized the class loader. So our new class loader looks like this:

```
public class MultiLoader extends JavaRunnerLoader {
    private static final String server = "support.xyz.com/";

    public MultiLoader(String url, ClassLoader parent) {
        super(url, parent);
    }

    protected Class findClass(String name) {
        URL codeURL;

        SecurityManager sm = System.getSecurityManager();
        if (sm != null) {
            int i = name.lastIndexOf('.');
            if (i >= 0)
                sm.checkPackageDefinition(name.substring(0, i));
        }

        try {
            String codeName = name.replace('.', '/') + ".class";
            if (name.startsWith("com.xyz.support"))
                codeURL = new URL("http://" + server + codeName);
            else codeURL = new URL(urlBase, codeName);
            if (printLoadMessages)
                System.out.println("Loading " + name);
            InputStream is = codeURL.openConnection().getInputStream();
            byte buf[] = getClassBytes(is);
            return defineClass(name, buf, 0, buf.length, null);
```

```
        } catch (Exception e) {
            return null;
        }
    }
}
```

If you're thinking clearly about the security ramifications of this code, then you've already spotted a potential error: just because we're asked to load a class named com.xyz.support.Car doesn't necessarily mean that we should contact our internal server to do so—we should only contact that internal server if the other classes that we are loading are also from our internal network. That is, if we use this class loader in a browser that is loading an applet from *www.EvilSite.org* that requests the class com.xyz.support.Car, we should attempt to load that class from *EvilSite* and not from our support group's server; we should only load com.xyz.support classes from *support.xyz.com* when the other classes in the program come from another machine in the *xyz.com* domain.

We could have put the logic to deal with that possibility into the class loader itself; however, it's equally possible to put that logic elsewhere into our application. The JavaRunner program, for example, must instantiate a new class loader for each program it loads, and it's simpler to instantiate a MultiLoader class loader when the program is being loaded from a machine within the *xyz.com* domain, and to instantiate a regular JavaRunnerLoader when the program is being loaded from a machine outside the *xyz.com* domain.

Note the different approach taken here and in the URLClassLoader class: in this case, we contact a second machine only when we have classes in a particular package that we expect to find on that machine. If we had constructed a URLClassLoader as follows:

```
URL urls[] = new URL[2];
urls[0] = new URL("http://hr.xyz.com/");
urls[1] = new URL("http://support.xyz.com/");
URLClassLoader ucl = new URLClassLoader(urls);
```

then we would have functionally achieved something similar. However, with the URL class loader, when we search for a class named com.xyz.support.Check, we'll always contact the HR server first, which is slightly less efficient. On the other hand, the technique used by the URL class loader is clearly more flexible than the approach we've outlined above. In addition, the present implementation of the URLClassLoader will not work with multiple HTTP-based URLs, so for the present, you must write your own class loader to handle that case.

A JAR File Class Loader

There is one important feature present in many class loaders that we haven't yet mentioned, and that is the ability to load a single file that contains many classes. JAR files have a significant advantage over individual class files: loading several classes in a single file can be orders of magnitude faster than loading those same classes through individual HTTP connections. The reason for this comes from a property of the HTTP protocol: it takes a relatively long time to set up an HTTP connection. In fact, the time it takes to transfer the data in a Java class file over a network is usually much shorter than the time required to set up the HTTP connection. Hence, JAR files are often preferred because they can greatly speed up the time it takes to download an applet.

In browsers based on 1.0.2, support for JAR files is browser-dependent; those browsers that support them refer to the JAR file as an archive. In browsers based on 1.1, support for JAR files is present within the JDK itself using classes in the java.util.zip package, because a JAR file is really just a zip file with some additional information. In Java 1.2, there is an additional set of classes in the java.util.jar package that can help to process these files as well (including the additional information in the JAR file).

Of course, there's a flip side to using JAR files. If you use a large word-processing program in Java, you'll probably want to avoid loading a lot of the classes when you download the program: there's no need to spend the time downloading all the class files that implement the spellchecker until it is actually time to check the document's spelling. With JAR files, you don't have that luxury; you must load all the classes in a single shot. Even in those browsers in which you can specify multiple JAR files, the class loader has no way of knowing which particular JAR file contains which particular classes, so it still has to load all of them at once.*

Nevertheless, JAR files are very popular, and they certainly have their place for programs where all (or at least most) of the classes are likely to be used every time the program is run. So we'll look into the additions that must be made to our class loader in order for it to support loading a JAR file. This may seem to be taking us somewhat far afield of our discussion about application security, but there is another reason JAR files are important: they provide the necessary support for digitally signed classes. We typically speak of a signed class as an entity unto itself;

---

* A Java application could be more clever about this: it could know to load the archive containing the classes to perform the spellcheck when it was time to run the spellchecker. But an applet cannot do that, because an applet has no mechanism that it can use to tell the browser to load a new archive.

in fact, a signed class can only be delivered as part of a JAR file. Hence, a class loader that can process JAR files is very important.

So, to complete our understanding of the class loader and to prepare us for those future examples, we'll show how to add JAR support to our custom class loader. In order to support a JAR file, we'll create a new class. Although the logic is similar to our JavaRunnerLoader class, we get no benefit from extending that class, so we'll show the full implementation here. Changes to the JavaRunnerLoader class are shown in bold.

```
public class JarLoader extends SecureClassLoader {
    private URL urlBase;
    public boolean printLoadMessages = true;
    Hashtable classArrays;

    public JarLoader(String base, ClassLoader parent) {
        super(parent);
        try {
            if (!(base.endsWith("/")))
                base = base + "/";
            urlBase = new URL(base);
            classArrays = new Hashtable();
        } catch (Exception e) {
            throw new IllegalArgumentException(base);
        }
    }

    private byte[] getClassBytes(InputStream is) {
        ByteArrayOutputStream baos = new ByteArrayOutputStream();
        BufferedInputStream bis = new BufferedInputStream(is);
        boolean eof = false;
        while (!eof) {
            try {
                int i = bis.read();
                if (i == -1)
                    eof = true;
                else baos.write(i);
            } catch (IOException e) {
                return null;
            }
        }
        return baos.toByteArray();
    }

    protected Class findClass(String name) {
        String urlName = name.replace('.', '/');
        byte buf[];
        Class cl;

        SecurityManager sm = System.getSecurityManager();
        if (sm != null) {
```

```
            int i = name.lastIndexOf('.');
            if (i >= 0)
                sm.checkPackageDefinition(name.substring(0, i));
        }

        buf = (byte[]) classArrays.get(urlName);
        if (buf != null) {
            cl = defineClass(name, buf, 0, buf.length, null);
            return cl;
        }

        try {
            URL url = new URL(urlBase, urlName + ".class");
            if (printLoadMessages)
                System.out.println("Loading " + url);
            InputStream is = url.openConnection().getInputStream();
            buf = getClassBytes(is);
            cl = defineClass(name, buf, 0, buf.length, null);
            return cl;
        } catch (Exception e) {
            System.out.println("Can't load " + name + ": " + e);
            return null;
        }
    }

    public void readJarFile(String name) {
        URL jarUrl = null;
        JarInputStream jis;
        JarEntry je;

        try {
            jarUrl = new URL(urlBase, name);
        } catch (MalformedURLException mue) {
            System.out.println("Unknown jar file " + name);
            return;
        }
        if (printLoadMessages)
            System.out.println("Loading jar file " + jarUrl);

        try {
            jis = new JarInputStream(
                        jarUrl.openConnection().getInputStream());
        } catch (IOException ioe) {
            System.out.println("Can't open jar file " + jarUrl);
            return;
        }

        try {
            while ((je = jis.getNextJarEntry()) != null) {
```

```
                String jarName = je.getName();
                if (jarName.endsWith(".class"))
                    loadClassBytes(jis, jarName);
                // else ignore it; it could be an image or audio file
                jis.closeEntry();
            }
        } catch (IOException ioe) {
            System.out.println("Badly formatted jar file");
        }
    }


    private void loadClassBytes(JarInputStream jis, String jarName) {
        if (printLoadMessages)
            System.out.println("\t" + jarName);
        BufferedInputStream jarBuf = new BufferedInputStream(jis);
        ByteArrayOutputStream jarOut = new ByteArrayOutputStream();
        int b;
        try {
            while ((b = jarBuf.read()) != -1)
                jarOut.write(b);
            classArrays.put(jarName.substring(0, jarName.length() - 6),
                            jarOut.toByteArray());
        } catch (IOException ioe) {
            System.out.println("Error reading entry " + jarName);
        }
    }


    public void checkPackageAccess(String name) {
        SecurityManager sm = System.getSecurityManager();
        if (sm != null)
            sm.checkPackageAccess(name);
    }
}
```

The bulk of the change in this example is the addition of two new methods (the readJarFile() and loadClassBytes() methods). These two new methods are used to process the JAR file.

The classes in the java.util.jar package handle all the details about the JAR file for us, and we're left with a simple implementation: we use the getNext-JarEntry() method to obtain each file in the archive and process each one sequentially. For maximum efficiency, we don't actually need to create the class from the bytes until necessary: the loadClassBytes() method just creates an array of bytes for each class in the JAR file.

This necessitates a slight change to the logic in our findClass() method: now when we need to provide a class that is not a system class, we check first to see if that class is in the classArrays hashtable. If it is, we obtain the bytes for the class from that hashtable (where they were stored in the readJarFile() method) rather than opening a URL to obtain the bytes for the class over the network.

If you need to produce a similar class loader under 1.1, you can use the java.util.zip package instead of the java.util.jar package. In this example, the two are functionally equivalent, and you may simply substitute Zip every time you see Jar (and zip for jar) with one exception: replace the get-NextJarEntry() method with the getNextEntry() method. Later, when we deal with signed JAR files, that substitution will not work: the difference between the two packages is that the jar package understands the signature format and mani-fest of the JAR file.

This implementation is similar to the procedure followed by the URLClassLoader class; in that case, the JAR files occur as elements in the array of URLs passed to the class.

Miscellaneous Class Loading Topics

There are a few details that we haven't yet covered. These details are not directly related to the security aspects of the class loader, which is why we've saved them until now. If you're interested in the complete details of the class loader, we'll fill in the last few topics here.

Delegation

Beginning with Java 1.2, class loading follows a delegation model. This new model permits a class loader to be instantiated with this constructor:

protected ClassLoader(ClassLoader delegate) ★

> Create a class loader that is associated with the given class loader. This class loader delegates all operations to the delegate first: if the delegate is able to fulfill the operation, this class loader takes no action. For example, when the class loader is asked to load a class via the loadClass() method, it first calls the loadClass() method of the delegate. If that succeeds, the class returned by the delegate will ultimately be returned by this class. If that fails, the class loader then uses its original logic to complete its task:

```
public Class loadClass(String name) {
    Class cl;
    cl = delegate.loadClass(name);
    if (cl != null)
        return cl;
    // else continue with the loadClass() logic
}
```

You may retrieve the delegate associated with a class loader with the following method.

public final ClassLoader getParent() ★

Return the class loader to which operations are being delegated. If there is no such class loader, return null.

You'll notice that we used delegation in all of our examples. This is pretty much a requirement: when the virtual machine starts, it creates a URL class loader that is based on the directories and JAR files present in your CLASSPATH. That class loader is the class loader that will be used to load the first class in your application (i.e., the JavaRunner class in our example).

That URL class loader is the only class loader that knows about the CLASSPATH. If the application will reference any other classes that are part of the CLASSPATH, you will be unable to find them unless you use the delegation model of class loading: the JavaRunner loader will first ask the URL class loader to load the class. If the class is on the CLASSPATH, the URL class loader will succeed; otherwise, the Java-Runner loader will end up loading the class itself. This logic is built into the load-Class() method; you do not need to concern yourself with it at a programming level, but it is the reason why you must use delegation.

This URL class loader is known as the system class loader, and it may be retrieved via the following method:

public static classLoader getSystemClassLoader() ★

Return the system class loader (the class loader that was used to load the base application classes). If a security manager is in place, you must have the getClassLoader runtime permission to use this method (see Chapter 5).

Hence, to set up a delegation class loader, you can use this call:

```
jrl = new JavaRunnerLoader(ClassLoader.getSystemClassLoader())
```

instead of the methods we showed earlier.

Loading Resources

A class loader can load not only classes, but any arbitrary resource: an audio file, an image file, or anything else. Instead of calling the loadClass() method, a resource is obtained by invoking one of these methods:

public URL getResource(String name)
public InputStream getResourceAsStream(String name)
public URL findResource(String name) ★

Find the named resource and return either a URL reference to it or an input stream from which it can be read. Implementations of class loaders should look for resources according to their internal rules, which are typically (but need not be) the same rules as are used to find classes. In our first JavaRunnerLoader class, that would mean simply constructing a URL based on the urlBase concatenated with the name parameter.

In 1.1, the default behavior for these methods is to return null.

In 1.2, the getResource() method calls the getSystemResource() method; if it does not find a system resource, it returns the object retrieved by a call to the findResource() method (which by default will still be null). The getResourceAsStream() method simply calls the getResource() method and, if a resource is found, open the stream associated with the URL.

public static URL getSystemResource(String name)
public static InputStream getSystemResourceAsStream(String name)
Find the named resource and return either a URL reference to it or an input stream from which it can be read. By default, these methods look for the resource on the CLASSPATH and return that resource (if found).

public final Enumeration getResources(String name) ★
public Enumeration findResources(String name) ★
Return an enumeration of resources with the given name. In the first method, an enumeration of the local resources of all delegated class loaders (including the present class loader) is returned; in the second method, only the local resources of the present class loader are returned.

Loading Libraries

In 1.2, a new method exists in the ClassLoader class:

protected String findLibrary(String libname) ★
Return the directory from which native libraries should be loaded.

This method is used by the System.loadLibrary() method to determine the directory in which the native library in question should be found. If this method returns null (the default), the native library must be in one of the directories specified by either the java.library.path or java.sys.library.path property; typically, these properties are set in a platform-specific way (e.g., from the LD_LIBRARY_PATH on Solaris or the PATH on Windows). That mimics the behavior that applies in 1.1 and earlier releases.

However, a 1.2 custom class loader can override that policy and require that libraries be found in some application-defined location. This prevents a user from overriding the runtime environment to specify an alternate location for that library, which offers a slight security advantage. Note that if the user can write to the hardwired directory where the library lives, this advantage no longer exists: the user can simply overwrite the existing library instead of changing an environment variable to point to another library; the end result is the same.

Summary

The class loading mechanism is integral to Java's security features. Typically this integration is considered in light of the relationship between the class loader and the security manager. However, the class loader is important in its own right. The class loader must enforce the namespace separation between classes that are loaded from different sites (especially when these different sites are untrusted). Newer versions of the class loader (in Java 1.2) provide an easier route for developers of class loaders, and they provide more hooks into the access controller.

For sites that need a more flexible security policy, a different class loader may be desirable. For example, a class loader that allows programs within a protected, internal network to load class files from several machines on that internal network is particularly useful for extending the advantages that the Java model brings to program distribution. Other variations on this theme are possible—as long as the implementor remembers to keep the security requirements of Java's namespace model in mind when such variations are designed.

In the next chapters, we'll look in depth at Java's security manager and Java's protection domains, and see how the class loader and these features together further enforce Java's security policies.

4

The Security Manager Class

When most people think of Java security, they think of the protections afforded to a Java program—and, more particularly, only by default to a Java applet—by Java's security manager. As we've seen, there are other important facets of Java's security story, but the role played by the security manager is of paramount importance in the degree to which your machine will be safe from malicious Java programs.

On one level, the Java security manager is simple to understand, and it's often summarized by saying that it prevents Java applets from accessing your local disk or local network. The real story is more complicated than that, however, with the result that Java's security manager is often misunderstood. In this chapter, we'll look into how the security manager actually works, what it can and can't do, and when it does—and doesn't—protect you. In this chapter, we're only going to look at the security manager in terms of its capabilities, with an emphasis on how those capabilities are used by popular browsers; we'll look into writing our own security manager in the next few chapters.

Overview of the Security Manager

On a simple level, the security manager is responsible for determining most of the parameters of the Java sandbox—that is, it is ultimately up to the security manager to determine whether many particular operations should be permitted or rejected. If a Java program attempts to open a file, the security manager decides whether or not that operation should be permitted. If a Java program wants to connect to a particular machine on the network, it must first ask permission of the security manager. If a Java program wants to alter the state of certain threads, the security manager will intervene if such an operation is considered dangerous.

The security manager is of particular concern to authors and users of Java applets. In general, Java applications do not have security managers—unless the author of the application has provided one. Historically, that's been a somewhat unusual occurrence, even though there are many times when you might want a security manager in your Java application; this stems from the fact that before Java 1.2,* writing a security manager was more difficult than it is now. Beginning in 1.2, there is a default, user-configurable security manager that is suitable for most applications, one which can even be installed via a command-line argument when starting an application. This brings the benefits of a security manager to an application without requiring any programming. And we'll show how to write your own (non-default) security manager for the JavaRunner program in Chapter 6.

But this point cannot be overemphasized: Java applications (at least by default) have no security manager, while Java applets (again, by default) have a very strict security manager. This leads to a common misconception that exists in the arena of Java security: it's common to think that because Java is said to be secure, it is always secure, and that running Java applications that have been installed locally is just as secure as running Java applets inside a Java-enabled browser. Nothing is further from the truth.

To illustrate this point, consider the following malicious code:

```
public class MaliciousApplet extends Applet {
    public void init() {
        try {
            Runtime.getRuntime().exec("/bin/rm -rf .");
        } catch (Exception e) {}
    }
    public static void main(String args[]) {
        MaliciousApplet a = new MaliciousApplet();
        a.init();
    }
}
```

If you compile this code, place it on your web server, and load it as an applet, you'll get an error reflecting a security violation. However, if you compile this code, place it in a directory, and run it as an application, you'll end up deleting all the files in your current directory.† As a user, then, it's crucial that you understand which security manager is in place when you run a Java program so that you understand just what types of operations you are protected against.

---

* 1.2 is now Java 2.

† The example will only delete the files in your current directory if you run it on a Unix system, but we could have included similar code for any other operating system.

Security Managers and the Java API

The security manager can be considered a partnership between the Java API and the implementor of a specific Java application or of a specific Java-enabled browser. There is a class in the Java API called SecurityManager (java.lang.SecurityManager) which is the linchpin of this partnership—it provides the interface that the rest of the Java API uses to check whether particular operations are to be permitted. The essential algorithm the Java API uses to perform a potentially dangerous operation is always the same:

1. The programmer makes a request of the Java API to perform an operation.

2. The Java API asks the security manager if such an operation is allowable.

3. If the security manager does not want to permit the operation, it throws an exception back to the Java API, which in turn throws it back to the user.

4. Otherwise, the Java API completes the operation and returns normally.

Let's trace this idea with the example that we first saw in Chapter 1:

```
public class Cat {
    public static void main(String args[]) {
        try {
            String s;
            FileReader fr = new FileReader(args[0]);
            BufferedReader br = new BufferedReader(fr);
            while ((s = br.readLine()) != null)
                System.out.println(s);
        } catch (Exception e) {
            System.out.println(e);
        }
    }
}
```

The FileReader object will in turn create a FileInputStream object, and constructing the input stream is the first step of the algorithm. When the input stream is constructed, the Java API performs code similar to this:

```
public FileInputStream(String name) throws FileNotFoundException {
    SecurityManager security = System.getSecurityManager();
    if (security != null) {
        security.checkRead(name);
    }
    try {
        open(name); // open() is a private method of this class
    } catch (IOException e) {
        throw new FileNotFoundException(name);
    }
}
```

This is step two of our algorithm and is the essence of the idea behind the security manager: when the Java API wants to perform an operation, it first checks with the security manager and then calls a private method (the open() method in this case) that actually performs the operation.

Meanwhile, the security manager code is responsible for deciding whether or not the file in question should be allowed to be read and, if not, for throwing a security exception:

```
public class SecurityManagerImpl extends SecurityManager {
    public void checkRead(String s) {
        if (theFileIsNotAllowedToBeRead)
            throw new SecurityException("checkRead");
    }
}
```

The SecurityException class is a subclass of the RuntimeException class. Remember that runtime exceptions are somewhat different than other exceptions in Java in that they do not have to be caught in the code—which is why the check-Read() method does not have to declare that it throws that exception, and the FileInputStream constructor does not have to catch it. So if the security exception is thrown by the checkRead() method, the FileInputStream constructor will return before it calls the open() method—which is simply to say that the input file will never be opened, because the security manager prevented that code from being executed.

Typically, the security exception propagates up through all the methods in the thread that made the call; eventually, the top-most method receives the exception, which causes that thread to exit. When the thread exits in this way, it prints out the exception and the stack trace of methods that led it to receive the exception. This leads to the messages that you've probably seen in your Java console:

```
sun.applet.AppletSecurityException: checkread
        at sun.applet.AppletSecurity.checkRead(AppletSecurity.java:427)
        at java.io.FileOutputStream.<init>(FileOutputStream.java)
        at Cat.init(Cat.java:7)
        at sun.applet.AppletPanel.run(AppletPanel.java:273)
        at java.lang.Thread.run(Thread.java)
```

If the security exception is not thrown—that is, if the security manager decides that the particular operation should be allowed—then the method in the security manager simply returns, and everything proceeds as expected.

Several methods in the SecurityManager class are similar to the checkRead() method. It is up to the Java API to call those methods at the appropriate time. You may want to call those methods from your own Java code (using the technique shown above), but that's never required. Since the Java API provides the interface to the virtual operating system for the Java program, it's possible to isolate all the necessary security checks within the Java API itself.

You Don't Know About All Security Violations

Since a violation of the rules of the security manager manifests itself as a security exception, it's possible to hide the attempted violation from the user running the program by catching that exception.

To portray this feature in a positive light, it allows the author of a Java program to provide a more intelligent program that might be delivered to an end user in different ways. If the program is delivered as an application, the author may want to save some state from the program in a file on the user's disk; if the program is delivered as an applet, the author will need to save that state by sending it to the web server. So the program might have code that looks like this:

```
OutputStream os;
try {
    os = new FileOutputStream("statefile");
} catch (SecurityException e) {
    os = new Socket(webhost, webport).getOutputStream();
}
```

Now the Java program has an appropriate output stream where it can save its data.

On the other hand, this technique can be used by the author of an applet to probe your browser's security manager without your knowledge—because the applet is catching the security exceptions, you'll never see them. This is one reason why it's important to understand the ramifications of adjusting your browser's security policy.

One exception to this guideline occurs when you extend the virtual operating system of the Java API, and it is important to ensure that your extensions are well-integrated into Java's security scheme. Certain parts of the Java API—the Toolkit class, the Provider class, the Socket class, and others—are written in such a way that they allow you to provide your own implementation of those classes. If you're providing your own implementation of any of these classes, you have to make sure that it calls the security manager at appropriate times.

It's important to note that there is (by design) no attempt in the Java API to keep any sort of state. Whenever the Java API needs to perform an operation, it checks with the security manager to see if the operation is to be allowed—even if that same operation has been permitted by the security manager before. This is because the context of the operation is often significant—the security manager might allow a `FileOutputStream` object to be opened in some cases (e.g., by certain classes) while it might deny it in other cases. The Java API cannot keep track of this contextual information, so it asks the security manager for permission to perform every operation.

Trusted and Untrusted Classes

In the discussion that follows, we make the distinction between trusted and untrusted classes. Generally, an implementation of a security manager allows more operations for trusted classes than for untrusted classes. Whether or not a class is trusted is a complex decision based upon many factors—not the least of which is the release of Java under which the program is running. The default notion of what constitutes a trusted class has changed significantly between releases of Java:

- In Java 1.0, a class that is loaded from the CLASSPATH is considered trusted, and a class that is loaded from a class loader is considered untrusted.

- In Java 1.1, that same rule applies, but a class that is loaded from a JAR file may carry with it a digital signature that allows it to be given extra privileges.

- In Java 1.2, a class that is loaded from the core API is considered trusted and may perform any operation it wants to. Otherwise, classes are (by default) given privileges based upon where they were loaded from, including if they were loaded from the CLASSPATH. However, this applies only when certain command-line arguments are present; in the default method of loading applications, items from the CLASSPATH are generally considered trusted.

Nothing inherent in the design of the security manager requires security to be enforced as an all-or-nothing proposition for each class. It's possible to write a security manager that gives access to certain parts of the filesystem only to certain classes (even classes that came from the network), or to write a security manager that prohibits classes loaded from the CLASSPATH from performing operations that are normally permitted to classes loaded from the filesystem. A security manager can be as simple or as sophisticated as its author desires, with the result that the security manager can enforce a simple binary yes-or-no policy for operations, or it can enforce a very specialized, very detailed policy. This is true of all security managers in all versions of Java, though as we'll see in Chapter 5, one of the prime benefits of Java 1.2 is that it makes it much easier to achieve fine-grained security policies.

However, even though a sophisticated security manager can enforce a very detailed security policy, most implementations of the security manager (especially implementations that occur within popular Java-enabled browsers) assume that a trusted class is one that has been loaded from the CLASSPATH, while an untrusted class is one that has been loaded from a class loader. Furthermore, trusted classes are normally permitted to perform any operation, while an untrusted class is normally subjected to the full extent of the provisions of the security manager.

This dichotomy is essentially the same as the one we normally make between applications and applets: since an application is loaded entirely through the CLASSPATH, all of its classes are considered trusted, and the application can perform any operation that it wants to. On the other hand, the classes that comprise an applet are generally loaded from the network; hence they are considered untrusted and denied any operation that has the potential to violate the browser's security policy.

Beginning with Java 1.1, this distinction became less clear (and Java 1.2 made it even fuzzier): classes now have the ability to be signed, and classes that are signed can be treated as trusted or untrusted. We discuss the rationale behind that idea in Chapter 7 and we fully explore signed classes in the last part of this book; for now, we'll just keep in mind that some classes are trusted and some are not.

Using the Security Manager

We're now going to examine the public methods of the security manager so that we may understand how the security manager is used by applications and by the Java API.

Setting a Security Manager

There are two methods in the System class that are used to work with the security manager itself:

public static SecurityManager getSecurityManager()
> Return a reference to the currently installed security manager object (or null if no security manager is in place). Once obtained, this object can be used to test against various security policies.

public static void setSecurityManager(SecurityManager sm)
> Set the system's security manager to the given object. This method can only be called once, and once installed, the security manager cannot be removed. Attempting to call this method after a security manger has already been installed will result in a SecurityException.

These methods operate with the understanding that there is a single security manager in the virtual machine; the only operations that are possible on the security manager are setting it (that is, creating an instance of the security manager class and telling the virtual machine that the newly created object should be the security manager), and getting it (that is, asking the virtual machine to return the object that is the security manager so that a method might be invoked upon it).

We've already seen how you might use the getSecurityManager() method to retrieve the security manager and invoke an operation on it. Setting the security manager is a predictably simple operation:

```
public class TestSecurityManager {
    public static void main(String args[]) {
        System.setSecurityManager(new SecurityManagerImpl());
        ... do the work of the application ...
    }
}
```

However, there's an important detail here: the setSecurityManager() method is written in such a way that it can only be called once. Once a particular security manager has been installed, that security manager will be used by every other class that runs in this virtual machine. Once the policy is established, it cannot be changed (although the policy itself might be very fluid).

This fact has two important ramifications. First, as the author, it's up to you to write a security manager that embodies all the security policies you want your Java application to have. Second, in a Java-enabled browser, the security manager is always set as the browser initializes itself. This makes it impossible for an applet to set the security manager—it must live with the policy established by the author of the browser. This, of course, is a crucial feature of the security manager: since the security manager is responsible for fencing in the applet, it would be a catastrophe if the applet could change the security manager and hence the security policies of the browser.

The real significance of this last point, however, is that it is up to the developer of a browser to set the security policy. There is no absolute security policy that is common to every Java-enabled browser; each company that supports one is free to develop its own security manager and, accordingly, the security policies of that browser.

Now that we have an understanding of how the security manager works, we'll look into what protection the security manager actually provides. We'll discuss the public methods of the security manager that perform security checks and when those methods are called, along with the rationale behind each of the methods. Since these methods are all public, they can be called anywhere, including in your own code, although as we've mentioned, that's a rare thing.

When we discuss the rationale for each of the methods in the SecurityManager class, we'll discuss them from the point of view of untrusted classes. For now, consider an untrusted class as one loaded from the network (i.e., as part of an applet), while a trusted class is one that has been loaded from the filesystem through the user's CLASSPATH (including the classes that are part of the Java-enabled browser itself).

Methods Relating to File Access

The most well-known methods of the security manager class handle access to files on the local network. This includes any files that are on the local disk as well as files that might be physically located on another machine but appear (through the use of NFS, NetWare, Samba, or a similar network-based filesystem) to be part of the local filesystem.

These are the methods the security manager uses to track file access:

public void checkRead(FileDescriptor fd)
public void checkRead(String file)
public void checkRead(String file, Object context)
> Check whether the program is allowed to read the given file. The last method in this list is not used by the Java API itself.

public void checkWrite(FileDescriptor fd)
public void checkWrite(String file)
> Check whether the program is allowed to write the given file.

public void checkDelete(String file)
> Check whether the program is allowed to delete the given file.

Interestingly, although as developers we tend to think of other file operations—such as creating a file or seeing when the file was last modified—as being distinct operations, as far as security is concerned, the Java API considers all operations to be either reading, writing, or deleting.

Table 4-1 lists the Java API interaction with the checkRead(), checkWrite(), and checkDelete() methods, listing when and why each check is invoked. In all the tables in this chapter, the syntax may imply that the calling methods are all static, but that of course is not the case: the entry File.canRead() means the canRead() method invoked on an instance of the File class.

This table lists only those classes that directly call the security manager method in question. There may be many routes through the Java API that lead to one of these checks; for example, when a FileReader object is constructed, it will construct a FileInputStream object, which will result in a call to checkRead().

Table 4-1. Check Methods

Method	Calling Methods	Rationale
checkRead()	File.canRead()	Test if the current thread can read the file
	FileInputStream() RandomAccessFile()	Constructing a file object requires that you must be able to read the file

Table 4-1. Check Methods (continued)

Method	Calling Methods	Rationale
	`File.isDirectory()` `File.isFile()`	Determining whether a file object is an actual file or a directory requires that you must be able to read the file
	`File.lastModified()`	Determining the modification date requires that you read the file's attributes
	`File.length()`	Determining the length requires that you read the files attributes
	`File.list()`	Determining the files in a directory requires that you read the directory
`checkWrite()`	`File.canWrite()`	Test if the current thread can write the file
	`FileOutputStream()` `RandomAccessFile()`	To construct a file object, you must be able to write the file
	`File.mkdir()`	To create a directory, you must be able to write to the filesystem
	`File.renameTo()`	To rename a file, you must be able to write to the directory containing the file
	`File.createTemp-` `File()` ★	To create a temporary file, you must be able to write the file
`checkDelete()`	`File.delete()`	Test if the current thread can delete a file
	`File.deleteOnExit()` ★	Test if the current thread can delete the file when the virtual machine exits

By default, in most Java-enabled browsers, untrusted classes are not allowed any sort of file access, for these reasons:

- If an untrusted class is allowed to read an arbitrary file, it might read your password file, or the data file from your tax preparation program, or the temporary file containing an edit log of the sensitive document you're working on.

- If an untrusted class is allowed to write an arbitrary file, it might overwrite data on your machine, essentially erasing the file. Worse, it might insert a virus into an existing file (or create a new file with a virus), with catastrophic results. Less damaging, but still a problem, would be the ability for the applet to completely fill the available disk space.

- If an untrusted class is allowed to delete files, it could destroy any data in your local filesystem.

Some Java developers consider this strict restriction on file access unnecessarily draconian—they'd seek a compromise where at least some access to some local files is possible. The types of suggested compromises are things like:

The Real Reason Applets Cannot Access Files

If you're a Java developer chafing at the restriction that an applet cannot access the user's local files, you're missing one of the points of developing in Java. The real reason your applet can't access local files is that there may not be any: what if your applet is being run on a network computer or a Java-enabled TV webtop? If your applet requires a local disk, it will be unable to run on the next generation of computing devices. Java is leading-edge technology; if you're riding the next wave, you may as well take full advantage of it—there is a wealth of middleware Java tools that will allow you to easily read and write files from and to a remote web server or file server.

- Untrusted classes should be allowed access to the system's temporary directory.

  The problem with this is that other programs might have left sensitive data in that directory. If I'm editing salary data on my machine, I wouldn't want some untrusted class to come along and see the edit log that exists in the system's temporary directory.

- A single directory could be set up for the exclusive use of untrusted classes.

  This does not prevent a bad untrusted class from accessing, erasing, or corrupting the data files of other untrusted programs.

- An individual directory could be set up for each applet (or for each package of untrusted classes).

  This would work in theory, but such a scheme would be unwieldy. It also leaves potential attack routes for an applet. On the Internet, one site can pretend to be another site by engaging in IP spoofing (see the discussion in "The Need for Authentication" in Chapter 7); applets from such sites could read data from the original applet. In addition, an applet could still fill the available disk space.

- The user could be prompted before an untrusted class accessed a file.

  This issue is less black-and-white. On the one hand, there's a persuasive argument that computer users are pretty intelligent, and they'll know whether or not a program should be allowed to access the file in question. In the real world, however, there are users who will not pay enough attention to such prompts and always grant access, to the detriment of their system's security. You may not have much sympathy for users on home computers who grant an applet access to the data file of their financial package, but the user on a corporate or campus network who allows an applet access to his or her password file harms other users of the network as well.

Nonetheless, as with all policies enforced by the security manager, it is up to the author of a particular program (or web browser) to establish the policy the security manager will enforce. Hence, while Netscape Navigator, Internet Explorer, and HotJava all have a default policy that prevents untrusted classes from all file access, some of them allow the user to configure a different policy. HotJava and the JDK's `appletviewer`, for example, allow the user to create a set of directories in which applets can read and write files, and some versions of Internet Explorer allow the user to grant file access to all untrusted classes.

There is one exception to the rule about file access: applets that are loaded from a CODEBASE that specifies file as its protocol (e.g., *file:/myapplets*) are allowed to read (but not create or delete) files in the CODEBASE directory (and any of its subdirectories). This is required to allow the applet to load other resources—audio files, images, as well as other classes—in the same manner in which it would load those resources through an HTTP-based URL.

If you carefully considered the list of methods in the tables above, you were probably surprised not to see an obvious method to check: the actual `read()` or `write()` methods of any of the `File` classes. The assumption here is that a trusted class is responsible for determining the security policy associated with any particular `File` object; if the trusted class decides that it is okay for an untrusted class to perform I/O on a particular `File*Stream` object, then it is free to deliver that object to the untrusted class, and the untrusted class is free to read or write to that object. This implementation also allows for much greater efficiency: if the program had to check with the security manager every time it called the `read()` or `write()` methods, I/O performance would drastically suffer.

Methods Relating to Network Access

Network access in Java is always accomplished by opening a network socket, whether directly through the `Socket` class or indirectly through another class like the `URL` class. An untrusted class can only (by default) open a •socket to the machine from which it was actually downloaded; typically, this is the location given by the CODEBASE tag in the HTML for the browser page containing the applet or— in the absence of such a tag—the web server for the page. In either case, the machine in question is a web server, so we'll use that terminology in this discussion.

This restriction on untrusted classes is designed to prevent two types of attack. The first attack concerns a rogue applet using your machine for malicious purposes by connecting to a third machine over the network. The canonical description of this attack is an applet that connects to the mail server on someone else's machine and sends people on that machine offensive email from your address. There are more severe attacks possible with this technique, however—such an applet could use a connection from your machine to break into a third computer; auditors on that third computer will think the break-in attempts are coming from you, which can cause you all sorts of legal problems.

The second sort of attack concerns network information on your local network that you might not want to be broadcast to the world at large. Typically, computers at corporations or campuses sit behind a firewall so that users on the Internet cannot access those computers (see Figure 4-1). The firewall allows only certain types of traffic through (e.g., HTTP traffic), so that users on the local network can access the Internet, but users on the Internet cannot glean any information about the local network.

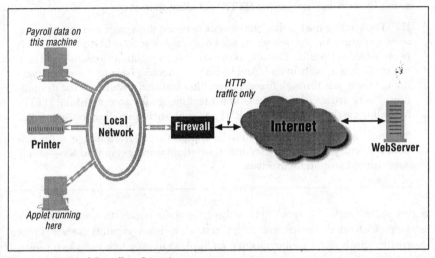

Figure 4-1. A typical firewall configuration

Now consider what happens if an applet downloaded onto a machine on the local network can connect to other machines on the local network. This allows the applet to gather all sorts of information about the local network topology and network services and to send that information (via HTTP, so that it will pass through the firewall) back out onto the Internet. Such an opportunity for corporate spying would be very tempting to would-be hackers. Worse, if the applet had access to arbitrary network services, it could break into the local HR database and steal employee data, or it could break into a network file server and steal corporate documents. Hence, applets (and untrusted classes in general) are prevented from arbitrary network access.

Network sockets can be logically divided into two classes: client sockets and server sockets. A client socket is responsible for initiating a conversation with an existing

The Real Reason Why Network Access Is Limited

Just when you realized that your applet couldn't access files in the new network computing model and thus had to send all its data over the network comes this restriction of limited network access.

But even if this restriction didn't exist in Java, the configuration of many sites dictates a harsher restriction for network access anyway—the corporate or campus firewall. The firewall often restricts all traffic between the applet's web server and the user's browser to a set of protocols and, possibly, a set of hosts. If you're going to write really effective network applets with Java, you have to take this into account anyway—which means that all your network access really needs to use something called HTTP-tunneling to work.

HTTP-tunneling means that all requests between the applet and the network service running on the web server are encapsulated to look like normal HTTP (web browsing) traffic. This allows the data to go through firewalls that filter out traffic based on protocol. And by only connecting back to the web server, the data will pass through firewalls that filter out traffic based on the destination. There are a variety of well-known techniques for accomplishing HTTP-tunneling via the URL class, and RMI gives you such tunneling transparently.

So, once again, if you're going to write applets that take advantage of the full power of Java, Java's network security restrictions won't get in your way—you'll have worked around them anyway.

server socket; server sockets sit idle waiting for these requests to come from client sockets. Untrusted classes are often restricted from creating server sockets. Normally, this is not a problem: since an applet can only talk to its web server, it could only answer requests from that machine—and the applet can already open a connection to that machine at will; there's no algorithmic or logistic reason why an operation between the applet and the web server cannot always start with the applet as the client. In situations where the applet is allowed to open client sockets to other machines, however, this reasoning doesn't apply, and the ability to create a server socket is often granted in such situations (and, sometimes, in all situations).

The security manager uses the following methods to check network access:

public void checkConnect(String host, int port)
public void checkConnect(String host, int port, Object context)

Check if the program can open a client socket to the given port on the given host. The second form of this method is never called directly from the Java API.

public void checkListen(int port)

Check if the program can create a server socket that is listening on the given port.

public void checkAccept(String host, int port)

Check if the program can accept (on an existing server socket) a client connection that originated from the given host and port.

public void checkMulticast(InetAddress addr)
public void checkMulticast(InetAddress addr, byte ttl)

Check if the program can create a multicast socket at the given multicast address (optionally with the given time-to-live value).

public void checkSetFactory()

Check if the program can change the default socket implementation. When the Socket class is used to create a socket, it gets a new socket from the socket factory, which typically supplies a standard TCP-based socket. However, a socket factory could be used to supply SSL-based sockets, or any other socket variant.

The instances where these methods are used and the rationale for such uses are shown in Table 4-2.

Table 4-2. Security Manager Methods to Protect Network Access

Method	Called by	Rationale
checkConnect()	DatagramSocket.send() DatagramSocket.receive() ☆ MulticastSocket.send() Socket()	Test if the untrusted class can create a client-side connection
checkConnect()	DatagramSocket.getLocalAddress() InetAddress.getHostName() InetAddress.getLocalHost() InetAddress.getAllByName()	Test if the untrusted class can see any hosts on the local network
checkListen()	DatagramSocket() MulticastSocket() ServerSocket()	Test if the untrusted class can create a server-side socket
checkMulticast()	DatagramSocket.send() DatagramSocket.receive() MulticastSocket.send() MulticastSocket.receive() MulticastSocket.joinGroup() MulticastSocket.leaveGroup()	Test if the untrusted class can operate on a multicast socket
checkAccept()	ServerSocket.accept() DatagramSocket.receive() ★	Test if the untrusted class can accept a server connection

Table 4-2. Security Manager Methods to Protect Network Access (continued)

Method	Called by	Rationale
checkSetFactory()	ServerSocket.setSocketFactory() Socket.setSocketFactory() URL.setURLStreamHandlerFactory() URLConnection.setContentHandler- Factory() RMI.setSocketFactory()	Test if the untrusted class can alter the manner in which all sockets are created
checkSetFactory()	HttpURLConnection.setFollowRedi- rects()	Test if the untrusted class can change redirection behavior

Some notes are in order. As in the case with file access, these methods sometimes check operations that are logically different from a programming view, but are essentially the same thing at a system view. Hence, the checkConnect() method not only checks the opening of a socket but also the retrieval of hostname or address information (on the theory that to know the name of a host, you need to be able to open a socket to that host). This last test may seem somewhat odd— under what circumstances, you might wonder, should an untrusted class not be able to know the name or address of the machine on which it is running? Recall that we want to prevent the outside world from knowing our network topology; this includes the name and address of the user's machine as well.*

There was a change in the default security policy supplied in 1.0 and in 1.1 with respect to untrusted classes and server sockets (either instances of class Server-Socket or datagram sockets that received data from any source). In 1.0, untrusted classes were typically not allowed to create a server socket at all, which meant that the checkListen() and checkAccept() methods always threw a security exception when an applet attempted such an operation. In 1.1 and later, untrusted classes are allowed to create a server socket so long as the port number of that socket is greater than the privileged port number on the machine (typically 1024). Note too that the receive() method of the DatagramSocket class in 1.2 now calls the checkAccept() rather than the checkConnect() method.

Some applet publishers consider it to be very inconvenient to have to put both the applet and any network services that the applet requires on the same machine (the applet's web server). When you're configuring a network of machines, it certainly is more natural to have a database server that is separate from the web server; the scaling and flexibility that such separation gives is the cornerstone of network computing. Hence, an applet that is running on the browser shown in Figure 4-2

---

* On the other hand, there's a good chance that the outside web server already knows that information, since our browser sent along a hostname and other information when it retrieved the file to begin with. If our request passed through a firewall or proxy server, there's a chance that some of this information was prevented from passing to the outside web server, but that's not necessarily the case either.

would consider it more convenient to access the database server directly. Sites with this configuration may therefore attempt to convince you to adjust your browser's network connection policy so their applet will work in this multitiered environment.

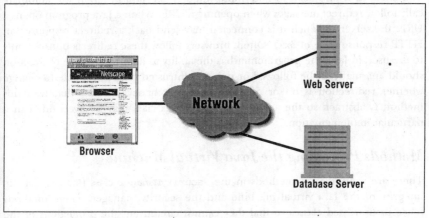

Figure 4-2. An untrusted class cannot directly connect to the database server

However, it's relatively trivial for applet publishers to set up a proxy service on their web server that forwards requests to the third machine, so that the applet only connects to the web server while the proxy service can connect to the third machine (e.g., the database server). Such a configuration may not be ideal—there's still a lot of traffic on the web server going through the proxy—but it's an effective compromise.

The requirement to use a proxy should not prove onerous to developers, either; it's common for network software providers to deliver such proxies with their Java code. Many JDBC-driver vendors, for example, provide such a proxy HTTP server that their JDBC drivers can access. Writing a simple proxy from scratch for other services is well within the grasp of good Java programmers.

Nonetheless, if in your view the reward of reduced network traffic outweighs the security considerations behind preventing arbitrary network access by untrusted classes, the Sun browsers (HotJava and `appletviewer`) and some versions of Internet Explorer allow you to configure them so that untrusted classes can connect to any host on the network.

The `checkSetFactory()` method of the security manager class is responsible for arbitrating the use of several low-level aspects of Java's network classes. Most of the tests made by this method have to do with whether or not the untrusted class is allowed to create some variety of socket factory. Socket factories are classes that are responsible for creating sockets that implement a particular interface while having a nonstandard feature: for example, a Java server might want to encrypt all of its traffic, so it would create and install a socket factory that creates only SSL-enabled sockets. Predictably, untrusted classes cannot change the socket factory in use.

This method is also used to determine whether the Java program will automatically follow redirect messages when opening a URL. When a Java program opens a URL, the server to which it is connected may send back a redirect response (an HTTP response code of 3xx). Often, browsers follow these redirects transparently to the user; in Java, the programmer has the ability to determine if the redirection should automatically be followed or not. An untrusted class is not able to change whether redirection is on or off. The HttpURLConnection class that uses this method is abstract, so the actual behavior of this class may be overridden in a particular implementation.

Methods Protecting the Java Virtual Machine

There are a number of methods in the SecurityManager class that protect the integrity of the Java virtual machine and the security manager. These methods fence in untrusted classes so that they cannot circumvent the protections of the security manager and the Java API itself. These methods are summarized in Table 4-3.

Table 4-3. Security Manager Methods Protecting the Virtual Machine

Method	Called by	Rationale
checkCreateClass-Loader()	ClassLoader()	Class loaders are protected since they provide information to the security manager
checkExec()	Runtime.exec()	Other processes might damage the user's machine
checkExec()	System.setIn() ☆ System.setOut() ☆ System.setErr() ☆	Don't let important messages be redirected away from the user
checkLink()	Runtime.load() Runtime.loadLibrary()	Don't let untrusted code import native code
checkExit()	Runtime.exit()	Don't let untrusted code halt the virtual machine
checkExit()	Runtime.runFinalizers-OnExit()	Don't let untrusted code change if finalizers are run
checkPermission() ★	many	See if the current thread has been granted a particular permission

public void checkCreateClassLoader()

The distinction we keep mentioning between trusted and untrusted classes is often based on the location from which the class was loaded (i.e., if the class came from the filesystem or from the network). As a result, the class loader we examined in Chapter 3 takes on an important role, since the security manager must ask the class loader where a particular class came from. The class loader is also responsible for marking certain classes as signed classes. Hence, an untrusted class is typically not allowed to create a class loader. This method is only called by the constructor of the ClassLoader class: if you can create a class loader (or if you obtain a reference to a previously created class loader), you can use it.

public void checkExec(String cmd)

This method is used to prevent execution of arbitrary system commands by untrusted classes—an untrusted class cannot, for example, execute a separate process that removes all the files on your disk.* In addition, this method is used to test whether a Java program is able to redirect the standard input, output, or error streams to another source—with the predictable result that untrusted classes are not allowed to perform such redirection.

In Java 1.2, this method is no longer used to determine whether the standard streams may be redirected. Redirection of those streams in 1.2 is determined instead by the checkPermission() method.

public void checkLink(String lib)

System commands aren't the only code that is out of reach of the security manager—any native (C language) code that is executed by the virtual machine cannot be protected by the security manager (or, in fact, by any aspect of the Java sandbox). Native code is executed by linking a shared library into the virtual machine; this method prevents an untrusted class from linking in such libraries.

It may seem as if this check is very important. It is, but only to a point: the programmatic binding from Java to C is such that Java code cannot just call an arbitrary C function—the C function must have a very specialized name that will not exist in an arbitrary library. So any C function that the untrusted class would like to call must reside in a library that you've downloaded and placed on your machine—and if the program's author can convince you to do that, then you don't really have a secure system anyway, and the author could find a different line of attack against you.

---

* The separate process would not need to be written in Java, of course, so there would be no security manager around to enforce the prohibition about deleting files.

public void checkExit(int status)

Next, there is the continuing processing of the virtual machine itself. This method prevents an untrusted class from shutting down the virtual machine. This method also prevents an untrusted class from changing whether or not all finalizers are run when the virtual machine does exit. This means that an untrusted class—and in particular, an applet—cannot guarantee that all the finalize methods of all the objects will be called before the system exits (which cannot be guaranteed in any case, since the browser can be terminated from the operating system without an opportunity to run the finalizers anyway).

public void checkPermission(Permission p) ★
public void checkPermission(Permission p, Object context) ★

Check to see if the current thread has the given permission. This method is at the heart of the access controller, which we'll explain in Chapter 5, where we'll also list when it is called. The second form of this method is never used by the Java API. The default for untrusted classes is to be given only a few explicit permissions, which we'll also list in Chapter 5.

Methods Protecting Program Threads

Java depends heavily on threads for its execution; in a simple Java program that uses images and audio, there may be a dozen or more threads that are created automatically for the user (depending on the particular implementation of the VM). These are system-level threads responsible for garbage collection, the various input and output needs of the graphical interface, threads to fetch images, etc. An untrusted class cannot manipulate any of these threads, because doing so would prevent the Java virtual machine from running properly, affecting other applets and possible even the browser itself.

The security manager protects threads with these methods:

public void checkAccess(Thread g)

Check if the program is allowed to change the state of the given thread.

public void checkAccess(ThreadGroup g)

Check if the program is allowed to change the state of the given thread group (and the threads that it holds).

public ThreadGroup getThreadGroup()

Supply a default thread group for newly created threads to belong to.

Table 4-4 shows the methods of the Java API that are affected by the policy set in the checkAccess() methods.

Table 4-4. Security Manager Methods Protecting Thread Access

Method	Called by	Rationale
CheckAccess(Thread g)	Thread.stop() Thread.interrupt() Thread.suspend() Thread.resume() Thread.setPriority() Thread.setName() Thread.setDaemon() Thread.setClassLoader() ★ Thread()	Untrusted classes may only manipulate threads that they have created
checkAccess(Thread-Group g)	ThreadGroup() ThreadGroup.setDaemon() ThreadGroup.setMaxPriority() ThreadGroup.stop() ThreadGroup.suspend() ThreadGroup.resume() ThreadGroup.destroy() ThreadGroup.interrupt() ★	Untrusted classes can only affect thread groups that they have created
getThreadGroup()	Thread()	Threads of untrusted classes must belong to specified groups
checkPermission(Permission p)	Thread.stop() ★	Stopping a thread could corrupt state of the virtual machine.

Most of the rationale behind these methods is straightforward: an untrusted class can manipulate its own threads, and it can manipulate threads that are in its thread group. This prevents an untrusted class from suspending the threads responsible for loading images; for example, those threads were not created by the untrusted class, and so the untrusted class cannot affect them.

Threads in a Java program are organized into a hierarchy (see Figure 4-3). In theory, the policy of the security manager should also apply to this hierarchy such that threads may only manipulate threads that are below them in the hierarchy. Hence, the calculating thread really should not be able to manipulate the state of the I/O reading thread—regardless of whether the calculating thread is executing trusted code or untrusted code. Similarly, the processing thread ought to be able to manipulate the state of the I/O reading thread even if the code to do so is in an untrusted class, since that implies that the untrusted class created the processing thread and the I/O thread anyway.

In practice, however, it does not work that way in Java 1.1: in that release, by default each applet is given an individual thread group, and the threads within that group can manipulate other threads within that group without respect to any hierarchy. In Java 1.2, the default is for the thread hierarchy to operate as expected.

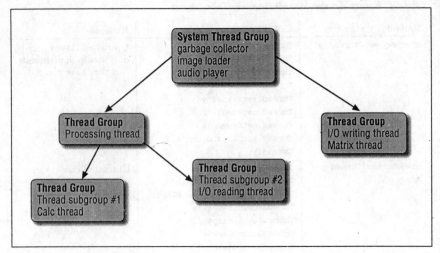

Figure 4-3. A Java thread hierarchy

Unlike the other public methods of the security manager, the getThreadGroup()
method is not responsible for deciding whether access to a particular resource
should be granted or not, and it does not throw a security exception under any
circumstances. The point of this method is to determine the default thread group
that a particular thread should belong to. When a thread is constructed and does
not ask to be placed into a particular thread group, the getThreadGroup()
method of the security manager is used to find a thread group to which the thread
should be assigned. By default, this is the thread group of the calling thread, but a
security manager can implement different logic so that the thread hierarchy we've
described above becomes possible.

The getThreadGroup() method is only present in Java 1.1 and subsequent
releases. In Java 1.0 (and browsers built on that release), thread security was generally non-existent: any thread could manipulate the state of any other thread, and
applets weren't able to create their own thread groups. This additional method
provided the infrastructure by which security managers built in Java 1.1 and later
releases can implement the security policy that we've described here.

In 1.2 the Thread class also calls the checkPermission() method of the security
manager whenever the stop() method is called, since stopping a thread is an
inherently dangerous operation (which has led the stop() method to become
deprecated). For backward compatibility, this permission is normally granted even
to untrusted classes, but an end user may change her environment so that the
security manager throws an exception whenever the stop() method is called.

Methods Protecting System Resources

The Java-enabled browser has access to certain system-level resources to which untrusted classes should not be granted access. The next set of methods (outlined in Table 4-5) in the SecurityManager class handles those system-level resources.

Table 4-5. Security Manager Protections of System Resources

Method	Called by	Rationale
checkPrintJobAccess()	Toolkit.getPrintJob()[a]	Untrusted classes can't initiate print jobs
checkSystemClipboardAccess()	Toolkit.getSystemClipboard()	Untrusted classes can't read the system clipboard
checkAwtEventQueueAccess()	EventQueue.getEventQueue()	Untrusted classes can't manipulate window events
checkPropertiesAccess()	System.getProperties() System.setProperties()	Untrusted classes can't see or set system properties
checkPropertyAccess()	System.getProperty()	Untrusted classes can't get a particular system property
checkPropertyAccess()	Locale.setDefault()	Can't change the locale unless the user.language property can be read
checkPropertyAccess()	Font.getFont()	Can't get a font unless its property can be read
checkTopLevelWindow()	Window()	Windows created by untrusted classes should have an indentifying banner

[a] The Toolkit class is abstract and hence may vary by implementation; it's assumed that the implementation on a particular platform will call the correct method of the security manager.

public void checkPrintJobAccess()

Untrusted classes are not allowed access to the user's printer. This is another example of a nuisance protection; you wouldn't want a rogue applet sending reams of nonsense data to your printer. This method is never actually called by the standard Java API—it's up to the platform-specific implementation of the AWT toolkit to call it.

Note that this doesn't prevent the user from initiating a print action from the browser—it only prevents an applet from initiating the print action. The utility of such a check is subtle: the user always has to confirm the print dialog box before anything is actually printed (at least with the popular implementations of the AWT toolkit). The only sort of scenario that this check prevents is this:

the user could surf to *www.EvilSite.org* and then to *www.sun.com*; although the applets from *EvilSite* are no longer on the current page, they're still active, and one of them could pop up the print dialog. The user will associate the dialog with the *www.sun.com* page and presumably allow it to print—and when the *EvilSite* applet then prints out offensive material, the user will blame the Sun page.

public void checkSystemClipboardAccess()

The Java virtual machine contains a system clipboard that can be used as a holder for copy-and-paste operations. Granting access to the clipboard to an untrusted class runs the risk that a class will come along, examine the clipboard, and find contents a previous program left there. Such contents might be sensitive data that the new class should not be allowed to read; hence, untrusted classes are prevented from accessing the system clipboard. This restriction applies only to the system clipboard: an untrusted class can still create its own clipboard and perform its own copy-and-paste operations to that clipboard. Untrusted classes can also share non-system clipboards between them.

This method is also never actually called by the Java API; it's up to the platform-specific implementation of the AWT toolkit to call it.

public void checkAwtEventQueueAccess()

Similarly, the Java virtual machine contains a system event queue that holds all pending AWT events for the system. An untrusted class that had access to such a queue would be able to delete events from the queue or insert events into the queue. This protects against the same sort of scenario we saw for printing—an applet on a previously visited page could insert events into the queue which would then be fed to an applet on the existing page.

Since this means that an untrusted class cannot get the system event queue, it is unable to call any of the methods of the EventQueue class—specifically the postEvent() and peekEvent() methods. Note, however, that an applet may still post events to itself using the dispatchEvent() method of the Component class.

public void checkPropertiesAccess()
public void checkPropertyAccess(String key)

The Java virtual machine has a set of global (system) properties that contains information about the user and the user's machine: login name, home directory, etc. Untrusted classes are generally denied access to some of this information in an attempt to limit the amount of spying that an applet can do. As usual, these methods only prevent access to the system properties; an untrusted class is free to set up its own properties and to share those properties with other classes if it desires.

Note that security managers are typically written to allow access to some system properties based on the name of the property.

public boolean checkTopLevelWindow(Object window)

Java classes, regardless of whether they are trusted or untrusted, are normally allowed to create top-level windows on the user's desktop. However, there is a concern that an untrusted class might bring up a window that looks exactly like another application on the user's desktop and thus confuse the user into doing something that ought not be done. For example, an applet could bring up a window that looks just like a telnet session and grab the user's password when the user responds to the password prompt. For that reason, top-level windows that are created by untrusted classes have some sort of identifying banner on them.

Note that unlike other methods in the security manager, this method has three outcomes: if it returns true, the window will be created normally; if it returns false, the window will be created with the identifying banner. However, this method could also throw a security exception (just like all the other methods of the security manager class) to indicate that the window should not be created at all. However, all the popular security manager implementations allow an untrusted class to bring up a window, subject to the identifying banner.

Methods Protecting Security Aspects

There are a number of methods in the security manager that protect Java's idea of security itself. These methods are summarized in Table 4-6.

Table 4-6. Security Manager Methods Protecting Java Security

Method	Called by	Rationale
checkMemberAccess()	Class.getFields() Class.getMethods() Class.getConstructors() Class.getField() Class.getMethod() Class.getConstructor() Class.getDeclaredClasses() Class.getDeclaredFields() Class.getDeclaredMethods() Class.getDeclaredConstructors() Class.getDeclaredField() Class.getDeclaredMethod() Class.getDeclardConstructor()	Untrusted classes can only inspect public information about other classes

Table 4-6. Security Manager Methods Protecting Java Security (continued)

Method	Called by	Rationale
checkPackageAc-cess()	not called	Check if the untrusted class can access classes in a particular package
checkPackageDef-inition()	not called	Check if the untrusted class can load classes in a partic-ular package
checkSecurityAc-cess()	Identity.setPublicKey() Identity.setInfo() Identity.addCertificate() Identity.removeCertificate() IdentityScope.setSystem-Scope() Provider.clear()[a] Provider.put() Provider.remove() Security.insertProviderAt() Security.removeProvider() Security.setProperty() Signer.getPrivateKey() Signer.setKeyPair() Identity.toString()[b] Security.getProviders() Security.getProvider() Security.getProperty()	Untrusted classes cannot manipulate security features

[a] The provider methods only call the security manager in 1.2.
[b] The last four methods in this list no longer call the security manager in 1.2.

public void checkMemberAccess(Class clazz, int which)

In Chapter 2, we examined the importance of the access modifiers to the integrity of Java's security model. Java's reflection API allows programs to inspect classes to determine the class's methods, variables, and constructors. The ability to access these entities can impact the memory integrity that Java provides.

The reflection API is powerful enough that, by inspection, a program can determine the private instance variables and methods of a class (although it can't actually access those variables or call those methods). Untrusted classes are allowed to inspect a class and find out only about its public variables and methods.

public void checkSecurityAccess(String action)

In the last half of this book, we'll be examining the details of the Java security package. This package implements a higher-order notion of security, including digital signatures, message digests, public and private keys, etc. The security package depends on this method in the security manager to arbitrate which classes can perform certain security-related operations. As an example, before a class is allowed to read a private key, this method is called with a string indicating that a private key is being read.

Predictably, an untrusted class is not allowed to perform any of these security-related operations, while a trusted class is.* Although the string argument gives the ability to distinguish what operation is being attempted, that argument is typically ignored in present implementations. As we discuss the features of the security package itself, we'll examine more in depth how the security package uses this method.

public void checkPackageAccess(String pkg)
public void checkPackageDefinition(String pkg)

These methods are used in conjunction with a class loader. When a class loader is asked to load a class with a particular package name, it will first ask the security manager if it is allowed to do so by calling the checkPackageAccess() method. This allows the security manager to make sure that the untrusted class is not trying to use application-specific classes that it shouldn't know about.

Similarly, when a class loader actually creates a class in a particular package, it asks the security manager if it is allowed to do so by calling the checkPackageDefinition() method. This allows the security manager to prevent an untrusted class from loading a class from the network and placing it into, for example, the java.lang package.

Note the distinction between these two methods: in the case of the checkPackageAccess() method, the question is whether the class loader can reference the class at all—e.g., whether we can call a class in the sun package. In the checkPackageDefinition() method, the class bytes have been loaded, and the security manager is being asked if they can belong to a particular package.

By default, these methods are never called. If you write a class loader, you should make sure that you call these methods as we indicated in Chapter 3.

That's all the methods of the security manager class that are used by the Java API to perform checks on certain operations. There are two more public methods of the SecurityManager class that we have not examined in this section; even though those methods are public, they are generally only used when you implement your

---

* This is not quite true: most browsers (including Netscape Communicator 4.0 and Internet Explorer 4.0) do not implement the Java security package at all. For classes loaded over the network, the effect is the same: you cannot use the methods of the security package. In these browsers, a trusted class in the browser's CLASSPATH, however, is also unable to use the security package.

own security manager, so we will defer their discussion. Remember that the discussion we followed in this chapter about the behavior of the system is based on a default set of behaviors exhibited by popular Java-enabled browsers—but since each browser is free to implement its own security policies, your particular browser may have a variation of the features we've just discussed.

Summary

In this chapter, we've had an overview of the most commonly known feature of Java's security story: the security manager. The security manager is responsible for arbitrating access to what we normally consider operating system features—files, network sockets, printers, etc. The goal of the security manager is to grant access to each class according to the amount of trust the user has in the class. Often, that means granting full access to trusted classes (that is, classes that have been loaded from the filesystem) while limiting access when the access is requested from an untrusted class (that is, a class that has been loaded from the network).

Although the security manager is the most commonly known feature of Java's security story, it's often misunderstood: there is no standard security manager among Java implementations, and Java applications, by default, have no security manager at all. Even with the popular Java-enabled browsers, the user often has latitude in what protections the security manager will be asked to enforce.

We examined in this chapter all the times when the security manager is asked to make a decision regarding access; such decisions range from the expected file and network access to more esoteric decisions, such as whether a frame needs a warning banner or what thread group a particular thread should belong to. This gave us a basic understanding of how the security manager can be used to enforce a specific policy, and the issues involved when defining such a policy. This knowledge will be used as a basis in the next few chapters, when we'll look at how to implement our own security manager.

5

The Access Controller

In this chapter, we're going to examine Java's access controller. While the security manager is the key to the security model of the Java sandbox, the access controller is the mechanism that the security manager actually uses to enforce its protections. The security manager may be king, but the access controller is really the power behind the throne.

The access controller is actually somewhat redundant. The purpose of the security manager is to determine whether or not particular operations should be permitted or denied. The purpose of the access controller is really the same: it decides whether access to a critical system resource should be permitted or denied. Hence, the access controller can do everything the security manager can do.

The reason there is both an access controller and a security manager is mainly historical: the access controller is only available in Java 1.2* and subsequent releases. Before the access controller existed, the security manager had to rely on its internal logic to determine the security policy that should be in effect, and changing the security policy required changing the security manager itself. Starting with 1.2, the security manager is able to defer these decisions to the access controller. Since the security policy enforced by the access controller can be specified in a file, this allows a much more flexible mechanism for determining policies. The access controller also gives us a much simpler method of granting fine-grained, specific permissions to specific classes. That process was theoretically possibly with the security manager alone, but it was simply too hard to implement.

But the large body of pre-1.2 Java programs dictates that the primary interface to system security—that is, the security manager—cannot change; otherwise, existing

---

* 1.2 is now Java 2.

code that implements or depends on the security manager would become obsolete. Hence, the introduction of the access controller did not replace the security manager—it supplemented the security manager. This relationship is illustrated in Figure 5-1. Typically, an operation proceeds through the program code into the Java API, through the security manager to the access controller, and finally into the operating system. In certain cases, however, the security manager may bypass the access controller. And native libraries are still outside the domain of either the security manager or the access controller (although the ability to load those libraries may be restricted, as we've seen).

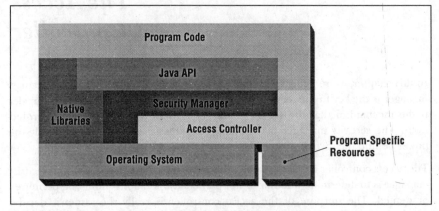

Figure 5-1. Coordination of the security manager and the access controller

The access controller plays another role in this picture as well: it allows a program to determine that access to any arbitrary resource must require explicit permission. A program that accesses employee payroll information from a corporate database may want to assign permission to each employee to access only his or her own data in the database. While global access to the database may be controlled by the security manager (e.g., because it's necessary to open a file or socket to get to the database), access to the particular record can be controlled by the access controller alone. Because the access controller (unlike the security manager) is easily extensible, it is simple for a program to use the same security framework to access both the general resources of the operating system and any specific resources of the program.

Keep in mind, however, that the core Java API never calls the access controller unless a security manager is in place, and that the access controller will not be initialized until it is called. If you call it directly for a program-specific resource, it will initialize itself automatically. But by default, Java applications run without a security manager will not use the access controller. We'll discuss later in this chapter and in Chapter 6 the use of the -Djava.security.manager flag to install a security manager into the application, which will initialize the access controller for us.

In this chapter, then, we'll look into the access controller, including its implementation and its use. This will give us the necessary knowledge of how the access controller works, how it can be used to change the security of a Java program without requiring code changes, and how it is used to implement the security manager. This last point will also give us the necessary information to write our own security manager. In Java 1.2, there are only rare cases where such a task is necessary.

The access controller is built upon four concepts:

- *Code sources*: An encapsulation of the location from which certain Java classes were obtained

- *Permissions*: An encapsulation of a request to perform a particular operation

- *Policies*: An encapsulation of all the specific permissions that should be granted to specific code sources

- *Protection domains*: An encapsulation of a particular code source and the permissions granted to that code source

Before we examine the access controller itself, we'll look each of these building blocks.

The CodeSource Class

When we examined class loaders, we introduced the notion of a code source. A code source is a simple object that merely reflects the URL from which a class was loaded and the keys (if any) that were used to sign that class. The `SecureClass-Loader` class (and its subclasses) are responsible for creating and manipulating these code source objects.

The `CodeSource` class (`java.security.CodeSource`) has a few interesting methods:

public CodeSource(URL url, Certificate cers[]) ★
> Create a code source object for code that has been loaded from the specified URL. The optional array of certificates is the array of public keys that have signed the code that was loaded from this URL. These certificates are typically obtained from reading a signed JAR file, which we'll show in Chapter 12; if the code was not signed, this argument should be null.

public boolean equals(Object o) ★
> Two code source objects are considered equal if they were loaded from the same URL (that is, the `equals()` method for the URL of the objects returns

true) and the array of certificates is equal (that is, a comparison of each certificate in the array of certificates will return true).

public final URL getLocation() ★
Return the URL that was passed to the constructor of this object.

public final Certificate[] getCertificates() ★
Return a copy of the array of certificates that were used to construct this code
source object. The original certificates are not returned so that they cannot be
modified accidentally (or maliciously).

public boolean implies(CodeSource cs) ★
Determine if the code source implies the parameter according to the rules of
the Permission class (see later in this chapter). One code source implies
another if it contains all the certificates of the parameter and if the URL of
the parameter is implied by the URL of the target.

That's the extent of the CodeSource class. When we discussed the SecureClass-
Loader class in Chapter 3, we showed that the defineClass() method expected a
CodeSource object as a parameter. It's up to the implementor of the Secure-
ClassLoader to provide this object. In the URLClassLoader class, this happens
automatically, based on the URL where the class was actually located. By default,
each URL in the URLClassLoader class will have its own distinct code source
object, so all classes that are loaded from that URL are considered to have the
same code source. This does not have to be the case (though it's much simpler);
you could have a different code source for each class, or even different code
sources for sets of classes from the same URL (although we question the wisdom
of doing that).

In Chapter 3, we didn't bother to create code sources, which meant that our
classes were assigned to a default code source. For the time being, we'll create
code sources in an URL-based class loader simply based on the URL we used to
construct the class loader; these classes will all be unsigned classes as a result. In
Chapter 12, we'll show how you can get the correct certificates with which to
construct a code source object for a signed class.

Permissions

The basic entity that the access controller operates on is a permission object—an
instance of the Permission class (java.security.Permission). The Permission
class itself is an abstract class that represents a particular operation. The nomen-
clature here is a little misleading, because a permission object can reflect two
things. When it is associated with a class (through a code source and a protection
domain), a permission object represents an actual permission that has been
granted to that class. Otherwise, a permission object allows us to ask if we have a
specific permission.

For example, if we construct a permission object that represents access to a file, possession of that object does not mean that we have permission to access the file. Rather, possession of the object allows us to ask if we have permission to access the file.

An instance of the Permission class represents one specific permission. A set of permissions—e.g., all the permissions that are given to classes signed by a particular individual—is represented by an instance of the Permissions class (java.security.Permissions). As developers and administrators, we'll make extensive use of these classes, so we'll need to investigate them in depth.

The Permission Class

Permissions have three properties:

A type

> All permissions carry a basic type that identifies what the permission pertains to. A permission object to access a file will have a type of FilePermission; an object to create a window will have a type of AWTPermission; permission to use the XYZ company payroll application would have a type of XYZPayrollPermission.

A name

> All permissions have a name that identifies the specific object that a permission relates to. A FilePermission has a name that is the name of the file to be accessed; an AWTPermission to create a window has a name of showWindow-WithoutWarningBanner; permission to access a particular employee's payroll record would have the name of that employee. Names are often based on wildcards, so that a single file permission object may represent permission to access several files, and so on.

> The name of a permission is fairly arbitrary. In the case of file permissions, the name is obviously the file. But the name of the showWindowWithoutWarning-Banner permission (among many others) is chosen by convention, and it is up to all Java programs to adhere to that convention. This is only a concern to programmers when dealing with your own permission classes; as a developer you rarely need to create permission objects for the types of permissions defined in the Java API.

> On the other hand, this naming convention is of concern to end users and administrators, who must know the name of the permission they want to grant to the programs they are going to run. These names must go into the policy file (which we'll discuss in just a bit).

Actions

> Some permissions carry with them one or more actions. The presence of these actions is dependent upon the semantics of the specific type of permission. A

file permission object has a list of actions that could include read, write, and delete; an XYZ payroll permission object could have a list of actions that includes view and update. On the other hand, a window permission does not have an action: you either have permission to create the window, or you don't. Actions can also be specified by wildcards. The terms used to specify a list of actions are also arbitrary and handled by convention.

Permissions can serve two roles. They allow the Java API to negotiate access to several resources (files, sockets, and so on). Those permissions are defined by convention within the Java API, and their naming conventions are wholly within the domain of the Java API itself. Hence, you can create an object that represents permission to read a particular file, but you cannot create an object that represents permission to copy a particular file, since the copy action is not known within the file permission class.

On the other hand, you can create arbitrary permissions for use within your own programs and completely define both the names of those permissions as well as the actions (if any) that should apply. If you are writing a payroll program, for example, you could create your own permission class that uses the convention that the name of the permission is the employee upon whose payroll information you want to act; you could use the convention that the permissible actions on the payroll permission are view and update. Then you can use that permission in conjunction with the access controller to allow employees to view their own payroll data and to allow managers to change the payroll data for their employees.

We'll look at both of these cases, starting with the classes that are provided within the Java API itself. These classes are used by the Java API (and in particular, by the security manager) to protect access to certain resources in ways that are fairly intuitive, given our knowledge of the security manager (but we'll examine that interaction in detail later).

Permissions of the Java API

There are 11 standard permissions in the Java API, each of which is implemented as a class:

1. The `FilePermission` class (`java.io.FilePermission`)

   This class represents permissions for files. This class implements two wildcard patterns for filenames: an asterisk matches all files in a given directory, and a hyphen matches all files that reside in an entire directory hierarchy. Valid actions for file permissions are read, write, delete, and execute.

   File permissions must be constructed with their platform-specific name. Hence, */myclasses/xyz* is a valid name for a file permission on a Unix system, but not on a Macintosh (where an equivalent name might be *System Disk:myclasses:xyz*). When these strings are specified programmatically, they are not too difficult to construct (using the file separator property); when these strings need to be specified in an external file, an appropriate syntax must be used.

Keep in mind the difference between an asterisk and a hyphen: an asterisk only traverses a single directory, while a hyphen traverses an entire filesystem. Hence */myclasses/** will not include */myclasses/xyz/HRApplet.class*, but */myclasses/-* will. A single asterisk will access all files in the current directory, and a single hyphen will access all files in the current directory and its subdirectories.

If you want to access all files on a particular machine, you specify the special token <<ALL FILES>>.

A FilePermission object is constructed by providing the name of the file and a list of actions on that file:

```
FilePermission p1 = new FilePermission("-", "execute");
FilePermission p2 = new FilePermission("/myclasses/*", "read, write");
FilePermission p3 = new FilePermission("<<ALL FILES>>", "read");
```

Here, p1 represents permission to execute all files that are in the filesystem hierarchy under the current directory, p2 represents permission to read and write all files that exist in the directory */myclasses*, and p3 represents permission to read all the files on the machine.

2. The SocketPermission class (java.net.SocketPermission)

This class represents permissions to interact with network sockets. The name of a socket permission is *hostname:port*, where each component of the name may be specified by a wildcard. In particular, the hostname may be given as a hostname (possibly DNS qualified) or an IP address. The leftmost position of the hostname may be specified as an asterisk, such that the host *piccolo.East.Sun.COM* would be matched by each of these strings:

```
piccolo
piccolo.East.Sun.COM
*.Sun.COM
*
129.151.119.8
```

The port component of the name can be specified as a single port number or as a range of port numbers (e.g., 1–1024). When a range is specified, either side of the range may be excluded:

```
1024 (port 1024)
1024- (all ports greater than or equal to 1024)
-1024 (all ports less than or equal to 1024)
1-1024 (all ports between 1 and 1024, inclusive)
```

Valid actions for a socket permission are accept, connect, listen, and resolve. These map into the socket API: accept is used by the ServerSocket class to see if it can accept an incoming connection from a particular host; connect is used by the Socket class to see if it can make a connection to a particular host, listen is used by the ServerSocket class to see if a server socket can be created at all, and resolve is used by the Socket class to see if the IP address for a particular host can be obtained.

Constructing a socket permission, then, is simply a matter of putting together the desired strings in the correct format:

```
SocketPermission s1 = new SocketPermission("piccolo:6000", "connect");
SocketPermission s2 = new SocketPermission("piccolo:1024-",
                                           "accept, listen");
```

Here s1 represents permission to connect to the X server (port 6000) on machine *piccolo*, and s2 represents permission for *piccolo* to start a server on any nonprivileged port.

3. The PropertyPermission class (java.util.PropertyPermission)

This class represents permissions for Java properties. Property permission names are specified as dot-separated names (just as they are in a Java property file); in addition, the last element can be a wildcard asterisk: *, a.*, a.b.*, and so on.

The valid actions for this class are read and write. Hence, to construct a property permission, you would do something like:

```
PropertyPermission p1 = new PropertyPermission("java.version", "read");
PropertyPermission p2 = new PropertyPermission("xyz.*", "read,write");
```

Here, p1 represents permission to read the version of the virtual machine that's in use, and p2 represents permission to read or write all properties that begin with the token xyz.

4. The RuntimePermission class (java.lang.RuntimePermission)

This class represents permissions for the Java runtime—essentially, permissions to perform any of the operations encapsulated by the Runtime class, including most thread operations. The names recognized by this class are dot-separated names and are subject to the same wildcard asterisk matching as the property permission class.

Runtime permissions have no associated actions—you either have permission to perform those operations, or you don't. Hence, a runtime permission is constructed as:

```
RuntimePermission r1 = new RuntimePermission("exitVM");
RuntimePermission r2 = new
    RuntimePermission("accessClassInPackage.java");
```

Here, r1 represents permission to exit the virtual machine, and r2 represents permission to access classes in the java package.

5. The AWTPermission class (java.awt.AWTPermission)

This class represents permissions to access certain windowing resources. In particular, as we might assume from the corresponding methods in the security manager, there are three conventional names in this class: showWindow-WithoutWarningBanner, accessClipboard, and accessEventQueue.

There are no actions associated with this class. In addition, this class technically supports wildcard matching, but since none of the conventional names are in dot-separated format, that facility is unused. Hence, an AWT permission is constructed like this:

```
AWTPermission a = new AWTPermission("showWindowWithoutWarningBanner");
```

6. The NetPermission class (java.net.NetPermission)

This class represents permissions to interact with two different classes. The first is the Authenticator class: there are no concrete implementations of the Authenticator class within the JDK, but implementations of that class provide HTTP authentication for password-protected web pages. The valid names associated with this class are setDefaultAuthenticator and requestPasswordAuthentication. Wildcard asterisk matching applies to these names.

In addition, this class encapsulates various URL-related permissions. Permission to specify a stream handler in the URL class is named specifyStreamHandler.

There are no associated actions with a net permission, so they are constructed as follows:

```
NetPermission n1 = new NetPermission("requestPasswordAuthentication");
```

7. The SecurityPermission class (java.security.SecurityPermission)

This class represents permission to use the security package. Names passed to this class are subject to wildcard asterisk matching, and there are no actions associated with this class. The valid names to this class include all the valid strings that can be passed to the checkSecurityAccess() method of the security manager; as we discuss the security API in the last half of this book, we'll list these names for each class.

8. The SerializablePermission class (java.io.SerializablePermission)

This class represents various permissions relating to the serialization and deserialization of an object. No wildcards or actions are accepted by this class. This permission has two valid names: enableSubstitution and enableSubclassImplementation. The first of these permissions allows the enableResolveObject() method of the ObjectInputStream and the enableReplaceObject() method of the ObjectOutputStream classes to function. The latter permission allows the ObjectInputStream and ObjectOutputStream classes to be subclassed, which would potentially override the readObject() and writeObject() methods.

9. The ReflectPermission class (java.lang.reflect.ReflectPermission)

This permission represents the ability to set the accessible flag on objects that are to be used with the reflection API. This class has a single name (suppressAccessChecks) and no actions.

10. The UnresolvedPermission class (java.security.UnresolvedPermission)

This class is used internally in the Java API to represent external permissions (i.e., permissions that are implemented by third-party APIs) before the class that defines that permission is found. This permission is only needed if you are writing an implementation of the Policy class.

11. The AllPermission class (java.security.AllPermission)

This class represents permission to perform any operation—including file, socket, and other operations that have their own permission classes. Granting this type of permission is obviously somewhat dangerous; this permission is usually given only to classes within the Java API and to classes in Java extensions. This class has no name or actions; it is constructed as follows:

```
AllPermission ap = new AllPermission();
```

Using the Permission Class

We'll now look into the classes upon which all these permissions are based: the Permission class. This class abstracts the notion of a permission and a name. From a programmatic standpoint, the Permission class is really used only to create your own types of permissions. It has some interesting methods, but the operations that are implemented on a permission object are not generally used in code that we write—they are used instead by the access controller. Hence, we'll examine this class primarily with an eye towards understanding how it can be used to implement our own permissions.

Permission is an abstract class that contains these public methods:

public Permission(String name) ★
 Construct a permission object that represents the desired permission.

public abstract boolean equals(Object o) ★
 Subclasses of the Permission class are required to implement their own test for equality. Often this is simply done by comparing the name (and actions, if applicable) of the permission.

public abstract int hashCode() ★

Subclasses of the Permission class are required to implement their own hash code. In order for the access controller to function correctly, the hash code for a given permission object must never change during execution of the virtual machine. In addition, permissions that compare as equal must return the same hash code from this method.

public final String getName() ★

Return the name that was used to construct this permission.

public abstract String getActions() ★

Return the canonical form of the actions (if any) that were used to construct this permission.

public String toString() ★

The convention for printing a permission is to print in parentheses the class name, the name of the permission, and the actions. For example, a file permission might return:

```
("java.io.FilePermission","/myclasses/xyz/HRApplet.class","read")
```

public abstract boolean implies(Permission p) ★

This method is one of the keys of the Permission class: it is responsible for determining whether or not a class that is granted one permission is granted another. This method is normally responsible for performing wildcard matching, so that, for example, the file permission */myclasses/-* implies the file permission */myclasses/xyz/HRApplet.class*. But this method need not rely on wildcards; permission to write a particular object in a database would probably imply permission to read that object as well.

public PermissionCollection newPermissionCollection() ★

Return a permission collection suitable for holding instances of this type of permission. We'll discuss the topic of permission collections in the next section. This method returns null by default.

public void checkGuard(Object o) ★

Call the security manager to see if the permission (i.e., the this variable) has been granted, generating a SecurityException if the permission has not been granted. The object parameter of this method is unused. We'll give more details about this method later in this chapter.

Implementing your own permission means providing a class with concrete implementations of these abstract methods. Note that the notions of wildcard matching and actions are not generally present in this class—if you want your class to support either of these features, you're responsible for implementing all of the necessary logic to do so (although the BasicPermission class that we'll look at next can help us with that).

Say that you are implementing a program to administer payroll information. You'll
want to create permissions to allow users to view their payment history. You'll also
want to allow the HR department to update the pay rate for employees. So we'll
need to implement a permission class to encapsulate all of that:

```java
public class XYZPayrollPermission extends Permission {

    protected int mask;
    static private int VIEW = 0x01;
    static private int UPDATE = 0x02;

    public XYZPayrollPermission(String name) {
        this(name, "view");
    }

    public XYZPayrollPermission(String name, String action) {
        super(name);
        parse(action);
    }

    private void parse(String action) {
        StringTokenizer st = new StringTokenizer(action, ",\t ");

        mask = 0;
        while (st.hasMoreTokens()) {
            String tok = st.nextToken();
            if (tok.equals("view"))
                mask |= VIEW;
            else if (tok.equals("update"))
                mask |= UPDATE;
            else throw new IllegalArgumentException(
                                "Unknown action " + tok);
        }
    }

    public boolean implies(Permission permission) {
        if (!(permission instanceof XYZPayrollPermission))
            return false;

        XYZPayrollPermission p = (XYZPayrollPermission) permission;
        String name = getName();
        if (!name.equals("*") && !name.equals(p.getName()))
            return false;
        if ((mask & p.mask) != p.mask)
            return false;
        return true;
    }

    public boolean equals(Object o) {
```

```
        if (!(o instanceof XYZPayrollPermission))
            return false;

        XYZPayrollPermission p = (XYZPayrollPermission) o;
        return ((p.getName().equals(getName())) && (p.mask == mask));
    }

    public int hashCode() {
        return getName().hashCode() ^ mask;
    }

    public String getActions() {
        if (mask == 0)
            return "";
        else if (mask == VIEW)
            return "view";
        else if (mask == UPDATE)
            return "update";
        else if (mask == (VIEW | UPDATE))
            return "view, update";
        else throw new IllegalArgumentException("Unknown mask");
    }

    public PermissionCollection newPermissionsCollection() {
        return new XYZPayrollPermissionCollection();
    }
}
```

The instance variables in this class are required to hold the information about the actions—even though our superclass makes references to actions, it doesn't provide a manner in which to store them or process them, so we have to provide that logic. That logic is provided in the parse() method; we've chosen the common convention of having the action string treated as a list of actions that are separated by commas and whitespace. Note also that we've stored the actual actions as bits in a single integer—this simplifies some of the later logic.

As required, we've implemented the equals() and hashCode() methods—and we've done so rather simply. We consider objects equal if their names are equal and their masks (that is, their actions) are equal, and construct a hash code accordingly.

Our implementation of the getActions() method is typical: we're required to return the same action string for a permission object that was constructed with an action list of "view, update" as for one that was constructed with an action list of "update, view". This requirement is one of the prime reasons why the actions are stored as a mask—because it allows us to construct this action string in the proper format.

Finally, the `implies()` method is responsible for determining how wildcard and other implied permissions are handled. If the name passed to construct our object is an asterisk, then we match any other name; hence, an object to represent the permissions of the HR department might be constructed as:

```
new XYZPayrollPermission("*", "view, update")
```

When the `implies()` method is called on this wildcard object, the name will always match, and because the action mask has the complete list of actions, the mask comparison will always yield the mask that we're testing against. If the `implies()` method is called with a different object, however, it will only return true if the names are equal and the object's mask is a subset of the target mask.

Note that we also might have implemented the logic in such a way that permission to perform an update implies permission to perform a view simply by changing the logic of testing the mask—you're not limited only to wildcard matching in the `implies()` method.

The BasicPermission Class

If you need to implement your own permission class, the `BasicPermission` class (`java.security.BasicPermission`) provides some useful semantics. This class implements a basic permission—that is, a permission that doesn't have actions. Basic permissions can be thought of as binary permission—you either have them, or you don't. However, this restriction does not prevent you from implementing actions in your subclasses of the `BasicPermission` class (as the `PropertyPermission` class does).

The prime benefit of this class is the manner in which it implements wildcards. Names in basic permissions are considered to be hierarchical, following a dot-separated convention. For example, if the XYZ corporation wanted to create a set of basic permissions, they might use the convention that the first word of the permission always be `xyz`: `xyz.readDatabase`, `xyz.writeDatabase`, `xyz.runPayrollProgram`, `xyz.HRDepartment.accessCheck`, and so on. These permissions can then be specified by their full name, or they can be specified with an asterisk wildcard: `xyz.*` would match each of these (no matter what depth), and `*` would match every possible basic permission.

The wildcard matching of this class does not match partial names: `xyz.read*` would not match any of the permissions we just listed. Further, the wildcard must be in the rightmost position: `*.readDatabase` would not match any basic permission.

The `BasicPermission` class is abstract, although it does not contain any abstract methods, and it completely implements all the abstract methods of the `Permission` class. Hence, a concrete implementation of the `BasicPermission` need only contain a constructor to call the correct constructor of the superclass (since there is no default constructor in the BasicPermission class). Subclasses must call one of these constructors:

public BasicPermission(String name) ★

Construct a permission with the given name. This is the usual constructor for this class, as basic permissions do not normally have actions.

public BasicPermission(String name, String action) ★

Construct a permission with the given name and action. Even though basic permissions do not usually have actions associated with them, you must provide a constructor with this signature in all implementations of the BasicPermission class due to the mechanism that is used to construct permission objects from the policy file (which we will see later in this chapter).

Permission Collections

The access controller depends upon the ability to aggregate permissions so that it can easily call the implies() method on all of them. For example, a particular user might be given permission to read several directories: perhaps the user's home directory (*/home/sdo/-*) and the system's temporary directory (*/tmp/-*). When the access controller needs to see if the user can access a particular file, it must test both of these permissions to see if either one matches. This can be done easily by aggregating all the file permissions into a single permission collection.

Every permission class is required to implement a permission collection, then, which is a mechanism where objects of the same permission class may be grouped together and operated upon as a single unit. This requirement is enforced by the newPermissionCollection() method of the Permission class.

The PermissionCollection class (java.security.PermissionCollection) is defined as follows:

public abstract class PermissionCollection

Implement an aggregate set of permissions. While permission collections can handle heterogeneous sets of permissions, a permission collection typically should be used to group together a homogeneous group of permissions (e.g., all file permissions or all socket permissions, etc.).

There are three basic operations that you can perform on a permission collection:

public abstract void add(Permission p) ★

Add the given permission to the permission collection.

public abstract boolean implies(Permission p) ★

Check to see if any permission in the collection implies the given permission. This can be done by enumerating all the permission objects that have been added to the collection and calling the implies() method on each of those objects in turn, but it is typically implemented in a more efficient manner.

public abstract Enumeration elements() ★

Return an enumeration of all the permissions in the collection.

The *javadoc* documentation of this class claims that a permission collection is a collection of heterogeneous permission objects. Forget that idea; introducing that notion into permission collections vastly complicates matters, and the issue of a heterogeneous collection of permission objects is better handled elsewhere (we'll see how a little bit later). As far as we're concerned, the purpose of a permission collection is to aggregate only permission objects of a particular type.

Permission collections are typically implemented as inner classes, or at least as classes that are private to the package in which they are defined. There is, for example, a corresponding permission collection class for the FilePermission class, one for the SocketPermission class, and so on.

None of these collections is available as a public class that we can use in our own program. Hence, in order to support the newPermissionCollection() method in our XYZPayrollPermission class, we'd need to do something like this:

```java
public class XYZPayrollPermissionCollection extends
                                PermissionCollection {
    private Hashtable permissions;
    private boolean addedAdmin;
    private int adminMask;

    XYZPayrollPermissionCollection() {
        permissions = new Hashtable();
        addedAdmin = false;
    }

    public void add(Permission p) {
        if (!(p instanceof XYZPayrollPermission))
            throw new IllegalArgumentException(
                            "Wrong permission type");
        XYZPayrollPermission xyz = (XYZPayrollPermission) p;
        String name = xyz.getName();
        XYZPayrollPermission other =
                    (XYZPayrollPermission) permissions.get(name);
        if (other != null)
            xyz = merge(xyz, other);
        if (name.equals("**")) {
            addedAdmin = true;
            adminMask = xyz.mask;
```

```
        }
        permissions.put(name, xyz);
    }

    public Enumeration elements() {
        return permissions.elements();
    }

    public boolean implies(Permission p) {
        if (!(p instanceof XYZPayrollPermission))
            return false;
        XYZPayrollPermission xyz = (XYZPayrollPermission) p;
        if (addedAdmin && (adminMask & xyz.mask) != xyz.mask)
            return true;
        Permission inTable = (Permission)
                            permissions.get(xyz.getName());
        if (inTable == null)
            return false;
        return inTable.implies(xyz);
    }

    private XYZPayrollPermission
            merge(XYZPayrollPermission a, XYZPayrollPermission b) {
        String aAction = a.getActions();
        if (aAction.equals(""))
            return b;
        String bAction = b.getActions();
        if (bAction.equals(""))
            return a;
        return new XYZPayrollPermission(a.getName(),
                            aAction + "," + bAction);
    }
}
```

Note the logic within the implies() method—it's the important part of this example. The implies() method must test each permission in the hashtable (or whatever other container you've used to store the added permissions), but it should do so efficiently. We could always call the implies() method of each entry in the hashtable, but that would clearly not be efficient—it's better to call only the implies() method on a permission in the table that has a matching name.

The only trick is that we won't find a matching name if we're doing wildcard pattern matching—if we've added the name "*" to the table, we'll always want to return true, even though looking up the name "John Smith" in the table will not return the administrative entry. Implementing this wildcard pattern matching efficiently is the key to writing a good permission collection.

When you use (or subclass) one of the concrete permission classes that we listed earlier, there is no need to provide a permission collection class—all concrete implementations provide their own collection. In addition, there are two other cases when you do not need to implement a permission collection:

- When you extend the Permission class, but do not do wildcard pattern matching.

    Hidden internally within the Java API is a PermissionsHash class, which is the default permission collection class for permission objects. The Permissions-Hash class stores the aggregated permissions in a hashtable, so the implementations of its add() and elements() methods are straightforward. The implementation of its implies() method is based on looking up the name of the permission parameter in the hashtable collection: if an entry is found, then the implies() method is called on that entry.

- When you extend the BasicPermission class and do not provide support for actions.

    The newPermissionClass() method of the BasicPermission class will provide a permission collection that handles wildcard pattern matching correctly (and efficiently).

If you implement your own PermissionCollection class, you must keep track of whether it has been marked as read-only. There are two methods involved in this:

public boolean isReadOnly() ★

    Return an indication of whether the collection has been marked as read-only.

public void setReadOnly() ★

    Set the collection to be read-only. Once the read-only flag has been set, it cannot be unset: the collection will remain read-only forever.

A permission collection is expected to throw a security exception from its add() method if it has marked as read-only. Note that the read-only instance variable is private to the PermissionCollection class, so subclasses will have to rely on the isReadOnly() method to test its value.

The Permissions Class

So far, we've spoken about permission collections as homogeneous collections: all permissions in the XYZPayrollPermissionCollection class are instances of the XYZPayrollPermission class; a similar property holds for other permission collections. This idea simplifies the implies() method that we showed above. But to be truly useful, a permission collection needs to be heterogeneous, so it can represent all the permissions a program should have. A permission collection really needs to be able to contain file permissions, socket permissions, and other types of permissions.

This idea is present within the `PermissionCollection` class; conceptually, however, it is best to think of heterogeneous collections of permissions as encapsulated by the `Permissions` class (`java.security.Permissions`):

public final class Permissions extends PermissionCollection
> Implement the `PermissionCollection` class. This class allows you to create a heterogeneous collection of permissions: the permission objects that are added to this collection need not have the same type.

This class contains a concrete implementation of a permission collection that organizes the aggregated permissions in terms of their individual, homogenous permission collections. You can think of a permissions object as containing an aggregation of permission collections, each of which contains an aggregation of individual permissions.

For example, let's consider an empty permissions object. When a file permission is added to this object, the permissions object will call the `newPermissionCollection()` method on the file permission to get a homogeneous file permission collection object. The file permission is then stored within this file permission collection. When another file permission is added to the permissions object, the permissions object will place that file permission into the already existing file permission collection object. When a payroll permission object is added to the permissions object, a new payroll permission collection will be obtained, the payroll permission added to it, and the collection added to the permissions object. This process will continue, and the permissions object will build up a set of permission collections.

When the `implies()` method of the permissions object is called, it will search its set of permission collections for a collection that can hold the given permission. It can then call the `implies()` method on that (homogenous) collection to obtain the correct answer.

The `Permissions` class thus supports any arbitrary grouping of permissions. There is no need to develop your own permission collection to handle heterogeneous groups.

The Policy Class

The third building block for the access controller is the facility to specify which permissions should apply to which code sources. We call this global set of permissions the security policy; it is encapsulated by the `Policy` class (`java.security.Policy`).

public abstract class Policy ★

> Establish the security policy for a Java program. The policy encapsulates a mapping between code sources and permission objects in such a way that classes loaded from particular locations or signed by specific individuals have the set of specified permissions.

A policy class is constructed as follows:

public Policy() ★

> Create a policy class. The constructor should initialize the policy object according to its internal rules (e.g., by reading the *java.policy* file, as we'll describe later).

Like the security manager, only a single instance of the policy class can be installed in the virtual machine at any time. However, unlike the security manager, the actual instance of the policy class can be replaced. These two methods install and retrieve the policy:

public static Policy getPolicy() ★

> Return the currently installed policy object.

public static void setPolicy(Policy p) ★

> Install the given policy object, replacing whatever policy object was previously installed.

Getting and setting the policy object requires going through the checkProperty() method of the security manager. By default, this succeeds only if you already have been granted a security permission with the name of getPolicy or setPolicy (as appropriate). There's a bootstrapping issue involved when setting the policy, since granting permissions requires the policy to have been set. Hence, the initial policy is typically set by a class in the core API, as those classes always have permission to perform any operation.

There are two other methods in the Policy class:

public abstract Permissions getPermissions(CodeSource cs) ★

> Create a permissions object that contains the set of permissions that should be granted to classes that came from the given code source (i.e., loaded from the code source's URL and signed by the keys in the code source).

public abstract void refresh() ★

> Refresh the policy object. For example, if the initial policy came from a file, re-read the file and install a new policy object based on the (presumably changed) information from the file.

In programmatic terms, writing a policy class involves implementing these methods. The default policy class is provided by the PolicyFile class (sun.security.provider.PolicyFile), which constructs permissions based on information found in a file on the user's local disk (a process we're just about to examine).

Unfortunately, the `PolicyFile` class that parses that file and builds up the set of permissions is a file in the sun package class; it is not accessible to us as programmers. Hence, while it's possible to write your own `Policy` class, it is a fairly involved process. You might want to write your own `Policy` class if you want to define a set of permissions through some other mechanism than a URL (e.g., loading the permissions via a policy server database). That implementation is fairly straightforward: you need only provide a mechanism to map code sources to a set of permissions. Then, for each code source, construct each of the individual permission objects and aggregate them into a permissions object to be returned by the `getPermissions()` method.

Property Expansion and the Policy Class

You'll notice an unusual syntax in the list of policy properties in the *java.security* file: `${foo.bar}`. This syntax uses property substitution to fill in the given target; for example, the string `${user.home}` might expand to */home/sdo* on my Unix desktop machine and to *C:* on my Windows desktop machine. As you might have guessed, the string `${/}` expands to the file separator character on the platform that is reading the file.

This property substitution allows us to use one set of configuration files no matter what the underlying platform, since we can use standard Java properties to hide those platform-specific details. This is particularly important when specifying filenames for file permissions in a policy file.

If the `policy.expandProperties` property in the *java.security* file is set to `false`, however, substitution will not occur and these strings should not be used. If they are used, they will be treated as literal strings and fail.

The Default Policy

The `Policy` and `PolicyFile` classes give system administrators or end users the ability to define in a file a security policy for any Java program; this allows changes to the security model for the program without modifying the program's code. The policy that you can specify in this file is extremely flexible, since it's based on the permission model we examined earlier. If you want a Java program to be able to read a single directory, you can specify the appropriate file permission in the policy file. If you want a Java program to be able to connect to particular hosts on the network, you can specify the appropriate socket permissions in the policy file. And if you want a Java program to be able to administer payroll records, you can specify the appropriate payroll permissions in the policy file.

By default, the policy for a Java program is read from two locations, but this is controlled by the system security file. This file is a set of properties that apply to the security package in general; it is named *$JAVAHOME/lib/security/java.security*.

In terms of the Policy class, here are the relevant entries in the *java.security* file:

```
policy.provider=sun.security.provider.PolicyFile
policy.expandProperties=true
policy.allowSystemProperty=true
policy.url.1=file:${java.home}/lib/security/java.policy
policy.url.2=file:${user.home}/.java.policy
```

The first of these properties defines the class that should be instantiated to provide the initial instance of the Policy class: in this case, the PolicyFile class (which implements the behavior we're now describing). Here's the algorithm that the PolicyFile class uses to read in policy files. The entire set of entries in the resulting policy is composed of all the specific entries read from all of the following files:

1. If the policy.allowSystemProperty property in the *java.security* file is set to true (which it is by default), then the first file to be read is a file specified on the command line with the -Djava.security.policy argument, which must be used with the -Djava.security.manager option. For example, the following command would first load the policy file from */globalfiles/java.policy*:

```
piccolo% java -Djava.security.manager \
        -Djava.security.policy=/globalfiles/java.policy Cat /etc/passwd
```

If the policy.allowSystemProperty property is set to false, then the -Djava.security.manager file will be ignored. On the other hand, if this property is set to true and the filename given as the -Djava.security.manager argument begins with an equals sign:

```
piccolo% java -Djava.security.manager \
        -Djava.security.policy==/globalfiles/java.policy Cat /etc/passwd
```

then the given file is the *only* policy file that will be read (and hence the only file that will define permissions).

Note that you may also specify the -Djava.security.manager flag with no additional arguments, in which case the policy files from the *java.security* file (see the next step) are used and no additional files are consulted:

```
piccolo% java -Djava.security.manager Cat /etc/passwd
```

This last example is the typical usage. Any of these examples set up the default sandbox for us in Java 1.2—the parameters of this sandbox are defined by the entries in the policy file.

2. Next, the PolicyFile class looks for properties of the form policy.url.n where n is an integer starting with 1. As it finds each property, it reads in the policy from the given URL; in the default set of properties we listed above, this

means that the first URL to be read is the *java.policy* file in the *$JAVA-HOME/lib/security* directory and the second URL to be read is the *.java.policy* file in the user's home directory. You may specify as many or as few of these URLs as desired, but they must be numbered consecutively starting with 1.

3. If no files have been loaded (because there was no –Djava.security.policy argument and there were no policy.url properties), then an internal static set of permissions is loaded (which is the same set of permissions defined by the default *java.policy* file we list below).

The policy files are designed to map code sources to sets of permissions. For example, this entry:

```
grant codeBase http://www.xyz.com/ {
    permission java.io.FilePermssion "${user.home}${/}docs${/}-",
                                      "read, write, delete";
};
```

means that any code loaded from the top-level directory of *www.xyz.com* is granted permission to use any files under the user's *docs* directory. The code base in this case is used to construct a code source with no public keys.

The above example is one case of a policy entry, also called a grant entry, and a policy file is a collection of policy entries. Each entry is specific to one code source and should list all the permissions for that code source—but a single policy file can have several entries and thus work effectively for code that originated from multiple sources. The syntax of a policy entry is as follows:

```
grant [signedBy <signer>] [, codeBase <code source>] {
    permission <class> [<name> [, <action list>]];
    ...
    permission <class> [<name> [, <action list>]];
};
```

As indicated by the bracket syntax, the signedBy and codeBase entries are optional. If both are missing, the list of permissions applies to a class with any code source. The signer entry should be a name that matches an entry in the system's key management system—a concept we'll explore in Chapter 11. The codeBase should be the URL that applies to the location from which the classes were loaded—including a file-based or HTTP-based URL.

Note that omitting the signedBy and codeBase fields in the policy file means that the given permissions should apply to all code sources. It does not mean that the listed permissions should apply only to classes that had a code source with no URL and no public key. This point about the code source is important: permissions given within the policy file apply only to classes that have a code source. Classes that are loaded by the primordial class loader do not have a code source—these classes are given permission to perform any operation. Hence, the Java API itself has no restrictions placed upon what operations it may perform.

The permissions themselves should have the fully package-qualified class name for the permission—including any permission classes (like the XYZPayrollPermission class) that you may have defined for your own application. The name will be used to construct the permission, along with the action list (if present). An internal (private) method of the PolicyFile class is used to construct the permission object; this method expects to find a constructor that takes both a name and an action. If the action is not present, then null will be passed to the constructor. This requirement forces you to include a constructor with both arguments in all your permission classes, including those that are extensions of the BasicPermission class.

Here's the default policy file that comes with the Java 1.2. This is the system security file (i.e., the one loaded from *$JAVAHOME/lib/security/java.policy*); there is no default file for each user. This is also the set that will be loaded when no policy files are found:

```
// Standard extensions get all permissions by default
grant codeBase "file:${java.home}/lib/ext/" {
    permission java.security.AllPermission;
};


// default permissions granted to all domains
grant {
    // allows anyone to listen on un-privileged ports
    permission java.net.SocketPermission "localhost:1024-", "listen";

    // "standard" properies that can be read by anyone
    permission java.util.PropertyPermission "java.version", "read";
    permission java.util.PropertyPermission "java.vendor", "read";
    permission java.util.PropertyPermission "java.vendor.url", "read";
    permission java.util.PropertyPermission
                            "java.class.version", "read";
    permission java.util.PropertyPermission "os.name", "read";
    permission java.util.PropertyPermission "os.version", "read";
    permission java.util.PropertyPermission "os.arch", "read";
    permission java.util.PropertyPermission "file.separator", "read";
    permission java.util.PropertyPermission "path.separator", "read";
    permission java.util.PropertyPermission "line.separator", "read";

    permission java.util.PropertyPermission
                            "java.specification.version", "read";
    permission java.util.PropertyPermission
                            "java.specification.vendor", "read";
    permission java.util.PropertyPermission
                            "java.specification.name", "read";

    permission java.util.PropertyPermission
                            "java.vm.specification.version", "read";
```

```
        permission java.util.PropertyPermission
                        "java.vm.specification.vendor", "read";
        permission java.util.PropertyPermission
                        "java.vm.specification.name", "read";
        permission java.util.PropertyPermission "java.vm.version", "read";
        permission java.util.PropertyPermission "java.vm.vendor", "read";
        permission java.util.PropertyPermission "java.vm.name", "read";
        permission java.lang.RuntimePermission "stopThread";
};
```

When you use this policy file, then, all classes that are loaded from the Java extensions directory will be granted all permissions. All other non-system classes will have read access to the system properties listed as well as being able to listen on a socket with a port number of 1024 or greater (which means that the class will be able to create a server socket on an unprivileged port). All other classes will also be able to call the stop() method on a thread.

A policy file may contain an additional entry:

```
keystore ".keystore";
```

This entry specifies the name of the URL that will be used to process the keystore in which public keys for the signers listed in the policy file should be found. This entry is missing from the default policy file, as it does not contain any entries that are signed. The name of this file is relative to the URL that was used to load the file; if the policy.url property was *file:/${user.home}/.java.policy,* the URL to load the keystore will be *file:/${user.home}/.keystore.* The keystore entry may be an absolute URL if desired.

Policy files may be constructed by hand, or you may use the policytool application that comes with the JDK to administer those files (see Appendix A).

Protection Domains

A protection domain is a grouping of a code source and permissions—that is, a protection domain represents all the permissions that are granted to a particular code source. In the default implementation of the Policy class, a protection domain is one grant entry in the file. A protection domain is an instance of the ProtectionDomain class (java.security.ProtectionDomain) and is constructed as follows:

public ProtectionDomain(CodeSource cs, PermissionCollection p) ★
    Construct a protection domain based on the given code source and set of permissions.

When associated with a class, a protection domain means that the given class was loaded from the site specified in the code source, was signed by the public keys specified in the code source, and should have permission to perform the set of operations represented in the permission collection object. Each class in the virtual machine may belong to one and only one protection domain, which is set by the class loader when the class is defined.

However, not all class loaders have a specific protection domain associated with them: classes that are loaded by the primordial class loader have no protection domain. In particular, this means that classes that exist as part of the system class path (that is, the Java API classes) have no explicit protection domain. We can think of these classes as belonging to the system protection domain.

A protection domain is set for a class inside the defineClass() method. A protection domain is assigned to a class depending upon one of the following cases:

- The defineClass() method accepts a protection domain as a parameter. In this case, the given protection domain is assigned to the class. This case is typically unused, since that method exists in only the ClassLoader class and not in the SecureClassLoader class.

- The defineClass() method accepts a code source as a parameter. In this case, the getPermissions() method of the SecureClassLoader is used to determine the protection domain for the code source. By default, this just uses the getPermissions() class of the Policy class to find the permissions that are defined for the given code base. A secure class loader (including a URL class loader) has the option of overriding the getPermissions() method to enhance the permissions a particular class might have. We'll see an example of this in Chapter 6, when we discuss network permissions in the class loader.

- The defineClass() method accepts neither of these parameters. In this case, a protection domain is defined based on a code source with null parameters and a set of permissions that have been defined by the system's security policy (retrieved with the getPermissions() method). This case will include the default grant entry we listed earlier.

There are three utility methods of the ProtectionDomain class:

public CodeSource getCodeSource() ★
Return the code source that was used to construct this protection domain.

public PermissionCollection getPermissions() ★
Return the permission collection object that was used to construct this protection domain.

public boolean implies(Permission p) ★
Indicate whether the given permission is implied by the permissions object contained in this protection domain.

The AccessController Class

Now we have all the pieces in place to discuss the mechanics of the access controller. The access controller is represented by a single class called, conveniently, AccessController. There are no instances of the AccessController class (java.security.AccessController)—its constructor is private, so that it cannot be instantiated. Instead, this class has a number of static methods that can be called in order to determine if a particular operation should succeed. The key method of this class takes a particular permission and determines, based on the installed Policy object, whether or not the permission should be granted:

public static void checkPermission(Permission p) ★

Check the given permission against the policy in place for the program. If the permission is granted, this method returns normally; otherwise, it throws an AccessControlException.

We can use this method to determine whether or not a specified operation should be permitted:

```
public class AccessTest extends Applet {
    public void init() {
        SocketPermission sp = new SocketPermission(
                        getParameter("host") + ":6000", "connect");
        try {
            AccessController.checkPermission(sp);
            System.out.println("Ok to open socket");
        } catch (AccessControlException ace) {
            System.out.println(ace);
        }
    }
}
```

Whether the access controller allows or rejects a given permission depends upon the set of protection domains that are on the stack when the access controller is called. Figure 5-2 shows the stack that might be in place when the init() method of the AccessTest applet is called. In the *appletviewer*, an applet is run in a separate thread—so the bottom method on the stack is the run() method of the Thread class.* That run() method has called the run() method of the Applet-Panel class. This second run() method has done several things prior to calling the init() method: it first created an HTTP-based class loader (from an internal class that is a subclass of the URLClassLoader class) and has used that class loader to load the AccessTest class. It then instantiated an instance of the AccessTest class and called the init() method on that object. This left us with the stack shown in

---

* In fact, the run() method is always the bottom method on a stack, since stacks apply on a per-thread basis.

the figure—the run() method of the Thread class has called the run() method of the AppletPanel class, which has called the init() method of the AccessTest class, which has called the checkPermission() method of the AccessController class.

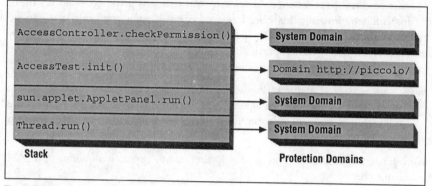

Figure 5-2. The stack and protection domains of a method

The reason we need to know the stack trace of the current thread is to examine the protection domains that are on the stack. In this example, only the AccessTest class has been loaded by a class loader: the AppletPanel class and the Thread class were loaded from the core API with the primordial class loader. Hence, only the AccessTest class has a nonsystem protection domain (associated with the URL from which we loaded it, *http://piccolo/* in this case).

The permissions for any particular operation can be considered to be the intersection of all permissions of each protection domain on the stack when the checkPermission() method is called. When the checkPermission() method is called, it checks the permissions associated with the protection domain for each method on the stack. It does this starting at the top of the stack, and proceeding through each class on the stack.

If this entry appeared in the policy file:

```
grant codeBase http://piccolo/ {
    permission java.net.SocketPermission "*:1024-", "connect";
}
```

the protection domain that applies to the AccessTest class will have permission to open the socket. Remember that the system domain implicitly has permission to perform any operation; as there are no other nonsystem protection domains associated with any class on the stack, the checkPermission() method will permit this operation—which is to say that it will silently return.

For most implementations of Java browsers, and many Java applications, there will only be a single nonsystem protection domain on the stack: all the classes for the applet will have come from a single CODEBASE (and hence a single protection domain). But the checkPermission() method is more general than that, and if you use a class loader that performs delegation, there will be multiple protection domains on the stack. This is a common occurrence if you're using a Java extension.

Let's say that you've written a payroll application that uses a class loader that loads classes from two sources: the server in the XYZ HR department and the server in the XYZ network services department.* This might lead to a call to the checkPermission() method with the stack shown in Figure 5-3. Note that this stack trace is a little more complicated than the one we've just shown—in this case, we're relying on the fact that the constructor of the Socket class will (indirectly) call the access controller. That is what actually happens, and we'll explore that process in our next chapter. For now, we'll just accept the fact that this is the correct stack trace.

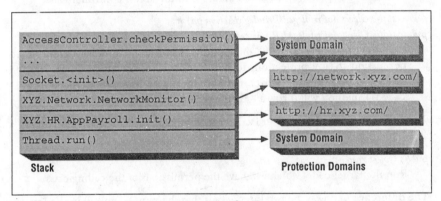

Figure 5-3. A stack with multiple nonsystem protection domains

In this example, the access controller first checks the protection domain for the Network class to see if a class loaded from *http://network.xyz.com/* is allowed to connect to the socket. If that succeeds, it then checks the protection domain of the PayrollApp class to see if a class loaded from *http://hr.xyz.com/* is allowed to connect to a the socket. Only if both code sources are granted permission in the policy file (either individually or via an entry that does not specify a code base at all) does the checkPermission() method succeed.

Whether or not this is the appropriate behavior depends upon your intent. Let's say that the policy file for the payroll application specifies that classes with a code

---

* We showed this example and class loaders to implement it in Chapter 3.

base of *http://network.xyz.com/* are allowed to create sockets, but that no other protection domains (other than the system protection domain, of course) are granted that permission. That leads to the situation where a class from the network services department might not be able to open a socket (even though it has that permission in the file): if there is any class in the HR protection domain on the stack, the operation will fail. All classes on the stack must have permission for an operation to succeed.

Often, however, you want a class to be temporarily given the ability to perform an action on behalf of a class that might not normally have that ability. In this case, we might want to establish a policy where the classes from the HR department cannot create a socket directly, but where they can call classes from the network services department that can create a socket.* In this case, you want to tell the access controller to grant (temporarily) the permissions of the network services department to any methods that it might call within the current thread.

That facility is possible with these two methods of the access controller class:

public static Object doPrivileged(PrivilegedAction pa) ★
public static Object doPrivileged(PrivilegedExceptionAction pae) ★
  Execute the run() method on any given object, temporarily granting its permission to any protection domains below it on the stack. In the second case, if the embedded run() method throws an exception, the doPrivileged() method will throw a PrivilegedActionException.

The PrivilegedAction and PrivilegedExceptionAction interfaces contain a single method:

public Object run() ★
  Run the target code, which will have the permissions of the calling class.

The difference between the two interfaces is that the run() method in the PrivilegedExceptionAction interface may throw an arbitrary exception. Note the unfortunate overloading between this method and the run() method of the Thread class and Runnable interface, which return void; a class cannot implement both the Runnable and PrivilegedAction interfaces.

The PrivilegedActionException class is a standard exception, so you must always be prepared to catch it when using the doPrivileged() method. If the embedded run() method does throw an exception, that exception will be wrapped into the PrivilegedActionException, where it may be retrieved with this call:

---

* Consider this in terms of writing a file: an applet might not be able to write a file, but it can call a method of the JDK to play audio data—which means that the JDK class must write to the audio device file.

public Exception getException()

Return the exception that was originally thrown to cause the `PrivilegedAc-tionException` to be thrown.

Let's see how all of this might work with our network monitor example:

```
public class NetworkMonitor {
    public NetworkMonitor() {
        try {
            class doSocket implements PrivilegedExceptionAction {
                public Object run() throws UnknownHostException,
                                           IOException {
                    return new Socket("net.xyz.com", 4000);
                }
            };
            doSocket ds = new doSocket();
            Socket s = (Socket) AccessContoller.doPrivileged(ds);
        } catch (PrivilegedActionException pae) {
            Exception e = pae.getException();
            if (e instanceof UnknownHostException) {
                // process host exception
            }
            else if (e instanceof IOException {
                // process IOException
            }
            else {
                // e must be a runtime exception
                throw (RuntimeException) e;
            }
        }
    }
}
```

Two points are noteworthy here. First, the code that needs to be executed with the privileges of the `NetworkMonitor` class has been encapsulated into a new class—the inner `doSocket()` class.

Second, the exception handling is somewhat new: we must list the exceptions that the socket constructor can throw in the `run()` method of our embedded class. If either of those exceptions is thrown, it will be encapsulated into a `PrivilegedAc-tionException` and thrown back to the network monitor, where we can retrieve the actual exception with the `getException()` method.

Let's examine the effect this call has on the access controller. The access controller begins the same way, by examining the protection domains associated with each method on the stack. But this time, rather than searching every class on the stack, the access controller stops searching the stack when it reaches the class that has called the `doPrivileged()` method. In the case of Figure 5-3, this means that the access controller does not continue searching the stack after the

NetworkMonitor class, so as long as the policy file has a valid entry for the
http://network.xyz.com/ code base, the monitor will be able to create its socket.

There's an important (but subtle) distinction to be made here: the doPrivi-
leged() method does not suddenly establish a global permission based on the
protection domain of the class that called it. Rather, it specifies a stopping point as
the access controller searches the list of protection domains on the stack. In the
previous example, we assumed that *http://network.xyz.com/* had permission to open
the socket. When the access controller searched the protection domains on the
stack, it first reached the protection domain associated with *http://network.xyz.com/*.
Since that domain had been marked as the privileged domain, the access
controller returned at that point: it never got to the point on the stack where it
would have checked (and rejected) the protection domain associated with
http://hr.xyz.com/.

Now consider what would happen if the permissions given to these protection
domains were reversed; that is, if the *http://network.xyz.com/* protection domain is
not given permission to open the socket, but the *http://hr.xyz.com/* protection
domain is. We might be tempted to write the PayrollApp class (knowing that it
will have permission to open the socket) like this:

```
public class PayrollApp {
    NetworkMonitor nm;
    public void init() {
        class doInit implements PrivilegedAction {
            public void run() {
                nm = new NetworkMonitor();
            }
        }
        doInit di = new doInit();
        AccessController.doPrivileged(di);
    }
}
```

When the code within the Socket constructor calls the checkPermission()
method, the access controller searches the same stack shown in Figure 5-3. When
the access controller reaches the protection domain associated with
http://network.xyz.com, it immediately throws an AccessControlException, because
that protection domain does not have permission to open sockets. Even though a
protection domain lower in the stack does have such a permission, and even
though that protection domain has called the doPrivileged() method of the
access controller, the operation is rejected when the access controller finds a
protection domain that does not have the correct permission assigned to it.

This means that a protection domain can grant privileges to code that has called
it, but it cannot grant privileges to code that it calls. This rule permits key opera-

tions of the Java virtual machine; if, for example, your nonprivileged class calls the Java API to play an audio clip, the Java API will grant permission to the calling code to write data to the audio device on the machine. When you write your own applications, however, it's important to realize that the permission granting goes only one way.

Guarded Objects

The notion of permissions and the access controller can be encapsulated into a single object: a guarded object, which is implemented by the GuardedObject class (java.security.GuardedObject). This class allows you to embed another object within it in such a way that all access to the object will first have to go through a guard (which, typically, is the access controller).

There are two methods in the GuardedObject class:

public GuardedObject(Object o, Guard g) ★

Create a guarded object. The given object is embedded within the guarded object; access to the embedded object will not be granted unless the guard allows it.

public Object getObject() ★

Return the embedded object. The checkGuard() method of the guard is first called; if the guard prohibits access to the embedded object, an AccessControlException will be thrown. Otherwise, the embedded object is returned.

The guard can be any class that implements the Guard interface (java.security.Guard). This interface has a single method:

public void checkGuard(Object o) ★

See if access to the given object should be granted. If access is not granted, this method should throw an AccessControlException; otherwise it should silently return.

Although you can write your own guards, the Permission class already implements the guard interface. Hence, any permission can be used to guard an object as follows:

```
public class GuardTest {
    public static void main(String args[]) {
        GuardedObject go = new GuardedObject(new XYZPayrollRequest(),
                        new XYZPayrollPermission("sdo", "view"));
        try {
            Object o = go.getObject();
            System.out.println("Got access to object");
        } catch (AccessControlException ace) {
            System.out.println("Can't access object");
        }
    }
}
```

When the getObject() method is called, it in turn calls the checkGuard() method of the XYZPayrollPermission class, which (as it inherits from the Permission class) will call the checkPermission() method of the access controller, passing the XYZ payroll request object as an argument.

Summary

In this chapter, we've looked at Java's access control mechanism. The access controller is the most powerful security feature of the Java platform: it protects most of the vital resources on a user's machine, and it allows users (or system administrators) to customize the security policy of a particular application simply by modifying entries in the *java.policy* (and/or other similar) files.

The access controller is able to control access to a well-established set of system resources (files, sockets, etc.), but it is extensible as well: you can create your own permission classes that the access controller can use in order to grant or to deny access to any resource that you like.

In the next chapter, we'll look into more details of implementing a security policy, including the important relationship between the access controller and the security manager. And, because the access controller is only available with Java 1.2, we'll look at how the security manager can be used to implement a security policy in earlier releases of Java as well.

6

Implementing Security Policies

In Chapter 4, we examined the security manager in the context of existing implementations of the security manager for use in Java-enabled browsers; we followed that with a discussion of the access control mechanism and Java's ability to define access policies.

In this chapter, we'll put that information together and look at how the security manager is actually implemented, and how you can implement your own security manager. There are three times when it's important to write your own security manager:

In an RMI server

RMI wants you to provide a security manager for all RMI servers; for RMI servers that load client classes, a security manager is required. There is a default RMI security manager that you may use for this purpose, or you may write your own.

In a customized browser

If you're writing your own Java-enabled browser, you'll want to provide a security manager. In addition, if you're using an existing browser, you may want to use a different security manager in that browser. Some browsers already allow the user to specify a different security manager via a property; other browsers can be licensed for this type of customization.

In a Java application

If you download, install, and run Java applications on your machine, you may want to provide a security manager to protect your system against those applications the same way that it is protected against Java applets. In Java 1.1 and earlier releases, this requires you to write a security manager. In Java 1.2,* you

---

* 1.2 is now Java 2.

can use the access control mechanism instead of writing a complete security manager. However, even in Java 1.2 you may need to write your own security manager in certain circumstances. There are methods (like the getThread-Group() method) of the security manager that are outside the scope of the access controller, and there are certain types of permissions (like those typically given to the checkConnect() method) that cannot be specified in a *java.policy* file.

Access Control and the Security Manager

When the access controller was introduced into Java 1.2, it made a big difference to the role of the security manager. Previously, the security manager was paramount in allowing or rejecting operations on files and sockets and other system resources. In Java 1.2, the security manager began to defer permission checking to the access controller.

However, the security manager remains an important interface to system security. The Java API still calls the methods of the security manager to enforce system security—and now most of these methods call the access controller. This allows for upward compatibility—if you wrote a 1.1-based security manager that implements your desired security policy, you can still use that security manager with Java 1.2; your program will run exactly the same as it used to. In this case, you needn't worry about policy files and code sources and secure class loaders—the security model that you've already encapsulated into your security manager will be respected.

Protected Methods of the Security Manager

We've often said that the distinction between trusted and untrusted code has its roots in information that the security manager must obtain from the class loader. There are two ways in which this happens: through a set of generic methods of the SecurityManager class that inform the security manager about the state of the class loader, and through an agreed-upon interface between the security manager and the class loader. We'll look at the first of these mechanisms in this section, and we'll discuss the second mechanism later when we actually develop a security manager.

The use of these protected methods is vital in Java 1.1 and previous releases. In Java 1.2, they are much less important—some of them have even been deprecated. This is not surprising, since the access controller now gives us much of the information that initially could only be obtained from the class loader. We'll give a complete overview of these methods here, although it is information that you'll only need to complete a 1.1-based security manager.

The methods of the security manager that provide us with generic information about the class loader are all protected methods of the security manager class; they are summarized in Table 6-1.

Table 6-1. Protected Methods of the Security Manager Class

Method	Purpose
getClassContext()	Return all the classes on the stack to see who has called us
currentClassLoader()	Return the most recent class loader
currentLoadedClass()	Return the class that was most recently loaded with a class loader
classLoaderDepth()	Return the depth in the call stack where the most recent class loader was found
classDepth()	Return the depth in the call stack of the given class
inClass()	Return true if the given class is on the stack
inClassLoader()	Return true if any class on the stack came from a class loader

protected native Class[] getClassContext()
    Return an array of all classes on the stack of the currently executing thread.

The first such method we'll discuss lets us retrieve all the classes involved in making the current call to the security manager. This method itself is rarely used in a security manager, but it is the basis for many of the methods we'll discuss in this section.

The getClassContext() method returns an array of Class objects in the order of the call stack for the current method. The first element of the array is always the Class object for the security manager class, the second element is the Class object for the method that called the security manager, and so on.

Accessing all the classes in this array is one way to determine whether the call originally came from code that is in the Java API or whether it came from other code. For example, we could put the following method into our custom security manager:

```java
public class MySecurityManager extends SecurityManager {
    public void checkRead(String s) {
        Class c[] = getClassContext();
        for (int i = 0; i < c.length; i++) {
            String name = c.getName();
            System.out.println(name);
        }
    }
}
```

If we then try to create a FileReader object:

```
public class Test {
    public static void main(String args[]) {
        System.setSecurityManager(new MySecurityManager());
        FileReader f = new FileReader("/etc/passwd");
    }
}
```

we see the following output from the checkRead() method:

```
MySecurityManager
java.io.FileInputStream
java.io.FileReader
Test
```

In other words, a method in the Test class invoked a method in the FileReader class, which invoked a method in the File InputStream class, which invoked a method (the checkRead() method, in fact) in the MySecurityManager class.

The policies you want to enforce determine how you use the information about these classes—just keep in mind that the first class you see is always your security manager class and the second class you see is normally some class of the Java API. This last case is not an absolute—it's perfectly legal, though rare, for any arbitrary class to call the security manager. And as we saw in Chapter 4, some methods are called by platform-specific classes that implement particular interfaces of the Java API (such as methods that implement the Toolkit class).

Also keep in mind that there may be several classes from the Java API returned in the class array—for example, when you construct a new thread, the Thread class calls the checkAccess() method; the classes returned from the getClassContext() method in that case are:

```
MySecurityManager
java.lang.Thread
java.lang.Thread
java.lang.Thread
java.lang.Thread
Test
Test
```

We get this output because the Thread class constructor calls three other internal methods before it calls the security manager. Our Test class has created a thread in an internal method as well, so the Test class also appears twice in the class array.

protected native ClassLoader currentClassLoader()

Search the array of classes returned from the getClassContext() method for the most recently called class that was loaded via a program-defined class loader, and return that class loader.

The objects in the class array returned from the getClassContext() method are generally used to inspect the class loader for each class—that's how the security manager can make a policy decision about classes that were loaded from disk versus classes that were loaded from the network (or elsewhere). The simplest test that we can make is to see if any of the classes involved in the current method invocation are loaded from the network, in which case we can deny the attempted operation. This is the method we use to do that.

To understand currentClassLoader(), we need to recall how the class loader works. The class loader first calls the findSystemClass() method, which attempts to find the class in the user's CLASSPATH (or system classpath in 1.2). If that call is unsuccessful, the class loader loads the class in a different manner (e.g., by loading the class over the network). As far as the Java virtual machine is concerned, the class loader associated with a class that was loaded via the findSystemClass() method is null. If an instance of the ClassLoader class defined the class (by calling the defineClass() method), then (and only then) does Java make an association between the class and the class loader. This association is made by storing a reference to the class loader within the class object itself; the getClassLoader() method of the Class object can be used to retrieve that reference.

Hence, the currentClassLoader() method is equivalent to:[*]

```
protected ClassLoader currentClassLoader() {
    Class c[] = getClassContext();
    for (int i = 1; i < c.length; i++)
        if (c[i].getClassLoader() != null)
            return c[i].getClassLoader();
    return null;
}
```

We can use this method to disallow writing to a file by any class that was loaded via a class loader:

```
public void checkWrite(String s) {
    if (currentClassLoader() != null)
        throw new SecurityException("checkWrite");
    }
}
```

With this version of checkWrite(), only the Java virtual machine can open a file for writing. When the Java virtual machine initializes, for example, it may create a thread for playing audio files. This thread will attempt to open the audio device on the machine by instantiating one of the standard Java API file classes. When the

---

[*] The truth is that the currentClassLoader() method is written in native code, so we don't know how it actually is implemented, but it is functionally equivalent to the code shown. This is true about most of the methods of this section, which for efficiency reasons are written in native code.

instance of this class is created, it (as expected) calls the checkWrite() method, but there is no class loader on the stack. The only methods that are involved in the thread opening the audio device are methods that were loaded by the Java virtual machine itself and hence have no class loader. Later, however, if an applet class tries to open up a file on the user's machine, the checkWrite() method is called again, and this time there is a class loader on the stack: the class loader that was used to load in the applet making the call to open the file. This second case will generate the security exception.

A number of convenience methods of the security manager class also relate to the current class loader:

protected boolean inClassLoader() ☆

Test to see if there is a class loader on the stack:

```
protected boolean inClassLoader() {
    return currentClassLoader() != null;
}
```

protected Class currentLoadedClass() ☆

Return the class on the stack that is associated with the current class loader:

```
protected Class currentLoadedClass() {
    Class c[] = getClassContext();
    for (int i = 0; i < c.length; i++)
        if (c[i].getClassLoader() != null)
            return c[i];
    return null;
}
```

protected native int classDepth(String name) ☆

Return the index of the class array from the getClassContext() method where the named class is found:

```
protected int classDepth(String name) {
    Class c[] = getClassContext();
    for (int i = 0; i < c.length; i++)
        if (c[i].getName().equals(name))
            return i;
    return -1;
}
```

protected boolean inClass(String name) ☆

Indicate whether the named class is anywhere on the stack:

```
protected boolean inClass(String name) {
    return classDepth(name) >= 0;
}
```

Many of these convenience methods revolve around the idea that an untrusted class may have called a method of a trusted class and that the trusted class should not be allowed to perform an operation that the untrusted class could not have performed directly. These methods allow you to write a Java application made up of trusted classes that itself downloads and runs untrusted classes. The HotJava browser is the best-known example of this sort of program. For example, the security manager of the HotJava browser does not allow an arbitrary applet to initiate a print job, but HotJava itself can.

HotJava initiates a print job when the user selects the "Print" item from one of the standard menus. Since the request comes from a class belonging to the HotJava application itself (that is, the callback method of the menu item), the browser is initiating the request (at least as far as the security manager is concerned). An applet initiates the request when it tries to create a print job.

In both cases, the getPrintJob() method of the Toolkit class calls the check-PrintJobAccess() method of the security manager. The security manager must then look at the classes on the stack and determine if the operation should succeed. If there is an untrusted (applet) class anywhere on the stack, the print request started with that class and should be rejected; otherwise, the print request originated from the HotJava classes and is allowed to proceed.

Note the similarity between this technique and the manner in which the access controller works. In Java 1.2, the HotJava classes belong to the system domain, so they are allowed to do anything; the classes that make up the applet, however, are prohibited from initiating the print job (unless, of course, an entry that enables printing for that applet's code source is in the policy file). This is why these methods have been deprecated in 1.2, where the access controller is the desired mechanism to provide this functionality.

The Class Loader Depth

The example that we just gave is typical of the majority of security checks the security manager makes. You can often make a decision on whether or not an operation should be allowed simply by knowing whether or not there is a class loader on the stack, since the presence of a class loader means that an untrusted class has initiated the operation in question.

There's a group of tricky exceptions to this rule, however, and those exceptions mean that you sometimes have to know the exact depth at which the class loader was found. Before we dive into those exceptions, we must emphasize: the use of the class loader depth is not pretty. Fortunately, beginning with Java 1.2, this method has been deprecated, and we need no longer concern ourselves with it. If you need to write a 1.1-compatible security manager, however, you need to use the information in this section.

The depth at which the class loader was found in the class context array can be determined by this method:

protected native int classLoaderDepth() ☆

Return the index of the class array from the `getClassContext()` method where the current class loader is found:

```
protected int classLoaderDepth() {
    Class c[] = getClassContext();
        for (int i = 0; i < c.length; i++) {
            if (c[i].getClassLoader() != null)
                return i;
        }
    return -1;
}
```

Let's look at this method in the context of the following applet:

```
public class DepthTest extends Applet {
    native void evilInterface();

    public void init() {
        doMath();
        infiltrate();
    }

    public void infiltrate() {
        try {
            System.loadLibrary("evilLibrary");
            evilInterface();
        } catch (Exception e) {}
    }

    public void doMath() {
        BigInteger bi = new BigInteger("100");
        bi = bi.add(new BigInteger("100"));
        System.out.println("answer is " + bi);
    }
}
```

Under normal circumstances, we would expect the `doMath()` method to inform us (rather inefficiently) that 100 plus 100 is 200. We would further expect the call to the `infiltrate()` method to generate a security exception, since an untrusted class is not normally allowed to link in a native library.

The security exception in this case is generated by the `checkLink()` method of the security manager. When the `infiltrate()` method calls the `System.loadLibrary()` method, the `loadLibrary()` method in turn calls the `checkLink()` method. If we were to retrieve the array of classes (via the `getClassContext()`

method) that led to the call to the checkLink() method, we'd see the following classes on the stack:

```
MySecurityManager (the checkLink() method)
java.lang.Runtime (the loadLibrary() method)
java.lang.System  (the loadLibrary() method)
DepthTest         (the infiltrate() method)
DepthTest         (the init() method)
... other classes from the browser ...
```

Because the untrusted class DepthTest appears on the stack, we are tempted to reject the operation and throw a security exception.

Life is not quite that simple in this case. As it turns out, the BigInteger class contains its own native methods and hence depends on a platform-specific library to perform many of its operations. When the BigInteger class is loaded, its static initializer attempts to load the math library (by calling the System.loadLibrary() method), which is the library that contains the code to perform these native methods.

Because of the way in which Java loads classes, the BigInteger class is not loaded until it is actually needed—that is, until the doMath() method of the DepthTest class is called. If you recall our discussion from Chapter 3 regarding how the class loader works, you'll remember that when the doMath() method is called and needs access to the BigInteger class, the class loader that created the DepthTest class is asked to find that class (even though the BigInteger class is part of the Java API itself). Hence, the applet class loader (that is, the class loader that loaded the DepthTest class) is used to find the BigInteger class, which it does by calling the findSystemClass() method. When the findSystemClass() method loads the BigInteger class from disk, it runs the static initializers for that class, which call the System.loadLibrary() method to load in the math library.

The upshot of all this is that the System.loadLibrary() method calls the security manager to see if the program in question is allowed to link in the math library. This time, when the checkLink() method is called, the class array from the getClassContext() method looks like this:

```
MySecurityManager      (the checkLink() method)
java.lang.Runtime      (the loadLibrary() method)
java.lang.System       (the loadLibrary() method)
java.math.BigInteger   (the static intializer)
java.lang.ClassLoader  (the findSystemClass() method)
AppletLoader           (the loadClass() method)
java.lang.ClassLoader  (the loadClassInternal() method)
DepthTest              (the doMath() method)
DepthTest              (the init() method)
... various browser classes ...
```

As we would expect, the first three elements of this list are the same as the first three elements of the previous list—but after that, we see a radical difference in the list of classes on the stack. In both cases, the untrusted class (DepthTest) is on the stack, but in this second case, it is much further down the stack than it was in the first case. In this second case, the untrusted class indirectly caused the native library to be loaded; in the first case the untrusted class directly requested the native library to be loaded. That distinction is what drives the use of the class-LoaderDepth() method.

So in this example, we need the checkLink() method to obtain the depth of the class loader (that is, the depth of the first untrusted class on the stack) and behave appropriately. If that depth is 3, the checkLink() method should throw an exception, but if that depth is 7, the checkLink() method should not throw an exception. There is nothing magical about a class depth of 7, however—that just happens to be the depth returned by the classLoaderDepth() method in our second example. A different example might well have produced a different number, depending on the classes involved.

Testing the Security Manager

If you want to know whether or not the security manager will permit a certain operation, you might be tempted to ask the security manager directly. If you want to know, for example, if you can change the state of a particular thread, you might be tempted to write this code:

```
SecurityManager sm = System.getSecurityManager();
boolean canModify = true;
if (sm != null) {
    try {
        sm.checkAccess(myThread);
    } catch (SecurityException se) {
        canModify = false;
    }
}
```

Sometimes this procedure works, and sometimes it doesn't. The methods of the security manager that depend on the depth of the class loader usually test for a specific value. In the code fragment above, the depth of the class loader is 1—which is a depth that most security managers will not complain about, so the canModify variable is set to true. When an actual operation on the thread is attempted, however, the depth of the class loader will be different, and the security manager will reacts differently.

Hence, the only certain way to know if the security manager will prohibit an operation is to attempt that operation and see if a security exception is thrown.

There is, however, something special about a class depth of 3 in this example: a class depth of 3 always means that the untrusted class called the `System.loadLibrary()` method, which called the `Runtime.loadLibrary()` method, which called the security manager's `checkLink()` method.* Hence, when there is a class depth of 3, it means that the untrusted class has directly attempted to load the library. When the class depth is greater than 3, the untrusted class has indirectly caused the library to be loaded. When the class depth is 2, the untrusted class has directly called the `Runtime.loadLibrary()` method—which is to say again that the untrusted class has directly attempted to load the library. When there is a class depth of 1, the untrusted class has directly called the `checkLink()` method—which is possible, but that is a meaningless operation. So in this case, a class depth that is 3 or less (but greater than -1, which means that no untrusted class is on the stack) indicates that the call came directly from an untrusted class and should be handled appropriately (usually meaning that a security exception should be thrown).

But while 3 is a magic number for the `checkLink()` method, it is not necessarily a magic number for all other methods. In general, for most methods the magic number that indicates that an untrusted class directly attempted an operation is 2: the untrusted class calls the Java API, which calls the security manager. Other classes have other constraints on them that change what their target number should be.

The class depth is therefore a tricky thing: there is no general rule about the allowable class depth for an untrusted class. Worse, there's no assurance that the allowable class depth may not change between releases of the JDK—the JDK could conceivably change its internal algorithm for a particular operation to add another method call, which would increase the allowable class depth by 1. This is one reason why the class depth is such a bad idea: it requires an intimate knowledge of all the trusted classes in the API in order to pick an appropriate class depth. Worse, a developer may introduce a new method into a call stack and completely change the class depth for a sensitive operation without realizing the effect this will have on the security manager.

Nonetheless, in order for certain classes of the Java API to work correctly, you need to put the correct information into your 1.1-based security manager (such as

---

* Theoretically, it could also mean that an untrusted class has called a trusted class that has called the `Runtime.loadLibrary()` method directly. However, the Java API never bypasses the `System.loadLibrary()` method, so that will not happen in practice. If you expect trusted classes in your Java application to work under the scenario we're discussing here, you must also follow that rule.

in the checkLink() method that we just examined). The methods that need such treatment are summarized in Table 6-2.

Table 6-2. Methods of the SecurityManager Class Affected by the Depth of the Class Loader

Method	Depth to Avoid	Remarks
checkCreateClass-Loader()	2	Java beans create a SystemClassLoader
checkPropertiesAccess()	2	Java API calls System.getProperties()
checkPropertyAccess()	2	Java API gets many properties
checkAccess(Thread t)	3	Java API manipulates its own threads
checkAccess(Thread-Group tg)	3 (sometimes 4)	Java API manipulates its own thread groups
checkLink()	2 or 3	Java API loads many libraries
checkMemberAccess()	3	Java API uses method reflection
checkExec()	2	Toolkit implementations of getPrintJob() may execute a print command
checkExit()	2	The application may call exit
checkWrite()	2	Toolkit implementations may create temporary files; the Java API needs to write to audio and other device files
checkDelete()	2	Toolkit implementations may need to delete temporary files
checkRead()	2	Java API needs to read property files
checkTopLevelWindow()	3	Trusted classes may need pop-up windows

In all cases in Table 6-2, the Java API depends on being allowed to perform an operation that would normally be rejected if an untrusted class performed it directly. The JavaBeans classes, for example, create a class loader (an instance of SystemClassLoader) in order to abstract the primordial class loader. So if an untrusted class creates a Java bean, that Java bean must in turn be allowed to create a class loader, or the bean itself won't work.

Note that not every target depth in this table is 2. In the case of the Thread and ThreadGroup classes, operations that affect the state of the thread call the check-Access() method of the Thread or ThreadGroup class itself, which in turn calls the checkAccess() method of the SecurityManager class. This extra method call results in an extra method on the stack and effectively increases the target depth by 1. Similarly, the checkTopLevelWindow() method is called from the constructor of the Window class, which in turn is called from the constructor of the Frame class, resulting in a target depth of 3.

Remember that this table only summarizes the methods of the security manager where the actual depth of the class loader matters to the core Java API. If you're writing your own application, you need to consider whether or not your application classes want to perform certain operations. If you want classes in your application to be able to initiate a print job, for example, and you don't want untrusted classes that your application loads to initiate a print job, you'll want to put a depth check of 2 into the checkPrintJobAccess() method. In general, for methods that aren't listed in the above table, a depth of 2 is appropriate if you want your application classes (i.e., classes from the CLASSPATH) to be able to perform those operations.

There is once again a nice similarity between these ideas and the access controller. When you call the doPrivileged() method of the access controller, you're achieving the same thing a security manager achieves by testing the class depth. The point to remember about the class depth is that it allows the security manager to grant more permissions to a class than it would normally have—just like the doPrivileged() method grants its permissions to all protection domains that have previously been pushed onto the stack. Of course, the access controller is a much smarter way to go about this, since it doesn't depend upon someone getting the class depth right; it only depends upon the actual characteristics of the stack during execution of the program.

Protected Instance Variables in the Security Manager

There is a single protected instance variable in the security manager class, and that is the inCheck instance variable:

protected boolean inCheck ☆
Indicate whether a check by the security manager is in progress.

The value of this variable can be obtained from the following method:

public boolean getInCheck() ☆
Return the value of the inCheck instance variable.

Since there is no corresponding public method to set this variable, it is up to the security manager itself to set inCheck appropriately.*

This variable has a single use: it must be set by the security manager before the security manager calls most methods of the InetAddress class. The reason for this is to prevent an infinite recursion between the security manager and the InetAddress class. This recursion is possible under the following circumstances.

---

* Don't get all excited and think that your untrusted class can use this method to see when the security manager is working. As we'll see, it's only set by the security manager in a rare case, and even if it were set consistently, there's no practical way for your untrusted class to examine the variable during the short period of time it is set.

1. An untrusted class attempts to open a socket to a particular host (e.g., *sun.com*). The expectation is that if the untrusted class was loaded from *sun.com* that the operation will succeed; otherwise, the operation will fail.

2. Opening the socket results in a call to the checkConnect() method, which must determine if the two hosts in question are the same. In the case of a class loaded from *sun.com* that is attempting to connect to *sun.com*, a simple string comparison is sufficient. If the names are the same, the checkConnect() method can simply return immediately. In fact, this is the only logic performed by some browsers—if the names do not literally match, the operation is denied immediately.

3. A complication arises if the two names do not match directly, but may still be the same host. My machine has a fully qualified name of *piccolo.East.Sun.COM*; browsers on my local area network can access my machine's web server as *piccolo, piccolo.East,* or *piccolo.East.Sun.COM*. If the untrusted class is loaded from a URL that contained only the string *piccolo,* and the class attempts to open a socket to *piccolo.East,* we may want that operation to succeed even though the names of the hosts are not equal.

   Hence, the checkConnect() method must retrieve the IP address for both names, and compare those IP addresses.

4. To retrieve the IP address for a particular host, the checkConnect() method must call the InetAddress.getByName() method, which converts a string to an IP address.

5. The getByName() method will not blithely convert a hostname to an IP address—it will only do so if the program in question is normally allowed to make a socket connection to that host. Otherwise, an untrusted class could be downloaded into your corporate network and determine all the IP addresses that are available on the network behind your firewall. So the getByName() method needs to call the checkConnect() method in order to ensure that the program is allowed to retrieve the information that is being requested.

We see the problem here: the getByName() method keeps calling the checkConnect() method, which in turn keeps calling the getByName() method. In order to prevent this recursion, the checkConnect() method is responsible for setting the inCheck instance variable to true before it starts and then setting it to false when it is finished. Similarly, the getByName() method is responsible for examining this variable (via the return from the getInCheck() method); it does not call the checkConnect() method if a security check is already in progress.

There may be other variations in this cooperation between the security manager and the InetAddress class—other methods of the InetAddress class also use the information from the getInCheck() method to determine whether or not to call the checkConnect() method. But this is the only class where this information is used directly. You can set the inCheck method within other methods of your security manager, but there is no point in doing so.

In 1.2, this variable and method are deprecated. The correct operation to perform in a 1.2-based security manager is to place the calls to the InetAddress in a class that can be used by the doPrivileged() method. In addition, the InetAddress class in 1.2 no longer calls the getInCheck() method.

If you implement a checkConnect() method that calls the InetAddress class and sets the inCheck variable, you must make the checkConnect() method and the getInCheck() methods synchronized. This prevents another thread from directly looking up an IP address at the same time that the security manager has told the InetAddress class not to call the checkConnect() method.

Security Managers and the Class Loader

In addition to the methods of the security manager class that we just examined, a second way by which the security manager can enforce policies is to ask that the class loader for a particular class provide more information on which the security manager may base its decision. This technique requires a coordination between the security manager and the class loader; there is no standard interface by which this information may be obtained (nor is there a limit to the type of information that may be exchanged). The details of the interface are completely at the discretion of the application developer. This technique is useful for both 1.1-based and (to a lesser extent) 1.2-based security managers.

In the last section, we showed an example of the checkWrite() method that threw a security exception only if there was a class loader on the stack; this effectively prevented any class that was loaded from the network from opening a file in order to write to it. A more sophisticated policy would be to allow certain classes loaded over the network to write files, but not other classes. If you recall our example from Chapter 3, XYZ Corporation is using a customized class loader that allows their applications to read classes both from the web server on which the application is hosted and from the centralized administration server. XYZ Corporation might want to establish a security policy whereby classes that are loaded from the administration server can write local files, but other classes cannot. This sort of policy requires some cooperation between the security manager and the class loader—the security manager must ask the class loader for the host the class was loaded from:

```
public void checkWrite(String s) {
    ClassLoader cl = currentClassLoader();
    if (cl != null) {
        MultiLoader ml = null;
```

```
        try {
            ml = (MultiLoader) cl;
        } catch (ClassCastException cce) {
            // This can't happen unless our class loader and our
            // security manager are out of sync
            throw new SecurityException("checkWrite out of sync");
        }
        if (!ml.getTrust(currentLoadedClass()))
            throw new SecurityException("checkWrite");
    }
}
```

This example only works with a class loader we have defined, since we need a
method called getTrust() in the class loader to let us know the origin of the class.
That getTrust() method might look like this:

```
public class MultiLoader extends SecureClassLoader {
    ...
    boolean getTrust(Class c) {
        String name = c.getName();
        if (supportClassesCache.get(name))
            return true;
        return false;
    }
}
```

Hence, we cast the class loader returned from getClassLoader() to be an
instance of MultiLoader. It's easy to keep the class loader and the security
manager in sync because the application must install both of them, but it always
pays to be sure. We use this class loader to check whether the particular class is to
be trusted; the class loader thinks classes that have been loaded from XYZ's
support machine are trusted and other classes are not. Note that if you are going
to use this technique in 1.2 that it is quite possible the class loader will not be your
multi loader—it might be one of the internal class loaders that is used to load
extension or API classes. In that case, instead of throwing a security exception
when the class cast fails, you should simply call the super.checkWrite() method,
which will do the correct thing in 1.2.

This sort of cooperation can be used between the class loader and the security
manager to support a variety of requirements—providing different access to
classes from different domains, or from different protocols, or anything else the
class loader knows about. It just requires that the security manager know about any
special interfaces the class loader might have to support these features.

The Class Loader and the Security Manager

The relationship between the security manager and class loader goes both ways—
not only is the class loader able to provide additional information about particular
classes to the security manager, the class loader is also responsible for calling the

security manager to see if particular classes are able to be loaded or defined. We showed the code a class loader uses to do this in Chapter 3.

When a class loader is asked to load a class, it must call the checkPackageAccess() method of the security manager so that the security manager can prevent certain classes from being loaded. This is chiefly used to prevent untrusted classes from directly accessing implementation-specific classes. If you ship an application with a set of classes in the com.XYZ package, you can ensure that untrusted classes do not directly call classes in that package by placing the appropriate logic into the checkPackageAccess() method. Java-enabled browsers typically do just that; for example, an applet cannot call any of the classes in the sun package within the HotJava browser.

Additionally, when a class loader is asked to define a class, it must call the checkPackageDefinition() method of the security manager so that the security manager can prevent an untrusted class from defining classes in a particular package. This should be used, for example, to prevent an untrusted class from loading a new class into the java.lang package. Otherwise, an untrusted class could create a class named java.lang.Foo that has access to all the default-protected methods and instance variables of the other classes within the java.lang package.

Implementation Techniques

We'll now turn our attention to implementing security policies. Our goal is to show how to write a security manager—one that can be used in conjunction with the access controller, and one that can stand alone. We'll plug these security managers into our JavaRunner program, and we'll also discuss the implementation of the security manager that comes with the Launcher and how that security manager may be installed.

Utility Classes

In order to make our implementation of the security manger a bit easier, we'll provide a few utility classes.

As we intimated above, there are many times when we want to reject an operation if there is any untrusted class on the stack. In order to simplify this operation, we define this method:

```
private void checkClassLoader(String ask, String ex) {
    // Use the ask string to prompt the user if the operation
    // should succeed
    if (inClassLoader()) {
        throw new SecurityException(ex);
    }
}
```

We've passed a string to this method that allows us to ask the user if the operation in question should be permitted; for example, the application could pop up a dialog window and give the user the opportunity to accept the operation. Whether or not that ability is a good idea is open to debate; we've left it to the reader to provide the logic to implement that feature (if desired).

There are a number of tests we want our security manager to reject if they are attempted directly by an untrusted class, but should succeed if they are attempted indirectly by an untrusted class. For these tests in Java 1.1, we have to rely on the class depth to tell us whether the call originated from an untrusted class or not. We use this method to help us with that task:

```
private void checkClassDepth(int depth, String ask, String ex) {
    int clDepth = classLoaderDepth();
    if (clDepth > 0 && clDepth <= depth + 1) {
        throw new SecurityException(ex);
    }
}
```

Note that we have to add 1 to the class depth for this method to succeed, since calling this method has pushed another method frame onto the stack.

Implementing Network Access

Regardless of the release on which your security manager is based, you typically must write the necessary methods to handle network access, because the default methods of the security manager are usually inadequate. In 1.1, the default behavior for the checkConnect() method is to throw a security violation.

In 1.2, the default behavior for the checkConnect() method is to use the access controller to see if the appropriate entry is in the policy file. This is very useful in some circumstances: we can, for example, specify that all code loaded from *network.xyz.com* can access any other machine in the *xyz.com* domain, but no other machines. But we cannot set up a general rule for the mode of network access we're most accustomed to. We cannot set up a rule saying that code loaded from a particular machine can only make a network connection back to that machine. The problem lies in the fact that we cannot pattern match entries in the policy file; we cannot say something like:

```
grant codeBase http://%template/ {
        permission java.net.SocketPermission "%template", "connect";
};
```

So if we want to implement a security policy where code can only make a connection back to the host from which it was loaded, we must provide a new implementation of the checkConnect() method:

```java
private ClassLoader getNonSystemClassLoader() {
    Class c[] = getClassContext();
    ClassLoader sys = ClassLoader.getSystemClassLoader();
    for (int i = 1; i < c.length; i++) {
        ClassLoader cl = c[i].getClassLoader();
        if (cl != null && !cl.equals(sys))
            return cl:
    }
    return null
}

public void checkConnect(String host, int port) {
    try {
        super.checkConnect(host, port);
        return;
    } catch (AccessControlException ace) {
        // continue
    }

    //In 1.1, use currentClassLoader() instead
    ClassLoader loader = getNonSystemClassLoader();
    String remoteHost;

    if (loader == null)
        return;
    if (!(loader instanceof JavaRunnerLoader))
        throw new SecurityException("Class loader out of sync");
    JavaRunnerLoader cl = (JavaRunnerLoader) loader;
    remoteHost = cl.getHost();

    if (host.equals(remoteHost))
        return;

    try {
        class testHost implements PrivilegedExceptionAction {
            String local, remote;
            testHost(String local, String remote) {
                this.local = local;
                this.remote = remote;
            }
            public Object run() throws UnknownHostException {
                InetAddress hostAddr = InetAddress.getByname(local);
                InetAddress remoteAddr = InetAddress.getByName(remote);
                if (hostAddr.equals(remoteAddr))
                    return new Boolean("true");
                return new Boolean("false");
            }
        }
        testHost th = new testHost(host, remoteHost);
        Boolean b = (Boolean) AccessController.doPrivileged(th);
```

```
        if (b.booleanValue())
            return;
    } catch (PrivilegedActionException pae) {
    //Must be an UnknownHostException; continue and throw exception
    }

    throw new SecurityException(
            "Can't connect from " + remoteHost + " to " + host);
}
```

First, we check our superclass to see if it allows the connection. This is only appropriate for 1.2-based security managers—calling the superclass checks the policy file to see if the connection should be made according to information in that file. If that's true, then we simply want to return: the check should succeed. Otherwise, we continue so we can make sure the destination machine is the same machine we loaded this particular class from. For 1.1, this test must be omitted; the superclass in 1.1 would immediately throw an exception.

If there is no class loader on the stack, we want to permit access to any host, so we simply return. Otherwise, we obtain the hostname the untrusted class was loaded from (via the getHost() method of the class loader) and compare that to the hostname the untrusted class is attempting to contact. If the strings are equal, we're all set and can return. Otherwise, we implement the logic we described earlier by obtaining the IP address for each hostname and comparing the two IP addresses.

Note that the logic here for allowing the InetAddress class to resolve the hostname to an IP address is based on the access controller. For a 1.1-based security manager, you would set the inCheck variable to true, execute the calls that are in the run() method of the testHost class, and then set inCheck to false. You would also need to synchronize this method and the getInCheck() methods.

This implementation requires yet another change to the class loader we're using. The class loader must now be able to provide us with the name of the host from which a particular class was loaded. Since our class loader is based on a URL, that's an easy method to implement: we simply return the host of the URL:

```
public class JavaRunnerLoader extends SecureClassLoader {
    URL urlBase;
    ... other code from previous examples ...
    String getHost() {
        return urlBase.getHost();
    }
}
```

If you choose to implement a different network security model for your checkConnect() method, there are a few things that you should be aware of:

- The checkConnect() method is frequently called with a port of -1. That usage comes primarily from the methods of the InetAddress class; in order to resolve the name of a machine, you must be able to make a connection to that machine. So if you want to restrict a connection to the privileged ports on your machine (those less than 1024), make sure you test to see that the port is between 0 and 1023, rather than simply less than 1024.

- The host argument passed to the checkConnect() method is frequently an IP address rather than a symbolic hostname. This is an artifact of the way in which the default socket implementation (that is, the PlainSocketImpl class) operates: this class actually generates two calls to the checkConnect() method. The first call contains the actual hostname and a port number of -1 (because the PlainSocketImpl class has called the InetAddress.get-ByName() method), and the second call contains the IP address and the actual port number.

- If you choose to disallow all network access by untrusted classes and you are using a network-based class loader to load classes, you cannot simply write a checkConnect() method that calls the inClassLoader() method and throws an exception if it returns true. The class loader must be allowed to open a socket in order to retrieve additional classes that are referenced by the untrusted class, and such a request will contain the untrusted class on the stack when the call is made. In Java 1.1, you can use the inClass() method to see if the class loader is attempting to open the socket, in which case you should let the operation succeed. In Java 1.2, you can use the doPrivileged() method of the access controller from within the class loader to attempt to open the URL.

- There is another checkConnect() method that accepts as arguments the hostname, the port number, and an arbitrary object (a context). Like the similar checkRead() method, this version of the checkConnect() method is never called by the Java API, so the easiest route to take is not to implement it at all. The type of information you might choose to encode within the context could be, for example, the hostname that was retrieved from the current class loader. However, since the security manager is responsible for obtaining the context in the first place, there's no reason why that information cannot be used directly rather than calling this second checkConnect() method.

You may want to implement a similar policy in the checkAccept() method so that a class can only accept a connection from the host from which it was loaded. Since we've just implemented that logic in the checkConnect() method, the easiest way to implement this method is:

```
public void checkAccept(String host, int port) {
    try {
        super.checkAccept(host, port);
```

```
        return;
    } catch (AccessControlException ace) {
        // continue
    }
    checkConnect(host, port);
}
```

Network Permissions in the Class Loader

In Java 1.2, there is another way to achieve the network permissions we just outlined. Instead of overriding the checkConnect() method of the security manager, we can arrange for the protection domain of each class to carry with it the permission to open a socket to the host it was loaded from. We can add this permission without regard to the permissions that might be in the policy file.

This implementation requires us to override the getPermissions() method of the SecureClassLoader class as follows:

```
protected PermissionCollection getPermissions(CodeSource cs) {
    if (!cs.equals(this.cs))
            return null;
    Policy pol = Policy.getPolicy();
    PermissionCollection pc = pol.getPermissions(cs);
    pc.add(new SocketPermission(urlBase.getHost(), "connect"));
    return pc;
}
```

As long as we use the correct code source to define the class, when the class loader resolves its permissions the appropriate socket permission will be added to the user-defined set of permissions.

Implementing Thread Security

Implementing a model of thread security requires that you implement the check-Access() methods as well as implementing the getThreadGroup() method. In 1.1, the checkAccess() methods by default throw a security exception. In 1.2, the default behavior of the security manager is to allow the checkAccess() method to succeed unless the target thread is a member of the system thread group or the target thread group is the system thread group. In those cases, the program must have been granted a runtime permission of modifyThread or modifyThreadGroup (depending on which checkAccess() method is involved) for the operation to succeed. Hence, any thread can modify any thread or thread group except for those belonging to the system thread group. Both releases return the thread group of the calling thread for the getThreadGroup() method.

We'll show an example that implements a hierarchical notion of thread permissions which fits well within the notion of the virtual machine's thread hierarchy (see Figure 6-1). In this model, a thread can manipulate any thread that appears within its thread group or within a thread group that is descended from its thread group. In the example, Program #1 has created two thread groups. The Calc thread can manipulate itself, the I/O thread, and any thread in the Program #1 thread groups; it cannot manipulate any threads in the system thread group or in Program #2's thread group. Similarly, threads within Program #1's thread subgroup #1 can only manipulate threads within that group.

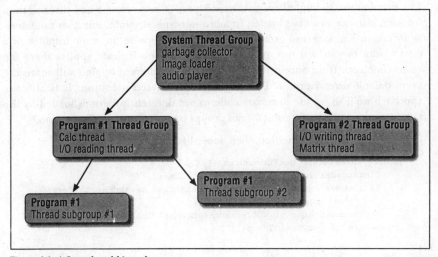

Figure 6-1. A Java thread hierarchy

This is a different security model than that which is implemented by the JDK's appletviewer and by some browsers in 1.1. In those models, any thread in any thread group of the applet can modify any other thread in any other thread group of the applet, but threads in one applet are still prevented from modifying threads in another applet or from modifying the system threads. But the model we'll describe fits the thread hierarchy a little better.

Note that this security model doesn't fit well within the idea of thread permissions and protection domains. An entry in the policy file granting permission to manipulate threads to the classes from which Program #1 is loaded will thus gran Program #1 permission to manipulate any threads in the virtual machine. The 1 default security manager checks for the modifyThread and modifyThreadGro permissions as described above.

The key to our model of thread security depends on the getThreadGro method. We can use this method to ensure that each class loader creat threads in a new thread group as follows:

- If the program attempts to create a thread in a particular thread gro checkAccess() method can throw a security exception if the thread question is not a descendant of the thread group that belongs to loader.

- If the program attempts to create a thread without specifying the thread group to which it should belong, we can arrange for the getThreadGroup() method to return the class loader's default thread group. This works because the constructors of the thread class call the getThreadGroup() method directly to obtain the thread group to which a thread should belong.

The simplest way to implement getThreadGroup() is to create a new thread group for each instance of a class loader. In a browser-type program, this does not necessarily create a new thread group for each applet, because the same instance of a class loader might load two or more different applets if those applets share the same codebase. If we adopt this approach, those different applets will share the same default thread group. This might be considered a feature. It is also the approach we'll show; the necessary code to put different programs loaded by the same class loader into different thread groups is a straightforward extension.

Our getThreadGroup() method, then, looks like this:

```java
public ThreadGroup getThreadGroup() {          .
    ClassLoader loader = currentClassLoader();
    if (loader == null || !(loader instanceof JavaRunnerLoader))
        return super.getThreadGroup();
    JavaRunnerLoader cl = (JavaRunnerLoader) loader;
    return cl.getThreadGroup();
}
```

We want each instance of a class loader to provide a different thread group. The simplest way to implement this logic is to defer to the class loader to provide the thread group. If there is no class loader, we'll use the thread group our superclass recommends (which, if we've directly extended the SecurityManager class, will be the thread group of the calling thread).

Of course, not every class loader has a getThreadGroup() method, so if the class loader we find isn't of the class that we expect, we again have to defer to our super-class to provide the correct thread group (which, by default, is the thread group of the calling thread). Otherwise, we can ask the class loader, which implies that we to provide a getThreadGroup() method within that class loader:

```java
 c class JavaRunnerLoader extends SecureClassLoader {
     vate ThreadGroup threadGroup;
     ate static int groupNum;

           roup getThreadGroup() {
            hreadGroup == null)
            eadGroup = new ThreadGroup("JavaRunner ThreadGroup-"
                             + groupNum++);
            eadGroup;
```

t part of our goal: when the program attempts to
ying a thread group that it should belong to, the

thread is assigned to the desired group. For the second part of our goal, we need to ensure that the checkAccess() method only allows classes from that class loader to create a thread within that thread group (or one of its descendent thread groups).

In order to achieve this second goal, we must implement the checkAccess() methods as follows:

```
public void checkAccess(Thread t) {
    ThreadGroup current = Thread.currentThread().getThreadGroup();
    if (!current.parentOf(t.getThreadGroup()))
        super.checkAccess(t);
}
public void checkAccess(ThreadGroup tg) {
    ThreadGroup current = Thread.currentThread().getThreadGroup();
    if (!current.parentOf(tg))
            super.checkAccess(tg);
}
```

This logic prevents threads in sibling thread groups from manipulating each other, as well as preventing threads in groups that are lower in the thread hierarchy from manipulating threads in their parent groups. Though that makes it more restrictive than the model employed by the 1.1 JDK, it matches the concept of a thread group hierarchy better than the JDK's model.

There are three caveats with this model. The first has to do with the way in which thread groups are created. When you create a thread group without specifying a parent thread group, the new thread group is placed into the thread hierarchy as a child of the thread group of the currently executing thread. For example, in Figure 6-1, when the Calc thread creates a new thread group, by default that thread group is a child of Program Thread Group #1 (e.g., it could be Program Subgroup #1). Hence, if you start a program, you must ensure that it starts by executing it in the thread group that would be returned by its class loader—that is, the default thread group of the program. That's why we included that logic at the beginning of our JavaRunner example.

The second caveat is that threads may not be expecting this type of enforcement of the thread hierarchy, since it does not match many popular browser implementations. Hence, programs may fail under this model, while they may succeed under a different model.

Finally, remember that in 1.2, the stop() method of the Thread class first calls the checkPermission() class of the security manager to see if the current stack has a runtime permission of "stopThread". For backward compatibility, all protection domains have that permission by default, but a particular user may change that in the policy file.

Implementing Package Access

A final area for which the default security manager is sometimes inadequate is the manner in which it checks for package access and definition. In 1.1, the default security manager rejects all package access and definition attempts.

In 1.2, the situation is complex. For package access, the security manager looks for a property defined in the *java.security* file named `package.access`. This property is a list of comma-separated package names for which access should be checked. If the class loader uses the `checkPackageAccess()` method (many do not) and attempts to access a package in the list specified in the *java.security* file, then the program must have a runtime permission with a name of `accessClassIn-Package.<packagename>`. For defining a class, the operation is similar; the property name in the *java.security* file is `package.definition`, and the appropriate runtime permission has a name of `defineClassInPackage.<packagename>`. This model works well, but it requires that the *java.security* file and all the *java.policy* files be coordinated in their attempts to protect package access and definition.

For that reason, and also to provide a better migration between releases (and because it's the only way to do it in 1.1), you may want to include the logic to process some policies within your new security manager. In that way, users will not need to make any changes on their system; in this case, the user will not have to put the appropriate `RuntimePermission` entries into the *java.policy* files by hand.

The `checkPackageAccess()` method is most often used to restrict untrusted classes from directly calling certain packages—e.g., you may not want untrusted classes directly calling the `com.xyz.support` pacakge of your application. Unfortunately, the only way to do that while relying on the security manager is to rely on the class depth, which we want to avoid.

One solution is to introduce a property for the application that defines packages that the untrusted classes in the application are not allowed to access. HotJava and the `appletviewer` do this by setting properties of the form:

```
package.restrict.access.pkgname = true
```

In the `checkPackageAccess()` method, you can use the parameter to construct this property (substituting for the `pkgname`) and see if the corresponding property is set: if it is, and if the `inClassLoader()` method returns `true`, you can throw the security exception. For our purposes, however, we will allow classes to access any package, and write our `checkPackageAccess()` method like this:

```
public void checkPackageAccess(String pkg) {
}
```

The `checkPackageDefinition()` method is somewhat different—you probably don't want untrusted classes defining things in the java package, for example. So we want to test for that package explicitly. But we also want to respect the permissions for the applications, so the general solution for cases such as this is, to first check with the access controller (via the security manager's superclass), and then to implement the original logic:

```
public void checkPackageDefinition(String pkg) {
    if (!pkg.startsWith("java."))
        return;
    try {
        super.checkPackageDefinition(pkg);
        return;
    } catch (AccessControlException ace) {
        // continue
    }
    if (inClassLoader())
        throw new SecurityException("Can't define java classes");
}
```

Note that the name in the test contains the period separator—you don't want an untrusted class to be able to define a class named java.lang.String, but you do want it to be able to define a class named javatest.myClass. On the other hand, you may or may not want to grant access to classes in the javax package. This method also requires a change to the class loader that we'll show at the end of the chapter.

Establishing a Security Policy in 1.2

We'll now give specific information on how to establish a security policy for 1.2. In Java 1.2, the SecurityManager class is a concrete class—you use it directly, or you may subclass it. The simplest implementation of the SecurityManager class is:

```
public class JavaRunnerManager extends SecurityManager {
}
```

The JavaRunnerManager class inherits the default behavior of the SecurityManager class for all its methods—but it's important to realize that this default behavior is not the behavior we discussed in Chapter 4. The behavior we discussed in that chapter stemmed from the security manager implementations of various popular browsers—that may be the security that is appropriate for your application, but the default behavior for the Security Manager class comes from the *java.policy* files.

The default behavior of the public methods of the SecurityManager class is to call the access controller with an appropriate permission. For example, the implementation of the checkExit() method is:

```
public void checkExit(int status) {
    AccessController.checkPermission(new RuntimePermission("exitVM"));
}
```

This is why the default security policy for the application can be specified via the *java.policy* files. Table 6-3 lists the methods of the security manager and the permission they construct when they call the access controller.

Table 6-3. The Relationship Between the Security Manager and the Access Controller

Method	Permission
checkCreateClassLoader()	RuntimePermission("createClass-Loader")
checkAccess(Thread t)	RuntimePermission("modifyThread")
checkAccess(ThreadGroup tg)	RuntimePermission("modifyThread-Group")
checkExit(int status)	RuntimePermission("exitVM")
checkExec(String cmd)	FilePermission(cmd, "execute")
checkLink(String lib)	RuntimePermission("loadLibrary." + lib)
checkRead(FileDescriptor fd)	RuntimePermission("readFileDe-scriptor")
checkRead(String file)	FilePermission(file, "read")
checkRead(String file, Object context)	FilePermission(file, "read");
checkWrite(FileDescriptor fd)	RuntimePermission("writeFileDe-scriptor")
checkWrite(String file)	FilePermission(file, "write")
checkDelete(String file)	FilePermission(file, "delete")
checkConnect(String h, int p)	*if port == -1* SocketPermission(h, "resolve") *otherwise* SocketPermission(h + ":" + p, "connect")
checkConnect(String h, int p, Object context)	*same as* checkConnect()
checkListen(int port)	*if port == 0* SocketPermission("localhost:1024-","listen") *otherwise* SocketPermission("localhost:" + port, "listen")
checkAccept(String host, int port)	SocketPermission(host + ":" + port, "accept")
checkMulticast() [both signatures]	SocketPermission(maddr.getHostAd-dress(), "accept,connect")
checkPropertiesAccess()	PropertyPermission("*", "read, write")
checkPropertyAccess(String key)	PropertyPermission(key, "read")
checkTopLevelWindow(Object w)	AWTPermission("showWindowWithout-WarningBanner")

Table 6-3. The Relationship Between the Security Manager and the Access Controller (continued)

Method	Permission
checkPrintJobAccess()	RuntimePermission("queuePrintJob")
checkSystemClipboardAccess()	AWTPermission("accessClipboard");
checkAwtEventQueueAccess()	AWTPermission("accessEventQueue");
checkPackageAccess(String pkg)	RuntimePermission("accessClassIn-Package." + pkg)
checkPackageDefinition(String pkg)	RuntimePermission("defineClassIn-Package." + pkg)
checkSetFactory()	RuntimePermission("setFactory")
checkMemberAccess(Class c, int which)	RuntimePermission("accessDeclared-Members")
checkSecurityAccess(String action)	SecurityPermission(action)
checkPermission(Permission p)	p (that is, the permission parameter)
checkPermission(Permission p, Object o)	p (that is, the permission parameter)

There are five slight exceptions to the rules laid out in Table 6-3:

- The checkAccess() methods only check for the given permission if the target thread (group) is in the system thread group.

- If the command passed to the checkExec() method is not a fully qualified pathname (that is, if the command will be found by examining the user's PATH variable), the string passed to create the file permission is "<<ALL FILES>>." The domain must have permission to execute all files in the filesystem in this case.

- The methods that use a context expect the context to be an instance of the AccessControlContext class. They then call the checkPermission() method of that context, using the same permission that would normally be used in that call (e.g., a file permission with a read action for the checkRead() method). As we mentioned, these methods are never called by the core API. If the context is not an access control context, then a SecurityException will be thrown.

- The checkTopLevelWindow() method catches the AccessControlException if it is thrown by the access controller. In this case, it returns false. This method does not (by default) throw an exception.

- The checkMemberAccess() method does not call the access controller if the program is inspecting public values (that is, if the which flag is Member.PUB-LIC) or if the current class loader is the same class that loaded the target class.

For the most part, it's possible to use the default security manager and the permission mappings we've just identified to support virtually any security policy. But there are certain useful exceptions a security manager will often define:

- Network permissions may want to follow the implementation outlined above.

- Package access and definition permissions may follow the implementation outlined above.

- Exit permissions may be summarily granted to all applications (unless the application is a server that should stick around).

- Thread permissions may follow the thread hierarchy rather than the default all-or-nothing policy.

For a complete 1.2-based security manager, then, you typically need to override only the methods involved with these four exceptions. The 1.2-based security manager we'll use for our JavaRunner program looks like this:

```
public class JavaRunnerManager extends SecurityManager {
    public void checkConnect(String host, int port) {
        .. follow implementation given above ..
    }
    public void checkPackageAccess(String pkg) {
        .. follow implementation given above ..
    }
    public void checkPackageDefinition(String pkg) {
        .. follow implementation given above ..
    }
    public void checkExit(int status) {
    }
    public void checkAccess(Thread t) {
        .. follow implementation given above ..
    }
    public void checkAccess(ThreadGroup tg) {
        .. follow implementation given above ..
    }
}
```

Establishing a 1.1 Security Policy

Establishing a security policy in 1.1 is done only by ensuring that the correct security manager is in place. In this section, we're going to discuss how a 1.1-based security manager can be implemented.

The RMI security manager

One of the times a security manager is often used in a Java application is in an RMI server. An RMI server has the capability of loading code from an RMI client located on a remote machine and executing that code on the server—essentially transforming the server (temporarily) into a client.* In essence, the security ramifications of using RMI servers are similar to those of an applet, but in reverse: you now want to protect your server machine from the side effects of untrusted code it got from a client.

In the most common case, you'll want your RMI server to have a simple security model. If the code it's executing was completely loaded from the server, the operation should succeed; if any of the code it's executing was loaded from the client, the operation should fail. Hence, the Java API provides the RMISecurityManager class, which implements just such a policy. In general, the methods of the RMISecurityManager class look like this:

```
public void checkAccess(Thread t) {
    if (inClassLoader())
        throw new SecurityException("checkAccess");
}
```

You can check the source code (java.rmi.RMISecurityManager) for exact details; this example is a conflation of code found there.

Hence, in the RMI security manager, all local code is trusted and all remote code is untrusted. There are certain methods of this class that have slightly different implementations, however. Because the RMISecurityManager provides a useful basis for a default implementation of your own security manager, we'll list those exceptions here so you can use the RMISecurityManager class and understand where you're starting out.

public void checkPropertyAccess(String key)
> An untrusted class can check properties only if a special property is set. If an untrusted class wants to check the property foo.bar, the property foo.bar.stub must be set to true.

public void checkRead(FileDescriptor fd)
public void checkWrite(FileDescriptor fd)
> An untrusted class can read or write a file if that file is a socket. Note that the untrusted class still cannot create the socket.

public void checkConnect(String host, int port)
> An untrusted class can connect a socket only if called from certain internal RMI classes. If you're using the RMISecurityManager class as the basis for a non-RMI application, the untrusted class is not able to make any connections.

---

* This used to be called "peer computing," although that term has fallen out of favor. But it's a useful concept: just because one machine has to initiate a request shouldn't mean that the roles of client and server have to be immutable.

public void checkTopLevelWindow(Object window)
> An untrusted class can create a separate window, but it will have the warning banner.

public void checkPackageAccess(String pkg)
> An untrusted class can access a package unless the external properties specifically prohibit such access.

public void checkPackageDefinition(String pkg)
> An untrusted class can access a package definition unless the external properties specifically prohibit such access.

public void checkSetFactory()
> Neither an untrusted class *nor* a trusted class can change a socket factory.

public void checkMemberAccess()
> An untrusted class can only check the member access for public members.

A complete 1.1 security manager

In Java 1.1, the SecurityManager class is abstract, so you can't directly instantiate a security manager object. However, none of the methods of SecurityManager is itself abstract, meaning that the simplest implementation of the SecurityManager class is this:

```
public class StrictSecurityManager extends SecurityManager {
}
```

The StrictSecurityManager class inherits the default behavior of the Security-Manager class for all its methods—but once again it's important to realize that this default behavior is not the behavior we discussed earlier in terms of what an untrusted class might or might not be allowed to do. The default behavior of the public methods in the SecurityManager class in 1.1—and hence of the StrictSe-curityManager class above—is to deny every operation to every class, trusted or not. Each of the public methods of the SecurityManager class looks similar to this:

```
public void checkAccess(Thread g) {
    throw new SecurityException();
}
```

Thus, if you want to implement your own security manager, you need only override the methods for which you want to provide a more relaxed security policy. If you want to allow (at least some) thread operations, you must override the check-Access() methods; if you do not override those methods, no thread operations will be allowed by any class.

A Null Security Manager

The default security manager class makes you override each method to create a relaxed security policy for that method, but sometimes it might be easier to start with a null security manager: one that provides a completely wide-open policy for every check. You could then override only those methods for which you wanted to tighten the security policy.

The Java API does not provide such a class, but one is available in source form with the Java API source files—if you copy the *SecurityManager.java* file from the API source directory and edit it, you'll find a `NullSecurityManager` class that implements each method with a wide-open security policy. You can edit out everything but this class, make it a public class, and use it for the basis of your customized security manager. This class was removed from the 1.2 source.

In typical usage, a 1.1-based security manager might want to deny a large number of operations if there is any untrusted class on the stack. These methods might be implemented with the `checkClassLoader()` method we discussed above. Candidates for this type of check are:

`checkAccept()`	`checkMemberAccess()`	`checkSecurityAccess()`
`checkAWTEventQueue-` `Access()`	`checkMulticast()`	`checkSystemClipboardAc-` `cess()`
`checkExit()`	`checkPrintJobAccess()`	
`checkListen()`	`checkSecurityAccess()`	

Similarly, there are a number of tests that we want to fail if they are attempted directly by an untrusted class, but that we want to succeed if they are attempted indirectly by an untrusted class. For these tests, we have to rely on the class depth to tell us whether the call originated from an untrusted class or not; we use the `checkClassDepth()` method to help us with that task. Here are the candidate methods for this test along with the depth that checked for each method:

`checkCreateClassLoader()`	2	`checkLink()`	3
`checkDelete()`	2	`checkPropertiesAccess()`	2
`checkExec()`	2	`checkPropertyAccess()`	2

Finally, there are some methods we must implement with their own logic. Although we've saved these for last, they are most interesting since these are the methods that you'll need to pay the most attention to when you write your own security manager.

Implementing the file access methods

If you are going to implement a security manager, you must determine a policy for reading and writing files and implement it in each of the checkRead() and check-Write() methods. The logic you put into each method is slightly different.

Allowing File Access

If you want to write a policy that allows some files on the local machine to be read or written, make sure that you use the File.getCanonicalPath() method to find out the actual name of the file before you grant access to that file. If, for example, you want programs to have access to the */tmp* directory on your machine, you want to make sure that access to */tmp/../etc/passwd* is still denied; the program must not be allowed to use the parent directory to jump out of the directory you've allowed. The getCanonicalPath() method removes all references to parent directories, as well as following all symbolic links, shortcuts, and aliases to find out the actual name of the file that's being referenced.

In the case where these methods take a single string argument, the logic is straightforward: the program is attempting to open a file with the given name, and you should either accept or reject that operation. We'll base our decision on the depth of the class loader. Untrusted classes may not directly open a file for reading or writing, but they may cause that to happen through the Java API:

```
public void checkRead(String file) {
    checkClassDepth(2, "Read the file " + file,
                    "Can't read local files");
}
public void checkWrite(String file) {
    checkClassDepth(2, "Write the file " + file,
                    "Can't write local files");
}
```

In the case where these methods take a FileDescriptor as an argument, the policy is a little harder to define. As far as the Java API is concerned, these methods are only called as a result of calling the Socket.getInputStream() or Socket.getOutputStream() methods—which means that the security manager is really being asked to determine if the socket associated with the given file descriptor should be allowed to be read or written. By this time, the socket has already been created and has made a valid connection to the remote machine, and the security manager has had the opportunity to prohibit that connection at that time.

What type of access, then, would you prohibit when you implement these methods? It partially depends on the types of checks your security manager made when the socket was created. We'll assume for now that a socket created by an untrusted class can only connect to the site from which the class was loaded, while a socket created by a trusted class can connect to any site. Hence, you might want to prohibit an untrusted class from opening the data stream of a socket created by a trusted class—although if the class is trusted, you typically want to trust that class's judgement, and if that class passed the socket reference to an untrusted class, the untrusted class should be able to read from or write to the socket.

On the other hand, it is important to be sure that these methods are actually being called from the socket class. An untrusted class could attempt to pass an arbitrary file descriptor to the File*Stream constructor, breaking into your machine.

Typically, then, the only checks you put into this method are to determine that the FileDescriptor object is valid and the FileDescriptor object does indeed belong to the socket class:

```
public void checkRead(FileDescriptor fd) {
    if (!inClassLoader())
        return;
    if (!fd.valid() || !inClass("java.net.SocketInputStream"))
        throw new SecurityException("Can't read a file descriptor");
}
public void checkWrite(FileDescriptor fd) {
    if (!inClassLoader())
        return;
    if (!fd.valid() || !inClass("java.net.SocketOutputStream"))
        throw new SecurityException("Can't write a file descriptor");
}
```

Implementing network, thread, and package access

A typical 1.1-based security manager would implement thread, network, and package access as we described above.

Implementing miscellaneous methods

There is one more method of the security manager that we must implement with slightly different rules: the checkTopLevelWindow() method. This method uses the standard class depth test for an untrusted class, but it shouldn't throw an exception, so it looks like this:

```
public boolean checkTopLevelWindow(Object window) {
    if (classLoaderDepth() == 3)
        return false;
    return true;
}
```

Running Secure Applications

In Chapter 1 we showed how JavaRunner and the Launcher can be used to run a Java application. Now that we have the final piece of the security policy story, we can put everything together and show how the policy applies to these applications.

The Secure JavaRunner Program

Running a program securely under the auspices of JavaRunner requires that we modify that program to accept a security manager:

```
public class JavaRunner implements Runnable {
    .. other methods are unchanged ..

    public static void main(String args[])
                            throws ClassNotFoundException {
        Class self = Class.forName("JavaRunner");
        System.setSecurityManager(new JavaRunnerManager());
        JavaRunnerLoader jrl = new JavaRunnerLoader(
                            args[0], self.getClassLoader());
        ThreadGroup tg = jrl.getThreadGroup();
        Thread t = new Thread(tg,
                new JavaRunner(jrl, args[1], getArgs(args)));
        t.start();
        try {
            t.join();
        } catch (InterruptedException ie) {
            System.out.println("Thread was interrupted");
        }
    }
}
```

This single-line change installs a security manager for us; the security manager provides the security policy for the target application. Because our security manager defers most of its checks to the access controller, we must have appropriate *java.policy* files somewhere (unless, of course, we have installed a different default Policy class). If these policy files are in the default locations (*$JAVA-HOME/lib/security/java.policy* and *$HOME/.java.policy*), no other steps are necessary. If that file is somewhere else, you must list that file in the *java.security* file as an alternate policy URL.

Note that we cannot use the -Djava.security.policy command-line argument: the -Djava.security.policy command-line argument installs the Launcher's security manager for us, which prevents our security manager from being installed. On the other hand, we could forego the use of the JavaRunnerManager class altogether and use the same security manager that the Launcher uses by specifying the -Djava.security.policy command-line argument.

In Java 1.2, installing this security manager has other ramifications upon the JavaRunner program. Since the JavaRunner class is loaded from the default URL class loader, it is subject to the permissions of the access controller. As a practical matter, this means that one of the *java.policy* files must have certain permissions in it that the JavaRunner program needs: it needs to open sockets (to open the URLs from which to retrieve the classes), create a class loader, and so on. The simplest way to achieve this is to put the JavaRunner class and its associated class files (the class loader and security manager it uses) into a single directory and grant all permissions to that directory. If, for example, we put those files into the */home/sdo/JavaRunner* directory, we would need to put this entry into a *java.policy* file:

```
grant codeBase "file:/home/sdo/JavaRunner" {
    permission java.security.AllPermission;
};
```

The Secure Java Launcher

In 1.2, when you run a program via the command line, no security manager is installed for you and the program has no sandbox (unless one is installed as we did for the JavaRunner program).

However, when you specify the -Djava.security.policy argument on the command line, a default security manager is installed; the effect of that argument is to install the Launcher's security manager. This security manager in turn initializes the access controller—as we mentioned in Chapter 5, the access controller is not initialized until it is first used, and it will not be used until the security manager calls it (unless, of course, your own code calls it). The Launcher's security manager asks the access controller to check for the appropriate permission (that is, the permission that we listed in Table 6-3) with the exceptions that we listed with that table and the additional exception that the checkExit(), check-PackageAccess(), and checkPackageDefinition() methods always succeed.

Remember when you use the Launcher that the security provisions only apply to classes that are loaded from the CLASSPATH and not from the Java API.

Summary

Implementing a security manager is a key step in defining a security policy for your own Java applications; the examples presented in this chapter should help you do that effectively. In Java 1.2, you can specify much of the security policy via an external policy file, although there are still instances where you need to write your own security manager in order to achieve specific (but common) policies. In Java 1.1 and previous releases, you need to write your own security manager that implements the security policy you feel is appropriate. Otherwise, your Java application will have no security policy at all.

If you don't feel comfortable running a third-party Java application without a security manager in place, the examples we've provided in this chapter are also key—they provide the cornerstone of the security features that are built into the JavaRunner program.

On the other hand, if you have a secured network and want to expand the parameters of the Java sandbox without resorting to the use and configuration of signed classes (the topic we'll explore for most of the rest of this book), writing your own security manager is also the way to go. For browsers that support it, you can then substitute the new security manager into them, or you can again use the Java-Runner program or Java's Launcher to run the program.

No matter what path you take, the security manager is the most important aspect of the Java sandbox. The methods of the security manager should help you be able to make the appropriate decisions when you implement your own security policies.

Introduction to Cryptography

So far, we've examined the basic level of Java's security paradigm—essentially, those features that make up the Java sandbox. We're now going to shift gears somewhat and begin our examination of the cryptographic features in the Java security package itself. The Java security package is a set of classes that were added to Java 1.1 (and expanded in 1.2*); these classes provide additional layers of security beyond the layers we've examined so far. Although these classes do play a role in the Java sandbox—they are the basis by which Java classes may be signed, and expanding the sandbox based on signed classes is a key goal of Java security—they may play other roles in secure applications.

A digital signature, for example, can authenticate a Java class so that the security policy can allow that class greater latitude in the operations it can perform, but a digital signature is a useful thing in its own right. An HR department may want to use a digital signature to verify requests to change payroll data, an online subscription service might require a digital signature to process a change order, and so on. Thus, while we'll examine the classes of the Java security package from the perspective of what we'll be able to do with a signed class, the techniques we'll show will have broader applicability.

In order to use the classes of the security package, you don't need a deep understanding of cryptographic theory. This chapter will explain the basic concepts of the operations involved, which should be sufficient to understand how to use the APIs involved. On the other hand, one feature of the security package is that different implementations of different algorithms may be provided by third-party vendors. We'll explain how to go about providing such implementations, but it is assumed that readers who are interested in writing such an implementation

---

* 1.2 is now Java 2.

already understand the mechanics of cryptography. Hence, we won't give any cryptographically valid examples in those sections.

If you already have an understanding of the basics of digital signatures, encryption, and the need for authentication, you can skip this chapter, which provides mainly background information.

The Need for Authentication

We are primarily concerned with one goal of the security package: the ability to authenticate classes that have been loaded from the network. The components of the Java API that provide authentication may have other uses in other contexts (including within your own Java applications), but their primary goal is to allow a Java application (and a Java-enabled browser) to load a class from the network and be assured of two things:

- The identity of the site from which the class was loaded can be verified (author authentication).

- The class was not modified in transit over the network (data authentication).

As we've seen, Java applications typically assume that all classes loaded over the network are untrusted classes, and these untrusted classes are generally given permissions consistent with that assumption. Classes that meet the above two criteria, however, need not necessarily be so constrained. If you walk into your local software store and buy a shrink-wrapped piece of software, you're generally confident that the software will not contain viruses or anything else that's harmful. This is part of the implied contract between a commercial software producer and a commercial software buyer. If you download code from that same software producer's web site, you're probably just as confident that the code you're downloading is not harmful; perhaps it should be given the same access rights as the software you obtained from that company through a more traditional channel.

There's a small irony here, because many computer viruses are spread through commercial software. That's one reason why the fact that a class has been authenticated does not necessarily mean it should be able to access anything on your machine that it wants to. It's also a reason why the fine-grained nature of the access controller is important: if you buy classes from *acme.com*, but only give them access to certain things on your machine, you are still somewhat protected if by mistake *acme.com* includes a virus in their software.

Even if all commercial software were virus free, however, there is a problem with assuming that code downloaded from a commercial site is safe to run on your machine. The problem with that assumption—and the reason that Java by default does not allow that assumption to be made—has to do with the way in which the code you execute makes its way through the Internet. If you load some code from *www.xyz.com* onto your machine, that code will pass through many machines that are responsible for routing the code between your site and XYZ's site. Typically, we like to think that the data that passes between our desktop and *www.xyz.com* enters some large network cloud; it's called a cloud because it contains a lot of details, and the details aren't usually important to us. In this case, however, the details are important. We're very interested to know that the data between our desktop and *xyz.com* passes through, for example, our Internet service provider, two other sites on the Internet backbone, and XYZ's Internet service provider. Such a transmission is shown in Figure 7-1. The two types of authentication that we mentioned above provide the necessary assurance that the data passing through all these sites is not compromised.

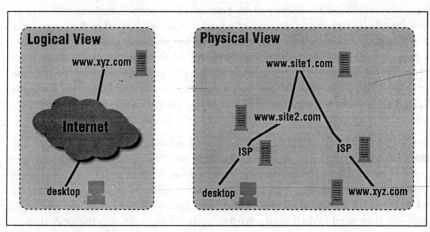

Figure 7-1. How data travels through a network

Author Authentication

First we must prove that the author of the data is who we expect it to be. When you send data that is destined for *www.xyz.com*, that data is forwarded to *site2*, who is supposed to forward it to *site1*, who should simply forward it to XYZ's Internet service provider. You trust *site1* to forward the data to XYZ's Internet service provider unchanged; however, there's nothing that causes *site1* to fulfill its part of this contract. A hacker at *site1* could arrange for all the data destined for *www.xyz.com* to be sent to the hacker's own machine, and the hacker could send back data through *site2* that looked as if it originated from *www.xyz.com*. The hacker is now successfully impersonating the *www.xyz.com* site. Hence, although the URL in your browser says *www.xyz.com*, you've been fooled: you're actually receiving whatever data the impersonator of XYZ Corporation wants to send to you.

There are a number of ways to achieve this masquerade, the most well-known of which is DNS (or IP) spoofing. When you want to surf to *www.xyz.com*, your desktop asks your DNS server (which is typically your Internet service provider) for the IP address of *www.xyz.com* and you then send off the request to whatever address you receive. If your Internet service provider knows the IP address of *www.xyz.com*, it tells your desktop what the correct address is; otherwise, it has to ask another DNS server (e.g., *site1*) for the correct IP address. If a hacker has control of a machine anywhere along the chain of DNS servers, it is relatively simple for that hacker to send out his own address in response to a DNS request for *www.xyz.com*.

Now say that you surf to *www.xyz.com* and request a Java class (or set of classes) to run a spellchecker for your Java-based word processor. The request you send to *www.xyz.com* will be misaddressed by your machine—your machine will erroneously send the request to the hacker's machine, since that's the IP address your machine has associated with *www.xyz.com*. Now the hacker is able to send you back a Java class. If that Java class is suddenly trusted (because, after all, it allegedly came from a commercial site), it has access that you wouldn't necessarily approve: perhaps while it's spellchecking your document, it is also searching your hard disk to find the data file of your financial planning software so that it can read that file and send its contents back over the network to the hacker's machine.

Yes, we've made this sound easier than it is—the hacker would have to have intimate knowledge of the *xyz.com* site to send you back the classes you requested, and those classes would have to have the expected interface in order for any of their code to be executed. But such situations are not difficult to set up either; if the hackers stole the original class files from *www.xyz.com*—which is usually extremely easy—all they need to do is set themselves up at the right place in the DNS chain.

In the strict Java security model we explored earlier, this sort of situation is possible, but it isn't dangerous. Because the classes loaded from the network are never trusted at all, the class that was substituted by the hackers is not able to damage anything on your machine. At worst, the substituted class does not behave as you expect and may in fact do something quite annoying—like play loud music on your machine instead of spellchecking your document. But the class is not able to do anything dangerous, simply because all classes from the network are untrusted.

In order to trust a class that is loaded from the network, then, we must have some way to verify that the class actually came from the site it said it came from. This authentication comes from a digital signature that comes with the class data—an electronic verification that the class did indeed come from *www.xyz.com*.

Data Authentication

The second problem introduced by the fact that our transmissions to *www.xyz.com* must pass through several hosts is the possibility of snooping. In this scenario, assume that *site2* on the network is under control of a hacker. When you send data to *www.xyz.com*, the data passes through the machine on *site2*, where the hacker can modify it; when data is sent back to you, it travels the same path, which means that the hacker on *site2* can again modify the data.

This lack of privacy in data transmission is one reason you might want data over the network to be encrypted—certainly if the spellchecking software you're using from *www.xyz.com* is something you must pay for, you don't want to send your unencrypted credit card through the network so that *site2* can read it. However, for authentication purposes, encrypting the data is not strictly necessary. All that is necessary is some sort of assurance that the data that has passed through the network has not been modified in transit. This can be achieved by various cryptographic algorithms even though the data itself is not encrypted. The simpler path is to use such a cryptographic algorithm (known as a message digest algorithm or a digital fingerprint) instead of encrypting the data.

Encryption Versus Data Authentication

When you send data through a public network, you can use a digital fingerprint of that data to ensure that the data was not modified while it was in transit over the network. This fingerprint is sufficient to prevent a snooper from substituting new data (e.g., a new Java class file) for the original data in your transmission.

However, this authentication does not prevent a snooper from reading the data in your transmission; authenticated data is not encrypted data. If you are worried about someone stealing your data, the security provided by data authentication is insufficient. Data authentication prevents writing of data, but not reading of data.

Java only provides authentication and not encryption because of export laws various countries apply to encryption technology. When we discuss the Java Cryptography Extension in Chapter 13, we'll expand upon these restrictions.

Without some cryptographic mechanism in place, the hacker at *site2* has the option of modifying the classes that are sent from *www.xyz.com*. When the classes are read by the machine at *site2*, the hacker could modify them in memory before they are sent back onto the network to be read by *site1* (and ultimately to be read by your machine). Hence, the classes that are sent need to have a digital fingerprint associated with them. As it turns out, the digital fingerprint is required to sign the class as well.

Java's Role in Authentication

When Java was first released and touted as being "secure," it surprised many people to discover that the types of attacks we've just discussed were still possible. As we've said, security means many things to many people, but a reasonable argument could be made that the scenarios we've just outlined should not be possible in a secure environment.

The reasons Java did not solve these problems in its first release are varied, but they essentially boil down to one practical reason and one philosophical reason.

The practical reason is that all the solutions we're about to explore depend to a high degree on technologies that are just beginning to become viable. As a practical matter, authentication relies on everyone having public keys available—and as we'll discuss in Chapter 11, that's not necessarily the case. Without a robust mechanism to share public keys, Java had two options:

- Provide no security at all, and allow applets full use of the resources of the user's computer. By now, we know all the possible problems with that route.

- Provide the very strict security that was implemented in 1.0-based versions of Java, with a view toward ways of enhancing that model as technologies evolved. While not the best of all possible worlds, this compromise allowed Java to be adopted much sooner than it would otherwise have been.

On a philosophical level, however, there's another argument: Java shouldn't solve these problems because they are not confined to Java itself. Even if Java classes were always authenticated, that would not prevent the types of attacks we've outlined here from affecting non-Java-related transmissions. If you surf to *www.xyz.com* and that site is subject to DNS spoofing, you'll be served whatever pages the spoofer wants to substitute. If you engage in a standard non-Java, forms-based transmission with *www.xyz.com*, a snooper along the way can steal and modify the data you're sending over the standard HTTP transmission mechanism.

In other words, the attacks we've just outlined are inherent in the design of a public network, and they affect all traffic equally—email traffic, web traffic, ftp traffic, Java traffic, and so on. In a perfect world, solving these problems at the Java level is inefficient, as it means that the same problem must still be solved for all the other traffic on the public network. Solving the problem at the network level, on the other hand, solves the problem once and for all, so that every protocol and every type of traffic are protected.

There are a number of popular technologies that solve this problem in a more general case. If all the traffic between your site and *www.xyz.com* occurs over SSL using an https-based URL, then your browser and the *www.xyz.com* web server will take care of the details of authentication of all web-based traffic, including the Java-related traffic. That solves the problem at the level of the web browser, but that still is not a complete solution. If the applet needs to open a connection back to *www.xyz.com*, it must use SSL for this communication as well. And we still have other, non-web-related traffic that is not authenticated.

It would be better still to solve this problem at the network level itself. There are many products from various vendors that allow you to authenticate (and encrypt) *all* data between your site and a remote site on the network. Using such a product is really the ideal from a design point of view; in that way, all data is protected, no matter what the source of the traffic is. Either of these solutions makes authentication and fingerprinting of Java classes redundant (and they may offer the benefit that the data is actually encrypted when it passes through the network).

Unfortunately, these solutions lead us back to practical considerations: if it's hard for Java environments to share digital keys and to manage cryptographic technology, it's harder still to depend on the network software to manage this process. So while it might be ideal for this problem to be solved for the network as a whole, it's impractical to expect such a solution. Hence, the Java security package offers a reasonable compromise: it allows you to deploy and use trusted (i.e., authenticated) classes, but their use is not mandated, in case you prefer to employ a broader solution to this problem.

The Role of Authentication

In the preceding discussion, we assumed that you want to load classes from *www.xyz.com* and that you want those classes to be trusted, so that they might have some special permission when they execute on your machine. For example, the spellchecking class might need to open up a local dictionary file to learn how to spellcheck names and other data you customized for the spellchecker.

Do not, however, make the assumption that all classes that are authenticated are therefore to be trusted, or even that all trusted classes should necessarily have the same set of permissions. There's nothing that prevents me from obtaining the necessary information and tools so that I can sign and encrypt all of my classes. When you download those classes, you know with certainty that the classes came from me—they carry my digital signature, and they've been fingerprinted to ensure that they haven't been tampered with.

But that's *all* the information that you know about these classes. In particular, just because the classes were authenticated does not mean that I didn't put a virus into them that's going to erase all the files on your hard disk. And just because you know that a particular Java applet came from me does not mean that you can necessarily track me down when something goes wrong. If you surf to my home page and run my authenticated applet, then surf to *www.sun.com* and run their authenticated applet, then surf to *www.EvilSite.org* and run their authenticated applet, and then two weeks later your hard disk is erased, how will you know which site planted the delayed virus onto your machine? How will you even remember which sites you had visited in the last two weeks (or longer)? If you have an adequate set of backups and other logs, it is conceivable that you might be able to re-create what happened and know at whom to point your finger (and whom to sue), but such a task would be arduous indeed. And if the virus affected your logs, the finger of suspicion might point to the incorrect site.

Hence, the role of authentication of Java classes is not to validate that those classes are trusted or to automatically give those classes special permissions. The role of authentication is to give the user (or, for a corporate network, the system or network administrator) more information on which to base a security policy. A reasonable policy might be that classes that are known to come from *www.SpellChecker.com* can read the user's personal dictionary file—but that doesn't mean they should necessarily be able to read anything else. A reasonable policy would also be that this type of exception to the general rule about permissions given to network classes is only to be granted in very specific cases to only a few well-known sites, and that unknown but authenticated sites are still considered untrusted.

The moral of the story is that authentication does not magically solve any problem; it is merely a tool that can be used in the pursuit of solutions.

Cryptographic Engines

In the next few chapters of this book, we're going to see how Java provides an interface to the algorithms required to perform the sort of authentications we've just talked about. We'll also explore the architecture Java provides for general implementation of these algorithms, including ones (such as encryption) that are not strictly required for authentication. If you're not familiar with the various cryptographic algorithms we've been alluding to so far in this chapter, the next section should sort that all out for you.

Essentially, all cryptographic operations are structured like the diagram in Figure 7-2. Central to this idea is the cryptographic algorithm itself, which is called an engine; the term "algorithm" is reserved to refer to particular implementations of the cryptographic operation. The engine takes some set of input data and (optionally) some sort of key and produces a set of output data. A few points are relevant to this diagram. There are engines that do not require a key as part of their input. In addition, not all cryptographic engines produce symmetric output—that is, it's not always the case that the original text can be reconstructed from the output data. Also, the size of the output is typically not the same as the size of the input. In the case of message digests and digital signatures, the output size is a small, fixed-size number of bytes; in the case of encryption engines, the output size is typically somewhat larger than the input size.

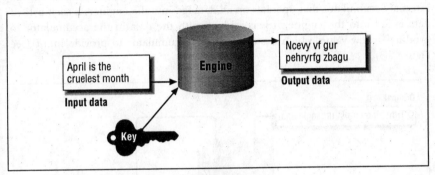

Figure 7-2. A cryptographic engine for encryption

In the Java security package, there are two standard cryptographic engines: a message digest engine and a digital signature engine. In addition, for some users, an optional engine is available to perform encryption. Finally, because keys are central to the use of most of these engines, there is a wide set of classes that operate on keys, including engines that can be used to generate certain types of keys. The term "engine" is also used within the security package to refer to other classes that support these operations.

Message Digests

Message digests are the first cryptographic engines we'll examine. A message digest is the digital fingerprint we alluded to earlier. Conceptually, a message digest is a small sequence of bytes that is produced when a given set of data is passed through the message digest engine. Unlike other cryptographic engines, a message digest engine does not require a key to operate. It takes a single stream of data as its input and produces a single output. We call the output a message digest (or simply a digest, or a hash), and we say that the digest represents the input data.

The digest that corresponds to a particular set of data does not reflect any information about that data—in particular, there is no way to tell from a digest how much data it represents, or what the data actually was. A message digest is useful only when the data it represents is also available. If you want to determine whether a particular digest represents a particular set of data, you must recalculate the digest and compare the newly calculated digest with the original digest. If the two are equal, you've verified that the original digest does indeed represent the given set of data.

Data that is fed into a message digest engine is always treated as an ordered set of bytes. If even one byte of the data is altered or absent (or presented out of order), the digest will be different. Hence, a typical message digest algorithm has an internal accumulator that operates on all data fed into the engine. As each byte of data is fed into the engine, it is combined with the data in the accumulator to produce a new value, which is stored in the accumulator to provide input (see Figure 7-3).

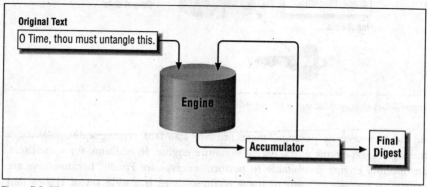

Figure 7-3. The message digest accumulator

As a simple example, consider a message digest algorithm based on the exclusive-or of all the input bytes. The accumulator starts with a value of 0. If the string "O Time, thou must untangle this" is passed to the engine, the engine considers the bytes one at a time.* The first byte, "O", has a value of 0x4f, which will *xor* with the accumulator to provide a value of 0x4f. The next byte, a space (0x20), will *xor* with the accumulator to produce a value of 0x6f. And so on, such that the final result of the accumulator is 0x67.

There are a few differences between this example and a real message digest algorithm. First, standard algorithms typically operate on 4- or 8-byte quantities, so the bytes that are fed into the engine are first grouped into ints or longs, with padding added if the input data is not a multiple of the desired quantity. Second,

---

* Don't be confused by the fact that we're dealing in bytes here, when the characters in a Java string are two bytes long. The data passed to the message digest engine is treated as arbitrary binary data—it doesn't matter if the data was originally ASCII (that is, byte-oriented) data, or a Java character string, or a binary class file.

they produce a digest that is usually 64 or 128 bits long, rather than a single byte; this final digest may be the value left in the accumulator, or it may be the value left in the accumulator subjected to additional operations.

The difference in the output size is one of the crucial differences. At best, the example we just walked through could produce 256 different digests. Any two given inputs have a 1 in 256 chance of producing the same digest, which is clearly not a sufficient guarantee that a digest represents a given set of data. In the example above, the string "O Time, thou must untangle this" produced a digest of 0x67—but so does the string "g". An algorithm that produces a 64-bit digest, on the other hand, produces over 18 quintillion unique digests, so that the odds that two data sequences will produce the same digest are very remote indeed.

This brings us to another of the crucial differences—a successful message digest algorithm must provide an assurance that it is computationally infeasible to find two messages that produce the same digest. This ensures that a new set of data cannot be substituted for the original data so that each produces the same digest.

Note also that a message digest in itself is not a secure entity. A digest is often provided with the data it represents; the recipient of the data then recalculates the digest to make sure that the data was not originally tampered with. But nothing in this scenario prevents someone from modifying both the original data and the digest, since both are transmitted, and since the calculation of the digest is a well-known operation requiring no key. Digests are an important piece of a digital signature, as we'll see in just a bit.

Cryptographic Keys

The second engine we'll look at generates cryptographic keys. Keys are the basis for many cryptographic operations. In its simplest sense, a key is a long string of numbers—not just any string of numbers, but a string of numbers that has very strict mathematical properties. The mathematical properties a key must have vary based on the cryptographic algorithms it is going to be used for, but there's an abstract (logical) set of properties all keys must have. It's this abstract set of properties that we'll see in the Java security package.

In the realm of cryptography, keys can either come alone (in which case they are called secret keys) or in pairs. A key pair has two keys, a public key and a private key. So altogether there are three types of keys—secret, public, and private—but from an algorithmic perspective, there are two types of keys, shared and secret.

When an algorithm requires a secret key, both parties using the algorithm will use the same key. Both parties must agree to keep the key secret, lest the security of the cryptography between the parties be compromised.

The secret key approach suffers from two problems. First, it requires a separate key for every pair of parties that need to send encrypted data. If you want to send your encrypted credit card data to ten different Internet stores, you would need ten different keys. Worse yet, if you operated an Internet store and had millions of customers, you would need literally millions of keys—one per customer. Management of such keys is a very hard problem.

The other problem with this approach is coming up with a method for sharing the keys. It's crucial that the key be kept secret, since anyone with the key can decrypt the data to be shared. Hence, you can't simply send the key over the network without somehow encrypting the key itself; doing so would be tantamount to sending the data itself unencrypted.

For these reasons, most keys in the security package are parts of public key/private key pairs (the exception to this is the encryption engine, which can use any type of key, and which provides a mechanism to share secret keys). Public and private keys can provide asymmetric operation to cryptographic engines. The public key can be used by one party participating in the algorithm, and the private key can be used by the other party.

The usefulness of this type of key pair is that one key can be published to the world. You can email your public key to your friends (and your enemies), you can put it on a global key server somewhere, you can broadcast it on the Internet—as long as you don't lose your private key, you can do anything you like with your public key.

Then, when someone wants to send you some sensitive information, they can use your public key to encrypt the data—and as long as you have kept your private key private, you'll be the only one who is actually able to decrypt the data. Similarly, when you want to send sensitive data to someone, all you need is their public key; when the data has been encrypted with the public key, you know that only the holder of the private key will be able to read what you've sent them. In the area of digital signatures, this key ordering is reversed: you sign a document with your private key, and the recipient of the document needs your public key in order to verify the digital signature.

Public key encryption is not without its key management problems as well, however. When you receive a digitally signed document, you need the public key of the signer of the document. The mechanism to obtain that key is very fluid; there are a number of proposals for centralized key warehouses that would hold public keys and for methods to access those keys, but the infrastructure to make this all a reality is not really in place. Hence, users of public keys have adopted a variety of techniques for obtaining the public keys.

Digital Signatures

The primary engine in the security package (at least as far as authentication goes) is the digital signature engine. Like a real signature, a digital signature is presumed to identify uniquely an entity (that is, an individual or an organization). Like a real signature, a digital signature can be forged, although it's much harder to forge a digital signature than a real signature.* Forging a digital signature requires access to the private key of the entity whose signature is being forged; this is yet another reason why it is important to keep your private keys private. Like a real signature, a digital signature can be "smudged" so that it is no longer recognizable. And because they're based on key certificates, digital signatures have other properties, such as the fact that they can expire.

Digital signatures rely on two things: the ability to generate a message digest, and the ability to encrypt that digest. The entire process is shown in Figure 7-4.

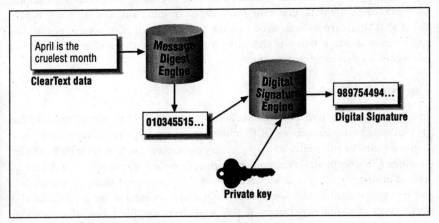

Figure 7-4. Generating a digital signature

The process is as follows:

1. A message digest is calculated that represents the input data.

2. The digest is then encrypted with the private key.

Note that encryption is performed on the digest and not on the data itself. In order to present this signature to another entity, you must present the original data with it—the signature is just a message digest, and, as we mentioned earlier, you cannot reconstruct the input data from the message digest.

---

* On the other hand, a forged digital signature is undetectable, unlike a forged real signature.

Verifying a digital signature requires the same path; the message digest of the original data must be calculated. This digest is then passed through the encryption engine, but this time, the public key of the signer is used. If the digital signature produced by this operation is the same as the digital signature that was presented, the digital signature is deemed valid. Alternately, for some digital signature algorithms, the signed digest could be decrypted with the public key, and the digests compared.

Nothing prevents the signed data from being intercepted. So the data that accompanies the digital signature cannot be sensitive data; the digital signature only verifies that the message came from a particular entity, but it does not actually protect that message.

However, just because someone can snoop the signed data does not mean that it can be tampered with—if the data is altered, it will not produce the same message digest, which in turn will not produce the same digital signature. And it's impossible to change the data, generate a new digest of that data, and then regenerate the digital signature without access to the private key. It is, however, possible to replace one message that was signed by a private key with another message that was signed by that same private key.

Encryption Engines

The final engine we'll discuss handles actual encryption. This engine is part of the Java Cryptography Extension (JCE) rather than the security package itself, and there are various rules on who may and may not obtain the JCE (at least from Sun or other U.S. companies). Encryption engines handle the encryption and decryption of arbitrary data, just as we would expect. An important thing to note is that the encryption engines that are part of the JCE are not used in the generation and verification of digital signatures—digital signatures use their own algorithms to encrypt and decrypt the message digest that are suitable only for manipulating data the size of a message digest. This difference allows the digital signature engine to be exportable, where the encryption engines are not.

Summary

Much of the Java security package is made up of a collection of engines, the basic properties of which we've outlined in this chapter. As a unit, these engines allow us primarily to create digital signatures—a useful notion that authenticates a particular piece of data. One thing that a digital signature can authenticate is a Java class file, which provides the basis for a security manager to consider a class to be trusted (at least to some degree), even though the class was loaded from the network.

The security package, like many Java APIs, is actually a fairly abstract interface that several implementations may be plugged into. Hence, another feature of the security package is its infrastructure to support these differing implementations. In the next chapter, we'll explore the structure of the security package and how it supports these differing implementations; we'll then proceed into how to use the engines of the security package.

8

Security Providers

The cryptographic engines in Java that provide for digital signatures, message digests, and the like are provided as a set of abstract classes in the Java security package. Concrete implementations of these classes are provided by Sun in the JDK, and you also have the option of obtaining third-party implementations of these engines. All of this is made possible through the security provider infrastructure. The provider infrastructure allows concrete implementations of various classes in the security package to be found at runtime, without any changes to the code. In terms of programming, the infrastructure provides a consistent API that can be used by all programs, regardless of who is providing the actual implementation.

Like many other tools discussed in this book, security providers are useful only to developers and users of Java applications. Java-enabled browsers do not implement the security provider infrastructure, nor do they implement any of the cryptographic engines we discuss in the remainder of this book. On the other hand, one of the key features of the Java Plug-in for Internet Explorer and Netscape Communicator is that it does implement the entire security provider infrastructure for use within a browser (subject to the restrictions that might be in place by the access controller and security manager). All the features discussed in this chapter are available in both Java 1.1 and 1.2,* with some slight differences we'll mention.

In terms of actual programming, the classes we're going to examine in this chapter are rarely used—hence, we will not delve much into programming. For most developers, end users, and administrators, this chapter focuses on the architecture of the security provider, since that gives us the ability to substitute new

---

* 1.2 is now Java 2.

implementations of the cryptographic engines we'll use in the rest of the book. Following that discussion, we'll move into the implementation of the architecture, for those readers who are interested in the details.

The Architecture of Security Providers

The security provider abstracts two ideas: engines and algorithms. In this context, "engine" is just another word for operation; there are certain operations the security provider knows about, and in Java, these operations are known as engines. An algorithm defines how a particular operation should be executed. An algorithm can be thought of as an implementation of an engine, but that can lead to confusion, because there may be several implementations of an algorithm.

As a simple example, the Java security package knows about message digests. A message digest is an engine: it is an operation a programmer can perform. The idea behind a message digest is independent of how any particular message digest may be calculated. All message digests share certain features, and the class that abstracts these common features into a single interface is termed an engine. Engines are generally abstract, and are always independent of any particular algorithm.

A message digest may be implemented by a particular algorithm, such as MD5 or SHA. An algorithm is generally provided as a concrete class that extends an abstract engine class, completing the definition of the class. However, there may be many classes that provide a particular algorithm; you may have an SHA class that came with your Java platform, and you may also have obtained an SHA class from a third party. Both classes should provide the same results, but their internal implementations may be vastly different.

Security providers are the glue that manages the mapping between the engines used by the rest of the security package (such as a message digest), the specific algorithms that are valid for those engines (such as an SHA digest), and the specific implementations of that algorithm/engine pair that might be available to any particular Java virtual machine. The goal of the security provider interface is to allow an easy mechanism where the specific algorithms and their implementations can be easily changed or substituted. The security provider allows us to change the implementation of the SHA digest algorithm that is in use, and to introduce a new algorithm to generate a digest.

Hence, a typical programmer only uses the engine classes to perform particular operations. You don't need to worry about the classes that actually perform the computation. The engine classes provide the primary interface to the security package.

Components of the Architecture

The architecture surrounding all of this has these components:

Engine classes

These classes come with the Java virtual machine as part of the core API.

Algorithm classes

At the basic level, there is a set of classes that implement particular algorithms for particular engines. A default set of these classes is provided by the supplier of the Java platform, and other third-party organizations (including your own) can supply additional sets of algorithm classes. These classes may implement one or more algorithms for one or more engines; it is not necessary for a set of classes from a particular vendor to implement all possible algorithms or all possible engines. A single algorithm class provides a particular algorithm for a particular engine.

The Provider class

Each set of algorithm classes from a particular vendor is managed by an instance of the class Provider. A provider knows how to map particular algorithms to the actual class that implements the operation.

The Security class

The Security class maintains a list of the provider classes and consulting each in turn to see which operations it supports.

In later chapters, we'll look at the individual algorithms and engines of this architecture; for now, we'll discuss the Provider and Security classes. These two classes together make up the idea of a security provider.

The security providers rely on cooperation between themselves and the rest of the Java security package in order to fulfill their purpose. The details of this cooperation are handled for us—when we use the MessageDigest class to generate a digest, for example, it's the responsibility of the MessageDigest class to ask the Security class which particular class to use to generate the digest. The Security class in turn asks each of the providers whether or not they can supply the desired digest.

So a typical program that wants to use the security package does not interact directly with the security provider. Instead, the security provider provides its usefulness transparently to the programmer and to the end user. An end user, a system administrator, or a developer can configure the security provider; this is a result of the security provider being based on a set of provider classes. While there is a default provider class, the end user or system administrator can replace the default provider with another class. In addition, a user or programmer can augment the default provider class by adding additional provider classes.

When the security package needs to perform an operation, it constructs a string representing that operation and asks the Security class for an object that can perform the operation with the given algorithm. For example, the idea of generating a message digest is represented by a particular engine; its name (i.e., MessageDigest) is the first component in the request to the security provider. There can be many algorithms that can provide a message digest. SHA-1 and MD5 are the two most common, though we'll explore other possibilities when we look in depth at the corresponding classes that handle digests in Java. So the name of the algorithm (e.g., MD5) forms the second component of the string provided to the security class. These components are concatenated into a single string separated by a dot (e.g., MessageDigest.MD5).

Nine cryptographic engines are supported in the Java security package. In addition, thirteen cryptographic algorithms are common enough to have standard names recognized by the Java security package. However, not every algorithm can be used to perform every operation; the valid combinations Java supports are listed in Table 8-1. Italicized entries are operations that the Java security specification defines as legal, but are not implemented by the default security provider.

Table 8-1. Security Features and Algorithms Expected in the Security API

Engine	Algorithm Name
AlgorithmParameters ★	DSA
AlgorithmParameterGenerator ★	DSA
CertificateFactory	X509
KeyFactory ★	DSA
KeyPairGenerator	DSA
KeyPairGenerator	*RSA*
KeyStore	JKS
MessageDigest	MD5
MessageDigest	SHA-1
MessageDigest	*MD2*
SecureRandom	SHA1PRNG
Signature	DSA[a]
Signature	*MD2/RSA*
Signature	*MD5/RSA*
Signature	*SHA-1/RSA*

[a] This becomes SHA/DSA in Java 1.2, though DSA is still accepted.

The names in this table are the strings passed to the security provider in order for it to find the class implementing the operation. In addition, the security provider can be passed certain alias strings that map an alias to one of these valid strings. For example, although the standard name of the secure hash algorithm is SHA-1 (to distinguish it from SHA-0, the first such algorithm, which is now obsolete), this algorithm is often referred to as SHA. So while

```
MessageDigest.SHA-1
```

is a valid string to pass to the security provider, there is a way to construct alias strings so that the alias refers to the original algorithm. Such a string has the form:

```
Alg.Alias.MessageDigest.SHA
```

This string specifies to the security provider that SHA is a valid name for the message digest operation implemented by this provider. We'll see an example of this alias in use when we discuss the Provider class.

A word about the algorithm names in Table 8-1: Though the documentation for the Java security package talks about these algorithm names as the valid names that are supported by Java, that notion is not very helpful. As the entries in italics show, not all pairs of engines and algorithm names are provided by the default JDK. So, even though it's reasonable to ask the Java security package for an engine that provides digital signatures using an RSA algorithm, you won't be successful in obtaining such an engine unless you've installed special software to provide it. Similarly, although these are the supported algorithm names, there's nothing that prevents us from using another name to refer to a new algorithm. If you develop a new algorithm that performs a message digest operation, you can give that algorithm whatever name you like and use that name freely within the Java security package.

As it happens, there are many standard algorithms that have well-known names which are not included in the set of names that the Java security specification defines; there are some six to eight well-known message digest algorithms even though the Java documentation mentions only three of them. Nothing prevents you from using any of these algorithms.

In fact, the default security provider in Sun's provider uses other names for the algorithms it does implement, although those names are undocumented. On the other hand, it is not very useful to have arbitrary names for algorithms; these other names that the Sun provider uses are known as OID names. OID stands for Object IDentifier and is a way that some algorithm names are standardized by the U.S. government. If you're used to dealing with algorithm definitions at that level, rest assured that the Sun provider has aliases for them, but for our purposes, we'll stick with the default names.

Choosing a Security Provider

When the Java virtual machine begins execution, it is responsible for consulting the user's properties in order to determine which security providers should be in place. These properties must be located in the file *$JAVAHOME/lib/security/java.security*. In the reference release of the JDK, this file contains this line (among others):

```
security.provider.1=sun.security.provider.Sun
```

This line tells us that there is at least one provider class that should be consulted, and that class should be an instance of the `sun.security.provider.Sun` class.

Each provider given in this file must be numbered, starting with 1. If you want to use an additional provider, you can edit this file and add that provider at the next number. Say that you obtain a security provider from XYZ Corporation. When you obtain this provider, you are told that the provider's class name is `com.xyz.XYZProvider`; hence, you add this line to the *java.security* file:

```
security.provider.2=com.xyz.XYZProvider
```

Note that there's no reason why the new provider class had to be added at position 2—it would have been perfectly acceptable to add the XYZProvider class as `security.provider.1` if the `sun.security.provider.Sun` class were changed to `security.provider.2` (or, alternately, removed altogether). The `Security` class keeps the instances of the providers in an array so that each class is found at the index specified in the *java.security* file. As long as the providers in the *java.security* file begin with 1 and are numbered consecutively, they may appear in any order.

The numbers in this example are significant; when the `Security` class is asked to provide a particular engine and algorithm, it searches the listed providers in order to find the first one that can supply the desired operation. All engine classes use the security class to supply objects. When the message digest engine is asked to provide an object capable of generating SHA message digests, the engine will ask the `Security` class which provider to use. If the first provider in the list can perform SHA message digests, that provider will be used. Otherwise, the second provider is checked, and so on, until there are no providers left (and an exception is thrown) or until a provider that implements the desired operation is found. Hence, the number that follows the `security.provider` string indicates the order in which providers will be searched for particular implementations.

For end users and administrators, that's all there is to adding new security providers. For developers, there is also a programmatic way in which a security provider may be added; we'll explore that when we discuss the interface of the `Security` class. But as we mentioned earlier, the programmatic interface provided by the two classes we're about to discuss is not often needed; you'd need them only if you wanted to supply your own security provider, or if you wanted to inspect or set programmatically the list of existing providers. Otherwise, the classes are interesting only because they are used by the engine classes we'll begin to examine in the next chapter.

The Provider Class

The first class we'll examine in depth is the Provider class (java.security.Provider).

public abstract class Provider extends Properties

This class forms the basis of the security provider architecture. There is normally a standard subclass that implements a default security feature set; other classes can be installed to implement other security algorithms.

In the core Java API, the Provider class is abstract, and there are no classes in the core Java API that extend the Provider class. The default provider class that comes with the reference JDK is the class Sun in the sun.security.provider package. However, since this class is in the sun package, there's no guarantee that it will be available with every implementation of the Java virtual machine.

In theory, this should not matter. The concepts of the security package will work according to the specification as long as the Java implementation provides an appropriate provider class and appropriate classes to perform the operations a Java program will expect. The exact set of classes a particular program may expect will depend, of course, on the program. In the next section, we'll discuss how different implementations of the Provider class may be loaded and used during the execution of the virtual machine.

Using the Provider Class

The Provider class is seldom used directly by a programmer. This class does contain a number of useful miscellaneous methods we'll review here; these methods are generally informational and would be used accordingly.

public String getName()

Return the name of the provider.

public double getVersion()

Return the version number of the provider.

public String getInfo()

Return the info string of the provider.

public String toString()

Return the string specifying the provider; this is typically the provider's name concatenated with the provider's version number.

As an extension of the `Properties` class, the `Provider` class also shares its public interface. Beginning in Java 1.2, the `Provider` class overrides three of those methods:

public synchronized void clear() ★
> If permission is granted, clear out all entries from the provider.

public synchronized Object put(Object key, Object value) ★
> If permission is granted, add the given property, keyed off the given key.

public synchronized Object remove(Object key) ★
> If permission is granted, remove the object associated with the given key.

Permission to perform these last three options is granted if the `checkSecurityAccess()` method grants permission based on the argument string (which is `clearProviderProperties`, `putProviderProperty`, and `removeProviderProperty`, respectively) as follows: `argument + getName()`.

Since the interface to this class is simple, we won't actually show how it is used, although we will use some of these methods later in this chapter. Note also that there is no public constructor for the `Provider` class—a provider can only be constructed under special circumstances we'll discuss later.

Implementing the Provider Class

If you're going to provide your own set of classes to perform security operations, you must extend the `Provider` class and register that class with the virtual machine. In this section, we'll explore how to do that. Most of the time, of course, you will not implement your own `Provider` class—you'll just use the default one, or perhaps install a third-party provider using the techniques that we explore in the next section.

Although the `Provider` class is abstract, none of its methods are abstract. This means that implementing a provider is, at first blush, simple: all you need do is subclass the `Provider` class and provide an appropriate constructor. The subclass must provide a constructor, since there is no default constructor within the `Provider` class. The only constructor available to us is:

protected Provider(String name, double version, String info)
> Construct a provider with the given name, version number, and information string.

Hence, the basic implementation of a security provider is:

```
public class XYZProvider extends Provider {
    public XYZProvider() {
        super("XYZ", 1.0, "XYZ Security Provider v1.0");
    }
}
```

Here we're defining the skeleton of a provider that is going to provide certain facilities based on various algorithms of the XYZ Corporation. Throughout the remainder of this book, we'll be developing the classes that apply to the XYZ's cryptographic methods, but they will be examples only—they lack the rigorous mathematical properties that these algorithms must have. In practice, you might choose to implement algorithms that correspond to the RSA algorithms for the cryptographic engines.

Note that we used a default constructor in this class rather than providing a constructor similar to the one found in the Provider class itself. The reason for this has to do with the way providers are constructed, which we'll discuss at the end of this section. When you write a provider, it must provide a constructor with no arguments.

This is a complete, albeit useless, implementation of a provider. In order to add some functionality to our provider, we must put some associations into the provider. The associations will perform the mapping that we mentioned earlier; it is necessary for the provider to map the name of an engine and algorithm with the name of a class that implements that operation. This is why the Provider class itself is a subclass of the Properties class—so that we can make each of those associations into a property.

The operations that our provider will be consulted about are listed in Table 8-2. In this example, we're going to be providing an SHA-1 algorithm for performing message digests, since that would be needed as part of the signature generation algorithm we want to implement. There's no absolute requirement for this; we could have depended on the default Sun security provider to supply this algorithm for us. On the other hand, there's no guarantee that the default security provider will be in place when our security provider is installed, so it's a good idea for a provider to include all the algorithms it will need.

Table 8-2. Properties Included by Our Sample Provider

Property	Corresponding Class
Signature.SHA-1/XYZ	XYZSignature
KeyPairGenerator.XYZ	XYZKeyPairGenerator
MessageDigest.XYZ	XYZMessageDigest
MessageDigest.SHA-1	SHA1MessageDigest

In order to make these associations from this table, then, our XYZProvider class needs to look like this:

```
public class XYZProvider extends Provider {
    public XYZProvider() {
        super("XYZ", 1.0, "XYZ Security Provider v1.0");
```

```
        put("Signature.SHA-1/XYZ", "com.xyz.XYZSignature");
        put("KeyPairGenerator.XYZ", "com.xyz.XYZKeyPairGenerator");
        put("MessageDigest.XYZ", "com.xyz.XYZMessageDigest");
        put("MessageDigest.SHA-1", "com.xyz.SHA1MessageDigest");
        put("Alg.Alias.MessageDigest.SHA", "SHA-1");
    }
}
```

The only properties a provider is required to put into its property list are the properties that match the engine name and algorithm pair with the class that implements that operation. In this example, that's handled with the first four calls to the put() method (but remember too that the provider can implement as few or as many operations as it wants to; it needn't implement more than a single engine with one algorithm, or it can implement dozens of engine/algorithm pairs). Note that the class name is the fully qualified package name of the class.

The provider also has the opportunity to set any other properties that it wants to use. If the provider wants to set aliases (as we've done with the final call to the put() method, using the syntax we showed earlier), it's free to do so. Our example allows the program using this provider to request an SHA message digest in addition to requesting an SHA-1 digest. Doing this for SHA is highly advisable, since that algorithm is typically referred to as SHA rather than SHA-1, but that's the only common case where that aliasing is needed.

A provider can set any other arbitrary properties that it wants as well. For instance, a provider class could set this property:

```
    put("NativeImplementation", "false");
```

if it wanted the classes that use the provider to be able to determine if this particular XYZ implementation uses native methods.* It can also use the convention that certain properties are preceded with the word Alg and contain the algorithm name, like this:

```
    put("Alg.NativeImplementation.XYZ", "false");
```

There's no advantage to setting any additional properties—nothing in the core JDK will use them. They can be set to make the classes that accompany your provider class easier to write—for example, your XYZSignature class might want to inquire which particular providers have a native method implementation of the XYZ algorithm. Whatever information you put into your provider and how your accompanying classes use that information is a design detail that is completely up to you. The Security class will help you manage the information in these proper-

---

* RSA algorithms often use native methods, because there are existing implementations of them that are written in C and have gone through an extensive quality acceptance test that many commercial sites have a level of confidence in. However, many third-party RSA implementations do not use native methods.

ties; this relationship to the Security class is the reason why we used a string value for the NativeImplementation property rather than a Boolean value.

There's one more nonpublic method of the Provider class that is used by the security API:

static Provider loadProvider(String className)
> Instantiate a provider that has as its type the given class. This method is provided mostly for convenience—it simply loads the given class and instantiates it. However, this method also ensures that the loaded class is an instance of the Provider class.

This method creates an instance of a provider. The importance of this method stems from how it performs its task: it creates the instance of the provider object by calling the newInstance() method of the Class class. In order for that operation to succeed, the provider class must therefore have a default constructor—that is, a constructor that requires no arguments. This is why in our example we provided such a constructor and had the constructor hardwire the name, version number, and information string. We could have provided an additional constructor that accepts those values as parameters, but it would never be called, since the only way in which the virtual machine uses providers is to load them via this method.

In the next section, we'll look into the details of how the virtual machine loads those provider classes we want to use.

The Security Class

The Security class (java.security.Security) is responsible for managing the set of provider classes that a Java program can use, and forms the last link in the architecture of the security provider. This class is final, and all its methods are static (except for its constructor, which is private). Like the System and Math classes, then, the Security class can never be created or subclassed; it exists simply to provide a placeholder for methods that deal with the java.security package.

Earlier, we explained how to add entries to the *java.security* file to add new providers to the security architecture. The same feat can be accomplished programmatically via these methods of the Security class:

public static int addProvider(Provider provider)
> Add a new provider into the list of providers. The provider is added to the end of the internal array of providers.

public static int insertProviderAt(Provider provider, int position)

> Add a new provider into the internal array of providers. The provider is added at the specified position; other providers have their index changed if necessary to make room for this provider. Position counting begins at 1.

The notion that these classes are kept in an indexed array is important; when the Security class is asked to provide a particular algorithm for an operation, the array is searched sequentially for a provider that can provide the requested algorithm for the requested operation.

As an example, let's use a modification of the XYZProvider class that we outlined earlier. This class comes with a set of classes to perform generation of key pairs, and it can generate key pairs according to two algorithms: DSA and XYZ. The XYZProvider class, according to an entry added to the *java.security* file, has been added at position 2. Additionally, let's say that our Java program has installed an additional provider class at position 3 called the FooProvider that can generate key pairs and digital signatures according to a single algorithm known as Foo. This

Table 8-3. Sample Security Providers

Sun Provider	XYZ Provider	Foo Provider

Signature Engines
    DSA
	Signature Engines
	    XYZ
	    DSA
		Signature Engines
		    Foo

Message Digest Engines
    MD5
	Message Digest Engines
	    XYZ
	    SHA
		Message Digest Engines
		    None

Key Pair Engines
    DSA
	Key Pair Engines
	    XYZ
	    DSA
		Key Pair Engines
		    Foo

leaves us with the set of provider classes listed in Table 8-3.

Now when our Java program needs to generate a key pair, the security provider is consulted as to which classes will implement the key pair generation we want. If we need to generate a DSA key, the security provider returns to us a class associated with the Sun provider class, since the Sun provider, at position 1, is the first class that says that it can perform DSA key generation. If we had reversed the order of indices in the *java.security* file so that the Sun provider was at position 2 and the XYZ provider was at position 1, a class associated with the XYZ provider would have been returned instead. Similarly, when we request a Foo key pair, a class associated with the Foo provider is returned to us, regardless of what index it occurs at, since that is the only provider class that knows how to perform Foo key generation.

Remember that this is a two-step process. The security class receives a string (like KeyPairGenerator.DSA) and locates a class that provides that service (such as `sun.security.provider.Sun`). The Sun class, as a provider class, does not actually know how to generate keys (or do anything else)—it only knows what classes in the Sun security package know how to generate keys. Then the security class must ask the provider itself for the name of the class that actually implements the desired operation. That process is handled by an internal method of the Security class—we'll use that method implicitly over the next few chapters when we retrieve objects that implement a particular engine and algorithm. Before we do that, though, we'll finish looking at the interface of the Security class.

There are a number of other methods in the Security class that provide basic information about the configuration of the security provider.

public static void removeProvider(String name)

Remove the named provider from the list of provider classes. The remaining providers move up in the array of providers if necessary. If the named provider is not in the list, this method silently returns (i.e., no exception is thrown).

public static Provider[] getProviders()

Return a copy of the array of providers on which the Security class operates. Note that this is a copy of the array; reordering its elements has no effect on the Security class.

public static Provider getProvider(String name)

Return the provider with the given name. If the named provider is not in the list held by the Security class, this method returns null.

public static String getProperty(String key)

Get the property of the Security class with the associated key. The properties held in the Security class are the properties that were read from the *java.security* file. In typical usage, one of the properties is security.provider.1 (as well as any other providers listed in the *java.security* file). Note, however, that properties of this sort may not reflect the actual order of the provider classes: when the addProvider(), insertProviderAt(), and removeProvider() methods are called, the order of the providers changes. These changes are not reflected in the internal property list.

The *java.security* file has a number of other properties within it; these other properties may also be retrieved via this method.

public static String setProperty(String key)

Set the property of the security class with the associated key.

public static String getAlgorithmProperty(String algName, String propName)☆

Search all the providers for a property in the form Alg.propName.algName and return the first match it finds. For example, if a provider had set the Alg.NativeImplementation.XYZ property to the string "false," a call to getAlgorithmName("XYZ", "NativeImplementation") returns the string "false" (which is why earlier we used a string value in the provider class).

Here's a simple example, then, of how to see a list of all the security providers in a particular virtual machine:

```
public class ExamineSecurity {
    public static void main(String args[]) {
        try {
            Provider p[] = Security.getProviders();
            for (int i = 0; i < p.length; i++) {
                System.out.println(p[i]);
                for (Enumeration e = p[i].keys(); e.hasMoreElements();)
                    System.out.println("\t" + e.nextElement());
            }
        }
        catch (Exception e) {
            System.out.println(e);
        }
    }
}
```

If we run this program with the 1.2 Sun security provider, we get this output:

```
SUN version 1.2
        Alg.Alias.MessageDigest.SHA
        Alg.Alias.Signature.SHAwithDSA
        Alg.Alias.Signature.1.3.14.3.2.13
        Alg.Alias.Signature.OID.1.2.840.10040.4.3
        Alg.Alias.Signature.SHA-1/DSA
        Alg.Alias.Signature.DSS
        Alg.Alias.Signature.SHA1withDSA
        Alg.Alias.Signature.OID.1.3.14.3.2.13
        AlgorithmParameters.DSA
        KeyFactory.DSA
        Alg.Alias.Signature.1.2.840.10040.4.3
        Alg.Alias.MessageDigest.SHA1
        AlgorithmParameterGenerator.DSA
        Alg.Alias.AlgorithmParameters.1.2.840.10040.4.1
        MessageDigest.MD5
        Alg.Alias.KeyPairGenerator.OID.1.2.840.10040.4.1
        MessageDigest.SHA-1
        Alg.Alias.KeyPairGenerator.OID.1.3.14.3.2.12
        Signature.DSA
        Alg.Alias.KeyPairGenerator.1.3.14.3.2.12
        Alg.Alias.KeyPairGenerator.1.2.840.10040.4.1
        Alg.Alias.Signature.1.3.14.3.2.27
        Alg.Alias.Signature.SHA/DSA
        KeyPairGenerator.DSA
        Alg.Alias.Signature.SHA1/DSA
```

```
Alg.Alias.Signature.OID.1.3.14.3.2.27
Alg.Alias.AlgorithmParameters.1.3.14.3.2.12
KeyStore.JKS
CertificateFactory.X509
Alg.Alias.CertificateFactory.X.509
SecureRandom.SHA1PRNG
```

Two things are readily apparent from this example. First, the strings that contain only an engine name and an algorithm implement the expected operations that we listed in Table 8-1. Second, as we mentioned in the section on the Provider class, security providers often leverage the fact that the Provider class is a subclass of the Properties class to provide properties that may make sense only to other classes that are part of the provider package. Hence, the signature algorithm 1.3.14.3.2.13 may make sense to one of the classes in the Sun security provider, but it is not a string that will necessarily make sense to other developers. In fact, those aliases—including the ones that are prefaced by OID—do have meanings within the cryptography standards world, but for our purposes we'll stick with the standard algorithm names that we listed earlier.

The Security Class and the Security Manager

All the public methods of the Security class call the checkSecurityAccess() method of the security manager. This gives the security manager the opportunity to intervene before an untrusted class affects the security policy of the virtual machine.

Recall that the checkSecurityAccess() method accepts a single string parameter. In the case of the methods in the Security class, the call that is made looks like this:

```
public static Provider getProvider(String name) {
    SecurityManager sec = System.getSecurityManager();
    if (sec != null)
        sec.checkSecurityAccess("java");
    ... continue to find the provider ...
}
```

The string parameter that is sent to the checkSecurityAccess() method has changed between releases of Java; the various methods and the strings they pass to the security manager are listed in Table 8-4.

In typical usage in 1.1, the security manager ignores this string altogether and simply allows all trusted classes to call these methods and prevents all untrusted classes from calling these methods. In 1.2, the security manager constructs a security permission for the given name and calls the access controller to see if the given permission has been granted.

Table 8-4. Security Checks of the Security Class

Method	1.2 Parameter	1.1 Parameter
insertProviderAt()	insertProvider. + provider.getName()	java
removeProvider()	removeProvider. + provider.getName()	java
getProviders()	– not called –	java
getProvider()	– not called –	java
getProperty()	getProperty. + key	java
setProperty()	setProperty. + key	java

The Architecture of Engine Classes

In the next few chapters, we'll discuss the engine classes that are part of the core Java API. All engine classes share a similar architecture that we'll discuss here.

Most programmers are only interested in using the engine classes to perform their desired operation; each engine class has a public interface that defines the operations the engine can perform. None of this is unusual: it is the basis of programming in Java.

However, the engine classes are designed so that users can employ third-party security providers (using the architecture we've just examined). For programmers who are interested in writing such providers, the engine classes have an additional interface called the security provider interface (SPI). The SPI is a set of abstract methods that a particular engine must implement in order to fulfill its contract of providing a particular operation.

The role of the SPI has changed between Java 1.1 and Java 1.2. In 1.1, the SPI was simply a convention. There were a set of protected, usually abstract, methods in each engine that made up the SPI. By convention, these methods begin with the word "engine"; implementing a 1.1 engine is a matter of implementing each of these protected methods.

In 1.2, the interface of an engine was split between two distinct classes: the engine class itself and the SPI class. For example, in 1.2 there is an engine class called MessageDigest, and its SPI class is called MessageDigestSpi. For historic reasons, there are differences in various engine classes between the engine class itself and the SPI.

There were three engine classes in 1.1. In 1.2, the SPI class for these classes is a superclass of the engine class; e.g., the MessageDigest class extends the Message-DigestSpi class. This allows the MessageDigest class in 1.2 to have the same interface as it does in 1.1, even though the class hierarchy to which it belongs has changed.

There are six new engine classes in 1.2, and for these classes, the SPI is unrelated to the class itself; e.g., there is a KeyFactory class and a KeyFactorySpi class, both of which simply subclass the Object class. In these cases, the engine class contains an instance of the SPI that it uses to carry out its operations. Table 8-5 summarizes the nine core Java engine classes and their corresponding SPI.

Table 8-5. Engine Classes in the Core Java API

Engine	SPI Class	Engine Superclass
AlgorithmParameters ★	AlgorithmParametersSpi	Object
AlgorithmParameterGenerator ★	AlgorithmParameterGeneratorSpi	Object
CertificateFactory ★	CertificateFactorySpi	Object
KeyFactory ★	KeyFactorySpi	Object
KeyPairGenerator	KeyPairGeneratorSpi	KeyPairGeneratorSpi
KeyStore ★	KeyStoreSpi	Object
MessageDigest	MessageDigestSpi	MessageDigestSpi
SecureRandom ★	SecureRandomSpi	Object
Signature	SignatureSpi	SignatureSpi

What this all means is that if you want to implement a security provider under Java 1.2, you would typically extend the SPI. This allows a developer to request a particular engine and receive the correct class according to the following algorithm:

1. The programmer requests an instance of a particular engine that implements a particular algorithm. Engine classes never have public constructors; instead, every engine has a getInstance() method that takes the name of the desired algorithm as an argument and returns an instance of the appropriate class.

2. The Security class is asked to consult its list of providers and provide the appropriate instance. For example, when the getInstance() method of the MessageDigest class is called, the Security class may determine that the appropriate provider class is called com.xyz.XYZMessageDigest.

3. If the retrieved class does not extend the appropriate SPI (e.g., java.security.MessageDigestSpi in this case), a NoSuchAlgorithmException is generated.

4. An instance of the retrieved class is created and returned to the getInstance() method (which in turn returns it to the developer).

For consistency, when you implement any engine class in 1.2, it is always possible to extend the appropriate SPI. However, when you implement one of the three engines that are part of 1.1, it may make more sense to extend the engine class (e.g., the MessageDigest class) rather than the SPI (e.g., the MessageDigestSpi class). This allows the implementation to be used under both 1.1 and 1.2. An engine class that directly subclasses its SPI in 1.2 cannot be used in 1.1, while an engine class that directly subclasses a Java engine class can be used in both 1.1 and 1.2. That is the convention we'll follow in our examples.

Summary

In this chapter, we've explored the architecture that forms the basis of the Java security API. This architecture is based on the Security and Provider classes, which together form a set of mappings that allow the security API to determine dynamically the set of classes it should use to implement certain operations.

Implementing a provider is trivial, but implementing the set of classes that must accompany a provider is much harder. We've shown a simple provider class in this chapter. Although we'll show the engine classes in the next few chapters, the mathematics behind designing and implementing a successful cryptographic algorithm are beyond the scope of this book. However, this architecture also allows users and administrators to buy or download third-party implementations of the security architecture and plug those implementations seamlessly into the Java virtual machine; a partial list of available third-party implementations appears in Appendix C.

In the next few chapters, we'll examine the specifics of the engine classes—that is, the operations—that this security provider architecture makes possible. In those chapters, we'll see how the engines are used, and the benefits each engine provides.

9

Message Digests

In this chapter, we're going to look at the API that implements the ability to create and verify message digests. The ability to create a message digest is one of the standard engines provided by the Sun default security provider. You can therefore reasonably expect every Java implementation to create message digests.

Message digests are the simplest of the standard engines that compose the security provider architecture, so they provide a good starting point in our examination of those engines. In addition, message digests provide the first link in creating and verifying a digital signature—the most important goal of the provider architecture. However, message digests are useful entities in their own right, since a message digest can verify that data has not been tampered with—up to a point. As we'll see, there are certain limitations on the security of a message digest that is transmitted along with the data it represents.

Message digests are implemented through a single class:

public abstract class MessageDigest extends MessageDigestSpi
Implement operations to create and verify a message digest.

In Java 1.1, there is no `MessageDigestSpi` class, and the `MessageDigest` class simply extends `Object`. That difference is important only if you want to implement your own message digest class, which we'll do later in the chapter.

Like all engines in the Java security package, the `MessageDigest` class (`java.security.MessageDigest`) is an abstract class; it defines an interface that all message digests must have, but the implementation details of a particular message digest class are hidden in the private classes that accompany a security provider. This allows a developer to use the message digest class without knowing the details of a message digest implementation by operating on the public methods of the message digest class, and it allows providers of a security package

196

to implement their own message digests by implementing the abstract methods of the class. We'll examine the message class from the perspectives of both developer and implementor in this chapter.

Using the Message Digest Class

For a developer who wants to operate on a message digest, the first step is to obtain an instance of the message digest class. Since the message digest class is abstract, this cannot be done directly; instead, the developer must use one of these methods:

public static MessageDigest getInstance(String algorithm)
public static MessageDigest getInstance(String algorithm, String provider)

> Return an instance of the message digest class that implements the given algorithm. In the first case, the security providers are searched in order following the process we outlined in Chapter 8; otherwise, only the given provider is searched. Valid names for the default Sun security provider are SHA, SHA-1, and MD5. If no provider can be found that implements the given algorithm, a NoSuchAlgorithmException is thrown. If the named provider cannot be found, a NoSuchProviderException is thrown.

Once a message digest object has been obtained, the developer can operate on that object with these methods:

public void update(byte input)
public void update(byte[] input)
public void update(byte[] input, int offset, int length)

> Add the specified data to the digest. The first of these methods adds a single byte to the data, the second adds the entire array of bytes, and the third adds only the specified subset of the array of data.

> These methods may be called in any order and any number of times to add the desired data to the digest. Consecutive calls to these methods append data to the internal accumulation of data over which the digest will be calculated.

public byte[] digest()
public byte[] digest(byte[] input)

> Compute the message digest on the accumulated data (optionally adding the specified data before performing the computation). The resulting digest is returned as a byte array. Once a digest has been calculated, the internal state of the algorithm is reset, so that the object may be reused at this point to create a new message digest.

public int digest(byte[] output, int offset, int len) ★

Compute the message digest on the accumulated data and place the answer into the provided array, starting at the given offset and copying at most len bytes. Most implementations do not return a partial digest, so if the amount of space in the buffer (taking into account its offset) is not sufficient to store the digest, a DigestException is thrown. This method returns the size of the digest.

public static boolean isEqual(byte digestA[], byte digestB[])

Compare two digests for equality. Two digests are considered equal only if each byte in the first digest is exactly equal to each byte in the second digest and the digests are the same length.

public void reset()

Reset the digest object by discarding all accumulated data and resetting the algorithm that is used to implement the digest. This is equivalent to creating a new instance of the object. In addition, this method throws away any information that the toString() method would have printed (see below).

public final String getAlgorithm()

Return the string representing the algorithm name (e.g., SHA).

public String toString()

A string representation of a digest by default contains the name of the class implementing the digest, the words "Message Digest," and the bytes that were returned by a previous call to the digest() method. If the digest() method has not been called, or if the reset() method has been called, then "<incomplete>" is printed instead of the digest. An example string looks like:

```
sun.security.provider.SHA Message Digest \
        <0a808982fee54fd74a86aae72eff7991328ff32b>
```

public Object clone() throws CloneNotSupportedException

Return a clone of the object. Message digest implementations need to implement the clone() method because some internal operations on the digest object require a call to the digest() method, which resets the digest. These operations are typically done on a clone of the object so that the state of the original object is not changed.

public final int getDigestLength() ★

Return the length of array of bytes that are returned from the digest() method. This value is usually constant (i.e., it does not depend on the amount of data that has been sent through the update() method).

Let's see an example of how all of this works. As a simple case, let's say that we want to save a simple string to a file, but we're worried that the file might be corrupted when we read the string back in. Hence, in addition to saving the string, we must save a message digest. We do this by saving the serialized string object followed by the serialized array of bytes that constitute the message digest.

In order to save the pieces of data, we use this code:

```
public class Send {
    public static void main(String args[]) {
        try {
            FileOutputStream fos = new FileOutputStream("test");
            MessageDigest md = MessageDigest.getInstance("SHA");
            ObjectOutputStream oos = new ObjectOutputStream(fos);
            String data = "This have I thought good to deliver thee, "+
                "that thou mightst not lose the dues of rejoicing " +
                "by being ignorant of what greatness is promised thee.";
            byte buf[] = data.getBytes();
            md.update(buf);
            oos.writeObject(data);
            oos.writeObject(md.digest());
        } catch (Exception e) {
            System.out.println(e);
        }
    }
}
```

That's all there is to creating a digest of some data. The call to the getInstance() method finds a message digest object that implements the SHA message digest algorithm. After creating our data—which in this case is a simple string—we pass that data to the update() method of the message digest. In practice, this code could be slightly more complicated, since all the data might not be available at once. As far as the message digest object is concerned, though, that situation would just require multiple calls to the update() method instead of a single call (it can also be handled with digest streams, which we'll examine next). Once we've loaded all the data into the object, it is a simple matter to create the digest itself (with the digest() method) and then save our data objects to the file.

Similarly, to retrieve this data we need only read the object back in and verify the message digest. In order to verify the message digest, we must recompute the digest over the data we received and test to make sure the digest is equivalent to the original digest:

```
public class Receive {
    public static void main(String args[]) {
        try {
            FileInputStream fis = new FileInputStream("test");
            ObjectInputStream ois = new ObjectInputStream(fis);
            Object o = ois.readObject();
            if (!(o instanceof String)) {
                System.out.println("Unexpected data in file");
```

```
                System.exit(-1);
            }
            String data = (String) o;
            System.out.println("Got message " + data);
            o = ois.readObject();
            if (!(o instanceof byte[])) {
                System.out.println("Unexpected data in file");
                System.exit(-1);
            }
            byte origDigest[] = (byte []) o;
            MessageDigest md = MessageDigest.getInstance("SHA");
            md.update(data.getBytes());
            if (MessageDigest.isEqual(md.digest(), origDigest))
                System.out.println("Message is valid");
            else System.out.println("Message was corrupted");
        } catch (Exception e) {
            System.out.println(e);
        }
    }
}
```

Once again, if the data was not available all at once, we would need to make multiple calls to the update() method as the data arrived. We do not, however, need to make sure that calls to the update() methods between the Send and Receive classes match in any sense; that is, if we called the update() method four times in the Send class, we do not need to call the update() method four times (with the same data) in the Receive class—we can call it once, five times, or whatever. The calculation of the digest is unaffected by how the data was placed into the message digest object—as long as the order of the bytes presented to the various calls to the update() methods is the same.

Secure Message Digests

As we stated in Chapter 7, the message digest by itself does not give us a very high level of security. We can tell whether somehow the output file in this example has been corrupted, because the text that we read in won't produce the same message digest that was saved with the file. But there's nothing to prevent someone from changing both the text and the digest stored in the file in such a way that the new digest reflects the altered text.

There are various ways in which a message digest can be made into a Message Authentication Code (MAC), but the Java security API does not provide any standard techniques for doing so. One popular way is to encrypt the message digest using the encryption engine (if one is available to you)—which, in fact, is really a variation of a digital signature.

If we are not able to encrypt the digest, all is not lost; we can also use a passphrase along with the message digest in order to calculate a secure message digest (or MAC). This requires that both the sender and receiver of the data have a shared passphrase that they have kept secret.

Using this passphrase, calculating a MAC requires that we:

1. Calculate the message digest of the secret passphrase concatenated with the data:

```
MessageDigest md = MessageDigest.getInstance("SHA");
String data = "This have I thought good to deliver thee, " +
              "that thou mightst not lose the dues of rejoicing " +
              "by being ignorant of what greatness is promised thee.";
String passphrase = "Sleep no more";
byte dataBytes[] = data.getBytes();
byte passBytes[] = passphrase.getBytes();
md.update(passBytes);
md.update(dataBytes);
byte digest1[] = md.digest();
```

2. Calculate the message digest of the secret passphrase concatenated with the just-calculated digest:

```
md.update(passBytes);
md.update(digest1);
byte mac[] = md.digest();
```

We can substitute this code into our original Send example, writing out the data string and the MAC to the file. Note that we can use the same message digest object to calculate both digests, since the object is reset after a call to the digest() method. Also note that the first digest we calculate is not saved to the file: we save only the data and the MAC. Of course, we must make similar changes to the Receive example; if the MACs are equal, the data was not modified in transit.

As long as we use exactly same data for the passphrase in both the transmitting and receiving class, the message digests (that is, the MACs) still compare as equal. That gives a certain level of security to the message digest, but it requires that the sender and the receiver agree on what data to use for the passphrase; the passphrase cannot be transmitted along with the text. In this case, the security of the message digest depends upon the security of the passphrase. Normally, of course, you would prompt for that passphrase rather than hardcoding into the source as we've done above.

Message Digest Streams

The interface to the message digest class requires that you supply the data for the digest as a series of single bytes or byte arrays. As we mentioned earlier, this is not always the most convenient way to process data, which may be coming from a file or other input stream. This brings us to the message digest stream classes. These classes implement the standard input and output filter stream semantics of Java streams so that data can be written to a digest stream that will calculate the digest as the data itself is written (or the reverse operation for reading data).

The DigestOutputStream Class

The first of these classes we'll examine is the DigestOutputStream class (java.security.DigestOutputStream). This class allows us to write data to a particular output stream and calculate the message digest of that data transparently as the data passes through the stream:

public class DigestOutputStream extends FilterOutputStream

Provide a stream that can calculate the message digest of data that is passed through the stream. A digest output stream holds two components internally: the output stream that is the ultimate destination of the data, and a message digest object that computes the data of the stream written to the destination.

The digest output stream is constructed as follows:

public DigestOutputStream(OutputStream os, MessageDigest md)

Construct a digest output stream that associates the given output stream with the given message digest. Data that is written to the stream is automatically passed to the update() method of the message digest.

In addition to the standard methods available to all output streams, a message digest output stream provides the following interface:

public MessageDigest getMessageDigest()

Return the message digest associated with this output stream.

public void setMessageDigest(MessageDigest md)

Associate the given message digest with this output stream. The internal reference to the original message digest is lost, but the original message digest is otherwise unaffected (i.e., if you still hold a reference to the original message digest object, you can still calculate the digest of the data that was written to the stream while that digest was in place).

public void write(int b)
public void write(byte b[], int off, int len)

Write the given byte or array of bytes to the underlying output stream, and also update the internal message digest with the given data (if the digest stream is marked as on). These methods may throw an IOException from the underlying stream.

public void on(boolean on)

Turn the message digest stream on or off. When data is written to a stream that is off, the data will be passed to the underlying output stream, but the message digest will not be updated.

Note that this last method does not affect the underlying output stream at all; data is still sent to the underlying stream even if the digest output stream is marked as off. The on/off state only affects whether the update() method of the message digest will be called as the data is written.

We can use this class to simplify the example we used earlier:

```
public class SendStream {
    public static void main(String args[]) {
        try {
            FileOutputStream fos = new FileOutputStream("test");
            MessageDigest md = MessageDigest.getInstance("SHA");
            DigestOutputStream dos = new DigestOutputStream(fos, md);
            ObjectOutputStream oos = new ObjectOutputStream(dos);
            String data = "This have I thought good to deliver thee, "+
                "that thou mightst not lose the dues of rejoicing " +
                "by being ignorant of what greatness is promised thee.";
            oos.writeObject(data);
            dos.on(false);
            oos.writeObject(md.digest());
        } catch (Exception e) {
            System.out.println(e);
        }
    }
}
```

The big change is in constructing the object output stream—we now want to wrap it around the digest output stream so that as each object is written to the file, the message digest will include those bytes. We also want to make sure that we turn off the message digest calculation before we send the digest itself to the file. Turning off the digest isn't strictly necessary in this case, since we don't use the digest object once we've calculated a single digest in this example, but it's good practice to keep the digest on only when strictly required.

Note that there is a subtle difference between the digest produced in this example and the previous example. In the first example, the digest was calculated over just the bytes of the string that we saved to the file. In the second example, the digest was calculated over the serialized string object itself—which includes some information regarding the class definition in addition to the bytes of the string.

The DigestInputStream Class

The symmetric operation to the digest output stream is the DigestInputStream class (java.security.DigestInputStream):

public class DigestInputStream extends FilterInputStream

Create an input stream that is associated with a message digest. When data is read from the input stream, it is also sent to the update() method of the stream's associated message digest.

The digest input stream has essentially the same interface as the digest output stream (with writing replaced by reading). There is a single constructor for the class:

public DigestInputStream(InputStream is, MessageDigest md)

Construct a digest input stream that associates the given input stream with the given message digest. Data that is read from the stream will also automatically be passed to the update() method of the message digest.

The interface provided by the digest input stream is symmetric to the digest output stream:

public MessageDigest getMessageDigest()

Return the message digest that is associated with this output stream.

public void setMessageDigest(MessageDigest md)

Associate the given message digest with this output stream. The internal reference to the original message digest is lost, but the original message digest is otherwise unaffected (e.g., you can still calculate the digest of the data that had been written to the stream while that digest was in place).

public void read(int b)
public void read(byte b[], int off, int len)

Read one or more bytes from the underlying output stream, and also update the internal message digest with the given data (if the digest stream is :narked as on). These methods may throw an IOException from the underlying stream.

public void on(boolean on)

Turn the message digest stream on or off. When data is read from a stream that is off, the message digest will not be updated.

Here's how we can use this class to read the file we created with the digest output stream:

```
public class ReceiveStream {
    public static void main(String args[]) {
        try {
```

```java
    FileInputStream fis = new FileInputStream("test");
    MessageDigest md = MessageDigest.getInstance("SHA");
    DigestInputStream dis = new DigestInputStream(fis, md);
    ObjectInputStream ois = new ObjectInputStream(dis);
    Object o = ois.readObject();
    if (!(o instanceof String)) {
        System.out.println("Unexpected data in file");
        System.exit(-1);
    }
    String data = (String) o;
    System.out.println("Got message " + data);
    dis.on(false);
    o = ois.readObject();
    if (!(o instanceof byte[])) {
        System.out.println("Unexpected data in file");
        System.exit(-1);
    }
    byte origDigest[] = (byte []) o;
    if (MessageDigest.isEqual(md.digest(), origDigest))
        System.out.println("Message is valid");
    else System.out.println("Message was corrupted");
} catch (Exception e) {
    System.out.println(e);
}
    }
}
```

Once again, constructing the input stream is a matter of providing a message digest. In this example, we've again turned off the digest input stream after reading the string object in the file. Turning off the stream is strictly required in this case. We want to make sure that the digest we calculate is computed only over the string object and not the stored byte array (that is, the stored message digest).

Implementing a MessageDigest Class

If you want to write your own security provider, you have the option of creating your own message digest engine. Typically, you'd do this because you want to ensure that a particular algorithm like SHA is available regardless of who the default security provider is; if you have a mathematics background, it's conceivable that you might want to implement your own algorithm.

In order to implement a message digest algorithm, you must provide a concrete subclass of the MessageDigest class. This essentially entails providing an implementation of most of the public methods we've just looked at. Although the public methods are not declared abstract, they typically do nothing more than call an internal (protected) method to accomplish their task.

The MessageDigest class exists in both Java 1.1 and 1.2,* which is why it extends its SPI (see Chapter 8). For our example, we'll directly subclass the MessageDigest class so that the resulting example will work under both releases, but remember that in 1.2 you have the option of extending the MessageDigestSpi class directly.

There is a single constructor in the MessageDigest class that is available to implementors:

protected MessageDigest(String name)
> Construct a message digest object. Classes that extend the MessageDigest class must call this constructor, as this is the only constructor in the class. As we'll see, however, the constructor of the subclass must take no arguments.

In order to write a message digest class, you must implement each of the following methods:

protected abstract void engineUpdate(byte input)
protected abstract void engineUpdate(byte[] input, int offset, int len)
> Add the given bytes to the data over which the digest will be calculated. Note that there is no method in this list that accepts simply an array of bytes; the update(byte[] b) method in the base class simply uses an offset of 0 and a length equal to the entire array.

protected abstract byte[] engineDigest()
> Calculate the digest over the accumulated data, resetting the internal state of the object afterwards. Note that there is no corresponding method that accepts an array of bytes as an argument; the digest() method in the base class simply calls the engineUpdate() method if needed before calling the engineDigest() method.

protected int engineDigest(byte buf[], int offset, int len) ★
> Calculate the digest, placing the output into the buf array (starting at the given offset and proceeding for len bytes) and returning the length of the calculated digest. The default implementation of this method simply calls the engineDigest() method and then copies the result into buf. The buffer passed to this method always has sufficient length to hold the digest, since if the buffer had been too short the digest() method itself would have thrown an exception.

protected abstract void engineReset()
> Reset the internal state of the engine, discarding all accumulated data and resetting the algorithm to an initial condition.

---

* 1.2 is now Java 2.

protected int engineGetDigestLength() ★

Return the digest length that is supported by this implementation. Unlike most of the protected methods in this class, this method is not abstract; it does not need to be overridden. However, the default implementation simply returns 0. If 0 is returned by this method, the getDigestLength() method attempts to create a clone of the digest object, calculate its digest, and return the length of the calculated digest. If a digest implementation does not override this method and does not implement the Cloneable interface, the getDigestLength() method will not operate correctly.

Each of these methods corresponds to a public method we just looked at, with the name of the public method preceded by the word "engine". The public methods that do not have a corresponding method in this list are fully implemented in the base class and do not need to be implemented in the message digest subclass.

We'll show a simple implementation of a message digest class here. This implementation is based on a hash algorithm that produces a 4-byte output. As bytes are accumulated by this algorithm, they are stored into a 4-byte value (that is, an int); when this value has all four bytes filled, it is XOR-ed to another integer that accumulates the hash.

```
package com.xyz;

public class XYZMessageDigest extends MessageDigest
                              implements Cloneable {
    private int hash;
    private int store;
    private int nBytes;

    public XYZMessageDigest() {
        super("XYZ");
        engineReset();
    }

    public void engineUpdate(byte b) {
        switch(nBytes) {
            case 0:
                store = (b << 24) & 0xff000000;
                break;
            case 1:
                store |= (b << 16) & 0x00ff0000;
                break;
            case 2:
                store |= (b << 8) & 0x0000ff00;
                break;
            case 3:
                store |= (b << 0) & 0x000000ff;
                break;
```

```
        }
        nBytes++;
        if (nBytes == 4) {
            hash = hash ^ store;
            nBytes = 0;
            store = 0;
        }
    }

    public void engineUpdate(byte b[], int offset, int length) {
        for (int i = 0; i < length; i++)
            engineUpdate(b[i + offset]);
    }

    public void engineReset() {
        hash = 0;
        store = 0;
        nBytes = 0;
    }

    public byte[] engineDigest() {
        while (nBytes != 0)
            engineUpdate((byte) 0);
        byte b[] = new byte[4];
        b[0] = (byte) (hash >>> 24);
        b[1] = (byte) (hash >>> 16);
        b[2] = (byte) (hash >>>  8);
        b[3] = (byte) (hash >>>  0);
        engineReset();
        return b;
    }
}
```

The implementation of this class is simple, which isn't surprising given the fact
that the algorithm itself is too simple to be considered an effective digest algorithm. The major points to observe are:

- The name of the class (XYZMessageDigest) and the name of the algorithm
  that it implements (XYZ) must match one of the strings in the provider package for this class to be found. Hence, in our provider class in Chapter 8, we
  included this property:

```
put("MessageDigest.XYZ", "com.xyz.XYZMessageDigest");
```

- Our constructor calls the only constructor available to us, and the string "XYZ"
  that we pass to that constructor takes on significance—it's the name of the
  algorithm we've implemented in this class. This in turn becomes the name
  that is registered in the security provider architecture; it must match the name
  of the algorithm we registered in our provider.

- In order for the getDigestLength() method to function, we chose to implement the Cloneable interface instead of overriding the engineGetDigestLength() method. Since there are no embedded objects in this class, we do not need to override the clone() method. The default implementation of that method (a shallow copy) is sufficient for this class.

- The engineUpdate() methods accumulate bytes of data until an integer has been accumulated, at which point that integer can be XOR-ed into the saved state held in the hash instance variable.

- The engineDigest() method converts the hash instance variable into a byte array and returns that to the programmer. Note that the engineDigest() method is responsible for resetting the internal state of the algorithm. In addition, the engineDigest() method is responsible for padding the data so that it is a multiple of four bytes (the size of a Java integer). This type of data padding is a common feature of message digest calculation.

- The engineReset() method initializes the algorithm to its initial state.

Once we have an implementation of a message digest, we must install it into the security provider architecture. If we use the XYZProvider class from Chapter 8, we can change our Send class above to use our new digest algorithm:

```java
public class SendXYZ {
    public static void main(String args[]) {
        try {
            Security.addProvider(new XYZProvider());
            FileOutputStream fos = new FileOutputStream("test.xyz");
            MessageDigest md = MessageDigest.getInstance("XYZ");
            ObjectOutputStream oos = new ObjectOutputStream(fos);
            String data = "This have I thought good to deliver thee, "+
                "that thou mightst not lose the dues of rejoicing " +
                "by being ignorant of what greatness is promised thee.";
            byte buf[] = data.getBytes();
            md.update(buf);
            oos.writeObject(data);
            oos.writeObject(md.digest());
        } catch (Exception e) {
            System.out.println(e);
        }
    }
}
```

Similar changes to the Receive class will allow us to accept the message that we've saved to the file *test.xyz*.

Summary

In this chapter, we've explored the first link in creating an authenticated and secure system: the message digest. The facility to calculate a message digest is straightforward and easy to use; the facility to write our own message digest class is equally straightforward.

The message digest by itself gives us some comfort about the state of the data it represents, but it does not give us a completely secure system. If we have a shared passphrase, we can construct a secure message digest (that is, a Message Authentication Code), but there are no easy means to share that passphrase. A MAC is similiar to a digital signature (where digital keys replace the passphrase); in the next few chapters, we'll continue our exploration of the API to provide the necessary components of a digital signature, beginning with an exploration of the keys required to create a digital signature.

10

Keys and Certificates

In this chapter, we discuss the classes in the Java security package that handle keys and certificates. Keys are a necessary component of many cryptographic algorithms—in particular, keys are required to create and verify digital signatures. The keys we're going to discuss in this chapter are public keys and private keys, since those are the keys most often used in a digital signature. Secret keys—used for encryption algorithms—are discussed in Chapter 13. We defer that discussion because secret keys do not come with standard Java implementations; they come only with the Java Cryptography Extension.

We also cover the implementation of certificates in this chapter. Certificates are used to authenticate keys; when keys are transmitted electronically, they are often embedded within certificates.

Keys and certificates are normally associated with some person or organization, and the way in which keys are stored, transmitted, and shared is an important topic in the security package. Management of keys is left for the next chapter, however; right now, we're just concerned about the APIs that implement keys and certificates. As usual, we'll show how a programmer interacts with keys and certificates, as well as how you might implement your own versions of each.

The classes and engines we discuss in this chapter are outlined in Figure 10-1. There are two engines that operate on keys:

- The KeyPairGenerator class generates keys from scratch. With no input (or, possibly, input to initialize it to a certain state), the generator can produce one or more pairs of keys.

- The KeyFactory class translates between key objects and their external representations, which may be either a byte array or a key specification; this translation goes both ways.

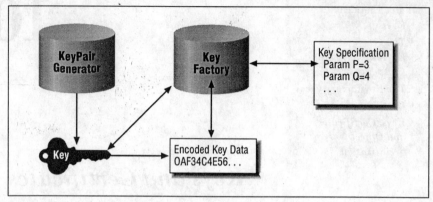

Figure 10-1. The interaction of key classes

There are a number of classes and interfaces we'll discuss to facilitate support for Figure 10-1; in addition to the engine classes themselves, there are several classes and interfaces that represent the key objects and the key specifications (the encoded key data is always an array of bytes). In an effort to provide the complete story, we'll delve into the details of all of these classes; for the most part, however, the important operations that most developers will need are:

- The ability to create a new pair of keys from scratch using the key pair generator

- The ability to export a key, either as a parameter specification or as a set of bytes, and the corresponding ability to import that data in order to create a key

This means that, for the most part, the data objects we explore in this chapter—the Key classes and interfaces as well as the various KeySpec classes (key specification classes)—can be treated by most programmers as opaque objects. We'll show their complete interface (which you might be curious about, and which is absolutely needed if you're writing your own security provider), but we'll try not to lose sight of the two goals of this chapter.

Also note that the idea of the key factory and key specifications is available only with Java 1.2.* In Java 1.1, you can get the encoded key data directly from a key, but that's a one-way operation.

Keys

Let's start with the various classes that support the notion of keys within Java.

---

* 1.2 is now Java 2.

The Key Interface

The concept of a key is modeled by the Key interface (java.security.Key):

public interface Key extends Serializable
> Model the concept of a single key. Because keys must be transferred to and from various entities, all keys must be serializable.

As we discussed in Chapter 8, there might be several algorithms available for generating (and understanding) keys, depending on the particular security providers that are installed in the virtual machine. Hence, the first thing a key needs to be able to tell us is what algorithm generated it:

public String getAlgorithm()
> Return a string describing the algorithm used to generated this key; this string should be the name of a standard key generation algorithm.

We listed the standard algorithm names for key generation in Chapter 8, but with the default provider with the JDK, this string is always DSA.

When a key is transferred between two parties, it is usually encoded as a series of bytes; this encoding must follow a format defined for the type of key. Keys are not required to support encoding—in which case the format of the data transferred between the two parties in a key exchange is either obvious (e.g., simply the serialized data of the key) or specific to a particular implementation. Keys tell us the format they use for encoding their output with this method:

public String getFormat()
> Return a string describing the format of the encoding the key supports.

For DSA keys produced by the Sun security provider, this format is always PKCS#8 for private keys and X.509 for public keys. The encoded data of the key itself is produced by this method:

public byte[] getEncoded()
> Return the bytes that make up the particular key in the encoding format the key supports. The encoded bytes are the external representation of the key in binary format.

Those are the only methods that a key is guaranteed to implement (other than methods of the Object class, of course; most implementations of keys override many of those methods). In particular, you'll note that there is nothing in the key interface that says anything about decoding a key. We'll say more about that later.

There are two additional key interfaces in the Java security API:

public interface PublicKey extends Key
public interface PrivateKey extends Key

These interfaces contain no additional methods. They are used simply for type convenience. A class that implements the PublicKey interface identifies itself as a public key, but it contains no methods that are different from any other key.

DSA keys

The keys supported by the Sun security provider are built around the DSA algorithm. DSA-generated keys are important enough to have several interfaces built around them; these interfaces enhance your ability to work with these specific types of keys. These interfaces are necessary because DSA keys have certain pieces of information that are not reflected in the default key interfaces: the DSA algorithm-specific parameters p, q, and g that are used to generate the keys. Knowledge of these variables is abstracted into the DSAParams interface (java.security.interfaces.DSAParams):

```
public interface DSAParams {
    public BigInteger getP();
    public BigInteger getQ();
    public BigInteger getG();
}
```

Keys that are generated by DSA will typically implement the DSAKey interface (java.security.interfaces.DSAKey):

public interface DSAKey

Provide DSA-specific information about a key.

Implementing this interface serves two purposes. First, it allows the programmer to determine if the key is a DSA key by checking its type. The second purpose is to allow the programmer to access the DSA parameters using this method in the DSAKey interface:

public DSAParams getParams()

Return the DSA parameters associated with this key.

These methods and interfaces allow us to do specific key manipulation like this:

```
public void printKey(Key k) {
    if (k instanceof DSAKey) {
        System.out.println("key is DSA");
        System.out.println("P value is " +
                    ((DSAKey) k).getParams().getP());
    }
    else System.out.println("key is not DSA");
}
```

The idea of a DSA key is extended even further by these two interfaces (both of which are in the java.security.interfaces package):

public interface DSAPrivateKey extends DSAKey
public interface DSAPublicKey extends DSAKey

These interfaces allow the programmer to retrieve the additional key-specific values (known as *y* for public keys and *x* for private keys in the DSA algorithm):

```
public void printKey(DSAKey k) {
    if (k instanceof DSAPublicKey)
        System.out.println("Public key value is " +
                                    ((DSAPublicKey) k).getY());
    else if (k instanceof DSAPrivateKey)
        System.out.println("Private key value is " +
                                    ((DSAPrivateKey) k).getX());
    else System.out.println("Bad key implementation");
}
```

DSA keys are often used in the Java world (and elsewhere in cryptography), and if you know you're dealing with DSA keys, these interfaces can be very useful. In particular, if you're writing a security provider that provides an implementation of DSA keys, you should ensure that you implement all of these interfaces correctly. For most programmers, however, keys are opaque objects, and the algorithm-specific features of DSA keys are not needed.

The KeyPair Class

There are no classes in the core JDK that implement any of the Key interfaces. However, there is one concrete class, the KeyPair class (java.security.KeyPair), that extends the abstraction of keys:

public final class KeyPair
    Model a data object that contains a public key and a private key.

The KeyPair class is a very simple data structure class, containing two pieces of information: a public key and a private key. When we need to generate our own keys (which we'll do next), we'll need to generate both the public and private key at once. This object will contain both of the necessary keys. If you're not interested in generating your own keys, this class may be ignored.

The KeyPair class contains only two methods:

public PublicKey getPublic()
public PrivateKey getPrivate()
    Return the desired key from the key pair.

A key pair object is instantiated through a single constructor:

public KeyPair(PublicKey pub, PrivateKey priv)
    Create a key pair object, initializing each member of the pair.

In theory, a key pair should not be initialized without both members of the pair being present; there is nothing, however, that prevents us from passing null as one of the keys. Similarly, there are no security provisions within the KeyPair class that prevent the private key from being accessed—no calls to the security manager are made when the getPrivate() method is invoked. Hence the KeyPair class should be used with caution.

The KeyPairGenerator Class

Generation of public and private keys is one of the standard engines that can be provided by a Java security provider. This operation is provided by the KeyPair-Generator class (java.security.KeyPairGenerator):

public abstract class KeyPairGenerator
    Generate and provide information about public/private key pairs.

    In Java 1.1, this class extends only the Object class; in Java 1.2, this class extends the KeyPairGeneratorSpi class (java.security.KeyPairGenera-torSpi). As is usual with this architecture, some of the methods we're going to use are methods of the KeyPairGenerator class in Java 1.1 and methods of the KeyPairGeneratorSpi class in 1.2; for the developer, the end result is the same.

Generating a key pair is a very time-consuming operation. Fortunately, it does not need to be performed often; much of the time, we obtain keys from a key management system rather than generating them. However, when we establish our own key management system in the next chapter, we'll need to use this class; it is often easier to generate your own keys from scratch rather than use a key management system as well.

Using the KeyPairGenerator Class

Like all engine classes, the KeyPairGenerator is an abstract class for which there is no implementation in the core API. However, it is possible to retrieve instances of the KeyPairGenerator class via these methods:

public static KeyPairGenerator getInstance(String algorithm)
public static KeyPairGenerator getInstance(String algorithm, String provider)
    Find the implementation of the engine that generates key pairs with the named algorithm. The algorithm should be one of the standard API algorithm

names; if an appropriate implementation cannot be found, this method throws a `NoSuchAlgorithmException`.

The first format of this method searches all available providers according to the rules we outlined in Chapter 8. The second method searches only the named provider, throwing a `NoSuchProviderException` if that provider has not been loaded.

These methods search the providers that have been registered with the security provider interface for a key pair generator that supports the named algorithm. In the Sun security provider, this method allows us to retrieve the key pair generator that generates keys using the DSA algorithm.

Once we have the key pair generator, we can invoke any of the following methods on it:

public String getAlgorithm()

Return the name of the algorithm that this key pair generator implements (e.g., DSA).

public void initialize(int strength)
public abstract void initialize(int strength, SecureRandom random)

Initialize the key pair generator to generate keys of the given strength. The idea of strength is common among key pair generator algorithms; typically it means the number of bits that are used as input to the engine to calculate the key pair, but the actual meaning may vary between algorithms.

Most key algorithms restrict on the values that are valid for `strength`. In the case of DSA, the strength must be between 512 and 1024 and it must be a multiple of 64. If an invalid number is passed for `strength`, an `InvalidParameterException` will be thrown.

Key pairs typically require a random number generator to assist them. You may specify a particular random number generator if desired; otherwise, a default random number generator (an instance of the `SecureRandom` class) is used.

In Java 1.2, the second of these methods is inherited from the `KeyPairGeneratorSpi` class.

public void initialize(AlgorithmParameterSpec params) ★
public void initialize(AlgorithmParameterSpec params, SecureRandom random) ★

Initialize the key pair generator using the specified parameter set (which we'll discuss a little later). By default, the first method simply calls the second method with a default instance of the `SecureRandom` class; the second method, by default, will throw an `UnsupportedOperationException`. The second of these methods is inherited from the `KeyPairGeneratorSpi` class.

public abstract KeyPair generateKeyPair()

public final KeyPair genKeyPair() ★

Generate a key pair, using the initialization parameters previously specified. A `KeyPairGenerator` object can repeatedly generate key pairs by calling one of these methods; each new call generates a new key pair. The `genKeyPair()` method simply calls the `generateKeyPair()` method.

In Java 1.2, the `generateKeyPair()` method is inherited from the SPI.

Using these methods, generating a pair of keys is very straightforward:

```
KeyPairGenerator kpg = KeyPairGenerator.getInstance("DSA");
kpg.initialize(512);
KeyPair kp = kpg.generateKeyPair();
```

According to the Java documentation, you are allowed to generate a key pair without initializing the generator; in this situation, a default strength and random number generator are to be used. However, this feature does not work with the Sun security provider in 1.1: a `NullPointerException` is thrown from within the `generateKeyPair()` method. Since it is possible that third-party providers may behave similarly, it is always best to initialize the key pair generator.

We'll show what to do with these keys in the next chapter, when we discuss the topic of key management.

Generating DSA Keys

The abstraction provided by the key pair generator is usually all we need to generate keys. However, sometimes the particular algorithm needs additional information to generate a key pair. When a DSA key pair is generated, default values for p, q, and g are used; in the Sun security provider, these values are pre-computed to support strength values of 512 and 1024. Precomputing these values greatly reduces the time required to calculate a DSA key. Third-party DSA providers may provide precomputed values for additional strength values.

It is possible to ask the key generator to use different values for p, q, and g if the key pair generator supports the `DSAKeyPairGenerator` interface (`java.security.interfaces.DSAKeyPairGenerator`):

public interface DSAKeyPairGenerator

Provide a mechanism by which the DSA-specific parameters of the key pair engine can be manipulated.

There are two methods in this interface:

public void initialize(int modlen, boolean genParams, SecureRandom random)

Initialize the DSA key pair generator. The modulus length is the number of bits used to calculate the parameters; this must be any multiple of 8 between

512 and 1024. If genParams is true, then the *p*, *q*, and *g* parameters will be generated for this new modulus length; otherwise, a precomputed value will be used (but precomputed values in the Sun security provider are available only for modlen values of 512 and 1024). If the modulus length is invalid, this method throws an InvalidParameterException.

public void initialize(DSAParams params, SecureRandom random)
Initialize the DSA key pair generator. The *p*, *q*, and *g* parameters are set from the values passed in params. If the parameters are not correct, an InvalidParameterException is generated.

As with the DSAKey interface, a DSA key pair generator implements the DSAKeyPairGenerator interface for two purposes: for type identification, and to allow the programmer to initialize the key pair generator with the desired algorithm-specific parameters:

```
KeyPairGenerator kpg = KeyPairGenerator.getInstance("DSA");
if (kpg instanceof DSAKeyPairGenerator) {
    DSAKeyPairGenerator dkpg = (DSAKeyPairGenerator) kpg;
    dkpg.initialize(512, true, new SecureRandom());
}
else kpg.initialize(512);
```

In sum, this interface allows us to use the generic key pair generator interface while providing an escape clause that allows us to perform DSA-specific operations.

Implementing a Key Pair Generator

If you want to implement your own key pair generator—either using a new algorithm or, more typically, a new implementation of a standard algorithm—you need to create a concrete subclass of the KeyPairGenerator class. In Java 1.2, you may create a subclass of the KeyPairGeneratorSpi class instead; in this case, the SPI is the superclass of the engine class.

To construct a key pair generator, there is a single protected method at your disposal:

protected KeyPairGenerator(String name)
Construct a key pair generator that implements the given algorithm.

As with the other engines in the security API, there is no default constructor available within the engine class. When the key pair generator is constructed, it must pass the name of the algorithm that it implements to its superclass so that the algorithm name may be correctly registered with the Security class.

There are two abstract public methods of the key pair generator (or its SPI) that we must implement in our key pair generator: the initialize() method and the generateKeyPair() method. For this example, we'll generate a simple key pair that could be used for a simple rotation-based encryption scheme. In this scheme, the key serves as an offset that we add to each ASCII character—hence, if the key is 1, an encryption based on this key converts the letter a to the letter b, and so on (the addition is performed with a modulus such that z will map to a). To support this encryption, then, we need to generate a public key that is simply a number between 1 and 25; the private key is simply the negative value of the public key.

We must also define a class to represent keys we're implementing.* We can do that with this class:

```
public class XYZKey implements Key, PublicKey, PrivateKey {
    int rotValue;

    public String getAlgorithm() {
        return "XYZ";
    }

    public String getFormat() {
        return "XYZ Special Format";
    }

    public byte[] getEncoded() {
        byte b[] = new byte[4];
        b[3] = (byte) ((rotValue << 24) & 0xff);
        b[2] = (byte) ((rotValue << 16) & 0xff);
        b[1] = (byte) ((rotValue <<  8) & 0xff);
        b[0] = (byte) ((rotValue <<  0) & 0xff);
        return b;
    }
}
```

The only data value our key class cares about is the value to be used as the index; for simplicity, we've made it a simple instance variable accessible only by classes in our package. Because this example is simple, we can use the same class as the interface for the public and the private key; normally, of course, public and private keys are not symmetric like this.

With these pieces in place, we're ready to define our key pair generation class:

```
public class XYZKeyPairGenerator extends KeyPairGenerator {
    SecureRandom random;

    public XYZKeyPairGenerator() {
```

---

* This is true even if you're implementing the DSA algorithm—the classes the Sun security provider uses to represent keys are not in the java package, so they are unavailable to us. So even if you're implementing DSA, you must still define classes that implement all the DSA interfaces we looked at earlier.

```
        super("XYZ");
    }

    public void initialize(int strength, SecureRandom sr) {
        random = sr;
    }

    public KeyPair generateKeyPair() {
        int rotValue = random.nextInt() % 25;
        XYZKey pub = new XYZKey();
        XYZKey priv = new XYZKey();
        pub.rotValue = rotValue;
        priv.rotValue = -rotValue;
        KeyPair kp = new KeyPair(pub, priv);
        return kp;
    }
}
```

As a last step, we must install this class using the security provider architecture that we examined in Chapter 8. Now obtaining a new key pair for the XYZ algorithm is as simple as substituting the string XYZ for the algorithm name in the example we gave earlier for DSA key pair generation.

The KeyFactory Class

Although there are times when you'll generate your own keys, they are more often obtained electronically. The next engine and related set of classes we'll examine show us how to import and export keys. The source or destination of these keys is not specified by any of these classes—you may have read the data from a file, or from a socket, or you may have typed it in manually. The classes in this section merely enable you to convert a key object to a known external representation and to perform the reverse conversion.

Key factories are available only in Java 1.2. Exporting keys in 1.1 is simple: the encoded bytes of the key can be obtained and transmitted in any manner that is convenient. But importing keys in 1.1 is very difficult, because there is no way to take the encoded bytes and produce a key from them. As a fallback measure, you can serialize a key object to export it and then deserialize that data to import the key, although that's not something we generally recommend (see "Keys, Certificates, and Object Serialization" later in this chapter).

There are two external representations by which a key may be transmitted—by its encoded format, or by the parameters that were used to generate the key. Either of these representations may be encapsulated in a key specification, which is used to interact with the KeyFactory class (java.security.KeyFactory) that actually imports and exports keys:

public class KeyFactory ★

Provide an infrastructure for importing and exporting keys according to the specific encoding format or parameters of the key.

Using the KeyFactory class

The KeyFactory class is an engine class, which provides the typical method of instantiating itself:

public static final KeyFactory getInstance(String alg) ★
public static final KeyFactory getInstance(String alg, String provider) ★

Create a key factory capable of importing and exporting keys that were generated with the given algorithm. The class that implements the key factory comes from the named provider or is located according to the standard rules for provider engines. If a key factory that implements the given algorithm is not found, a NoSuchAlgorithmException is generated. If the named provider is not found, a NoSuchProviderException is generated.

A key factory presents the following public methods:

public final Provider getProvider() ★

Return the provider that implemented this particular key factory.

public final PublicKey generatePublic(KeySpec ks) ★
public final PrivateKey generatePrivate(KeySpec ks) ★

These methods are used to import a key: they create the key based on the imported data that is held in the key specification object. If the key cannot be created, an InvalidKeySpecException is thrown.

public final KeySpec getKeySpec(Key key, Class keySpec) ★

This method is used to export a key: it creates a key specification based on the actual key. If the key specification cannot be created, an InvalidKeySpecException is thrown.

public final Key translateKey(Key key) ★

Translate a key from an unknown source into a key that was generated from this object. This method can be used to convert the type of a key that was loaded from a different security provider (e.g., a DSA key generated from the XYZ provider—type com.XYZ.DSAPrivateKey—could be converted to a DSA key generated from the Sun provider—type sun.security.provider.DSAPrivateKey). If the key cannot be translated, an InvalidKeyException is generated.

public final String getAlgorithm() ★

Return the algorithm this key factory supports.

We'll defer examples of these methods until we discuss the KeySpec class later.

Implementing a Key Factory

Like all engines, the key factory depends on a service provider interface class: the KeyFactorySpi class (java.security.KeyFactorySpi):

public abstract class KeyFactorySpi ★

Provide the set of methods necessary to implement a key factory that is capable of importing and exporting keys in a particular format.

However, since the KeyFactory class did not exist in 1.1, its SPI is unrelated in the class hierarchy. Implementing a key factory therefore requires that we subclass the SPI rather than subclassing the KeyFactory class directly. The KeyFactorySpi class is required to implement a key factory because the KeyFactory class contains only this constructor:

protected KeyFactory(KeyFactorySpi keyFacSpi, Provider provider, String algorithm)

Construct a key factory based on the given factory service provider class that is implemented by the given provider and that provides keys of the given algorithm.

This constructor is called by the Security class itself; all we need to do is ensure that the class we register with the security provider interface is a subclass of the KeyFactorySpi class.

The KeyFactorySpi class contains the following methods; since each of these methods is abstract, our class must provide an implementation of all of them:

protected abstract PublicKey engineGeneratePublic(KeySpec ks) ★
protected abstract PrivateKey engineGeneratePrivate(KeySpec ks) ★

Generate of the public or private key. Depending on the key specification, this means either decoding the data of the key or regenerating the key based on specific parameters to the key algorithm. If the key cannot be generated, an InvalidKeyException should be thrown.

protected abstract KeySpec engineGetKeySpec(Key key, Class keySpec) ★

Export the key. Depending on the key class specification, this means either encoding the data (e.g., by calling the getEncoded() method) or saving the parameters that were used to generate the key. If the specification cannot be created, an InvalidKeySpecException should be thrown.

protected Key engineTranslateKey(Key key) ★

Perform the actual translation of the key. This is typically performed by translating the key to its specification and back. If the key cannot be translated, an InvalidKeyException should be thrown.

Although we show how to use a key factory later, we won't show how to implement one; the amount of code involved is large and relatively uninteresting. However, the online examples do contain a sample key factory implementation if you're interested in seeing one.

Key Specifications

Importing and exporting a key are based on classes that implement the KeySpec interface (java.security.spec.KeySpec):

public interface KeySpec ★
> Identify a class as one that is able to hold data that can be used to generate a key.

The KeySpec interface is an empty interface; it is used for type identification only. This interface in turn forms the basis of two interfaces, each of which handles one method of importing a key.

The EncodedKeySpec class

Earlier, we mentioned that the Key class must provide a getEncoded() method for the key that outputs a series of bytes in a format specific to the type of key; this format is generally part of the specification for the key algorithm. For DSA keys, for example, the encoding format might be PKCS#8 or X.509. An encoded key specification holds the encoded data for a key and is defined by the EncodedKey-Spec class (java.security.spec.EncodedKeySpec):

public abstract class EncodedKeySpec implements KeySpec ★
> Provide an object to hold the encoded data of a key.

An encoded key specification can be operated on via these methods:

public abstract byte[] getEncoded() ★
> Return the actual encoded data held by the object.

public abstract String getFormat() ★
> Return the string that represents the format of the encoded data (e.g., PKCS#8).

There are two core classes that provide a concrete implementation of this class (both of which are in the java.security.spec package):

public class PKCS8EncodedKeySpec extends EncodedKeySpec ★
public class X509EncodedKeySpec extends EncodedKeySpec ★
> Provide an implementation of the encoded key specification. The PCKS8 encoded key specification is used for DSA private keys, and the X509 encoded key specification is used for DSA public keys.

Both of these classes are constructed by passing in the encoded data:

public PKCS8EncodedKeySpec(byte data[]) ★
public X509EncodedKeySpec(byte data[]) ★

> Construct an encoded key specification object that holds the given encoded data. The format of the data is not checked for validity. The input data is saved within the object to be returned via the getEncoded() method.

Taken together, the methods of these classes allow us to import and export keys. Keys are exported via the getEncoded() method, and they are imported by constructing an object based on the encoded bytes.

The AlgorithmParameterSpec interface

In addition to their encoded format, keys are typically able to be specified by providing the parameters to the algorithm that produced the key. Specifying keys in this manner is a function of the AlgorithmParameterSpec interface (java.security.spec.AlgorithmParameterSpec):

public interface AlgorithmParameterSpec ★

> Provide an infrastructure for specifying keys based on the parameters used to generate them.

Like the KeySpec interface, this interface provides no methods and is used only for type identification. The DSAParameterSpec class (java.security.spec.DSAParameterSpec) is the single core class that implements this interface:

public class DSAParameterSpec implements AlgorithmParameterSpec, DSAParams ★

> Provide a class that holds the parameters used to generate a DSA key.

As we mentioned earlier, there are three parameters that are common to all DSA keys: p, q, and g. Hence, an instance of this class can be constructed as follows:

public DSAParameterSpec(BigInteger p, BigInteger q, BigInteger g) ★

> Create an object that holds the common parameters used to generate a DSA key.

The only methods of this class are used to retrieve those parameters:

public BigInteger getP() ★
public BigInteger getQ() ★
public BigInteger getG() ★

> Return the parameter held by the specification object.

While those three parameters are common to every DSA key, a DSA public key has an additional parameter (y) and a DSA private key has a different additional parameter (*x*). Hence, to represent a DSA key fully requires one of these classes (both of which are in the `java.security.spec` package):

public class DSAPublicKeySpec implements KeySpec ★
public class DSAPrivateKeySpec implements KeySpec ★

Provide an object to hold all parameters of a DSA public or private key.

Instances of these classes are constructed by providing all parameters:

public DSAPublicKeySpec(BigInteger y, BigInteger p, BigInteger q, BigInteger g) ★
public DSAPrivateKeySpec(BigInteger x, BigInteger p, BigInteger q, BigInteger g) ★

Create an object that holds all the parameters used to generate a DSA key.

This final parameter can be retrieved via a class-specific method (`getX()` or `getY()` as appropriate).

Once again, these classes in total allow us to export keys (via the various `get*()` methods) and to import keys via the constructors.

A Key Factory Example

As we mentioned at the beginning of this section, the prime reason for key factories is that they give us the ability to import and export keys. Exporting a key specification is typically done by transmitting the individual data elements of the key specification (those individual elements vary by the type of key). Importing a key specification typically involves constructing the specification with the transmitted elements as parameters to the constructor.

Here's an example using a DSA algorithmic parameter specification. We'll look first at exporting a key:

```
public class Export {
    public static void main(String args[]) {
        try {
            KeyPairGenerator kpg = KeyPairGenerator.getInstance("DSA");
            kpg.initialize(512, new SecureRandom());
            KeyPair kp = kpg.generateKeyPair();
            Class spec = Class.forName(
                            "java.security.spec.DSAPrivateKeySpec");
            KeyFactory kf = KeyFactory.getInstance("DSA");
            DSAPrivateKeySpec ks = (DSAPrivateKeySpec)
                            kf.getKeySpec(kp.getPrivate(), spec);
            FileOutputStream fos = new FileOutputStream("exportedKey");
            ObjectOutputStream oos = new ObjectOutputStream(fos);
            oos.writeObject(ks.getX());
            oos.writeObject(ks.getP());
            oos.writeObject(ks.getQ());
            oos.writeObject(ks.getG());
```

```
        } catch (Exception e) {
            e.printStackTrace();
        }
    }
}
```

Two items are interesting in this code. First, one argument to the getKeySpec() method is a class object, requiring us to construct the class object using the forName() method (a somewhat unusual usage). Then, once we have the key specification itself, we have to figure out how to transmit the specification. Since in this case, the specification is an algorithmic specification, we chose to write out the individual parameters from the specification.* If we had used an encoded key specification, we simply would have written out the byte array returned from the getEncoded() method.

We can import this key as follows:

```
public class Import {
    public static void main(String args[]) {
        try {
            FileInputStream fis = new FileInputStream("exportedKey");
            ObjectInputStream ois = new ObjectInputStream(fis);
            DSAPrivateKeySpec ks = new DSAPrivateKeySpec(
                    (BigInteger) ois.readObject(),
                    (BigInteger) ois.readObject(),
                    (BigInteger) ois.readObject(),
                    (BigInteger) ois.readObject());
            KeyFactory kf = KeyFactory.getInstance("DSA");
            PrivateKey pk = kf.generatePrivate(ks);
            System.out.println("Got private key");
        } catch (Exception e) {
            e.printStackTrace();
        }
    }
}
```

This example is predictably symmetric to exporting a key.

Certificates

When you are given a public and private key, you often need to provide other people with your public key. If you sign a digital document (using your private key), the recipient of that document will need your public key in order to verify your digital signature.

---

* The DSAPrivateKeySpec class—like all key specification classes—is not serializable itself. But for reasons that we'll discuss later, it's better not to serialize key classes that are to be imported into another Java VM anyway.

The inherent problem with a key is that it does not provide any information about the identity to which it belongs; a key is really just a sequence of seemingly arbitrary numbers. If I want you to accept a document that I digitally signed, I could mail you my public key, but you normally have no assurance that the key (and the original email) came from me at all. I could, of course, digitally sign the e-mail so that you knew that it came from me, but there's a circular chain here—without my public key, you cannot verify the digital signature. You would need my public key in order to authenticate the public key I've just sent you.

Certificates solve this problem by having a well-known entity (called a certificate authority, or CA) verify the public key that is being sent to you. A certificate can give you the assurance that the public key in the certificate does indeed belong to the entity that the certificate authority says it does. However, the certificate only validates the public key it contains: just because Fred sends you his public key in a valid certificate does not mean that Fred is to be trusted; it only means that the public key in question does in fact belong to Fred.

In practice, the key may not belong to Fred at all; certificate authorities have different levels at which they assess the identity of the entity named in the certificate. Some of these levels are very stringent and require the CA to do an extensive verification that Fred is who he says he is. Other levels are not stringent at all, and if Fred can produce a few dollars and a credit card, he is assumed to be Fred. Hence, one of the steps in the process of deciding whether or not to trust the entity named in the certificate includes the level at which the certificate authority generated the certificate. Each certificate authority varies in its approach to validating identities, and each publishes its approach to help you understand the potential risks involved in accepting such a certificate.

A certificate contains three pieces of information (as shown in Figure 10-2):

- The name of the entity for whom the certificate has been issued. This entity is referred to as the subject of the certificate.

- The public key associated with the subject.

- A digital signature that verifies the information of the certificate. The certificate is signed by the issuer of the certificate.

Because the certificate carries a digital signature of the certificate authority, we can verify that digital signature—and if the verification succeeds, we can be assured that the public key in the certificate does in fact belong to the entity the certificate claims (subject to the level at which the CA verified the subject).

We still have a bootstrapping problem here—how do we obtain the public key of the certificate authority? We could have a certificate that contains the public key of the certificate authority, but who is going to authenticate *that* certificate?

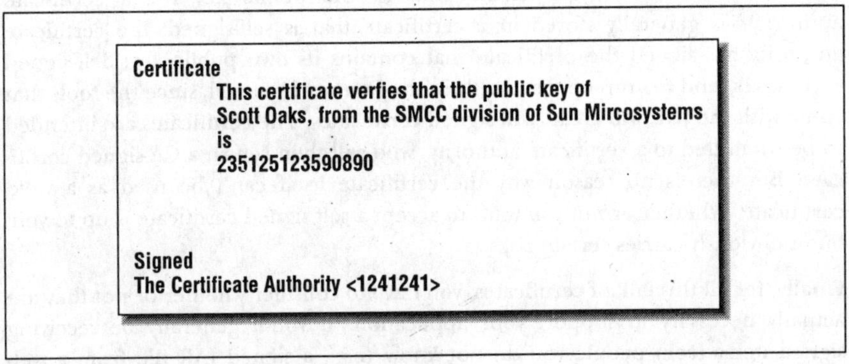

```
Certificate
    This certificate verfies that the public key of
    Scott Oaks, from the SMCC division of Sun Mircosystems
    is
    235125123590890



Signed
The Certificate Authority <1241241>
```

Figure 10-2. Logical representation of a certificate

This bootstrapping problem is one reason why key management (see Chapter 11) is such a hard topic. Most Java-enabled browsers solve this problem by providing the public keys for certain well-known certificate authorities along with the browser. This has worked well in practice, though it clearly is not an airtight solution (especially when the browser is downloaded from some site on the Internet— theoretically, the certificates that come with the browser could be tampered with as they are in transit). Although there are various proposals to strengthen this model, for now we will assume that the certificate of at least one well-known certificate authority is delivered along with the Java application. This situation allows me to mail you a certificate containing my public key; if the certificate is signed by a certificate authority you know about, you are assured that the public key actually belongs to me.

There are many well-known certificate authorities—and therein lies another problem. I may send you a certificate that is signed by the United States Post Office, but that certificate authority may not be one of the certificate authorities you recognize. Simply sending a public key in a certificate does not mean that the recipient of the public key will accept it. A more important implication of this is that a key management system needs to be prepared to assign multiple certificates to a particular individual, potentially one from each of several certificate authorities.

Another implication of this profusion of certificate authorities is that certificates are often supplied as a chain. Let's say that you have the certificate of the U.S. Post Office certificate authority, and I want to send you my certificate that has been generated by the Acme Certificate company. In order for you to accept this certificate, I must send you a chain of certificates: my certificate (certified by the Acme Certificate company), and a certificate for the Acme Certificate company (certified by the U.S. Post Office). This chain of certificates may be arbitrarily long.

The last certificate in this chain—that is, the public key for a certificate authority—is generally stored in a certificate that is self-signed: the certificate authority has signed the certificate that contains its own public key. Self-signed certificates tend to crop up frequently in the Java world as well, since the tools that come with the JDK will create self-signed certificates. The certificates are intended to be submitted to a certificate authority, who will then return a CA-signed certificate. But there's no reason why the certificate itself can't be used as a valid certificate. Whether or not you want to accept a self-signed certificate is up to you, but it obviously carries certain risks. ·

Finally, for all this talk of certificates, you have to consider whether or not they are actually necessary to support your application. If you'll generally be receiving signed items from people you do not know (e.g., a signed JAR file from a web site), then they are absolutely necessary. On the other hand, large-scale computer installations often consider using certificates to authenticate and validate their employees; this results in a computer system that has much better internal security than one that relies solely on passwords. But it is not the certificate that generates the security advantage, it is the use of public key cryptography. The computer installation can achieve the same level of security without using a certificate infrastructure.

Consider the security necessary to support XYZ Corporation's payroll application. When an employee wants to view her payroll statements, she must submit a digitally signed request to do so. Hence, XYZ should distribute to each employee a private key to be used to create the digital signature. XYZ can also store the employee's public keys in a database; when a request comes that claims to be from a particular employee, the payroll server can simply examine the database to obtain that employee's public key and verify the signature. No certificate is required in this case—and in general, no certificate is required when the recipient of the digital signature is already known to have the public key of the entity that signed the data. For applications within a corporation, this is almost always the case.

We issue this caveat about certificates being necessary because certificate support in Java (even in Java 1.2) is not fully complete—while it is possible to set up your own certificate authority to distribute the certificates for your company, it's very hard to write the necessary code to do that in Java (at present). Hence, we'll focus our discussion of the certificate API on accepting (i.e., validating) existing certificates.

The Certificate Class

There are many formats that a certificate can take (depending on the cryptographic algorithms used to produce the certificate). Hence, the Java API abstracts

Certificate: Class or Interface

There's an unfortunate ambiguity in Java's use of the term "certificate." In Java 1.1, an interface called java.security.Certificate was introduced and used by the javakey utility and by the appletviewer when they used signed classes. The Certificate interface was implemented by platform-specific classes.

In Java 1.2, there is a new class called java.security.cert.Certificate. This class is the preferred class for all interactions with certificates, and is used by the utilities provided with the 1.2 JDK. The java.security.Certificate interface has been deprecated starting with Java 1.2.

One problem where this manifests itself is with import statements. If you import the following packages:

```
import java.security.*;
import java.security.cert.*;
```

the compiler will be unable to reconcile the definition of Certificate. When dealing with certificates, you'll either need to refer to them by their fully qualified name or only import those classes in the security package that you explicitly need.

In the main text of this book, whenever we talk about a certificate object, we mean an instance of the java.security.cert.Certificate class (or one of its subclasses). Except for some examples in Appendix B, we will not show usage of the Certificate interface.

---

the generic notion of a certificate with the Certificate class (java.security.cert.Certificate):

public abstract class Certificate ★

Provide the necessary (and very basic) operations to support a certificate.

Like many classes in the Java security package, the Certificate class is abstract; it relies upon application-specific classes to provide its implementation. In the case of the JDK, there are classes in the sun package that implement certain certificate formats (but more about that in just a bit).

There are three essential operations that you can perform upon a certificate:

public abstract byte[] getEncoded() ★

Return a byte array of the certificate. All certificates must have a format in which they may be transmitted as a series of bytes, but the details of this encoding format are specific to the type of the certificate. If the encoding cannot be generated, a `CertificateEncodingException` is thrown.

public abstract void verify(PublicKey pk) ★
public abstract void verify(PublicKey pk, String provider) ★

Verify that the certificate is valid. In order to verify a certificate, you must have the public key of the certificate authority that issued it; a valid certificate is one in which the signature of the certificate authority is valid. A valid certificate does not imply anything about the trustworthiness of the certificate authority or the subject to which the certificate belongs; it merely means that the signature in the certificate is valid for the supplied public key. If the certificate is invalid, this method throws a `CertificateException`.

The signature is verified according to the digital signature details we'll examine in Chapter 12. The process of creating an object to verify the digital signature as well as the actual verification of the signature may thrown a `NoSuchProviderException`, a `NoSuchAlgorithmException`, an `InvalidKeyException`, or a `SignatureException`.

public abstract PublicKey getPublicKey() ★

Extract the public key from the certificate—that is, the key that belongs to the subject the certificate vouches for.

These are the basic operations that are valid for any certificate. Notice that while we can encode a certificate into a byte array in order to transmit the certificate, there is nothing in the basic API that allows us to create a certificate from such a byte array. In fact, there's no practical way to instantiate a certificate object at all; the `Certificate` class is usually used as a base class from which individual certificate types are derived. Fortunately, the next class allows us to import certificates.

The CertificateFactory Class

If you need to import a certificate into a program, you do so by using the `CertificateFactory` class (`java.security.cert.CertificateFactory`). That class is an engine class, and it has the following interface:

public static CertificateFactory getInstance(String type) ★
public static CertificateFactory getInstance(String type, String provider) ★

Return a certificate factory that may be used to import certificates of the specified type (optionally implemented by the given provider). A `CertificateException` will be thrown if the given factory cannot be found or created; if the given provider is not found, a `NoSuchProviderException` will be thrown. The default Sun security provider has one certificate factory that works with certificates of type X509.

public String getProvider()★

Return the provider that implemented this factory.

public String getType()★

Return the type of certificates that this factory can import.

public final Certificate generateCertificate(InputStream is)★

Return a certificate that has been read in from the specified input stream. For the default Sun security provider, the input stream must be an X509 certificate in RFC 1421 format (that is, a DER-encoded certificate that has been translated into 7-bit ASCII characters); this is the most common format for transmission of X509 certificates.

public final Collection generateCertificates(InputStream is)★

Return a collection of certificates that have been defined in the given input stream. For the default Sun provider, the input stream in this case may have a single RFC 1421 formatted certificate, or it may contain a certificate chain in PKCS#7 format.

public final CRL generateCRL(InputStream is)★

Define a certificate revocation list from the data in the input stream.

public final Collection generateCRLs(InputStream is)★

Define a collection of CRLs from the data in the input stream.

Note that the `CertificateFactory` class cannot generate a new certificate—it may only import a certificate from an input stream. This is one reason why it's hard to provide a certificate authority based solely on the standard Java API. In the next section, we'll see an example of reading a certificate through this interface.

The `CertificateFactory` is an engine class, so it has a companion SPI class—the `CertificateFactorySpi` class—that can be used if you want to implement your own certificate factory. Implementing such a class follows the familiar rules of engine classes: you must define a constructor that takes the type name as a parameter and then, for each of the public methods listed above, you must implement a corresponding engine method with the same parameters. Certificates are complicated things, and parsing their encoding is a complicated procedure, so we won't bother showing an example of the engine class.

The X509Certificate Class

As we mentioned, there are many certificate formats that could be in use by a key management system; one of the most common of these is the X509 format. X509 has gone through a few revisions; the version supported by the Java API is version 3. This format is an ANSI standard for certificates, and while there are PGP and other certificate formats in the world, the X509 format is dominant. This is the only format of certificate for which Java provides a standard API; if you want to support another certificate format, you must implement your own subclass of Certificate.

The X509Certificate class (java.security.cert.X509Certificate) is defined as follows:

public abstract class X509Certificate extends Certificate implements X509Extension ★

Provide an infrastructure to support X509 version 3 formatted certificates.

An X509 certificate has a number of properties that are not shared by its base class:

- A start and end date: An X509 certificate is valid only for a certain period of time, as specified by these dates.

- A version: Various versions of the X509 standard exist; the default implementation of this class supports version 3 of the standard.

- A serial number: Each certificate that is issued by a certificate authority must have a unique serial number. The serial number is only unique for a particular authority, so that the combination of serial number and certificate authority guarantee a unique certificate.

- The distinguished name* of the certificate authority.

- The distinguished name of the subject represented by the certificate.

These properties can be retrieved with the following set of methods:

public abstract void checkValidity() ★
public abstract void checkValidity(Date d) ★

Check that the specified date (or today if no date is specified) is within the start and end dates for which the certificate is valid. If the specified date is before the start date of the certificate, a CertificateNotYetValidException is thrown; if it is after the end date of the certificate, a CertificateExpiredException is thrown.

public abstract int getVersion() ★

Return the version of the X509 specification that this certificate was created with. For the Sun implementation, this will be version 3.

public abstract BigInteger getSerialNumber() ★

Return the serial number of the certificate.

---

* See the sidebar "What's in a Name?" in Chapter 11 for an explanation of distinguished names.

public abstract Principal getIssuerDN() ★

Extract the distinguished name of the certificate authority from the certificate and use that name to instantiate a principal object.

public abstract Principal getSubjectDN() ★

Extract the distinguished name of the subject entity in the certificate and use that name to instantiate a principal object.

public abstract Date getNotBefore() ★

Return the first date on which the certificate is valid.

public abstract Date getNotAfter() ★

Return the date after which the certificate is invalid.

From a programmatic view, these are the most useful of the attributes of a certificate. If your X509 certificate is contained in the file *sdo.cer*, you could import and print out information about the certificate as follows:

```java
public class PrintCert {
    public static void main(String args[]) {
        try {
            FileInputStream fr = new FileInputStream("sdo.cer");
            CertificateFactory cf =
                    CertificateFactory.getInstance("X509");
            X509Certificate c = (X509Certificate)
                            cf.generateCertificate(fr);
            System.out.println("Read in the following certificate:");
            System.out.println("\tCertificate for: " +
                                    c.getSubjectDN());
            System.out.println("\tCertificate issued by: " +
                                    c.getIssuerDN());
            System.out.println("\tThe certificate is valid from " +
                        c.getNotBefore() + " to " + c.getNotAfter());
            System.out.println("\tCertificate SN# " +
                                    c.getSerialNumber());
            System.out.println("\tGenerated with " +
                                    c.getSigAlgName());
        } catch (Exception e) {
            e.printStackTrace();
        }
    }
}
```

Running this program would produce the following output:

```
Read in the following certificate:
    Certificate for:
        CN=Scott Oaks, OU=SMCC, O=Sun Microsystems, L=NY, S=NY, C=US
    Certificate issued by:
        CN=Scott Oaks, OU=SMCC, O=Sun Microsystems, L=NY, S=NY, C=US
    The certificate is valid from Sun Oct 19 11:40:24 EDT 1997 to
```

```
         Sat Jan 17 10:40:24 EST 1998
       Certificate SN# 3895020084
       Generated with SHA1withDSA
```

Advanced X509Certificate Methods

There are a number of other methods of the X509Certificate class. For the purposes of this book, these methods are not generally useful; they enable you to perform more introspection on the certificate itself. We'll list these methods here simply as a matter of record.

public abstract byte[] getTBSCertificate() ★

Get the DER-encoded TBS certificate. The TBS certificate is the body of the actual certificate; it contains all the naming and key information held in the certificate. The only information in the actual certificate that is not held in the TBS certificate is the name of the algorithm used to sign the certificate and the signature itself.

The TBS certificate is used as the input data to the signature algorithm when the certificate is signed or verified.

public abstract byte[] getSignature() ★

Get the raw signature bytes of the certificate. These bytes could be used to verify the signature explicitly (e.g., using the methods we'll describe in Chapter 12) instead of relying upon the verify() method to do so.

public abstract String getSigAlgName() ★

Return the name of the algorithm that was used to sign the certificate. For the Sun implementation, this will always be SHA1withDSA.

public String getSigAlgOID() ★

Return the OID of the signature algorithm used to produce the certificate.

public abstract byte[] getSigAlgParams() ★

Return the DER-encoded parameters that were used to generate the signature. In general, this will return null, since the parameters are usually specified by the certificate authority's public key.

public abstract byte[] getIssuerUniqueID() ★

Return the unique identifier for the issuer of the certificate. The presence of a unique identifier for each issuer allows the names to be reused, although in general it is recommended that certificates not make use of the unique identifier.

public abstract byte[] getSubjectUniqueID() ★

Return the unique identifier for the subject of the certificate (again, this is unused in general).

public abstract BitSet getKeyUsage() ★

> Return the key usage extension, which defines the purpose of the key: the key may be used for digital signing, nonrepudiation, key encipherment, data encipherment, key agreement, certificate signing, and more. The key usage is an extension to the X509 specification and need not be present in all X509 certificates.

public abstract int getBasicConstraints() ★

> An X509 certificate may contain an optional extension that identifies whether the subject of the certificate is a certificate authority. If the subject is a CA, this extension returns the number of certificates that may follow this certificate in a certification chain.

Revoked Certificates

Occasionally, a certificate authority needs to revoke a certificate it has issued—perhaps the certificate was issued under false pretenses, or maybe the user of the certificate has engaged in illegal conduct using the certificate. Under circumstances such as these, the expiration date attached to the certificate is insufficient protection; the certificate must be immediately invalidated.

This invalidation occurs as the result of a CRL—a certificate revocation list. Certificate authorities are responsible for issuing certificate revocation lists that contain (predictably) a list of certificates the authority has revoked. Validators of certificates are required to consult this list before accepting the validity of a certificate.

Unfortunately, the means by which an authority issues a CRL is one of those areas that is in flux, and while the interfaces to support revoked certificates have been established, they are not completely integrated into most certificate systems. In particular, the `validate()` method of the `Certificate` class does not automatically consult any CRL. The CRL itself is typically obtained in an out-of-band fashion (just as the certificates of the authority were obtained); once you have a CRL, you can check to see if a particular certificate in which you are interested is on the list.

While the notion of revoked certificates in not necessarily specific to an X509 certificate, the Java implementation is. Revoked certificates themselves are represented by the X509CRLEntry class (`java.security.cert.X509CRLEntry`):

public abstract class X509CRLEntry implements X509Extension★

The methods of this class are simple and are based upon the fields present in a revoked X509 certificate:

public abstract BigInteger getSerialNumber() ★

> Return the serial number of the revoked certificate.

public abstract Date getRevocationDate() ★

Return the date on which the certificate was revoked.

public abstract boolean hasExtensions() ★

Indicate whether the implementation of the class has any X509 extensions.

Revoked certificates are modeled by the X509CRL class (java.secu-rity.cert.X509CRL):

public abstract class X509CRL implements X509Extension ★

Provide the support for an X509-based certificate revocation list.

Instances of the X509CRLEntry class are obtained by the getInstance() method of the CertificateFactory. Once the class has been instantiated, you may operate upon it with these methods. As you can see, there is a strong synergy between the methods that are used to operate upon an X509 certificate and those used to operate upon a CRL:

public abstract void verify(PublicKey pk) ★
public abstract void verify(PublicKey pk, String sigProvider) ★

Verify that the signature that accompanied the CRL is valid (based on the standard signature verification we'll look at in Chapter 12). The public key should be the public key of the certificate authority that issued the CRL.

An error in the underlying signature object may generate a NoSuchAlgo-rithmException, a NoSuchProviderException, an InvalidKeyExcep-tion, or a SignatureException.

public abstract int getVersion() ★

Return the version of the CRL. The present version of the X509 CRL specifica-tion is 2.

public abstract Principal getIssuerDN() ★

Extract the distinguished name of the issuer of the CRL and return a prin-cipal object that contains that name.

public abstract Date getThisUpdate() ★

Extract and return the date when the authority issued this CRL.

public abstract Date getNextUpdate() ★

Extract and return the date when the authority expects to issue its next CRL. This value may not be present in the CRL, in which case null is returned.

public abstract X509CRLEntry getRevokedCertificate(BigInteger bn) ★

Instantiate and return a revoked certificate object based on the given serial number. If the serial number is invalid, a CRLException is thrown.

public abstract Set getRevokedCertificates() ★

Instantiate a revoked certificate object for each certificate in the CRL and return the set of those objects. This method may throw a CRLException.

public abstract byte[] getEncoded() ★

Return the DER-encoded CRL itself. This method may throw a CRLException.

public abstract byte[] getTBSCertList() ★

Return the DER-encoded TBS certificate list—that is, all the data that came with the CRL aside from the name of the algorithm used to sign the CRL and the digital signature itself. This data can be used to verify the signature directly. Parsing of the underlying data may throw a CRLException or an X509ExtensionException.

public abstract byte[] getSignature ★

Return the actual bytes of the signature.

public abstract String getSigAlgName() ★

Return the name of the signature algorithm that was used to sign the CRL.

public abstract String getSigAlgOID() ★

Return the OID string of the signature algorithm that was used to sign the CRL.

public abstract byte[] getSigAlgParams() ★

Return the DER-encoded algorithms used in the signature generation. This generally returns null, as those parameters (if any) usually accompany the authority's public key.

There is one more method of the X509CRL class, which it inherits from its super-class, the CRL class (java.security.cert.CRL):

public abstract boolean isRevoked(Certificate c)★

Indicate whether or not the given certificate has been revoked by this CRL.

When all is said and done, the point of the CRL class (and the revoked certificate class) is to provide you with the tools necessary to see if a particular certificate has been invalidated. This checking is up to your application to perform; you might choose to implement it as follows:

```
public Certificate importCertificate(byte data[])
                                    throws CertificateException {
    X509Certificate c = null;
    try {
        CertificateFactory cf = CertificateFactory.getInstance("X509");
        ByteArrayInputStream bais = new ByteArrayInputStream(data);
        c = (X509Certificate) cf.generateCertificate(bais);
        Principal p = c.getIssuerDN();
        PublicKey pk = getPublicKey(p);
```

```
            c.verify(pk);
            InputStream crlFile = lookupCRLFile(p);
            cf = CertificateFactory.getInstance("X509CRL");
            X509CRL crl = (X509CRL) cf.generateCRL(crlFile);
            if (crl.isRevoked(c))
                throw new CertificateException("Certificate revoked");
        } catch (NoSuchAlgorithmException nsae) {
            throw new CertificateException("Can't verify certificate");
        } catch (NoSuchProviderException nspe) {
            throw new CertificateException("Can't verify certificate");
        } catch (SignatureException se) {
            throw new CertificateException("Can't verify certificate");
        } catch (InvalidKeyException ike) {
            throw new CertificateException("Can't verify certificate");
        } catch (CRLException ce) {
            // treat as no crl
        }
        return c;
    }
}
```

This method encapsulates importing a certificate and checking its validity. It is passed the DER-encoded data of the certificate to check (this data must have been read from a file or other input stream, as we showed earlier). Then we consult the certificate to find out who issued it, obtain the public key of the issuer, and validate the certificate. Before we return, however, we obtain the latest CRL of the issuing authority and ensure that the certificate we're checking has not been revoked; if it has been, we throw a CertificateException.

We've glossed over two details in this method: how we obtain the public key of the authority that issued the certificate, and how we get the CRL list associated with that authority. Implementing these methods is the crux of a key/certificate management system, and we'll show some ideas on how to implement the key lookup in Chapter 11. Obtaining the CRL is slightly more problematic, since you must have access to a source for the CRL data. Once you have that data, however, it's trivial to create the CRL via the generateCRL() method.

Keys, Certificates, and Object Serialization

Before we conclude this chapter, a brief word on object serialization, keys, and certificates. Keys and certificates are often transmitted electronically, and a reasonable mechanism for transmitting them between Java programs is to send them as serialized objects. In theory—and, most of the time, in practice—this is a workable solution. If you modify some of the examples in this chapter to save and restore serialized keys or certificates, that will certainly work in a testing environment.

A problem arises, however, when you send these serialized objects between virtual machines that have two different security providers. Let's take the case of a DSA public key. When you create such a key with the Sun security provider, you get an instance of the sun.security.provider.DSAPublicKey class. When you create such a key with a third-party security provider, you may get an instance of the com.xyz.XYZPublicKey class. Although both public keys are extensions of the PublicKey class, they cannot be interchanged by object serialization. Serializing a public key created with the Sun security provider requires that the sun.security.provider.DSAPublicKey class be used, and deserialization creates an object of that type, no matter what security providers the deserializing virtual machine has installed. Whether or not the Sun security provider has been installed in the destination virtual machine is irrelevant. The process of deserializing the object uses that class if it is available, and deserialization fails if that class is not available.

Hence, while they are serializable objects, keys and certificates should only be transmitted as encoded data. For keys, you also have the option of transmitting the data contained in the key specification as we did earlier; the key specification classes are not serializable themselves, so you still have to rely on transmitting only the data that those objects contain.

This rule applies not only to keys and certificates that stand alone, but also to classes that embed one of those objects. Take, for example, this class:

```
public class Message implements Serializable {
    String msg;
    X509Certificate cert;
    byte signature[];
}
```

If you want to send an object of this class to a remote virtual machine (or save the object to a file), you should override the writeObject() and readObject() methods of the class so that when it is transmitted, the certificate is transmitted only as its encoded data and not as an instance of the sun.security.x509.X509CertImpl class. We'll do just that in Chapter 12.

Summary

Keys are a basic feature of any cryptographic system; they provide one of the inputs required to produce a digital signature (as well as other potential cryptographic operations). In this chapter, we looked at the basic classes that implement the notion of a key within the Java security package.

Keys are closely tied to the notion of certificates; a certificate contains a public key as well as an assurance from some known entity that the public key belongs to a specific entity. In a general sense, there are a great many things you can do with certificates, but for our purposes, we're interested in certificates only from the perspective of the certificate's user—that is, we want to be able to import and verify a certificate, but we're not too interested in creating our own certificates or in becoming a certificate authority.

Given that the operations we want to perform on keys and certificates are simple— importing and exporting those certificates—you'd expect that we could leave our discussion of keys for the time being. Unfortunately, the topic of finding a key for a particular entity (which is really just a case of importing a key) is a particularly troublesome topic, which we'll examine in the next chapter.

In this chapter:
• *Overview of Key Management*
• *The KeyStore Class*
• *A Key Management Example*

11

Key Management

In this chapter, we're going to discuss key management, and the facilities in Java that enable key management. The problem of key management turns out to be a hard one to solve: there is no universally accepted approach to key management, and although many features in Java (and on the Internet) are available to assist with key management, all key management techniques remain very much works in progress.

The fluidity of key management is evident in the progress of Java itself. Key management with the 1.1 API is very different from key management in 1.2.* Further complicating this picture is the fact that no Java-enabled browser (including HotJava, but not including the Java Plug-In) uses the technique for key management that comes with the JDK. Each requires keys to be kept in a different key database, and each uses a different technique to store and retrieve keys from that application-specific database. Key management remains application-specific.

In this chapter, we'll discuss the basic features of Java that are available for key management, including the default key management features of the JDK. We'll conclude with an example of implementing your own key management system. The key management features we're going to discuss apply primarily to Java 1.2. If you must implement a key management system under Java 1.1, you'll need to use the IdentityScope class as discussed in Appendix B. The IdentityScope class has been deprecated in 1.2.

---

* 1.2 is now Java 2.

Overview of Key Management

Keys are important to Java's security model because they allow us to create or verify a digital signature. In the sandbox model, we usually think of the use of digital signatures in the context of a signed JAR file. When a JAR file is signed, we are assured that the classes contained in that file were actually provided by the entity (the person or corporation) that signed the JAR file. This allows us to grant privileges to the signed classes because we know that the classes have not been forged by a third party. Of course, digital signatures have many other uses in a particular application.

We'll discuss the details of digital signatures in Chapter 12. For now, it's enough to know that a digital signature is created with a private key, then transferred electronically (along with the data it signed). When the digital signature is received, it must be verified, which requires a public key that corresponds to the private key that generated the signature.

The purpose of a key management system is two-fold. When you need to digitally sign something, the key management system must provide your private key for the code that creates the digital signature. When you need to verify a digital signature, the key management system must provide the public key that will be used for verification. A key management system may encompass other operations (it may, for example, provide information about the degree to which a particular individual should be trusted), but it exists primarily to serve up keys.

Hence, there are three elements of a key management system:

Keys

 The keys in a key management system can be used for several cryptographic operations, but in general we will use them to sign data, such as a JAR file. An entity in the key management database can have no keys, a public key, or both a public key and a private key.

Certificates

 Certificates are used to verify that the association between a public key and an entity is valid. Verification of a digital signature requires the public key that belongs to the entity that created the digital signature; a certificate verifies that the public key itself has not been forged and does indeed belong to the desired identity.

Identities

 Identities are an abstraction of individuals, companies, or any other entity that might have a key. The purpose of a key management system is to associate identities with their keys. This association must be stored somewhere; we refer to the database in which these associations are stored as the key database or the keystore.

Java 1.1 comes with a key management system that is based upon the javakey utility. Javakey has several limitations; in particular, it stores public and private keys in the same, unprotected location (often called an identity database). This allows anyone with access to the javakey database to determine all the keys that were stored in the file. Since access is required to obtain your own private key to generate your own digital signature, this essentially gives all users access to each other's keys. This problem was a limitation of the javakey utility itself. It's possible to use the 1.1 classes to write a key database in such a way that your private key is held separately from a group of public keys (see Appendix B).

The javakey utility was an interim solution to the key management problem; it is no longer available. In 1.2, javakey has been replaced by a new utility called keytool. Keytool is a much better tool, in that individual private and public keys can be stored in the same database, and retrieval of each key can be made subject to a password. The keytool database is often referred to as the keystore.

Unfortunately, the default implementation of the keytool database still has certain limitations; in particular, it is difficult to share the keys in a keytool database among a widely dispersed group of people (like all the employees of XYZ Corporation). We can, however, use the framework that the keytool database uses to create a key management system that has whatever features we require.

That framework is the ultimate goal of this chapter. First, however, let's take a brief look at the notion of the identity to whom a key belongs. In Java's key management model, the association between a key and its owner is application-specific. There is an Identity class in Java that was used for this purpose in 1.1, but it has been deprecated (because, among other things, it used the wrong Certificate class). However, there is still one interface that can be useful in your own applications that use keys: the Principal interface.

Principals

Classes that are concerned with identities and key management in the Java security package generally implement the Principal interface (java.security.Principal):

public interface Principal
> Provide an interface that supports the notion of an entity. In particular, principals have a name, but little else.

There is a single method that implementors of the Principal interface must implement:

public String getName()

> Return the name of the principal. This is typically an X.500 distinguished name, but it may be any arbitrary name.

The only idea that the Principal interface abstracts is that principals have a name. The Java documentation claims that a principal is anything that can have an identity, but don't be confused by that statement; the word "identity" is being overloaded in this context. The deprecated Identity class is a principal, but there are classes implementing the Principal interface that are unrelated to the Identity class.

Further confusion about this interface can arise because there are two principal objects in Java 1.2: the java.security.Principal interface (introduced in 1.1), and the org.omg.CORBA.Principal class (introduced in 1.2). These classes are unrelated, and we'll discuss only the java.security.Principal interface throughout this book.

The name that is stored in a principal is often an X.500 distinguished name (DN). That is particularly true when a principal is used in certain certificates (like X509 certificates); it is not an absolute requirement by any means.

There are other methods listed in the Principal interface—namely, the equals(), toString(), and hashCode() methods. There's no reason for those methods to be listed in the Principal interface, since every class already inherits those methods from the Object class. If you implement the Principal interface, the only method you must implement is the getName() method. You should make sure that the other methods of the Principal interface are implemented correctly—but you should ensure that these methods of the Object class are implemented correctly for all your classes, not just those that implement the Principal interface.

The KeyStore Class

Now that we understand the pieces that make up a key management system, we can look at the topic of key management itself. From an administrative perspective, the primary tool that provides key management for Java 1.2 is the keytool utility. Keytool operates upon a file (or other storage system) containing a set of private keys and certificates for those keys. The keytool file contains a set of entries; each entry may have the following attributes:

- An alias. This is a name you can use to reference the entity in the database. For example, an alias for my entry might be sdo, or ScottOaks.

- One or more certificates that vouch for the identity of the entry. These certificates also provide the public key for the entry.

What's in a Name?

X509 certificates (and many other ANSI standards) make use of the idea of a distinguished name (usually referred to as a DN). The distinguished name of an individual includes these fields:

Common Name (CN)
   The (full) common name of the individual

Organizational Unit (OU)
   The unit the individual is associated with

Organization (O)
   The organization the individual is associated with

Location (L)
   The city where the individual is located

State (S)
   The state/province where the individual is located

Country (C)
   The country where the individual is located

The DN specification allows other fields as well, although these are the fields used internally in Java. The organization that is associated with an individual is typically the company the individual works for, but it can be any other organization (and of course, you may not be associated with an organization under a variety of circumstances).

The idea behind a DN is that it limits to some extent name duplication. There are other Scott Oakses in the world, but only one who has a DN of:

```
CN=Scott Oaks, OU=SMCC, O=Sun Microsystems, L=NY, S=NY,
C=US
```

On the other hand, this is not absolute; there are many non-unique DNs.

- Optionally, a private key. If present, the private key can be protected by a password.

We'd be tempted to call the entries in this database identities, but that's potentially confusing: the entries stored in the keytool database are not instances of the Identity class (although we could create an identity object based on the information retrieved from the database).

Figure 11-1 shows the role of the keytool database in the creation and execution of a signed JAR file. The jarsigner utility consults the keytool database for the private key of the entity that is signing the JAR file. Once the signed JAR file is produced, it is placed on a web server, where it can be downloaded into an applet-viewer or other Java-enabled browser.* When the JAR file is read on the remote system, the keytool database is consulted in order to retrieve the public key of the entity that signed the JAR file so that the JAR file's signature can be verified.

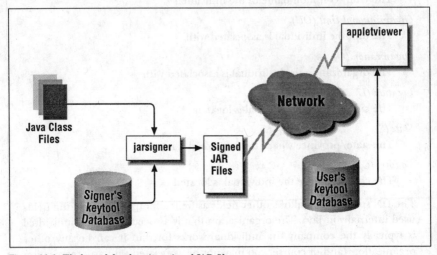

Figure 11-1. The keytool database in a signed JAR file

Note that the two keytool databases in this example are (probably) separate data-bases, on separate machines. They probably have completely different entries as well—even for the entry that represents the signer. The signer's entry in her own database must have the private key of the signer, while the signer's entry in the user's database needs only a certificate (public key) for the signer. However, the *keytool* database could (in this and all examples) be a shared database—but more about that later. The default keytool database is the file *.keystore* that is held in the user's home directory.

The class that implements the keytool database is the KeyStore class (java.security.KeyStore):

---

* As we mentioned, however, Netscape Navigator, Internet Explorer, and HotJava at present all use a dif-ferent key management system than the keytool database, so the appletviewer is the best example here.

public class KeyStore ★

> Represent a set of private keys, aliases (entities), and their corresponding certificates. A keystore object is typically one that has been read in from disk; that is, the keystore object is an in-memory representation of the keytool database.

The KeyStore class is an engine class; there is a corresponding KeyStoreSpi class that you can use to write your own keystore (more about that a little later). By default, the Sun security provider implements a keystore called JKS (for Java KeyStore). Hence, instances of the KeyStore class are predictably obtained via this method:

public static final KeyStore getInstance(String type) ★
public static final KeyStore getInstance(String type, String provider) ★

> Return an instance of the KeyStore class that implements the given algorithm, supplied by the given provider, if applicable. In the Sun security provider, the default algorithm name is "JKS".

If you do not want to hardwire the name of the keystore algorithm into your application, you may use this method to return the string that should be passed to the getInstance() method:

public static final String getDefaultType() ★

> Return the default keystore algorithm for the environment. This value is obtained by looking for a property called keystore.type in the *java.security* file.

When the keystore object is created, it is initially empty. Although the getInstance() method has constructed the object, it is not expected that the object's constructor will read in a keystore from any particular location. The interaction between the keystore object and the keytool database comes via these two methods:

public final void load(InputStream is, char[] password) ★

> Initialize the keystore from the data provided over the given input stream. The integrity of the keystore is typically protected by using a message digest: when the keystore is stored, a message digest that represents the data in the keystore is also stored. Before the digest is created, the password is added to the digest data; this means that the digest cannot be re-created from a tampered keystore without knowledge of the password. The password for this method can be null, in which case the keystore is loaded and not verified.

> This use of the password is a property of the Sun implementation of the KeyStore class; the password could be used for anything else (including encrypting the entire keystore) if you were to write your own implementation. To call this parameter a password is somewhat misleading (although that's

what the javadoc documentation calls it), since Sun's implementation lets you read the entire keystore without it. The Sun implementation of the KeyStore class requires another password to access each private key in the keystore, so this isn't a potential security hole; all you're reading is public certificates.

You cannot require a password for load() to succeed, since the Sun implementation of the Policy class calls this method without a password when it constructs the information needed for the access controller. You may, of course, provide your own implementation of the Policy class that provides a password if desired.

In the Sun implementation, if the class required to support the underlying message digest is not available, a NoSuchAlgorithmException is thrown. An error in reading the data results in an IOException, and generic format errors in the data result in a CertificateException.

public final void store(OutputStream os, char[] password) ★

Store the keystore to the given output stream. The password is typically included in a digest calculation of the keystore; this digest is then written to the output stream as well (but again, your own implementation of this class could use the password differently).

The Sun implementation of this method may throw an IOException if the output stream cannot be read, a NoSuchAlgorithmException if the class used to create the digest cannot be found, or a CertificateException if the keystore object contains a certificate that cannot be parsed.

There is no default file that holds the keystore. Within the core Java API, the only class that opens the keystore is PolicyFile, and that opens the keystore that is listed in the *java.policy* file. The tools that use the keystore (the jarsigner and keytool tools) allow you to use a command-line argument to specify the file that contains the keystore; by default, that file is *.keystore* in the user's home directory. This is the convention your own programs will need to use. If your application needs to open the keystore (for example, to obtain a private key to sign an object), it should provide either a command-line argument or a property to specify the name of the file to open. By convention, we'll use the *.keystore* file in the user's home directory in our examples.

While we mentioned that the keystore may not be encrypted, the private keys themselves typically are encrypted so that if someone gains access to the keystore file, they do not have access to the private keys in that file without the password used to encrypt those keys. If you provide a keystore implementation that supplies keys from a protected location, you do not necessarily need to store the private keys in encrypted format. When private keys are delivered over the network, you probably want to make sure that the transmission of those keys is encrypted so that no one can snoop the network and discover the private key.

A keystore is arranged in terms of alias names. Aliases are arbitrarily assigned to an entry; while the name embedded in the certificate for a particular entry may be a long, complicated, distinguished name, the alias for that entry can provide a shorter, easier-to-remember name. There are a number of simple methods in the KeyStore class that deal with these alias names:

public final String getType() ★
Return the name of the algorithm that this keystore implements.

public final String getProvider() ★
Return the name of the provider that supplied this keystore implementation.

public final Date getCreationDate(String alias) ★
Return the date on which the entry referenced by the given alias was created.

public final void deleteEntry(String alias) ★
Delete the entry referenced by the given alias from the keystore.

public final Enumeration aliases() ★
Return an enumeration of all the aliases in the keystore.

public final boolean containsAlias(String alias) ★
Indicate whether the keystore contains an entry referenced by the given alias.

public final int size() ★
Return the number of entries/aliases in the keystore.

Note that this list has a method to delete an entry but not one to create an entry—creating an entry in the keystore depends upon the type of entry you want to create.

The keystore holds two types of entries: certificate entries and key entries. A certificate entry is an entry that contains only a public key (encapsulated in a certificate) and can be used only to verify a digital signature, while a key entry is an entry that contains both a private and a public key and can be used to create and to verify a digital signature. Hence, you may think of a key entry as a signer and a certificate entry as an identity, although those classes are not used in the keystore interface (they may be used in the keystore implementation).

There are two basic differences between key entries and certificate entries:

• A key entry contains a private key, while a certificate entry does not.

• A key entry may contain a chain of certificates that verifies it, while a certificate entry contains a single certificate.

For a given alias, you can determine what type of entry it represents via these two methods:

public final boolean isKeyEntry(String alias) ★
public final boolean isCertificateEntry(String alias) ★

Indicate whether the given alias represents a key entry or a certificate entry.

For a given alias, you cannot retrieve an object that represents the entire entry. You may use these methods to retrieve information about the entry represented by an alias:

public final Key getKey(String alias, char[] password) ★

Return the private key for the entry associated with the given alias. For a certificate entry, this method returns null. An UnrecoverableKeyException is thrown if the key cannot be retrieved (e.g., if the key has been damaged).

Retrieving a private key typically requires a password; this may or may not be the same password that was used to read the entire keystore. This allows private keys to be stored encrypted so they cannot be read without the appropriate password. If the class that provides encryption cannot be found, this method throws a NoSuchAlgorithmException.

public final Certificate[] getCertificateChain(String alias) ★

Return the certificate chain that verifies the entry associated with the given alias, which must represent a key entry. For an alias that represents a certificate entry, this method returns null.

public final Certificate getCertificate(String alias) ★

Return the certificate associated with the given alias. If the alias represents a key entry, the certificate returned is the user's certificate (that is, the first certificate in the entry's certificate chain); certificate entries have only a single certificate.

public final String getCertificateAlias(Certificate cert) ★

Return the alias that corresponds to the entry that matches the given certificate (using the equals() method of certificate comparison). If no matches occur, null is returned.

Finally, in order to create or modify an entry, you may use one of these methods. All of these methods create a new entry if the given alias does not exist:

public final void setKeyEntry(String alias, byte key[], Certificate chain[]) ★
public final void setKeyEntry(String alias, Key k, char[] password, Certificate chain[]) ★

Assign the given private key and certificate chain to the key entry represented by the given alias, creating a new key entry if necessary. Any previous private key and certificate chain for this entry are lost; if the previous entry was a certificate entry, it now becomes a key entry.

A KeyStoreException is thrown if the key entry cannot be encrypted by the internal encrypting algorithm of the keystore. In the Sun implementation, when the key is passed in as a series of bytes, it is not encrypted—in this case, you are expected to have performed the encryption yourself.

public final void setCertificateEntry(String alias, Certificate c) ★

Assign the given certificate to the certificate entry represented by the given alias. If an entry for this alias already exists and is a key entry, a KeyStoreException is thrown. Otherwise, if an entry for this alias already exists, it is overwritten.

These are the basic methods by which we can manage a keystore. We'll see examples of many of these methods throughout the rest of this book; for now, let's look at a simple example that looks up a given entry in the keystore:

```
public class KeyStoreLookup {
    public static void main(String args[]) {
        try {
            KeyStore ks =
                        KeyStore.getInstance(KeyStore.getDefaultType());
            String fname = System.getProperty("user.home") +
                                File.separator + ".keystore";
            FileInputStream fis = new FileInputStream(fname);
            ks.load(fis, null);
            if (ks.isKeyEntry(args[0])) {
                System.out.println(args[0] +
                            " is a key entry in the keystore");
                char c[] = new char[args[1].length()];
                args[1].getChars(0, c.length, c, 0);
                System.out.println("The private key for" + args[0] +
                            " is " + ks.getKey(args[0], c));
                Certificate certs[] = ks.getCertificateChain(args[0]);
                if (certs[0] instanceof X509Certificate) {
                    X509Certificate x509 = (X509Certificate) certs[0];
                    System.out.println(args[0] + " is really " +
                        x509.getSubjectDN());
                }
                if (certs[certs.length - 1] instanceof
                                X509Certificate) {
                    X509Certificate x509 = (X509Certificate)
                                certs[certs.length - 1];
                    System.out.println(args[0] + " was verified by " +
                        x509.getIssuerDN());
                }
            }
            else if (ks.isCertificateEntry(args[0])) {
                System.out.println(args[0] +
                            " is a certificate entry in the keystore");
                Certificate c = ks.getCertificate(args[0]);
```

```
            if (c instanceof X509Certificate) {
                X509Certificate x509 = (X509Certificate) c;
                System.out.println(args[0] + " is really " +
                    x509.getSubjectDN());
                System.out.println(args[0] + " was verified by " +
                    x509.getIssuerDN());
            }
        }
        else {
            System.out.println(args[0] +
                " is unknown to this keystore");
        }
    } catch (Exception e) {
        e.printStackTrace();
    }
    }
}
```

This program expects two arguments: the name of the entity in the keystore for which information is desired, and the password that was used to encrypt the private key.

There are a number of points to pick out from this example. First, note that we constructed the keystore using the convention we mentioned earlier—the *.keystore* file in the user's home directory.

After we've read in the data, the first thing we do is determine if the entry that we're interested in is a key entry or a certificate entry—mostly so that we can handle the certificates for these entries differently. In the case of a key entry, we obtain the entire certificate chain, and use the first entry in that chain to print out the Distinguished Name (DN) for the entry, while the last entry in the chain is used to print out the DN for the last certificate authority in the chain. For a certificate entry, our task is simpler: there is a single certificate, and we simply print out its information.

A Key Management Example

The Sun implementation of the keytool utility is useful in many circumstances where users have disjoint databases. In Figure 11-1 we showed just such an example, and we mentioned that this example was set up in such a way that the code signer and the end user could have different key databases.

This is not to say, however, that those two databases could not have been the same database—that is, one that is shared by the signer and the end user. Since access to the private key of the signer is protected by a password, the signer and the end user are able to share a single database without concern that the end user may obtain access to the signer's private key (assuming that she keeps her password secret, of course). In the case of a corporate network, this flexibility is important, since an enterprise may want to maintain a single database that contains the private keys of all of its employees as well as the certificates of all known external entities.

We could have these users share the keystore by using the appropriate filename in the application and the *java.policy* files. But sharing the keytool database by a file is somewhat inefficient. If the global file is on a machine in New York and is referenced by a user in Tokyo, you'll want to use a better network protocol to access it than a file-based protocol. In addition, the load() method reads in the entire file. If there are 10,000 users in your corporate keystore database, you shouldn't need to read each entry into memory to find the one entry you are interested in using.

Hence, for many applications, you'll want to provide your own implementation of the KeyStore class. We'll show a very simple example here as a starting point for your own implementations. For the payroll application being deployed by XYZ Corporation, a database containing each employee in the corporation is necessary. The HR department could set up its own keystore for this purpose, but a similar keystore will be needed by the finance department to implement its 401K application; a better solution is to have a single keystore that is shared between all departments of XYZ Corporation.

In this case, the question becomes how best to share this keystore. A single global file would be too large for programs to read into memory and too unwieldy for administrators to distribute to all locations of XYZ Corporation. A better architecture is shown in Figure 11-2. Here, the application uses the security provider architecture to instantiate a new keystore object (of a class that we'll sketch out below). Unknown to the users of this object, the keystore class uses RMI (or CORBA, or any other distributed computing protocol) to talk to a remote server, which accesses the 10,000 employee records from a database set up for that purpose.

Without getting bogged down in the details of the network and database programming required for this architecture, let's look at how the KeyStore class itself would be designed.

Implementing a keystore requires that we write a KeyStoreSpi class, just as any other engine class. For most methods in the KeyStore class, there is a corresponding abstract engine method in the KeyStoreSpi class that you must provide an implementation for. A complete list of these methods is given in Table 11-1.

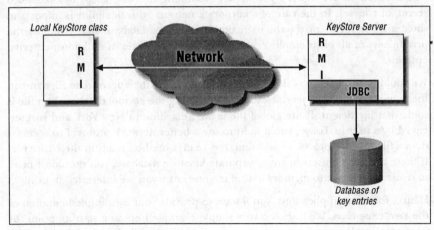

Figure 11-2. A distributed keystore example

Table 11-1. Engine methods in the KeyStoreSpi class

KeyStore Class	KeyStoreSpi class
aliases	engineAliases
containsAlias	engineContainsAlias
deleteEntry	engineDeleteEntry
getCertificate	engineGetCertificate
getCertificateAlias	engineGetCertificateAlias
getCertificateChain	engineGetCertificateChain
getCreationDate	engineGetCreationDate
getKey	engineGetKey
isCertificateEntry	engineIsCertificateEntry
isKeyEntry	engineIsKeyEntry
load	engineLoad
setCertificateEntry	engineSetCertificateEntry
setKeyEntry	engineSetKeyEntry
size	engineSize
store	engineStore

Many of the methods of our new class are simple passthroughs to the remote server. If the handle to the remote server is held in the instance variable rks, a typical method looks like this:

```
public Date engineGetCreationDate(String alias) {
    return rks.getCreationDate(alias);
}
```

The methods that could be implemented in this manner are:

```
engineGetKey()
engineGetCertificateChain()
engineGetCertificate()
engineGetCreationDate()
engineAliases()
engineContainsAlias()
engineSize()
engineIsKeyEntry()
engineIsCertificateEntry()
engineGetCertificateAlias()
```

On the other hand, many methods should probably throw an exception—especially those methods that are designed to alter the keystore. In an architecture such as this one, changes to the keystore should probably be done through the database itself—or at least through a different server than the server used by all employees in the corporation. So many functions may look simply like this:

```
public void engineSetKeyEntry(String alias, Key key,
                    char[] passphrase, Certificate chain[])
                        throws KeyStoreException {
    throw new KeyStoreException("Can't change the keystore");
}
```

Methods that could be implemented in this manner are:

```
engineSetKeyEntry()
engineSetCertificateEntry()
engineDeleteEntry()
engineStore()
```

Note that we did not include the engineLoad() method in the above list. The engineLoad() method is useful to us, because it allows the application to require a password from the user before a connection to the remote server can be made. This differs slightly from normal programming for this class. Typically, the engineLoad() method is called with the input stream from which to read the keystore. In this case, the engineLoad() method is expected to be called with a null input stream, and sets up the connection to the remote server itself:

```
public void engineLoad(InputStream is, char[] password)
        throws IOException, NoSuchAlgorithmException,
            CertificateException {
    rks = Naming.lookup("rmi://KSServer/DistributedKeyServer");
    if (!rks.authenticate(password)) {
        rks = null;
        throw new IOException("Incorrect password");
    }
}
```

Since the keystore database in this architecture cannot be written through the server, there is some question as to whether a password should be required to access the keystore at all (since there are individual passwords on the private keys). Every employee will potentially have access to the password (unless it is embedded into the application itself); you can decide if a password really adds security in that case. If no password is desired, the engineLoad() method could be empty and the connection to the remote server could be made in the constructor.

On the server side, implementation of the required methods is simply a matter of making appropriate database calls:

```
public int engineSize() {
    int sz = -1;
    try {
        Connection conn = connectToDatabase();
        Statement st = conn.createStatement();
        boolean restype = st.execute("select count(*) from entries");
        if (restype) {
            ResultSet rs = st.getResultSet();
            sz = Integer.parseInt(rs.getString(1));
        }
        st.cancel();
    } catch (Exception e) {
        ...
    }
    finally {
        return sz;
    }
}
```

This architecture works well because it allows the passwords for each of the private keys to be held in the database itself, so retrievals of private keys can easily test the password via a simple string comparison. Implementations of file-based keystores are more problematic: if the file is readable by the user, obviously the password cannot be stored in the file as a simple string. File-based keystores must store their passwords and their private keys in encrypted form, perhaps using the encryption APIs we'll examine in Chapter 13. Assuming that the database machine is secured, such encryption is not required in this architecture.

There are unlimited possibilities in the implementation of a keystore. One technique might be to create a floppy for each employee that contains only that employee's entry and to write a keystore class that looks for key entries from the file on the floppy and for certificate entries from a global file somewhere.* This type of implementation is very simple. The new keystore can contain two instances of the Sun KeyStore class that have read in both files, and it can use object delegation to implement all of its methods.

---

* Of course, we don't want to use a floppy for this—we want to use a Java-enabled smart card, though of course we don't all have smart card readers on our computers. At least, not yet...

Encrypting Private Keys

In this section, we've discussed the need for private keys to be stored encrypted whenever those keys are stored in a location that is generally accessible to other users. The Sun implementation of the KeyStore class does this using an internal algorithm to perform the encryption.

The strength of this encryption is limited; because it is part of the standard Sun distribution, the encryption must be weak enough to be exportable from the United States. "Weak" is a relative term in this context; it still requires some effort for the encryption to be broken, but it can be done.

In your own KeyStore class, if you need to encrypt the private keys you'll want to use the strongest form of encryption that is suitable for your situation. If you're a multinational organization, this encryption will not be very strong, and you're better off storing your private keys on a private database as we've described here.

Note that this type of two-tiered system is really the ideal. If the private keys are transmitted over the network, as in our previous case, then internal spies on the network might snoop the password used to retrieve the key or the private key that is sent back. If the private key is held locally, however, and only the public keys are retrieved from the remote key store, you have a much better implementation.

Installing a KeyStore Class

In order to use an alternate keystore implementation, you must install your new class into a security provider. If necessary, you'll need to establish a convention by which the input stream that is opened for the load() method is created—unless your keystore does not require one at all (as, for example, our RMI-based keystore would not).

The Policy class uses the keystore in a predictable manner. Given this entry in the *java.policy* file:

```
grant signedBy, "sdo", codeBase "http://piccolo/" {
    . . .
}
```

the Policy class uses the keystore to look up the alias for sdo, retrieve sdo's public key, and use that public key to verify any signature that comes from the site *piccolo*. Remember, however, that the Sun implementation of the Policy class requires an entry in the *java.policy* file that specifies the URL from which to load the keystore.

Summary

In this chapter we examined the key management facilities of Java. Key management revolves around keys and certificates—ideas we've already discussed—but it also depends upon the notion of an identity—an individual or a corporation—and the idea that a particular identity can be certified.

Key management in Java can be handled either programmatically with the standard Java API or with the key management tool keytool. Keytool itself is a good example of how the programming API can be used, although there are some trade-offs involved here; for example, loading a large keystore is not necessarily the most appropriate choice for a thin-client application. Fortunately, the security package gives us the necessary tools to implement our own keystore when that is appropriate.

For all the time we've spent on them, keys are not interesting by themselves. They are interesting for what they allow us to do, which among other things includes the ability to operate on a digital signature. In the next chapter, we'll look at digital signatures, their relationship to keys, and the operations that keys and digital signatures enable us to perform.

Digital Signatures

In the previous few chapters, we've examined various aspects of Java's security package with an eye toward the topics of this chapter: the ability to generate and to verify digital signatures. We've now reached the fruits of that examination. In this chapter, we'll explore the mechanisms of the digital signature.

The use and verification of digital signatures is another standard engine that is included in the security provider architecture. Like the other engines we've examined, the classes that implement this engine have both a public interface and an SPI for implementors of the engine.

In the JDK, the most common use of digital signatures is to create signed classes; users have the option of granting additional privileges to these signed classes using the mechanics of the access controller. In addition, a security manager and a class loader can use this information to change the policy of the security manager; this technique is quite useful in 1.1. Hence, we'll also show an example that reads a signed JAR file.

The Signature Class

Operations on digital signatures are abstracted by the Signature class (java.security.Signature):

public abstract class Signature extends SignatureSpi
Provide an engine to create and verify digital signatures. In Java 1.1, there is no SignatureSpi class, and this class simply extends the Object class.

The Sun security provider includes a single implementation of this class that generates signatures based on the DSA algorithm.

Using the Signature Class

As with all engine classes, instances of the Signature class are obtained by calling one of these methods:

public static Signature getInstance(String algorithm)
public static Signature getInstance(String algorithm, String provider)

Generate a signature object that implements the given algorithm. If no provider is specified, all providers are searched in order for the given algorithm as discussed in Chapter 8; otherwise, the system searches for the given algorithm only in the given provider. If an implementation of the given algorithm is not found, a NoSuchAlgorithmException is thrown. If the named security provider cannot be found, a NoSuchProviderException is thrown.

Beginning in 1.2,* if the algorithm string is "DSA", the string "SHA/DSA" is substituted for it. Hence, implementors of this class that provide support for DSA signing must register themselves appropriately (that is, with the message digest algorithm name) in the security provider.

Once a signature object is obtained, the following methods can be invoked on it:

public void final initVerify(PublicKey publicKey)

Initialize the signature object, preparing it to verify a signature. A signature object must be initialized before it can be used. If the key is not of the correct type for the algorithm or is otherwise invalid, an InvalidKeyException is thrown.

public final void initSign(PrivateKey privateKey)

Initialize the signature object, preparing it to create a signature. A signature object must be initialized before it can be used. If the key is not of the correct type for the algorithm or is otherwise invalid, an InvalidKeyException is thrown.

public final void update(byte b)
public final void update(byte[] b)
public final void update(byte b[], int offset, int length)

Add the given data to the accumulated data the object will eventually sign or verify. If the object has not been initialized, a SignatureException is thrown.

public final byte[] sign()
public final int sign(byte[] outbuf, int offset, int len) ★

Create the digital signature, assuming that the object has been initialized for signing. If the object has not been properly initialized, a SignatureException is thrown. Once the signature has been generated, the object is reset so

---

* 1.2 is now Java 2.

that it may generate another signature based on some new data (however, it is still initialized for signing; a new call to the initSign() method is not required).

In the first of these methods, the signature is returned from the method. Otherwise, the signature is stored into the outbuf array at the given offset, and the length of the signature is returned. If the output buffer is too small to hold the data, an IllegalArgumentException will be thrown.

public final boolean verify(byte[] signature)

Test the validity of the given signature, assuming that the object has been initialized for verification. If the object has not been properly initialized, then a SignatureException is thrown. Once the signature has been verified (whether or not the verification succeeds), the object is reset so that it may verify another signature based on some new data (no new call to the initVerify() method is required).

public final String getAlgorithm()

Get the name of the algorithm this object implements.

public String toString()

A printable version of a signature object is composed of the string "Signature object:" followed by the name of the algorithm implemented by the object, followed by the initialized state of the object. The state is either <not initialized>, <initialized for verifying>, or <initialized for signing>. However, the Sun DSA implementation of this class overrides this method to show the parameters of the DSA algorithm instead.

public final void setParameter(String param, Object value) ☆
public final void setParameter(AlgorithmParameterSpec param) ★

Set the parameter of the signature engine. In the first format, the named parameter is set to the given value; in the second format, parameters are set based on the information in the param specification.

In the Sun implementation of the DSA signing algorithm, the only valid param string is KSEED, which requires an array of bytes that will be used to seed the random number generator used to generate the k value. There is no way to set this value through the parameter specification, which in the Sun implementation always returns an UnsupportedOperationException.

public final Object getParameter(String param) ☆

Return the named parameter from the object. The only valid string for the Sun implementation is KSEED.

public final Provider getProvider() ★

Return the provider that supplied the implementation of this signature object.

It is no accident that this class has many similarities to the MessageDigest class; a digital signature algorithm is typically implemented by performing a cryptographic operation on a private key and the message digest that represents the data to be signed. For the developer, this means that generating a digital signature is virtually the same as generating a message digest; the only difference is that a key must be presented in order to operate on a signature object. This difference is important, however, since it fills in the hole we noticed previously: a message digest can be altered along with the data it represents so that the tampering is unnoticeable. A signed message digest, on the other hand, can't be altered without knowledge of the key that was used to create it. The use of a public key in the digital signature algorithm makes the digital signature more attractive than a message authentication code, in which there must be a shared key between the parties involved in the message exchange.

Let's take our example from Chapter 9 where we saved a message and its digest to a file; we'll modify it now to save the message and the digital signature. We can create the digital signature like this:

```
public class Send {
    public static void main(String args[]) {
        String data;
        data = "This have I thought good to deliver thee, " +
                "that thou mightst not lose the dues of rejoicing " +
                "by being ignorant of what greatness is promised thee.";

        try {
            FileOutputStream fos = new FileOutputStream("test");
            ObjectOutputStream oos = new ObjectOutputStream(fos);
            KeyStore ks =
                        KeyStore.getInstance(KeyStore.getDefaultType());
            ks.load(new FileInputStream(
                            System.getProperty("user.home") +
                            File.separator + ".keystore"), null);
            char c[] = new char[args[1].length()];
            args[1].getChars(0, c.length, c, 0);
            PrivateKey pk = (PrivateKey) ks.getKey(args[0], c);

            Signature s = Signature.getInstance("DSA");
            s.initSign(pk);

            byte buf[] = data.getBytes();
            s.update(buf);
            oos.writeObject(data);
            oos.writeObject(s.sign());
        } catch (Exception e) {
            e.printStackTrace();
        }
    }
}
```

This example puts together many of the examples from the past few chapters. In order to create the digital signature we must accomplish the following:

1. Obtain the private key that is used to sign the data. Here we're using the conventional keystore database (*$HOME/.keystore*) and the command-line arguments to obtain the alias and password of the private key we want to use.

2. Obtain a signing object via the getInstance() method and initialize it. Since we're creating a signature in this example, we use the initSign() method for initialization.

3. Pass the data to be signed as a series of bytes to the update() method of the signing object. Multiple calls could be made to the update() method even though in this example we only need one.

4. Obtain the signature by calling the sign() method. We save the signature bytes and write them to a file with the data so that the data and the signature can be retrieved at a later date.

Reading the data and verifying the signature are similar:

```java
public class Receive {
    public static void main(String args[]) {
        try {
            String data = null;
            byte signature[] = null;
            FileInputStream fis = new FileInputStream("test");
            ObjectInputStream ois = new ObjectInputStream(fis);
            Object o = ois.readObject();
            try {
                data = (String) o;
            } catch (ClassCastException cce) {
                System.out.println("Unexpected data in file");
                System.exit(-1);
            }
            o = ois.readObject();
            try {
                signature = (byte []) o;
            } catch (ClassCastException cce) {
                System.out.println("Unexpected data in file");
                System.exit(-1);
            }
            System.out.println("Received message");
            System.out.println(data);

            KeyStore ks =
                    KeyStore.getInstance(KeyStore.getDefaultType());
            ks.load(new FileInputStream(
                    System.getProperty("user.home") +
                    File.separator + ".keystore"), args[1]);
```

```
Certificate c = ks.getCertificate(args[0]);
PublicKey pk = c.getPublicKey();
Signature s = Signature.getInstance("DSA");
s.initVerify(pk);
s.update(data.getBytes());
if (s.verify(signature)) {
    System.out.println("Message is valid");
}
else System.out.println("Message was corrupted");
} catch (Exception e) {
System.out.println(e);
}
}
}
```

The process of verifying the signature still requires four steps. The major differences are that in step two, we initialize the signing object for verification by using the initVerify() method, and in step four, we verify (rather than create) the existing signature by using the verify() method. Note that we still have to know who signed the message in order to look up the correct key—but more about that a little later.

The SignedObject Class

In our last example, we had to create an object that held both the data in which we are interested and the signature for that data. This is a common enough requirement that Java provides the SignedObject class (java.security.SignedObject) to encapsulate an object and its signature:

public final class SignedObject implements Serializable ★

Encapsulate an object and its digital signature. The encapsulated object must be serializable so that a serialization of a signed object can do a deep copy of the embedded object.

Signed objects are created with this constructor:

public SignedObject(Serializable o, PrivateKey pk, Signature engine) ★

Create a signed object based on the given object, signing the serialized data in that object with the given private key and signature object. The signed object contains a copy of the given object; this copy is obtained by serializing the object parameter. If this serialization fails, an IOException is thrown.

It's very important to realize that this constructor makes, in effect, a copy of its parameter; if you create a signed object based on a string buffer and later change the contents of the string buffer, the data in the signed object remains unchanged. This preserves the integrity of the object encapsulated with its signature.

Here are the methods we can use to operate on a signed object:

public Object getContent() ★

Return the object embedded in the signed object. The object is reconstituted using object serialization; an error in serialization may cause either an IOException or a ClassNotFoundException to be thrown.

public byte[] getSignature() ★

Return the signature embedded in the signed object.

public String getAlgorithm() ★

Return the name of the algorithm that was used to sign the object.

public boolean verify(PublicKey pk, Signature s) ★

Verify the signature within the embedded object with the given key and signature engine. The signature engine parameter may be obtained by calling the getInstance() method of the Signature class. The underlying signature engine may throw an InvalidKeyException or SignatureException.

We'll use this class in examples later in this chapter.

Signing and Certificates

In the previous examples, we specified on the command line the name of the entity that we assumed generated the signature in the file. This was necessary because the file contained only the actual signature of the entity and the data that was signed; it did not contain any information about who the signer actually is. That's fine for an example, but it is not always appropriate in a real application. We could have asked the user for the name of the entity that was supposed to have signed the data, but that course is fraught with potential errors:

- The user could have no idea what names are in the keystore of the application. Especially in a corporate environment, users may not know what data the keystore database might contain.

- The user could get the name of the keystore alias wrong. Say that the application asks the user to enter the name of the signer; the user, knowing that the data came from me, may enter "sdo" as the alias of the identity.

  What the user may not remember is that when the keystore was first created, she received a public key from the San Diego Oil company; that public key was entered into the keystore with the alias "sdo." When my identity was added to the keystore, a different alias had to be chosen, so my public key was added with the alias "ScottOaks." But that was a long time ago, now forgotten, and because I use the sdo moniker all over my writings, the user assumes that I am the sdo in the keystore. And so the wrong alias will be chosen, and the signature verification will fail when it should have succeeded.

For these reasons, it makes more sense to include the public key with the signature and the signed data. This allows the application to find the identity based on the unique public key in order to determine who the signer of the data is.

We could do that by simply sending the encoded public key with the signature and data. A better solution, however, would be to send the certificate that verifies the public key. That way, if the public key is not found in the database, the credentials of the certificate can be presented to the user, and the user can have the opportunity to decide on the fly if the particular entity should be trusted.

Although an embedding of signature, data, and certificate is very common, the SignedObject class does not include the capability to contain a certificate. So we'll use the SignedObject class in this example, but we'll still need an object that contains the signed object and the certificate. We'd like to do this by extending the SignedObject class, but since that class is final we're forced to adopt this approach:

```
public class Message implements Serializable {
    SignedObject object;
    transient Certificate certificate;

    private void writeObject(ObjectOutputStream out)
                                throws IOException {
        out.defaultWriteObject();
        try {
            out.writeObject(certificate.getEncoded());
        } catch (CertificateEncodingException cee) {
            throw new IOException("Can't serialize object " + cee);
        }
    }

    private void readObject(ObjectInputStream in)
                        throws IOException, ClassNotFoundException {
        in.defaultReadObject();
        try {
            byte b[] = (byte []) in.readObject();
            CertificateFactory cf =
                        CertificateFactory.getInstance("X509");
            certificate = cf.generateCertificate(new
                            ByteArrayInputStream(b));
        } catch (CertificateException ce) {
            throw new IOException("Can't de-serialize object " + ce);
        }
    }
}
```

We've made the certificate variable in this class transient and have explicitly serialized and deserialized it using its external encoding. As we discussed in

Chapter 10, whenever we have an embedded certificate or key, we must follow a procedure like this to ensure that the receiving party is able to deserialize the class.

As it turns out, the X509 certificate implementation that comes with the JDK (that is, the sun.security.x509.X509CertImpl class) also overrides the writeObject() and readObject() methods, so if we serialize a certificate explicitly, the encoded data is written to or read from the file. It is not sufficient to rely upon that, however—if we use the default serialization methods for the Message class, a reference to the sun.security.x509.X509CertImpl class is embedded into the serialized stream. A user with another security provider (and hence a different implementation of the X509Certificate class) would not be able to deserialize the stream because there is no access to the Sun implementation of the X509Certificate class. Explicitly serializing and deserializing the certificate as we've done here avoids embedding any reference to the provider class and makes the data file more portable.

When we save the message to the file, we now have to make sure that we save a certificate with it. Other than that, changes to the class are minor:

```java
public class SendObject {
    public static void main(String args[]) {
        try {
            FileOutputStream fos = new FileOutputStream("test.obj");
            ObjectOutputStream oos = new ObjectOutputStream(fos);
            KeyStore ks =
                    KeyStore.getInstance(KeyStore.getDefaultType());
            char c[] = new char[args[1].length()];
            args[1].getChars(0, c.length, c, 0);
            ks.load(new FileInputStream(
                    System.getProperty("user.home") +
                    File.separator + ".keystore"), c);

            Certificate certs[] = ks.getCertificateChain(args[0]);
            PrivateKey pk = (PrivateKey) ks.getKey(args[0], c);
            Message m = new Message();
            m.object = new SignedObject(
              "This have I thought good to deliver thee, " +
              "that thou mightst not lose the dues of rejoicing " +
              "by being ignorant of what greatness is promised thee.",
                        pk, Signature.getInstance("DSA"));
            m.certificate = certs[0];
            oos.writeObject(m);
        } catch (Exception e) {
            System.out.println(e);
        }
    }
}
```

Retrieving the data is now more complicated, since we must verify both the signature in the signed object and the identity of the authority that signed the embedded certificate:

```
public class ReceiveObject {
    private static void verifySigner(Certificate c, String name)
                                    throws CertificateException {
        Certificate issuerCert = null;
        X509Certificate sCert = null;
        KeyStore ks = null;

        try {
            ks = KeyStore.getInstance(KeyStore.getDefaultType());
            ks.load(new FileInputStream(
                        System.getProperty("user.home") +
                        File.separator + ".keystore"), null);
        } catch (Exception e) {
            throw new CertificateException("Invalid keystore");
        }

        try {
            String signer = ks.getCertificateAlias(c);
            if (signer !=null){
                System.out.println("We know the signer as " + signer);
                return;
            }
            for (Enumeration alias = ks.aliases();
                            alias.hasMoreElements();){
                String s = (String) alias.nextElement();
                try {
                    sCert = (X509Certificate) ks.getCertificate(s);
                } catch (Exception e) {
                    continue;
                }
                if (name.equals(sCert.getSubjectDN().getName())){
                    issuerCert = sCert;
                    break;
                }
            }
        } catch(KeyStoreException kse) {
            throw new CertificateException("Invalid keystore");
        }
        if (issuerCert == null) {
            throw new CertificateException("No such certificate");
        }
        try {
            c.verify(issuerCert.getPublicKey());
        } catch (Exception e) {
            throw new CertificateException(e.toString());
```

```
        }
    }

    private static void processCertificate(X509Certificate x509)
                                throws CertificateParsingException {
        Principal p;
        p = x509.getSubjectDN();
        System.out.println("This message was signed by " +
                            p.getName());
        p = x509.getIssuerDN();
        System.out.println("This certificate was provided by " +
                            p.getName());
        try {
            verifySigner(x509, p.getName());
        } catch (CertificateException ce) {
            System.out.println("We don't know the certificate signer");
        }
        try {
            x509.checkValidity();
        } catch (CertificateExpiredException cee) {
            System.out.println("That certificate is no longer valid");
        } catch (CertificateNotYetValidException cnyve) {
            System.out.println("That certificate is not yet valid");
        }
    }

    public static void main(String args[]) {
        try {
            FileInputStream fis = new FileInputStream("test.obj");
            ObjectInputStream ois = new ObjectInputStream(fis);
            Object o = ois.readObject();
            if (o instanceof Message) {
                Message m = (Message) o;
                System.out.println("Received message");
                processCertificate((X509Certificate) m.certificate);
                PublicKey pk = m.certificate.getPublicKey();
                if (m.object.verify(pk, Signature.getInstance("DSA"))) {
                    System.out.println("Message is valid");
                    System.out.println(m.object.getObject());
                }
                else System.out.println("Message signature is invalid");
            }
            else System.out.println("Message is corrupted");
        } catch (Exception e) {
            e.printStackTrace();
        }
    }
}
```

We've seen most of this code in previous chapters; in particular, the processCer-tificate() method uses the standard certificate methods to extract and print information about the certificate. The new code for us is primarily in the verify-Signer() method, where we search the entire keystore for a name that matches the issuer of the certificate that was sent to us. If we find a match, we use the corresponding public key to verify the certificate we received.

This method shows yet another need for an alternate implementation of the KeyStore class—if you have to search the entire list of keys for a matching certificate like this, you clearly don't want to perform a linear search each time. An alternate keystore could provide a more efficient means of searching for certificates.

Signed Classes

One of the primary applications of digital signatures in Java is to create and verify signed classes. Signed classes allow the expansion of Java's sandbox in two different ways:

- The policy file can insist that classes coming from a particular site be signed by a particular entity before the access controller will grant that particular set of permissions. In the policy file, such an entry contains a signedBy directive:

```
grant signedBy "sdo", codeBase "http://piccolo.East.Sun.COM/" {
        java.io.FilePermission "-", "read,write";
}
```

  This entry allows classes that are loaded from *piccolo.East.Sun.COM* to read and write any local files under the current directory only if the classes have been signed by sdo.

- The security manager can cooperate with the class loader in order to determine whether or not a particular class is signed; the security manager is then free to grant permissions to that class based on its own internal policy. This technique is far more important in Java 1.1, since most Java 1.2 security managers simply defer decisions to the access controller.

In this section, we'll explore the necessary components behind this expansion of the Java sandbox. This example in the rest of the section fills in the remaining details of the JavaRunner program by showing us how to use a signed class.

There are three necessary ingredients to expand the Java sandbox with signed classes:

- A method to create the signed class. The jarsigner utility is used for this (see Appendix A).

- A class loader that knows how to understand the digital signature associated with the class. The URLClassLoader class knows how to do this, but we'll show an example of how to do that for our JavaRunnerLoader class as well.

- A security manager or access controller that grants the desired permissions based on the digital signature. The default access controller will do this for us; we'll show how the security manager might do this directly.

Reading Signed JAR Files

Signed classes in the Java-browser world are typically delivered as signed JAR files; there are various tools (javakey for Java 1.1 and jarsigner for Java 1.2) that can take an ordinary JAR file and attach a digital signature to it. A signed JAR file has three special elements:

- A manifest (MANIFEST.MF), containing a listing of the files in the archive that have been signed, along with a message digest for each signed file.

- A signature file (XXX.SF, where XXX is the name of the entity that signed the archive) that contains signature information. The data in this file is comprised of message digests of entries in the manifest file.

- A block file (XXX.DSA, where XXX is the name of the entity that signed the archive and DSA is the name of the signature algorithm used to create the signature). The block file contains the actual signature data in a format known as PKCS7.

There are many advantages to this format, not the least of which is that the PKCS7 block file (that is, the signature itself) is a standard format for external signatures. Unfortunately, the necessary classes to create PKCS7 blocks are not part of Java's public API; if you want to be able to write a signed JAR file, you'll need to write the classes to create the signature block yourself.

However, we can read a signed JAR file using the core API. This means that the class loader we've been using for the JavaRunner program can be modified to read a standard JAR file and associate the digital signature of that archive with the classes it loads.

We'll enhance the JarLoader class loader that we first developed in Chapter 3 in order to read the signature. For reference, we'll show the entire class again here, although only the highlighted portions of it have changed (it also contains some methods that we added in Chapter 6):

```
public class JarLoader extends SecureClassLoader {
    private URL urlBase;
    public boolean printLoadMessages = true;
    Hashtable classArrays;
```

```
Hashtable classIds;
static int groupNum = 0;
ThreadGroup threadGroup;

public JarLoader(String base, ClassLoader parent) {
    super(parent);
    try {
        if (!(base.endsWith("/")))
            base = base + "/";
        urlBase = new URL(base);
        classArrays = new Hashtable();
        classIds = new Hashtable();
    } catch (Exception e) {
        throw new IllegalArgumentException(base);
    }
}

private byte[] getClassBytes(InputStream is) {
    ByteArrayOutputStream baos = new ByteArrayOutputStream();
    BufferedInputStream bis = new BufferedInputStream(is);
    boolean eof = false;
    while (!eof) {
        try {
            int i = bis.read();
            if (i == -1)
                eof = true;
            else baos.write(i);
        } catch (IOException e) {
            return null;
        }
    }
    return baos.toByteArray();
}

protected Class findClass(String name) {
    String urlName = name.replace('.', '/');
    byte buf[];
    Class cl;

    SecurityManager sm = System.getSecurityManager();
    if (sm != null) {
        int i = name.lastIndexOf('.');
        if (i >= 0)
            sm.checkPackageDefinition(name.substring(0, i));
    }

    buf = (byte[]) classArrays.get(urlName);
    if (buf != null) {
        Certificate ids[] = (Certificate) classIds.get(urlName);
```

```
            CodeSource cs = new CodeSource(urlBase, ids);
            cl = defineClass(name, buf, 0, buf.length, cs);
            return cl;
        }

        try {
            URL url = new URL(urlBase, urlName + ".class");
            if (printLoadMessages)
                System.out.println("Loading " + url);
            InputStream is = url.openConnection().getInputStream();
            buf = getClassBytes(is);
            CodeSource cs = new CodeSource(urlBase, null);
            cl = defineClass(name, buf, 0, buf.length, cs);
            return cl;
        } catch (Exception e) {
            System.out.println("Can't load " + name + ": " + e);
            return null;
        }
    }

    public void readJarFile(String name) {
        URL jarUrl = null;
        JarInputStream jis;
        JarEntry je;

        try {
            jarUrl = new URL(urlBase, name);
        } catch (MalformedURLException mue) {
            System.out.println("Unknown jar file " + name);
            return;
        }
        if (printLoadMessages)
            System.out.println("Loading jar file " + jarUrl);

        try {
            jis = new JarInputStream(
                        jarUrl.openConnection().getInputStream());
        } catch (IOException ioe) {
            System.out.println("Can't open jar file " + jarUrl);
            return;
        }

        try {
            while ((je = jis.getNextJarEntry()) != null) {
                String jarName = je.getName();
                if (jarName.endsWith(".class"))
                    loadClassBytes(jis, jarName, je);
                // else ignore it; it could be an image or audio file
                jis.closeEntry();
```

```
            }
        } catch (IOException ioe) {
            System.out.println("Badly formatted jar file");
        }
    }

    private void loadClassBytes(JarInputStream jis,
                                String jarName, JarEntry je) {
        if (printLoadMessages)
            System.out.println("\t" + jarName);
        BufferedInputStream jarBuf = new BufferedInputStream(jis);
        ByteArrayOutputStream jarOut = new ByteArrayOutputStream();
        int b;
        try {
            while ((b = jarBuf.read()) != -1)
                jarOut.write(b);
            String className = jarName.substring(0, jarName.length() -
6);
            classArrays.put(className, jarOut.toByteArray());
            Certificate c[] = je.getCertificates();
            if (c == null)
                c = new Certificate[0];
            classIds.put(className, c);
        } catch (IOException ioe) {
            System.out.println("Error reading entry " + jarName);
        }
    }

    public void checkPackageAccess(String name) {
        SecurityManager sm = System.getSecurityManager();
        if (sm != null)
            sm.checkPackageAccess(name);
    }

    ThreadGroup getThreadGroup() {
        if (threadGroup == null)
            threadGroup = new ThreadGroup(
                        "JavaRuner ThreadGroup-" + groupNum++);
        return threadGroup;
    }

    String getHost() {
        return urlBase.getHost();
    }
}
```

Interestingly enough, all the details of the digital signature are handled for us by the classes in the jar package. All that we're left to do is obtain the array of signers when we read in each JAR entry and then use that array of signers when we construct the code source we use to define the class. Remember that each file in a JAR file may be signed by a different group of identities and that some may not be signed at all. This is why we must construct a new code source object for each signed class that was in the JAR file.

The Signed JAR File and Security Policies

The last item in our examination of signed JAR files involves the security policy and its interaction with the signed JAR file. In the case where the security policy is completely determined by the access controller, the class loader has already done all our work for us; the access controller depends on each class to have an appropriate code source, and permissions for that code will be completely defined in the policy file.

In Java 1.1, the mechanism is different; we can't use the JAR classes to parse a signed JAR file, and we can't use the defineClass() method to set the signers for a particular signed class. The first of these problems is harder to overcome; it requires that you implement the equivalent of the java.util.jar package. We've presented all the background information you'd need to do that, but it is a lot of code to write (so we won't). The second of these problems means that your class loader must define a class as follows:

```
if (isSecure(urlName)) {
    cl = defineClass(name, buf, 0, buf.length);
    if (ids != null)
        setSigners(cl, ids);
}
else cl = defineClass(name, buf, 0, buf.length);
```

The isSecure() method in this case must base its decision on information obtained from reading the manifest of the JAR file and verifying the signature that is contained in the signature file. The array of ids will need to be created by constructing instances of the Identity class to represent the signer of the class.

The reason for setting the signers in this way is to allow the security manager to retrieve those signatures easily. When the security manager does not defer all permissions to the access controller—and, hence, in all Java 1.1 programs—the security manager will need to take advantage of signed class information to base its decisions. This is typically done by programming the security manager to retrieve the keys that were used to sign a class via the getSigners() method. This allows the security manger to function with any standard signature-aware class loader. The security manager could then do something like this:

```
public void checkAccess(Thread t) {
    Class cl = currentLoadedClass();
    if (cl == null)
        return;
```

```
    Identity ids[] = (Identity[]) cl.getSigners();
    for (int i = 0; i < ids.length; i++) {
        if (isTrustedId(ids[i]))
            return;
    }
    throw new SecurityException("Can't modify thread states");
}
```

The key to this example is writing a good isTrustedId() method. A possible implementation is to use the information stored in the keystore (for 1.2) or identity database (for 1.1) to grant a level of trust to an entity; such an implementation requires that you have a non-default implementation of these databases. Alternately, your application could hardwire the public keys of certain entities (like the public key of the HR group of XYZ corporation) and use that information as the basis of its security decisions.

Implementing a Signature Class

Now that we've seen how to use the Signature class, we'll look at how to implement our own class. The techniques we'll see here should be very familiar from our other examples of implementing an engine in the security provider architecture. In particular, since in 1.2 the Signature class extends its own SPI, we can implement a single class that extends the Signature class.

To construct our subclass, we must use the following constructor:

protected Signature(String algorithm)
> This is the only constructor of the Signature class, so all subclasses of this class must use this constructor. The string passed to the constructor is the name that will be registered with the security provider.

Once we've constructed our engine object, we must implement the following methods in it:

protected abstract void engineInitVerify(PublicKey pk)
> Initialize the object to prepare it to verify a digital signature. If the public key does not support the correct algorithm or is otherwise corrupted, an InvalidKeyException is thrown.

protected abstract void engineInitSign(PrivateKey pk)
> Initialize the object to prepare it to create a digital signature. If the private key does not support the correct algorithm or is otherwise corrupted, an InvalidKeyException is thrown.

protected abstract void engineUpdate(byte b)
protected abstract void engineUpdate(byte b[], int off, int len)

Add the given bytes to the data that is being accumulated for the signature. These methods are called by the update() methods; they typically call the update() method of a message digest held in the engine. If the engine has not been correctly initialized, a SignatureException is thrown.

protected abstract byte[] engineSign()
protected int engineSign(byte[] outbuf, int offset, int len) ★

Create the signature based on the accumulated data. If there is an error in generating the signature, a SignatureException is thrown.

protected abstract boolean engineVerify(byte b[])

Return an indication of whether or not the given signature matches the expected signature of the accumulated data. If there is an error in validating the signature, a SignatureException is thrown.

protected abstract void engineSetParameter(String p, Object o) ☆
protected abstract void engineSetParameter(AlgorithmParameterSpec p) ★

Set the given parameters, which may be algorithm-specific. If this parameter does not apply to this algorithm, this method should throw an InvalidParameterException.

protected abstract Object engineGetParameter(String p) ☆

Return the desired parameter, which is algorithm-specific. If the given parameter does not apply to this algorithm, this method should throw an. InvalidParameterException.

In addition to those methods, there are a few protected instance variables that keep track of the state of the signature object—whether it has been initialized, whether it can be used to sign or to verify, and so on:

protected final static int UNINITIALIZED
protected final static int SIGN
protected final static int VERIFY
protected int state

These variables control the internal state of signature object. The state is initially UNITIALIZED; it is set to SIGN by the initSign() method and to VERIFY by the initVerify() method.

These variables are not normally used by the subclasses of Signature, since the logic to maintain them is already implemented in the Signature class itself.

Here is an implementation of a signature class. Note that the XYZSign class depends on other aspects of the security architecture—in this example, the message digest engine to create an SHA message digest, and the DSA key interfaces to handle the public and private keys. This is very typical of signature algorithms—even to the point where the default name of the algorithm reflects the underlying components. The actual encryption of the message digest will use a simple XOR-based algorithm (so that we can, as usual, avoid the mathematics involved with a secure example).

```
public class XYZSign extends Signature implements Cloneable {
    private DSAPublicKey pub;
    private DSAPrivateKey priv;
    private MessageDigest md;

    public XYZSign() throws NoSuchAlgorithmException {
        super("XYZSign");
        md = MessageDigest.getInstance("SHA");
    }

    public void engineInitVerify(PublicKey publicKey)
                                throws InvalidKeyException {
        try {
            pub = (DSAPublicKey) publicKey;
        } catch (ClassCastException cce) {
            throw new InvalidKeyException("Wrong public key type");
        }
    }

    public void engineInitSign(PrivateKey privateKey)
                                throws InvalidKeyException {
        try {
            priv = (DSAPrivateKey) privateKey;
        } catch (ClassCastException cce) {
            throw new InvalidKeyException("Wrong private key type");
        }
    }

    public void engineUpdate(byte b) throws SignatureException {
        try {
            md.update(b);
        } catch (NullPointerException npe) {
            throw new SignatureException("No SHA digest found");
        }
    }

    public void engineUpdate(byte b[], int offset, int length)
                                throws SignatureException {
        try {
            md.update(b, offset, length);
        } catch (NullPointerException npe) {
            throw new SignatureException("No SHA digest found");
        }
    }
```

```java
public byte[] engineSign() throws SignatureException {
    byte b[] = null;
    try {
        b = md.digest();
    } catch (NullPointerException npe) {
        throw new SignatureException("No SHA digest found");
    }
    return crypt(b, priv);
}

public boolean engineVerify(byte[] sigBytes)
                                throws SignatureException {
    byte b[] = null;
    try {
        b = md.digest();
    } catch (NullPointerException npe) {
        throw new SignatureException("No SHA digest found");
    }
    byte sig[] = crypt(sigBytes, pub);
    return MessageDigest.isEqual(sig, b);
}

public void engineSetParameter(String param, Object value) {
    throw new InvalidParameterException("No parameters");
}

public void engineSetParameter(AlgorithmParameterSpec aps) {
    throw new InvalidParameterException("No parameters");
}

public Object engineGetParameter(String param) {
    throw new InvalidParameterException("No parameters");
}

public void engineReset() {
}

private byte[] crypt(byte s[], DSAKey key) {
    DSAParams p = key.getParams();
    int rotValue = p.getP().intValue();
    byte d[] = rot(s, (byte) rotValue);
    return d;
}

private byte[] rot(byte in[], byte rotValue) {
    byte out[] = new byte[in.length];
    for (int i = 0; i < in.length; i++) {
        out[i] = (byte) (in[i] ^ rotValue);
```

```
        }
        return out;
    }
}
```

Like all implementations of engines in the security architecture, this class must have a constructor that takes no arguments, but it must call its superclass with its name. The constructor also is responsible for creating the instance of the underlying message digest using whatever algorithm this class feels is important. It is interesting to note that this requires the constructor to specify that it can throw a NoSuchAlgorithmException (in case the SHA algorithm can't be found).

The keys for this test algorithm are required to be DSA public and private keys. In general, the correspondence between an algorithm and the type of key it requires is very strong, so this is a typical usage. Hence, the two engine initialization methods cast the key to make sure that the key has the correct format. The engine initialization methods are not required to keep track of the state of the signature object—that is, whether the object has been initialized for signing or for verifying. That logic, since it is common to all signature objects, is present in the generic initialization methods of the Signature class itself.

The methods that update the engine can simply pass their data to the message digest, since the message digest is responsible for providing the fingerprint of the data that this object is going to sign or verify. Hence, the only interesting logic in this class is that employed by the signing and verification methods. Each method uses the message digest to create the digital fingerprint of the data. Then, to sign the data, the digest must be encrypted or otherwise operated upon with the previously defined private key—this produces a unique digest that could only have been produced by the given data and the given private key. Conversely, to verify the data, the digest must be decrypted or otherwise operated upon with the previously defined public key; the resulting digest can then be compared to the expected digest to test for verification.

Clearly, the security of this algorithm depends on a strong implementation of the signing operations. Our example here does not meet that definition—we're simply XORing every byte of the digest with a byte obtained from the parameters used to generate the keys. This XOR-encryption provides a good example, since it's both simple and symmetric; a real digital signature implementation is much more complex.

These engine signing and verification methods are also responsible for setting the internal state of the engine back to an initialization state, so that the same object can be used to sign or verify multiple signatures. In this case, no other work needs to be done for that; the message digest object itself is already reset once it creates its digest, and there is no other internal state inside the algorithm that needs to be reset. But if there were another state, it would need to be reset in those methods.

Summary

We've now completed our look at the basic engines that comprise the default security architecture on the Java platform. The digital signatures we've examined in this chapter form the pinnacle of that architecture, since they are the mechanism by which the parameters of the Java security sandbox can be extended: a digital signature gives the user the assurance that particular Java classes were provided by known entities. The user is then free to adopt a security policy for those classes based on the user's assessment of the trustworthiness of the entity that provided the classes.

The digital signature engine is interesting also because it requires the use of the other engines we've looked at in earlier chapters—the message digest engine to generate the fingerprint of the data that the digital signature will sign, and the key pair engine (and its related classes) to provide the necessary keys to feed into this engine. In sum, then, the engines provided with Java can really be thought of as having a single purpose: creating and verifying digital signatures. A digital signature thus becomes the basis of the advanced Java security model.

Important as digital signatures are, however, they do not complete what many people would expect from a security provider, in that the data communicated with a digital signature is itself not encrypted. This data is therefore vulnerable to being read by anyone. In the next chapter, we'll delve into an optional engine that can be loaded into the Java virtual machine—the engine to provide encryption of arbitrary streams of data. Although that engine cannot be used universally, it does provide (in those situations where it can be used) this last piece of security.

13

In this chapter:
• *Export Restrictions*
• *The Sun Security Provider in the JCE*
• *Key Types in the JCE*
• *Secret Key Engines*
• *Encrypting Data*
• *Cipher Streams*
• *Symmetric Key Agreement*
• *Sealed Objects*

Encryption

In this chapter, we'll examine the Java Cryptography Extension, which provides (among other things) an engine to perform encryption of arbitrary data. This engine allows developers to send and receive encrypted streams of data over the network or through a filesystem (subject to some export restrictions we'll also discuss).

The encryption engine we'll discuss in this chapter does not come with the JDK. Information in this chapter is based on the early access 2 release for JDK 1.2* of the Java Cryptography Extension (JCE); because it is an early access release, the information is subject to change when JCE is officialy released (tentatively scheduled for mid-1998). The JCE introduces four new engine classes to the Java security architecture—one to perform encryption, and three that handle keys for encryption—and it comes with a new security provider to implement those classes. We'll discuss all of these features in this chapter.

Export Restrictions

Use of the JCE is strictly limited by the export restrictions of the U.S. government. Sun Microsystems is headquartered in the United States, so the export of the JCE is controlled by the U.S. government. Because this implementation is capable of strong encryption, the only countries where it may be used are the United States and Canada.

There are ongoing legal challenges to this position as well as increasing negotiations with the U.S. government to change this policy; at the same time, there are increasing efforts to prohibit the use of this technology even within the United

---

* 1.2 is now Java 2.

States. The official policy regarding export of encryption software has changed a few times over the past few years and is likely to change frequently in the next few years as various parties attempt to reach a coherent policy. Right now, the U.S. government will grant an exemption for certain types of companies to use encryption in their global business; what will happen in the future is anyone's guess.

In addition, the U.S. is not the only government that is hostile to the use of encryption, and encryption software can face import restrictions as well as export restrictions. In France, for example, it is illegal to import the JCE without a license. Other countries have regulations for cryptography, but in most cases they are less onerous than those of the United States. However, it is always wise to check your local policies to be sure (see Appendix C for resources to find more information about these limitations).

According to the letter of the restrictions, technical information regarding the JCE also cannot be exported except in the form of published books such as this one (because the book is protected by the first amendment to the U.S. Constitution). This has not prevented several companies and groups outside the United States from reimplementing the JCE encryption APIs, with the result that there are now several third-party security providers that include their own implementations of the JCE and are available outside the United States (the list of third-party security providers in Appendix C includes some of these implementations).

Many of the popular algorithms that are used by the encryption engine (and some of the other cryptographic engines that we've looked at) are patented algorithms, which also restricts their use. RSA Data Security, Inc., holds a patent in the U.S. on several algorithms involving RSA encryption and digital signatures; Ascom System AG in Switzerland holds both U.S. and European patents on the IDEA method of performing encryption. If you live in a country where these patents apply, you cannot use these underlying algorithms without paying a license to the patent holder. In particular, this means that many of the third-party security providers and third-party implementations of the JCE cannot be used within the United States because of patents held by RSA (although some of them have reached a licensing agreement with RSA Data Security, Inc.—again, it is best to check with the provider to see what restrictions might apply).

For at least the time being, then, Java programmers are faced with the following restrictions on use of the JCE:

- The JCE must be procured separately from the JDK. The official JCE from Sun may only be procured by citizens of the United States and Canada, but third-party implementations of the JCE may be obtainable elsewhere.

- Electronic documentation of the JCE is subject to the same restriction. In practice, the restriction about electronic documentation of encryption techniques—which applies to many things other than the JCE—is rarely enforced and widely violated.

- Code that uses the APIs we are going to discuss in this chapter and that was developed inside the United States or Canada may not be distributed electronically outside the United States and Canada. Hence, if you are a resident of the United States or Canada, you cannot use these APIs to develop applets that you put on the Internet, or to develop applications that you send outside the United States and Canada.

  Since no browser currently implements the JCE, the impact of this restriction on browsers is somewhat muted. However, some third-party implementations of the JCE will be compatible with popular browsers; these third-party implementations could be downloaded and installed manually by the user, who could then use cryptography only in applets that were developed outside the United States and Canada or that are available only on private networks wholly within the United States and Canada.

  This restriction also means that, unlike the other examples in this book, the examples in this chapter may not be downloaded from the O'Reilly ftp site.

- Questions about these APIs cannot be answered via email (although this is another rule that applies in general to encryption algorithms and is—again, at least presently—rarely enforced in the general case).

These APIs, then, will typically be used:

- To develop applications for use on a private intranet that is located wholly within the United States and Canada. XYZ Corporation may want to use this technology for their payroll application; without this technology, although payroll data may only be retrieved upon a valid signed request, that data is still shipped over the network unencrypted, where an inside corporate spy could snoop the wire and obtain the data.

  With the APIs we'll discuss in this chapter, we could encrypt the payroll data as it is passed over the network. This completes the security protection that such an application really needs. We are assured that the payroll data is only being sent to an authorized user, and we are assured that no one can decode the data while it is in transit.

- By developers outside the United States, who are effectively in a much better position to take advantage of them than are their U.S. counterparts. These developers, however, will be dependent upon third-party implementations of the JCE.

You'll notice that this is the only part of this book where we've discussed export restrictions. Somewhat surprisingly, that is because this is the only instance in

Encryption and Weaponry

The prohibitions we've been discussing here occur because strong encryption is considered by the U.S. government to be a munitions-grade weapon. While this position is often questioned, it comes from a long tradition in computer science.

During WWII, the Allies waged a successful and pivotal campaign in the Atlantic against the Axis navy. The success of this campaign was greatly due to the work of Alan Turing, who with his colleagues broke the German encryption algorithm known as Enigma. Turing was also one of the founding fathers of modern computer science, much of which was based on the work he developed in service to his country during the war.

Ironically, the reward that Turing reaped for his efforts was that some years after the war, he was arrested and forced to undergo harmful chemical treatments because he was gay. There's an odd parallel here: many of the harsh restrictions that are presently placed on encryption technology make no more sense in a world with a global Internet than did England's persecution of Alan Turing in the 1950s. But the links between encryption and military security run deep and are not likely to be broken anytime soon.

which the export restrictions of the U.S. government apply. Encryption of arbitrary data is considered a weapons-grade munition, but message digests and digital signatures are not. Hence, the APIs that allow us to calculate a message digest and a digital signature are freely exportable, but the APIs that allow us to encrypt and decrypt data are not.

Note also that the restriction here is not only on the algorithms that perform encryption, but on the APIs themselves. Like other engines we've examined, the encryption engine allows us to plug in any arbitrary algorithm to perform the encryption. This includes a weak encryption algorithm (that is, one that can be broken) that by itself would be exportable. But since the API allows a strong encryption algorithm to be used as well, the export restrictions apply to the API itself, even if the strong encryption implementation is not provided. Hence, the JCE may not be exported in its present form.

The Sun Security Provider in the JCE

The JCE follows the same security provider infrastructure as does the rest of the Java security architecture; the JCE comes with an additional security provider that includes implementations of the engines of the JCE. In normal use, this security provider supplements the default security provider of the JDK; the security provider within the JCE contains implementations only of the engines of the JCE. Hence, to use the Sun JCE security provider, you need to add the SunJCE class (com.sun.crypto.provider.SunJCE) to your *java.security* file like this:

```
security.provider.2=com.sun.crypto.provider.SunJCE
```

Alternately, you may use the addProvider() or insertProviderAt() methods of the Security class. You may, of course, insert this provider at any position in the list of providers.

There are five new engine classes in the JCE: the Cipher, KeyAgreement, KeyGenerator, Mac, and SecretKeyFactory engines. Table 13-1 lists the engines and algorithms that are provided by the SunJCE security provider. In addition to implementations of the new engines, the SunJCE security provider gives us a key factory and a key pair generator for Diffie-Hellman (DH) keys as well as a new engine for working with keystores. As always, there may be additional algorithm names in third-party security providers. Also note that the algorithm name for the cipher engine may be more complex than we've shown here.

Table 13-1. Engine Classes of the JCE

Engine Name	Algorithm
Cipher	DES
Cipher	DESede
Cipher	PBEWithMD5AndDES
KeyAgreement	DH
KeyFactory	DH
KeyGenerator	DES
KeyGenerator	DESede
KeyPairGenerator	DH
SecretKeyFactory	DES
SecretKeyFactory	DESede
SecretKeyFactory	PBE
Mac	HmacSHA1
Mac	HmacMD5
KeyStore	JCEKS

Key Types in the JCE

The JCE introduces many new types of keys. Some of these are new types of public and private keys that extend our previous exploration of keys, and some of these are a new type of key: a secret key.

The new public and private key types are defined in the `javax.crypto.inter-`faces package of the JCE as new interfaces:

public interface DHKey
public interface DHPrivateKey extends DHKey, PrivateKey
public interface DHPublicKey extends DHKey, PublicKey

This set of interfaces defines keys suitable for use in Diffie-Hellman algorithms. In the SunJCE provider, they are used for the key agreement engine.

Like their DSA-based counterparts (the `DSAKey`, `DSAPublicKey`, and `DSAPri-`vateKey classes), these interfaces all have specific methods to retrieve the values of certain parameters of the key. Since they are all keys, they support a byte-encoded format as well. For our purposes, however, we'll treat their data as opaque objects. The Diffie-Hellman keys are used in the key agreement protocol we discuss later in this chapter.

Secret Keys

The new type of key in the JCE is a secret key. A secret key is a key that is shared between two parties in a cryptographic operation.

Until now, we've used public key/private key pairs for all our operations. For instance, the digital signature algorithms we explored in Chapter 12 all depended on public key cryptography to alter the message digest of the data they signed. These algorithms chose to use public key encryption because it simplified the way in which keys were exchanged, as well as reducing the number of keys that needed to be exchanged between parties. It is possible to use public and private key pairs to perform encryption of data using the APIs in this chapter; because two different keys are involved, this type of encryption is called asymmetric encryption.

Cryptographic algorithms can also implement symmetric operations, in which case only a single key is necessary. In symmetric encryption, the same key that was originally used to encrypt the data can also be used to decrypt the data. Hence, for these encryption algorithms, only a single key is necessary. This single key is also called a secret key, since the key itself must be kept secret by the parties who are exchanging the encrypted data. Anyone who has access to the key and to the encrypted data also has access to the data.

The key used by the encryption engine—whether it is used by a symmetric or an asymmetric encryption algorithm—is still an instance of the class `java.secu-`rity.Key. Just as there were interfaces that identified types of keys as public (`PublicKey`) or private (`PrivateKey`), there is a new `SecretKey` interface (`javax.crypto.SecretKey`) that is used by symmetric keys.

public interface SecretKey extends Key

> Identify a class as being a symmetric 'key. Like other extensions of the Key interface, this interface has no methods and is used strictly for type identification.

As usual, there are no classes in the javax package that implement this interface, though some are provided in the sun package. A simple implementation of this interface must include the usual methods that are in the Key interface:

```
public class XORKey implements SecretKey {
    byte value;

    public XORKey(byte b) {
        value = b;
    }

    public String getAlgorithm() {
        return "XOR";
    }

    public String getFormat() {
        return "XOR Special Format";
    }

    public byte[] getEncoded() {
        byte b[] = new byte[1];
        b[0] = value;
        return b;
    }
}
```

Unlike public and private keys, secret keys are not associated with identities and are not integrated into a key management system. Secret keys must therefore be managed with different techniques, which we'll examine at the end of this chapter.

Secret Key Engines

In the JCE, there are new ways to generate keys. Since the existing key engines only operate on public and private keys, the JCE introduces two new engines that can operate on secret keys. Note also in Table 13-1 that the SunJCE security provider implements a new algorithm to generate key pairs for Diffie-Hellman key agreement; that algorithm uses the standard KeyPairGenerator class we explored in Chapter 10.

The KeyGenerator Class

The first engine we'll look at is the KeyGenerator class (javax.crypto.Key-Generator); this class is used to generate secret keys. This class is very similar to the KeyPairGenerator class except that it generates instances of secret keys instead of pairs of public and private keys:

public class KeyGenerator
> Generate instances of secret keys for use by a symmetric encryption algorithm.

The KeyGenerator class is an engine within the JCE. As such, it has all the hallmarks of a cryptographic engine. It has a complementary SPI and a set of public methods that are used to operate upon it, and its implementation must be registered with the security provider.

Using the KeyGenerator class

Like other engine classes, the KeyGenerator class does not have any public constructors. An instance of a KeyGenerator is obtained by calling one of these methods:

public static final KeyGenerator getInstance(String algorithm)
public static final KeyGenerator getInstance(String algorithm, String provider)
> Return an object capable of generating secret keys that correspond to the given algorithm. These methods use the standard rules of searching the list of security providers in order to find an object that implements the desired algorithm. If the generator for the appropriate algorithm cannot be found, a NoSuchAlgorithmException is thrown; if the named provider cannot be found, a NoSuchProviderException is thrown.

Once an object has been obtained with these methods, the generator must be initialized by calling one of these methods:

public final void init(SecureRandom sr)
public final void init(AlgorithmParameterSpec aps)
public final void init(AlgorithmParameterSpec aps, SecureRandom sr)
public final void init(int strength)
public final void init(int strength, SecureRandom sr)
> Initialize the key generator. Like a key pair generator, the key generator needs a source of random numbers to generate its keys (in the second method, a default instance of the SecureRandom class will be used). In addition, some key generators can accept an algorithm parameter specification to initialize their keys (just as the key pair generator); however, for the DES-style keys generated by the SunJCE security provider, no algorithm parameter specification may be used.

A key generator does not have to be initialized explicitly, in which case it is initialized internally with a default instance of the SecureRandom class. However, it is up to the implementor of the engine class to make sure that this happens correctly; it is better to be sure your code will work by always initializing your key generator.

A secret key can be generated by calling this method:

public final SecretKey generateKey()

Generate a secret key. A generator can produce multiple keys by repeatedly calling this method.

There are two additional methods in this class, both of which are informational:

public final String getAlgorithm()

Return the string representing the name of the algorithm this generator supports.

public final Provider getProvider()

Return the provider that was used to obtain this key generator.

In the next section, we'll show the very simple code needed to use this class to generate a secret key.

Implementing a KeyGenerator class

Implementing a key generator requires implementing its corresponding SPI. Like all engines that are not available in Java 1.1, the SPI for the KeyGenerator class is unrelated in the class hierarchy to the KeyGenerator class itself, and the class that we register with the security provider must extend the KeyGeneratorSpi class (javax.crypto.KeyGeneratorSpi):

public abstract class KeyGeneratorSpi

This class forms the service provider interface class for the KeyGenerator class.

There are three protected methods of this class that we must implement if we want to provide an SPI for a key generator:

protected abstract SecretKey engineGenerateKey()

Generate the secret key. This method should use the installed random number generator and (if applicable) the installed algorithm parameter specification to generate the secret key. If the engine has not been initialized, it is expected that this method will initialize the engine with a default instance of the SecureRandom class.

protected abstract void engineInit(SecureRandom sr)
protected abstract void engineInit(AlgorithmParameterSpec aps, SecureRandom sr)
public final void engineInit(int strength, SecureRandom sr)

Initialize the key generation engine with the given random number generator and, if applicable, algorithm parameter specification. If the class does not support initialization via an algorithm parameter specification, or if the specification is invalid, an InvalidAlgorithmParameterException should be thrown.

Hence, a complete implementation might look like this:

```
public class XORKeyGenerator extends KeyGeneratorSpi {
    SecureRandom sr;

    public void engineInit(SecureRandom sr) {
        this.sr = sr;
    }

    public void engineInit(AlgorithmParameterSpec ap, SecureRandom sr)
                    throws InvalidAlgorithmParameterException {
        throw new InvalidAlgorithmParameterException(
            "No parameters supported in this class");
    }

    public SecretKey engineGenerateKey() {
        if (sr == null)
            sr = new SecureRandom();

        byte b[] = new byte[1];
        sr.nextBytes(b);
        return new XORKey(b[0]);
    }
}
```

Keys, of course, are usually longer than a single byte. However, unlike a public key/private key pair, there is not necessarily a mathematical requirement for generating a symmetric key. Such a requirement depends on the encryption algorithm the key will be used for, and some symmetric encryption algorithms require a key that is just an arbitrary sequence of bytes.

The SecretKeyFactory Class

The second engine that we'll look at is the SecretKeyFactory class (javax.crypto.SecretKeyFactory). Like the KeyFactory class, this class can convert from algorithmic or encoded key specifications to actual key objects and can translate key objects from one implementation to another. Unlike the

KeyFactory class, which can only operate on public and private keys, the Secret-KeyFactory class can operate only on secret keys:

public class SecretKeyFactory

Provide an engine that can translate between secret key specifications and secret key objects (and vice versa). This allows for secret keys to be imported and exported in a neutral format.

The interface to the SecretKeyFactory class is exactly the same at a conceptual level as the interface to the KeyFactory. At a programming level, this means that while most of the methods between the two classes have the same name and perform the same operation, they may require slightly different parameters: a secret key, rather than a public or private key. In addition, instead of methods to generate public or private keys, the SecretKeyFactory class contains this method:

public final SecretKey generateSecret(KeySpec ks)

Generate the secret key according to the given specification. If the specification is invalid, an InvalidKeySpecException is thrown.

Because of its similarity to the KeyFactory class, we won't show an example of how to use it; you may use examples from Chapter 10 and simply substitute this new method.

Secret key specifications

The specifications used to import and export secret keys depend on the underlying algorithm that generated the secret key. As a result, the JCE provides twelve new key specifications that deal with the new keys the JCE provides:

public class DESKeySpec implements KeySpec

This class provides the encoded and algorithmic parameter specifications for DES keys.

public class DESedeKeySpec implements KeySpec

This class provides the encoded specification for DESede keys.

public class DHGenParameterSpec implements AlgorithmParameterSpec
public class DHParameterSpec implements AlgorithmParameterSpec

These classes implement algorithm specifications for Diffie-Hellman keys.

public class DHPrivateKeySpec implements KeySpec
public class DHPublicKeySpec implements KeySpec

These classes implement the encoded key specifications for Diffie-Hellman keys.

public class PBEKeySpec implements KeySpec
public class PBEParameterSpec implements AlgorithmParameterSpec

These classes implement the encoded and algorithm key specifications for the password-based cipher algorithm (the PKCS#5 standard).

public class IvParameterSpec implements AlgorithmParameterSpec

This class implements an initialization vector. Initialization vectors are used in many algorithms; notably in DES.

public class RC2ParameterSpec implements AlgorithmParameterSpec
public class RC5ParameterSpec implements AlgorithmParameterSpec

These classes implement the algorithm parameter specifications for RC2 and RC5 encryption.

public class SecretKeySpec implements KeySpec

This class implements a key specification for the new class of secret keys.

We typically treat the values contained in these specifications as opaque values. Table 13-2 lists the methods for each class needed to import and export each of these key specifications. As usual for key specifications, exporting a specification involves transmitting the individual data elements of the class, while importing a specification involves constructing the specification with the correct values.

Table 13-2. Importing and Exporting Values from the Key Specification Classes

Key Specifications	Methods to Export Data	Methods to Import Data
DESKeySpec	byte[] getKey()	DESKeySpec(byte[] buf) DESKeySpec(byte[] buf, int offset)

IvParameterSpec	byte[] getIV()	IvParameterSpec(
		      byte[] buf)
		IvParameterSpec(
		      byte[] buf, int
		offset)

DESedeKeySpec	byte[] getKey()	DESedeKeySpec(byte[] buf) DESedeKeySpec(byte[] buf, int offset)

DHGenParameter-
Spec
	int getPrimeSize()
	int getExponentSize()
		DHGenParameterSpec(
		    int primeSize,
		    int exponentSize)

Table 13-2. Importing and Exporting Values from the Key Specification Classes (continued)

Key Specifications	Methods to Export Data	Methods to Import Data

DHParameterSpec	BigInteger getP()
	BigInteger getG()
	int getL()
		DHParameterSpec(
		    BigInteger p,
		    BigInteger g)
		DHParameterKeySpec(
		    BigInteger p,
		    BigInteger g,
		    int l)

DHPrivateKeySpec	BigInteger getX()
	BigInteger getP()
	BigInteger getG()
	int getL()
		DHPrivateKeySpec(
		    BigInteger x,
		    BigInteger p,
		    BigInteger g)
		DHPrivateKeySpec(
		    BigInteger x,
		    BigInteger p,
		    BigInteger g, int l)

DHPublicKeySpec	BigInteger getY()
	BigInteger getP()
	BigInteger getG()
	int getL()
		DHPublicKeySpec(
		    BigInteger x,
		    BigInteger p,
		    BigInteger g)
		DHPublicKeySpec(
		    BigInteger x,
		    BigInteger p,
		    BigInteger g, int l)

PBEKeySpec	String getPassword()	PBEKeySpec(String pw)
PBEParameterSpec	int getIterationCount() byte[] getSalt()	PBEParameterSpec(byte[] salt, int count)
RC2ParameterSpec	byte[] getIV() int getEffectiveKey- Bits()	RC2ParameterSpec(int effec- tive) RC2ParameterSpec(int effec- tive, byte[] iv) RC2ParameterSpec(int effec- tive, byte[] iv, int offset)
RC5ParameterSpec	byte[] getIV() int getRounds() int getVersion() int getWordSize()	RC5ParameterSpec(int version, int rounds, int wordSize) RC5ParameterSpec(int version, int rounds, int wordSize, byte[] iv) RC5ParameterSpec(int version, int rounds, int wordSize, byte[] iv, int offset)
SecretKeySpec	byte[] getEncoded()	SecretKeySpec(byte[] key, String Algorithm) SecretKeySpec(byte[] key, int offset, String Algo- rithm)

The secret key factory SPI

Like all engines, the secret key engine is implemented via an SPI; if you want to implement your own secret key factory you must extend the SecretKeyFactorySpi class (javax.crypto.SecretKeyFactorySpi):

public abstract class SecretKeyFactorySpi
>   This class is the SPI for the SecretKeyFactory class. As this class is only available as an extension to 1.2, the SPI is unrelated to the engine class; providers must extend this class directly to provide a secret key factory.

Implementation of this class follows the implementation of a key factory SPI, except that the methods of this class must operate upon secret keys rather than public or private keys. If you want to implement a secret key factory SPI, you can use the sample key factory SPI as a model.

Encrypting Data

In this section, we'll look at the engine that performs encryption within the JCE. This engine is called the Cipher class (javax.crypto.Cipher); it provides an interface to encrypt and decrypt data either in arrays within the program or as that data is read or written through Java's stream interfaces:

public class Cipher implements Cloneable
>   Perform encryption and decryption of arbitrary data, using (potentially) a wide array of encryption algorithms.

Like all security engines, the cipher engine implements named algorithms. However, the naming convention for the cipher engine is different, in that cipher algorithms are compound names that can include the name of the algorithm along with the name of a padding scheme and the name of a mode. Padding schemes and modes are specified by names—just like algorithms. In theory, just as you may pick a new name for an algorithm, you may specify new names for a padding scheme or a mode, although the SunJCE security provider specifies several standard ones.

Modes and padding schemes are present in the Cipher class because that class implements what is known as a block cipher; that is, it expects to operate on data one block (e.g., 8 bytes) at a time. Padding schemes are required in order to ensure that the length of the data is an integral number of blocks.

Modes are provided to further alter the encrypted data in an attempt to make it harder to break the encryption. For example, if the data to be encrypted contains a number of similar patterns—repeated names, or header/footer information, for example—any patterns in the resulting data may aid in breaking the encryption.

Different modes of encrypting data help prevent these sorts of attacks. Depending upon the mode used by a cipher, it may need to be initialized in a special manner when the cipher is used for decryption. Some modes require initialization via an initialization vector.

Modes also enable a block cipher to behave as a stream cipher; that is, instead of requiring a large, 8-byte chunk of data to operate upon, a mode may allow data to be processed in smaller quantities. So modes are very important in stream-based operations, where data may need to be transmitted one or two characters at a time.

The modes specified by the SunJCE security provider are:

ECB

This is the electronic cookbook mode. ECB is the simplest of all modes; it takes a simple block of data (8 bytes in the SunJCE implementation, which is standard) and encrypts the entire block at once. No attempt is made to hide patterns in the data, and the blocks may be rearranged without affecting decryption (though the resulting plaintext will be out of order). Because of these limitations, ECB is recommended only for binary data; text or other data with patterns in it is not well-suited for this mode.

ECB mode can only operate on full blocks of data, so it is generally used with a padding scheme.

ECB mode does not require an initialization vector.

CBC

This is the cipher block chaining mode. In this mode, input from one block of data is used to modify the encryption of the next block of data; this helps to hide patterns (although data that contains identical initial text—such as mail messages—will still show an initial pattern). As a result, this mode is suitable for text data.

CBC mode can only operate on full blocks of data (8-byte blocks in the SunJCE implementation), so it is generally used with a padding scheme.

CBC mode requires an initialization vector for decryption.

CFB

This is the cipher-feedback mode. This mode is very similar to CBC, but its internal implementation is slightly different. CBC requires a full block (8 bytes) of data to begin its encryption, while CFB can begin encryption with a smaller amount of data. So this mode is suitable for encrypting text, especially when that text may need to be processed a character at a time. By default, CFB mode operates on 8-byte (64-bit) blocks, but you may append a number of bits after CFB (e.g., CFB8) to specify a different number of bits on which the mode should operate. This number must be a multiple of 8.

CFB requires that the data be padded so that it fills a complete block. Since that size may vary, the padding scheme that is used with it must vary as well. For CFB8, no padding is required, since data is always fed in an integral number of bytes.

CFB mode requires an initialization vector for decryption.

OFB

This is the output-feedback mode. This mode is also suitable for text; it is used most often when there is a possibility that bits of the encrypted data may be altered in transit (e.g., over a noisy modem). While a 1-bit error would cause an entire block of data to be lost in the other modes, it only causes a loss of 1 bit in this mode. By default, OFB mode operates on 8-byte (64-bit) blocks, but you may append a number of bits after OFB (e.g., OFB8) to specify a different number of bits on which the mode should operate. This number must be a multiple of 8.

OFB requires that the data be padded so that it fills a complete block. Since that size may vary, the padding scheme that is used with it must vary as well. For OFB8, no padding is required, since data is always fed in an integral number of bytes.

OFB mode requires an initialization vector for decryption.

PCBC

This is the propagating cipher block chaining mode. This mode is popular in a particular system known as Kerberos; if you need to speak to a Kerberos version 4 system, this is the mode to use. However, this mode has some known methods of attack, and Kerberos version 5 has switched to using CBC mode. Hence, PCBC mode is no longer recommended.

PCBC mode requires that the input be padded to a multiple of 8 bytes.

PCBC mode requires an initialization vector for decryption.

The padding schemes specified by the SunJCE security provider are:

PKCS5Padding

This padding scheme ensures that the input data is padded to a multiple of 8 bytes.

NoPadding

When this scheme is specified, no padding of input is done. In this case, the number of input bytes presented to the encryption cipher must be a multiple of the block size of the cipher; otherwise, when the cipher attempts to encrypt or decrypt the data, it generates an error.

Remember that these uses of mode and padding are specific to the SunJCE security provider. The modes and padding schemes are based upon accepted standards and are thus likely to be implemented in this manner by third-party security providers as well, but you should check your third-party provider documentation to be sure.

The mode and padding scheme specified for decryption must match the mode and padding scheme specified for encryption, or the decryption will fail.

Using the Cipher Class

In order to obtain an instance of the Cipher class, we call one of these methods:

public static Cipher getInstance(String algorithmName)
public static Cipher getInstance(String algorithmName, String provider)

Obtain a cipher engine that can perform encryption and decryption by implementing the named algorithm. The engine is provided by the given security provider, or the list of installed security providers is searched for an appropriate engine.

If an implementation of the given algorithm cannot be found, a NoSuchAlgorithmException is thrown. If the named provider cannot be found, a NoSuchProviderException is thrown.

The algorithm name passed to the getInstance() method may either be a simple algorithm name (e.g., DES), or it may be an algorithm name that specifies a mode and padding in this format: algorithm/mode/padding (e.g., DES/ECB/PKCS5Padding). If the mode and padding are not specified, they default to an implementation-specific value; in the SunJCE security provider, the mode defaults to ECB and padding defaults to PKCS5.

Once you've obtained a cipher object, you must initialize it. An object can be initialized for encryption or decryption, but in either case, you must provide a key. If the algorithm is a symmetric cipher, you should provide a secret key; otherwise, you should provide a public key to encrypt data and a private key to decrypt data (in fact, the key must match the algorithm type: a DES cipher must use a DES key, and so on). Initialization is achieved with one of these methods:

public final void init(int op, Key k)
public final void init(int op, Key k, AlgorithmParameterSpec aps)
public final void init(int op, Key k, AlgorithmParameterSpec aps, SecureRandom sr)
public final void init(int op, Key k, SecureRandom sr)
public final void init(int op, Key k, AlgorithmParameters ap)
public final void init(int op, Key k, AlgorithmParameters ap, SecureRandom sr)

Initialize the cipher to encrypt or decrypt data. If op is Cipher.ENCRYPT_MODE, the cipher is initialized to encrypt data; if op is Cipher.DECRYPT_MODE, the cipher is initialized to decrypt data. (In practice, other values will initialize the cipher for encryption rather than generating an exception; this is arguably a bug in the early-access implementation of the JCE.)

These calls reset the engine to an initial state, discarding any previous data that may have been fed to the engine. Hence, a single cipher object can be used to encrypt data and then later to decrypt data.

Many algorithm modes we discussed earlier require an initialization vector to be specified when the cipher is initialized for decrypting. In these cases, the initialization vector must be passed to the init() method within the algorithm parameter specification or algorithm parameters; the IvParameterSpec class is typically used to do this for DES encryption.

In the SunJCE security provider, specifying an initialization vector for a mode that does not support it will eventually lead to a NullPointerException. Failure to specify an initialization vector for a mode that requires one will generate incorrect decrypted data.

After an engine has been initialized, it must be fed data. There are two sets of methods to accomplish this. The first set can be used any number of times:

public final byte[] update(byte[] input)
public final byte[] update(byte[] input, int offset, int length)
public final int update(byte[] input, int offset, int length, byte[] output)
public final int update(byte[] input, int offset, int length, byte[] output, int outOffset)

Encrypt or decrypt the data in the input array (starting at the given offset for the given length, if applicable). The resulting data is either placed in the given output array (in which case the size of the output data is returned) or returned in a new array. If the cipher has not been initialized, an Illegal-StateException is thrown.

If the length of the data passed to this method is not an integral number of blocks, any extra data is buffered internally within the cipher engine; the next call to an update() or doFinal() method processes that buffered data as well as any new data that is just being provided.

If the given output buffer is too small to hold the data, a ShortBufferException is thrown. The required size of the output buffer can be obtained from the getOutputSize() method. A ShortBufferException does not clear the state of the cipher: any buffered data is still held, and the call can be repeated (with a correctly sized buffer) with no ill effects.

This second set of methods should only be called once:

public final byte[] doFinal()
public final int doFinal(byte[] output, int offset)
public final byte[] doFinal(byte[] input)

public final byte[] doFinal(byte[] input, int offset, int length)
public final int doFinal(byte[] input, int offset, int length, byte[] output)
public final int doFinal(byte[] input, int offset, int length, byte[] output, int outOffset)

Encrypt or decrypt the data in the input array as well as any data that has been previously buffered in the cipher engine. This method behaves exactly the same as the `update()` method, except that this method signals that all data has been fed to the engine. If the engine is performing padding, the padding scheme will be used to process the pad bytes (i.e., add padding bytes for encryption and remove padding bytes for decryption). If the cipher engine is not performing padding and the total of all processed data is not a multiple of the mode's block size, an `IllegalBlockSizeException` is thrown.

These methods throw an `IllegalStateException` or a `ShortBufferException` in the same circumstances as the `update()` methods.

In order to initialize some ciphers for decryption, you need to specify an initialization vector; this initialization vector must be the same vector that was used when the cipher was initialized for encryption. For encryption, you may specify the initialization vector, or you may use a system-provided initialization vector. In order to retrieve this vector for later use (e.g., to send it to someone who will eventually need to decrypt the data), you may use this method:

public final byte[] getIV()

Return the initialization vector that was used to initialize this cipher. If a system-provided initialization vector is used, that vector is not available until after the first call to an `update()` or `doFinal()` method.

In order to preallocate an output buffer for use in the `update()` and `doFinal()` methods, you must know its size, which is returned from this method:

public final int getOutputSize(int inputLength)

Return the output size for the next call to the `update()` or `doFinal()` methods, assuming that one of those methods is called with the specified amount of data. Note that the size returned from this call includes any possible padding that the `doFinal()` method might add. A call to the `update()` method may actually generate less data than this method would indicate, because it will not create any padding.

Finally, there are two miscellaneous methods of this class:

public final Provider getProvider()

Return the provider class that defined this engine.

public final int getBlockSize()

Get the block size of the mode of the algorithm that this cipher implements.

Let's put this all together into a simple example:

```java
public class CipherTest {
    public static void main(String args[]) {
        try {
            KeyGenerator kg = KeyGenerator.getInstance("DES");
            Cipher c = Cipher.getInstance("DES/CBC/PKCS5Padding");
            Key key = kg.generateKey();

            c.init(Cipher.ENCRYPT_MODE, key);
            byte input[] = "Stand and unfold yourself".getBytes();
            byte encrypted[] = c.doFinal(input);
            byte iv[] = c.getIV();

            IvParameterSpec dps = new IvParameterSpec(iv);
            c.init(Cipher.DECRYPT_MODE, key, dps);
            byte output[] = c.doFinal(encrypted);
            System.out.println("The string was ");
            System.out.println(new String(output));
        } catch (Exception e) {
            e.printStackTrace();
        }
    }
}
```

We've reused the single engine object to perform both the encryption and the decryption. Since DES is a symmetric encryption algorithm, we generated a single key that is used for both operations. Within the try block, the second block of code performs the encryption:

1. We initialize the cipher engine for encrypting.

2. We pass the bytes we want to encrypt to the doFinal() method. Of course, we might have had any number of calls to the update() method preceding this call, with data in any arbitrary amounts. Since we've specified a padding scheme, we don't have to worry about the size of the data we pass to the doFinal() method.

3. Finally, we save the initialization vector the system provided to perform the encryption. Note that this step would not be needed for ECB mode.

Performing the decryption is similar:

1. First, we initialize the cipher engine for decrypting. In this case, however, we must provide an initialization vector to initialize the engine in order to get the correct results (again, this would be unnecessary for ECB mode).

2. Next, we pass the encrypted data to the doFinal() method. Again, we might have had multiple calls to the update() method first.

In typical usage, of course, encryption is done in one program and decryption is done in another program. In the example above, this entails that the initialization vector and the encrypted data must be transmitted to a receiver; this may be done via a socket or a file or any other convenient means. There is no security risk in transmitting the initialization vector, as it has the same properties as the rest of the encrypted data.

In this example, we used the PKCS5 padding scheme to provide the necessary padding. This is by far the simplest way. If you want to do your own padding—if, for example, you're using a CFB32 mode for some reason—you need to do something like this:

```
Cipher c = Cipher.getInstance("DES/CFB32/NoPadding");
c.init(Cipher.ENCRYPT_MODE, desKey);
int blockSize = c.getBlockSize();
byte b[] = "This string has an odd length".getBytes();
byte padded[] = new byte[b.length + blockSize -(b.length % blockSize)];
System.arraycopy(b, 0, padded, 0, b.length);
for (int i = 0; i < blockSize - (b.length % blockSize); i++)
    padded[b.length + i] = 0;
byte output[] = c.doFinal(padded);
```

The problem with this code is that when the data is decrypted, there is no indication of how many bytes should be discarded as padding. PKCS5 and other padding schemes solve this problem by encoding that information into the padding itself.

The NullCipher Class

The JCE includes one subclass of the Cipher class: the NullCipher class (javax.crypto.NullCipher). This class performs no encryption. Data passes through the null cipher unchanged, and no padding or blocking is performed (the getBlockSize() method will return 1). Unlike a traditional cipher engine, instances of the NullCipher class must be constructed directly:

```
Cipher c = new NullCipher();
```

This class can be used to test the logic of your program without actually encrypting or decrypting the data.

Cipher Algorithms

The SunJCE security provider supports three cipher algorithms:

- *DES*, the Data Encryption Standard algorithm, a standard that has been adopted by various organizations, including the U.S. government. There are known ways to attack this encryption, though they require a lot of computing power to do so; despite widespread predictions about the demise of DES, it continues to be used in many applications and is generally considered secure. The examples in this chapter are mostly based on DES encryption.

- *DESede*, also known as triple-DES or multiple-DES. This algorithm uses multiple DES keys to perform three rounds of DES encryption or decryption; the added complexity greatly increases the amount of time required to break the encryption. It also greatly increases the amount of time required to encrypt and to decrypt the data.

  From a developer's perspective, DESede is equivalent to DES; only the algorithm name passed to the key generator and cipher engines is different. Although DESede requires multiple keys, these keys are encoded into a single secret key. Hence, the programming steps required to use DESede are identical to the steps required to use DES.

- *PBEWithMD5AndDES*, the password-based encryption defined in PKCS#5. This algorithm entails using a password, a byte array known as *salt*, and an iteration count along with an MD5 message digest to produce a DES secret key; this key is then used to perform DES encryption or decryption. PKCS#5 was developed by RSA Data Security, Inc., primarily to encrypt private keys, although it may be used to encrypt any arbitrary data.

  From a developer's perspective, this algorithm requires some special programming to obtain the key. A password-based cipher cannot be initialized without special data that is passed via the algorithm specification. This data is known as the salt and iteration count. Hence, a password-based cipher is initialized as follows:

```
String password = "Come you spirits that tend on mortal thoughts";
byte[] salt = { (byte) 0xc9, (byte) 0x36, (byte) 0x78, (byte) 0x99,
                (byte) 0x52, (byte) 0x3e, (byte) 0xea, (byte) 0xf2 };
PBEParameterSpec paramSpec = new PBEParameterSpec(salt, 20);
PBEKeySpec keySpec = new PBEKeySpec(password);
SecretKeyFactory kf = SecretKeyFactory.getInstance("PBEWithMD5AndDES");
SecretKey key = kf.generateSecret(keySpec);
Cipher c = Cipher.getInstance("PBEWithMD5AndDES");
c.init(Cipher.ENCRYPT_MODE, key, paramSpec);
```

The rationale behind this system is that it allows the password to be shared verbally (or otherwise) between participants in the cipher; rather than coding the password as we've done above, the user would presumably enter the password. Since these types of passwords are often easy to guess (a string comparison of the above password against the collected works of Shakespeare would guess the password quite easily, despite its length), the iteration and salt provide a means to massage the password into something more secure. The salt itself should be random, and the higher the iteration count, the more expensive a brute-force attack against the key becomes (though it also takes longer to generate the key itself).

Of course, despite the presence of the salt and iteration, the password chosen in the method should not be easy to guess in the first place: it should contain special characters, not be known quotes from literature, and follow all the other usual rules that apply to selecting a password.

Implementing the Cipher Class

As in all 1.2-based engines, the SPI for the Cipher class is a separate class: the CipherSpi class (javax.crypto.CipherSpi):

public abstract class CipherSpi

The SPI for the Cipher class. This class is responsible for performing the encryption or decryption according to its internal algorithm. Support for various modes or padding schemes must be handled by this class as well.

There is very little intelligence in the Cipher class itself; virtually all of its methods are simply passthough calls to corresponding methods in the SPI. The one exception to this is the getInstance() method, which is responsible for parsing the algorithm string and removing the mode and padding strings if present. If it finds a mode and padding specification, it calls these methods of the SPI:

public abstract void engineSetMode(String s)

Set the mode of the cipher engine according to the specified string. If the given mode is not supported by this cipher, a NoSuchAlgorithmException should be thrown.

public abstract void engineSetPadding(String s)

Set the padding scheme of the cipher engine according to the specified string. If the given padding scheme is not supported by this cipher, a NoSuchPaddingException should be thrown.

Remember that the mode and padding strings we looked at earlier are specific to the implementation of the SunJCE security provider. Hence, while ECB is a common mode specification, it is completely at the discretion of your implementation whether that string should be recognized or not. If you choose to implement a common mode, it is recommended that you use the standard strings, but you may use any naming convention that you find attractive. The same is true of padding schemes.

Complicating this matter is the fact that there are no classes in the JCE that assist you with implementing any mode or padding scheme. So if you need to support a mode or padding scheme, you must write the required code from scratch.

The remaining methods of the SPI are all called directly from the corresponding methods of the Cipher class:

public abstract int engineGetBlockSize()

Return the number of bytes that comprise a block for this engine. Unless the cipher is capable of performing padding, input data for this engine must total a multiple of this block size (though individual calls to the update() method do not necessarily have to provide data in block-sized chunks).

public abstract byte[] engineGetIV()

Return the initialization vector that was used to initialize the cipher. If the cipher was in a mode where no initialization vector was required, this method should return null.

public abstract int engineGetOutputSize(int inputSize)

Return the number of bytes that the cipher will produce if the given amount of data is fed to the cipher. This method should take into account any data that is presently being buffered by the cipher as well as any padding that may need to be added if the cipher is performing padding.

public void engineInit(int op, Key key, SecureRandom sr)
public void engineInit(int op, Key key, AlgorithmParameterSpec aps, SecureRandom sr)
public void engineInit(int op, Key key, AlgorithmParameters ap, SecureRandom sr)

Initialize the cipher based on the op, which will be either Cipher.ENCRYPT_MODE or Cipher.DECRYPT_MODE. This method should ensure that the key is of the correct type and throw an InvalidKeyException if it is not (or if it is otherwise invalid), and use the given random number generator (and algorithm parameters, if applicable) to initialize its internal state. If algorithm parameters are provided but not supported or are otherwise invalid, this method should throw an InvalidAlgorithmParameterException.

public abstract byte[] engineUpdate(int input[], int offset, int len)
public abstract int engineUpdate(int input[], int offset, int len, byte[] output, int outOff)

Encrypt or decrypt the input data. The data that is passed to these methods will is not necessarily an integral number of blocks. It is the responsibility of these methods to process as much of the input data as possible and to buffer the remaining data internally. Upon the next call to an engineUpdate() or engineDoFinal() method, this buffered data must be processed first, followed by the input data of that method (and again leaving any leftover data in an internal buffer).

public abstract byte[] engineDoFinal(int input[], int offset, int len)
public abstract int engineDoFinal(int input[], int offset, int len, byte[] output, int outOff)

Encrypt or decrypt the input data. Like the update() method, this method must consume any buffered data before processing the input data. However, since this is the final set of data to be processed, this method must make sure that the total amount of data has been an integral number of blocks; it should not leave any data in its internal buffers.

If the cipher supports padding (and padding was requested through the engineSetPadding() method), this method should perform the required padding; an error in padding should cause a BadPaddingException to be thrown. Otherwise, if padding is not being performed and the total amount of data has not been an integral number of blocks, this method should throw an IllegalBlockSizeException.

Using our typical XOR strategy of encryption, here's a simple implementation of a cipher engine:

```
public class XORCipher extends CipherSpi {
    byte xorByte;

    public void engineInit(int i, Key k, SecureRandom sr)
                        throws InvalidKeyException {
        if (!(k instanceof XORKey))
            throw new InvalidKeyException("XOR requires an XOR key");
        xorByte = k.getEncoded()[0];
    }

    public void engineInit(int i, Key k, AlgorithmParameterSpec aps,
                    SecureRandom sr) throws InvalidKeyException,
                            InvalidAlgorithmParameterException {
        throw new InvalidAlgorithmParameterException(
            "Algorithm parameters not supported in this class");
    }

    public void engineInit(int i, Key k, AlgorithmParameters ap,
            SecureRandom sr) throws InvalidKeyException,
            InvalidAlgorithmParameterException {
        throw new InvalidAlgorithmParameterException(
            "Algorithm parameters not supported in this class");
    }

    public byte[] engineUpdate(byte in[], int off, int len) {
        return engineDoFinal(in, off, len);
    }

    public int engineUpdate(byte in[], int inoff, int length,
                            byte out[], int outoff) {
        for (int i = 0; i < length; i++)
            out[outoff + i] = (byte) (in[inoff + i] ^ xorByte);
        return length;
    }

    public byte[] engineDoFinal(byte in[], int off, int len) {
        byte out[] = new byte[len - off];
```

```
            engineUpdate(in, off, len, out, 0);
            return out;
    }

    public int engineDoFinal(byte in[], int inoff, int len,
                             byte out[], int outoff) {
        return engineUpdate(in, inoff, len, out, outoff);
    }

    public int engineGetBlockSize() {
        return 1;
    }

    public byte[] engineGetIV() {
        return null;
    }

    public int engineGetOutputSize(int sz) {
        return sz;
    }

    public void engineSetMode(String s)
                    throws NoSuchAlgorithmException {
        throw new NoSuchAlgorithmException("Unsupported mode " + s);
    }

    public void engineSetPadding(String s)
                    throws NoSuchPaddingException {
        throw new NoSuchPaddingException("Unsupported padding " + s);
    }
}
```

The bulk of the work of any cipher engine will be in the engineUpdate() method, which is responsible for actually providing the ciphertext or plaintext. In this case, we've simply XORed the key value with every byte, a process that works both for encryption as well as decryption. Because the work done by the engineUpdate() method is so symmetric, we don't need to keep track internally of whether we're encrypting or decrypting; for us, the work is always the same. For some algorithms, you may need to keep track of the state of the cipher by setting an internal variable when the engineInit() method is called.

Similarly, because we can operate on individual bytes at a time, we didn't have to worry about padding and buffering internal data. Such an extension is easy, using the code we showed earlier that uses the modulus operator to group the input arrays into blocks.

To use this class, we would need to add these two lines to the XYZProvider class we developed in Chapter 8:

```
put("Cipher.XOR", "XORCipher");
put("KeyGenerator.XOR", "XORKeyGenerator");
```

Then it is a simple matter of installing the XOR security provider and getting an instance of this cipher engine:

```
Security.addProvider(new XYZProvider());
KeyGenerator kg = KeyGenerator.getInstance("XOR");
Cipher c = Cipher.getInstance("XOR");
```

Note that "XOR" is the only valid algorithm name for this implementation since we do not support any modes or padding schemes.

Cipher Streams

In the Cipher class we just examined, we had to provide the data to be encrypted or decrypted as multiple blocks of data. This is not necessarily the best interface for programmers: what if we want to send and receive arbitrary streams of data over the network? It would often be inconvenient to get all the data into buffers before it can be encrypted or decrypted.

The solution to this problem is the ability to associate a cipher object with an input or output stream. When data is written to such an output stream, it is automatically encrypted, and when data is read from such an input stream, it is automatically decrypted. This allows a developer to use Java's normal semantics of nested filter streams to send and receive encrypted data.

The CipherOutputStream Class

The class that encrypts data on output to a stream is the CipherOutputStream class (javax.crypto.CipherOutputStream):

public class CipherOutputStream extends FilterOutputStream
Provide a class that will encrypt data as it is written to the underlying stream.

Like all classes that extend the FilterOutputStream class, constructing a cipher output stream requires that an existing output stream has already been created. This allows us to use the existing output stream from a socket or a file as the destination stream for the encrypted data:

public CipherOutputStream(OutputStream outputStream, Cipher cipher)
Create a cipher output stream, associating the given cipher object with the existing output stream. The given cipher must already have been initialized, or an IllegalStateException will be thrown.

The output stream may be operated on with any of the methods from the `Filter-OutputStream` class—the `write()` methods, the `flush()` method, and the `close()` method, which all provide the semantics you would expect. Often, of course, these methods are never used directly—for example, if you're sending text data over a socket, you'll wrap a cipher output stream around the socket's output stream, but then you'll wrap a print writer around that; the programming interface then becomes a series of calls to the `print()` and `println()` methods. You can use any similar output stream to get a different interface.

It does not matter if the cipher object that was passed to the constructor does automatic padding or not—the `CipherOutputStream` class itself does not make that restriction. As a practical matter, however, you'll want to use a padding cipher object, since otherwise you'll be responsible for keeping track of the amount of data passed to the output stream and tacking on your own padding.

Usually, the better alternative is to use a byte-oriented mode such as CFB8. This is particularly true in streams that are going to be used conversationally: a message is sent, a response received, and then another message is sent, etc. In this case, you want to make sure that the entire message is sent; you cannot allow the cipher to buffer any data internally while it waits for a full block to arrive. And, for reasons we're just about to describe, you cannot call the `flush()` method in this case either. Hence, you need to use a streaming cipher (or, technically, a block cipher in streaming mode) in this case.

When the `flush()` method is called on a `CipherOutputStream` (either directly, or because the stream is being closed), the padding of the stream comes into play. If the cipher is automatically padding, the padding bytes are generated in the `flush()` method. If the cipher is not automatically padding and the number of bytes that have been sent through the stream is not a multiple of the cipher's block size, then the `flush()` method (or indirectly the `close()` method) throws an `IllegalBlockSizeException` (note that this requires that the `IllegalBlockSizeException` be a runtime exception).

If the cipher is performing padding, it is very important not to call the `flush()` method unless it is immediately followed by a call to the `close()` method. If the `flush()` method is called in the middle of processing data, padding is added in the middle of the data. This means the data does not decrypt correctly. Remember that certain output streams (especially some types of `PrintWriter` streams) flush automatically; if you're using a padding cipher, don't use one of those output streams.

We can use this class to write some encrypted data to a file like this:

```
public class Send {
    public static void main(String args[]) {
        try {
```

```
        KeyGenerator kg = KeyGenerator.getInstance("DES");
        kg.init(new SecureRandom());
        SecretKey key = kg.generateKey();
        SecretKeyFactory skf = SecretKeyFactory.getInstance("DES");
        Class spec = Class.forName("javax.crypto.spec.DESKeySpec");
        DESKeySpec ks = (DESKeySpec) skf.getKeySpec(key, spec);
        ObjectOutputStream oos = new ObjectOutputStream(
                    new FileOutputStream("keyfile"));
        oos.writeObject(ks.getKey());

        Cipher c = Cipher.getInstance("DES/CFB8/NoPadding");
        c.init(Cipher.ENCRYPT_MODE, key);
        CipherOutputStream cos = new CipherOutputStream(
                    new FileOutputStream("ciphertext"), c);
        PrintWriter pw = new PrintWriter(
                    new OutputStreamWriter(cos));
        pw.println("Stand and unfold yourself");
        pw.close();
        oos.writeObject(c.getIV());
        oos.close();
    } catch (Exception e) {
        System.out.println(e);
    }
  . }
}
```

There are two steps involved here. First, we must create the cipher object, which means that we must have a secret key available. The problem of secret key management is a hard one to solve; we'll discuss it a little farther along. For now, we're just going to save the key object to a file that can later be read by whomever needs the key. Note that we've gone through the usual steps of writing the data produced by the secret key factory so that the recipient of the key need not use the same provider we use.

After we generate the key, we must create the cipher object, initialize it with that key, and then use that cipher object to construct our output stream. Once the data is sent to the stream, we close the stream, which flushes the cipher object, performs any necessary padding, and completes the encryption.

In this case, we've chosen to use CFB8 mode, so there is no need for padding. But in general, this last step is important: if we don't explicitly close the PrintWriter stream, when the program exits, data that is buffered in the cipher object itself will not get flushed to the file. The resulting encrypted file will be unreadable, as it won't have the correct amount of data in its last block.*

---

* Closing the output stream is necessary whenever the stream performs buffering, but it is particularly important to remember in this context.

The CipherInputStream Class

The output stream is only half the battle; in order to read that data, we must use the CipherInputStream class (javax.crypto.CipherInputStream):

public class CipherInputStream extends FilterInputStream
> Create a filter stream capable of decrypting data as it is read from the underlying input stream.

A cipher input stream is constructed with this method:

public CipherInputStream(InputStream is, Cipher c)
> Create a cipher input stream that associates the existing input stream with the given cipher. The cipher must previously have been initialized.

All the points we made about the CipherOutputStream class are equally valid for the CipherInputStream class. You can operate on it with any of the methods in its superclass, although you'll typically want to wrap it in something like a buffered reader, and the cipher object that is associated with the input stream needs to perform automatic padding or use a mode that does not require padding (in fact, it must use the same padding scheme and mode that the output stream that is sending it data used).

The CipherInputStream class does not directly support the notion of a mark. The markSupported() method returns false unless you've wrapped the cipher input stream around another class that supports a mark.

Here's how we could read the data file that we created above:

```
public class Receive {
    public static void main(String args[]) {
        try {
            ObjectInputStream ois = new ObjectInputStream(
                    new FileInputStream("keyfile"));
            DESKeySpec ks = new DESKeySpec((byte[]) ois.readObject());
            SecretKeyFactory skf = SecretKeyFactory.getInstance("DES");
            SecretKey key = skf.generateSecret(ks);

            Cipher c = Cipher.getInstance("DES/CFB8/NoPadding");
            c.init(Cipher.DECRYPT_MODE, key,
            newIvParameterSpec((byte[]) ois.readObject()));
            CipherInputStream cis = new CipherInputStream(
                    new FileInputStream("ciphertext"), c);
            cis.read(new byte[8]);
            BufferedReader br = new BufferedReader(
                    new InputStreamReader(cis));
            System.out.println("Got message");
            System.out.println(br.readLine());
        } catch (Exception e) {
            System.out.println(e);
```

```
        )
      )
    )
```

In this case, we must first read the secret key from the file where it was saved, and then create the cipher object initialized with that key. Then we can create our input stream and read the data from the stream, automatically decrypting it as it goes.

SSL Encryption

In the world of the Internet, data encryption is often achieved with SSL—the Secure Socket Layer protocol. These sockets use encryption to encrypt data as it is written to the socket and to decrypt that data as it is read from the socket.

SSL encryption is built into many popular web browsers and web servers; these programs depend on SSL to provide the necessary encryption to implement the https protocol. For Java applet developers who want to use SSL, there are three options:

1. Use the URL class.

   The URL class can be used to open a URL that the applet can read data from. If the URL is a POST URL, the applet can send some initial data before it reads the data. On browsers that will support it, you can specify an https protocol when the URL is constructed, in which case the data exchanged by the applet and the remote web server will be encrypted. Note that this is not supported by the JDK itself.

   There are a few limitations with this method. First, the data exchange is limited to the web server and the applet using the single request-response protocol of HTTP. Data cannot be streamed in this way, and you must write an appropriate back-end cgi-bin script, servlet, or other program to process the data. Second, not all browsers support the https protocol, and those that do support https may not support a Java applet opening an https URL. On the other hand, this will tunnel data through a firewall, which is one of the main reasons why it is used.

2. Use an SSLSocket class.

   There are a number of vendors who supply SSLSocket and SSLServerSocket classes that extend the Socket and ServerSocket classes; these classes provide all the semantics of their java.net counterparts with the additional feature that the data they exchange is encrypted with the SSL algorithm.

   These classes are generally subject to import and export restrictions; in particular, Sun's SSLSocket and SSLServerSocket classes (which come with the Java Server product) cannot be exported, and certain countries will not allow these implementations to be imported. There are SSL implementations that have been written outside the United States, so they have fewer restrictions (but they may contain implementations of RSA that may not be used within the United States).

3. Use an RSA-based security provider.

The `Cipher` class that we examined above has the ability to support RSA encryption. Many third-party security providers will have RSA implementations; some of these are listed in Appendix C.

For now, none of these solutions is completely attractive. The technique of using URLs is well known and demonstrated in any book on Java network programming, but suffers from the limitations we discussed above. The SSL-based `Socket` classes have a known interface and are simple to use, but suffer from availability questions (although no more than the JCE itself).

Symmetric Key Agreement

When we discussed public and private key pairs, we talked about the bootstrapping issue involved with key distribution: the problem of obtaining the public key of a trusted certificate authority. In the case of key pairs, keeping the private key secret is of paramount importance. Anyone with access to the private key will be able to sign documents as the owner of the private key; he or she will also be able to decrypt data that is intended for the owner of the private key. Keeping the private key secret is made easier because both parties involved in the cryptographic transfer do not need to use it.

With the symmetric key we introduced in this chapter, however, the bootstrapping issue is even harder to solve because both parties need access to the same key. The question then becomes how this key can be transmitted securely between the two parties in such a way that only those parties have access to the key.

One technique to do this is to use traditional (i.e., nonelectronic) means to distribute the key. The key could be put onto a floppy disk, for example, and then mailed or otherwise distributed to the parties involved in the encryption. Or the key could be distributed in paper format, requiring the recipient of the key to type in the long string of hex digits (the password-based encryption algorithm makes this easier, of course). This is the type of technique we used in the section on cipher data streams. In those examples, the key was saved in a file that was created when the ciphertext was generated (although the key could have been pregenerated, and the `Send` class could have also read it from a file).

Another technique is to use public key/private key encryption to encrypt the symmetric key, and then to send the encrypted key over the network. This allows the key to be sent electronically and then to be used to set up the desired cipher engine. This is a particularly attractive option, because symmetric encryption is usually much faster than public key encryption. You can use the slower encryption to send the secret key, and then use the faster encryption for the rest of your data. This option requires that your security provider implement a form of public key encryption (which the SunJCE security provider does not).

The final option is to use a key agreement algorithm. Key agreement algorithms exchange some public information between two parties so they each can calculate a shared secret key. However, they do not exchange enough information that eavesdroppers on the conversation can calculate the same shared key.

In the JCE, these algorithms are represented by the KeyAgreement class (javax.crypto.KeyAgreement):

public class KeyAgreement

Provide an engine for the implementation of a key agreement algorithm. This class allows for two cooperating parties to generate the same secret key while preventing parties unrelated to the agreement from generating the same key.

As an engine class, this class has no constructors, but it has the usual method to retrieve instances of the class:

public final KeyAgreement getInstance(String algorithm)
public final KeyAgreement getInstance(String algorithm, String provider)

Return an instance of the KeyAgreement class that implements the given algorithm, loaded either from the standard set of providers or from the named provider. If no suitable class that implements the algorithm can be found, a NoSuchAlgorithmException is generated; if the given provider cannot be found, a NoSuchProviderException is generated.

The interface to this class is very simple (much simpler than its use would indicate, as our example will show):

public final void init(Key k)
public final void init(Key k, SecureRandom sr)
public final void init(Key k, AlgorithmParameterSpec aps)
public final void init(Key k, AlgorithmParameterSpec aps, SecureRandom sr)

Initialize the key agreement engine. The parameter specifications (if present) will vary depending upon the underlying algorithm; if the parameters are invalid, of the incorrect class, or not supported, an InvalidAlgorithmParameterException is generated. This method will also perform the first phase of the key agreement protocol.

public final Key doPhase(Key key, boolean final)

Execute the next phase of the key agreement protocol. Key agreement protocols usually require a set of operations to be performed in a particular order. Each operation is represented in this class by a particular phase, which usually requires a key to succeed. If the provided key is not supported by the key agreement protocol, is incorrect for the current phase, or is otherwise invalid, an InvalidKeyException will be thrown.

The number of phases, along with the types of keys they require, vary drastically from key exchange algorithm to algorithm. Your security provider must document the types of keys required for each phase. In addition, you must specify which is the final phase of the protocol.

public final byte[] generateSecret()
public final int generateSecret(byte[] secret, int offset)

Generate the bytes that represent the secret key; these bytes can then be used to create a SecretKey object. The type of that object will vary depending upon the algorithm implemented by this key agreement. The bytes are either returned from this argument or placed into the given array (starting at the given offset). In the latter case, if the array is not large enough to hold all the bytes a ShortBufferException is thrown. If all phases of the key agreement protocol have not been executed, an IllegalStateException is generated.

After this method has been called, the engine is reset and may be used to generate more secret keys (starting with a new call to the init() method).

public final String getAlgorithm()

Return the name of the algorithm implemented by this key agreement object.

public final Provider getProvider()

Return the provider that implemented this key agreement.

Despite its simple interface, using the key agreement engine can be very complex. The SunJCE security provider implements one key agreement algorithm: Diffie-Hellman key agreement. This key agreement is based on the following protocol:

1. Alice (the first party in the exchange) generates a Diffie-Hellman public key/private key pair.

2. Alice transmits the public key and the algorithm specification of the key pair to Bob (the second party in the exchange).

3. Bob uses the algorithm specification to generate his own public and private keys; he sends the public key to Alice.

4. Alice uses her private key and Bob's public key to create a secret key. In the KeyAgreement class, this requires two phases: one that uses her private key and one that uses her public key.

5. Bob performs the same operations with his private key and Alice's public key. Due to the properties of a Diffie-Hellman key pair, this generates the same secret key Alice generated.

6. Bob and Alice convert their secret keys into a DES key.

7. Alice uses that key to encrypt data that she sends to Bob.

8. Bob uses that key to decrypt data that he reads.

These last two steps, of course, are symmetric: both Bob and Alice can encrypt as well as decrypt data with the secret key. They can both send and receive data as well.

Nothing in this key agreement protocol prevents someone from impersonating Bob—Alice could exchange keys with me, I could say that I am Bob, and then Alice and I could exchange encrypted data. So even though the transmissions of the public keys do not need to be encrypted, they should be signed for maximum safety.

This algorithm works because of the properties of the Diffie-Hellman public key/private key pair. These keys are not suitable for use in an encryption algorithm; they are used only in a key agreement such as this.

Here's how a key agreement might be implemented:

```
public class DHAgreement implements Runnable {
    byte bob[], alice[];
    boolean doneAlice = false;
    byte[] ciphertext;

    BigInteger aliceP, aliceG;
    int aliceL;

    public synchronized void run() {
        if (!doneAlice) {
            doneAlice = true;
            doAlice();
        }
        else doBob();
    }

    public synchronized void doAlice() {
        try {
            // Step 1: Alice generates a key pair
            KeyPairGenerator kpg = KeyPairGenerator.getInstance("DH");
            kpg.initialize(1024);
            KeyPair kp = kpg.generateKeyPair();

            // Step 2: Alice sends the public key and the
            //         Diffie-Hellman key parameters to Bob
```

```
            Class dhClass = Class.forName(
                           "javax.crypto.spec.DHParameterSpec");
        DHParameterSpec dhSpec = (
                     (DHPublicKey) kp.getPublic()).getParams();
        aliceG = dhSpec.getG();
        aliceP = dhSpec.getP();
        aliceL = dhSpec.getL();
        alice = kp.getPublic().getEncoded();
        notify();

        // Step 4 part 1: Alice performs the first phase of the
        //      protocol with her private key
        KeyAgreement ka = KeyAgreement.getInstance("DH");
        ka.init(kp.getPrivate());

        // Step 4 part 2: Alice performs the second phase of the
        //      protocol with Bob's public key
        while (bob == null) {
            wait();
        }
        KeyFactory kf = KeyFactory.getInstance("DH");
        X509EncodedKeySpec x509Spec = new X509EncodedKeySpec(bob);
        PublicKey pk = kf.generatePublic(x509Spec);
        ka.doPhase(pk, true);

        // Step 4 part 3: Alice can generate the secret key
        byte secret[] = ka.generateSecret();

        // Step 6: Alice generates a DES key
        SecretKeyFactory skf = SecretKeyFactory.getInstance("DES");
        DESKeySpec desSpec = new DESKeySpec(secret);
        SecretKey key = skf.generateSecret(desSpec);

        // Step 7: Alice encrypts data with the key and sends
        //      the encrypted data to Bob
        Cipher c = Cipher.getInstance("DES/ECB/PKCS5Padding");
        c.init(Cipher.ENCRYPT_MODE, key);
        ciphertext = c.doFinal(
                "Stand and unfold yourself".getBytes());
        notify();
    } catch (Exception e) {
        e.printStackTrace();
    }
}

public synchronized void doBob() {
    try {
        // Step 3: Bob uses the parameters supplied by Alice
        //      to generate a key pair and sends the public key
```

```
                while (alice == null) {
                    wait();
                }
                KeyPairGenerator kpg = KeyPairGenerator.getInstance("DH");
                DHParameterSpec dhSpec = new DHParameterSpec(
                                     aliceP, aliceG, aliceL);
                kpg.initialize(dhSpec);
                KeyPair kp = kpg.generateKeyPair();
                bob = kp.getPublic().getEncoded();
                notify();

                // Step 5 part 1:  Bob uses his private key to perform the
                //      first phase of the protocol
                KeyAgreement ka = KeyAgreement.getInstance("DH");
                ka.init(kp.getPrivate());

                // Step 5 part 2:  Bob uses Alice's public key to perform
                /       the second phase of the protocol.
                KeyFactory kf = KeyFactory.getInstance("DH");
                X509EncodedKeySpec x509Spec =
                                     new X509EncodedKeySpec(alice);
                PublicKey pk = kf.generatePublic(x509Spec);
                ka.doPhase(pk, true);
                ka.doPhase(1, k

                // Step 5 part 3:  Bob generates the secret key
                byte secret[] = ka.generateSecret();

                // Step 6:  Bob generates a DES key
                SecretKeyFactory skf = SecretKeyFactory.getInstance("DES");
                DESKeySpec desSpec = new DESKeySpec(secret);
                SecretKey key = skf.generateSecret(desSpec);

                // Step 8:  Bob receives the encrypted text and decrypts it
                Cipher c = Cipher.getInstance("DES/ECB/PKCS5Padding");
                c.init(Cipher.DECRYPT_MODE, key);
                while (ciphertext == null) {
                    wait();
                }
                byte plaintext[] = c.doFinal(ciphertext);
                System.out.println("Bob got the string " +
                            new String(plaintext));
        } catch (Exception e) {
            e.printStackTrace();
        }
    }

    public static void main(String args[]) {
        DHAgreement test = new DHAgreement();
```

```
          new Thread(test).start();// Starts Alice
          new Thread(test).start();// Starts Bob
     }
   }
```

In typical usage, of course, Bob and Alice would be executing code in different classes, probably on different machines. We've shown the code here using two threads in a shared object so that you can run the example more easily (although beware: generating a Diffie-Hellman key is an expensive operation, especially for a size of 1024; a size of 512 will be better for testing). Our second reason for showing the example like this is to make explicit the points at which the protocol must be synchronized: Alice must wait for certain information from Bob, Bob must wait for certain information from Alice, and both must perform the operations in the order specified. Once the secret key has been created, however, they may send and receive encrypted data at will.

Otherwise, despite its complexity, this example merely reuses a lot of the techniques we've been using throughout this book. Keys are generated, they are transmitted in neutral (encoded) format, they are re-formed by their recipient, and both sides can continue.

Sealed Objects

The final class in the JCE that we'll investigate is the SealedObject class (javax.crypto.SealedObject). This class is very similar to the SignedObject class we examined in Chapter 12, except that the stored, serialized object is encrypted rather than signed:

public class SealedObject
   A class that can embed within it a serializable object in an encrypted form.

Constructing a sealed object is achieved as follows:

public SealedObject(Serializable obj, Cipher c)
   Construct a sealed object. The sealed object serializes the given object to an embedded byte array, effectively making a copy of the object. It then uses the given cipher to encrypt the embedded byte array. If the object is unable to be serialized, an IOException is thrown; an error in encrypting the byte array results in an IllegalBlockSizeException. If the cipher object has not been initialized, an IllegalStateException is generated.

To retrieve the object, we use this method:

public Object getObject(Cipher c)
   Decrypt the embedded byte array and deserialize it, returning the reconstituted object. The cipher must have been initialized with the same mode and

key as the cipher that was passed to the constructor when the object was first created, otherwise a `BadPaddingMethodException` or an `IllegalBlockSize-Exception` is thrown. If the cipher was not initialized, an `IllegalStateException` is generated; failure to find the serialized class results in a `ClassNotFoundException`, and generic deserialization errors results in an `IOException`.

These are the only two operations that may be performed upon a sealed object. Just keep in mind that the embedded object in this class is a serialized instance of the original object: the technique the object uses to perform serialization may affect the resulting object that is retrieved from the sealed object. This class can help us prevent someone from tampering with our serialized object, but the reconstituted object may be lacking transient fields or other information (depending, of course, on the implementation of the object itself).

Summary

In this chapter, we explored the final engine of the Java security package—the encryption engine. The encryption engine is part of the Java Cryptography Extension (JCE). Due to export limitations, the JCE from Sun is available only within the United States and Canada. Third-party implementations of the JCE are available elsewhere. No matter where you get it from, the JCE must be obtained separately from the rest of the Java platform.

The encryption engine performs encryption of arbitrary chunks or streams of data according to various algorithms. Though support for RSA and other popular algorithms is possible within the provider architecture, the SunJCE security provider supplies only DES encryption. DES encryption has a different requirement for keys than the other cryptographic engines we've examined—DES encryption depends on both parties in the cryptographic exchange using the same key. Hence the JCE also provides a new key type known as a secret key (or symmetric key), as well as an engine to generate these keys.

Secret keys pose an interesting distribution problem—they cannot be distributed electronically unless the secret key itself is encrypted. This problem is often solved by relying on public key encryption to deliver the encrypted key, after which the symmetric key can be used to create the type of cipher that we've discussed in this chapter. The JCE also includes support for key agreement protocols to accomplish key sharing, one of which (the Diffie-Hellman key agreement protocol) is implemented in the SunJCE security provider.

The encryption engine finally provides what many people envision as the ultimate goal in security: the ability to send arbitrary encrypted data streams in a conversational manner across the network. Although its use is limited by governmental restrictions, it provides the last piece of the Java security puzzle that we outlined at the beginning of this book.

A

Security Tools

In this appendix, we'll discuss the tools that come with the JDK that allow developers, end users, and system administrators to deal with the security aspects of the Java platform. These tools are only available in Java 1.2,* since they primarily deal with operations that require the support of 1.2.† As Java's security model advances, these tools have become primary interfaces to establishing a secure sandbox for Java applications.

To a lesser extent, these tools have become an interface for establishing a secure sandbox for Java applets as well. However, as we've seen, not all the security features of the Java platform have yet been uniformly adopted by all browsers. In part, it is a problem with logistics. As this book went to press, Java 1.2 was still a new release. Clearly it will take some time before these new features can be propagated to browsers. Part of the problem, though, lies in the fact that Java applications (and Java browsers) ultimately decide upon their own security features.

This last fact is true of your own applications as well: you can certainly use the keytool utility that comes with the JDK to manage your public key/private key databases. But if it is appropriate, you may want to replace (or at least supplement) the keytool with your own key management tool that handles some of the situations we discussed in Chapter 11.

---

* 1.2 is now Java 2.

† The javakey utility in 1.1 can be used to sign JAR files and to operate like the keytool; that utility is obsolete in 1.2.

The keytool

In Chapter 11 we discussed the KeyStore class, which provides an interface to a key management system. The Java platform comes with a tool—keytool—that provides an administrative interface to that class. Keytool allows end users and system administrators to add, delete, and modify entries in the keystore (provided that they have sufficient permissions, of course).

When we discussed the KeyStore class, we mentioned that it had some limitations that may lead you to write your own implementation of that class. The good news is that if you write such a class, you may still use keytool to administer your set of keys. Since keytool uses the standard interface provided by the KeyStore class, it will be (mostly) compatible with any new class that you install into that interface (we'll remind you how to do that at the end of this appendix). However, there are some exceptions to this: keytool itself places some restrictions upon the algorithms that may be used to support particular keys.

Before we examine the workings of keytool, let's review a few objects that we talked about in Chapter 11. When we discussed the KeyStore class, we defined the following terms:

keystore

> The keystore is the file that actually holds the set of keys; keytool operates on this file. In other implementations of the KeyStore class, the keystore may not be a file—the keys in that implementation may be held in a database or some other structure. Regardless, we refer to the set of keys on disk (or wherever they are located) as the keystore.
>
> In keytool, this file is called *.keystore* and is held in the directory specified by the property user.home. On Unix systems, this directory defaults to the user's home directory (e.g., *$HOME*); on Windows systems, this directory defaults to the concatenation of the HOMEDRIVE and HOMEPATH environment variables (e.g., *C:*).

alias

> An alias is a shortened, keystore-specific name for an entity that has a key in the keystore. I choose to store my public and private key in my local keystore under the alias "sdo"; if you have a copy of my public key, you may use that alias, or you may use another alias (like "ScottOaks"). The alias used for a particular entity is completely up to the discretion of the individual who first enters that entity into the keystore.

DN (distinguished name)

> The distinguished name for an entity in the keystore is a subset of its full X.500 name. This is a long string; for example, my DN is:
>
> ```
> CN=Scott Oaks, OU=SMCC, O=Sun Microsystems, L=New York, S=NY, C=US
> ```

DNs are used by certificate authorities to refer to the entities to whom they supply a certificate. Hence, unlike an alias, the DN for a particular key is the same no matter what keystore it is located in: if I send you my public key, it will have the DN encoded in the public key's certificate.

However, nothing prevents me from having two public keys with different DNs (I might have one for personal use that omits references to my place of employment). And there is no guarantee that two unrelated individuals will not share the same DN (in fact, you can count on this type of namespace collision to occur).

key entries and certificate entries

There are two types of entries in the keystore: key entries and certificate entries. A key entry is an entry that has a private key as well as a corresponding public key. The public key in this case is embedded in a certificate, and there is a chain of certificates that vouch for the public key.

A certificate entry, on the other hand, does not contain a private key; it contains only a public key held in a certificate. In addition, there is only a single certificate associated with this entry.

With that in mind, we'll look at the various commands that keytool provides. At present, keytool only has a command-line interface; we'll look at the typical commands that add, modify, list, and delete entries in the keystore.

Global Options to keytool

Keytool implements a number of global options—options that are available to most of its commands. We'll list these as appropriate for each command, but here's an explanation of what they do:

-alias alias

Specify the alias the operation should apply to (e.g., -alias sdo). The default for this value is "mykey."

-dname distinguishedName

Specify the distinguished name. There is no default for this value, and if you do not specify it on the command line, you will be prompted to enter it when it is needed. Letting keytool prompt you is generally easier, since the tool will prompt for the name one field at a time. Otherwise, you must enter the entire name in one quoted string, e.g.:

```
-dname \
"CN=Scott Oaks, OU=SMCC, O=Sun Microsystems, L=New York, S=NY, C=US"
```

-keypass password

> Specify the password used to protect the entire keystore. Access to any element in the keystore requires this global password (programmatically, this is the password that is passed to the load() method of the KeyStore class). If this password is not provided on the command line, you will be prompted for it. This is generally more secure than typing it on a command line or in a script where others might see it. Passwords must be at least six characters long.
>
> Note that even though the KeyStore class allows you to read entries from the keystore without this password, keytool does not.

-keystore filename

> Specify the name of the file that holds the keystore (programmatically, this file will be opened and passed as the input stream argument to the load() method of the KeyStore class). The default value of this is the *.keystore* file described above.

-storepass password

> Specify the password used to protect a particular entry's private key. This is usually not (and should not be) the same as the global password. There should be a different password for each private key that is specific to that entry. This allows the keystore to be shared among many users. If this password is not provided on the command line, you will be prompted for it, which is generally the more secure way to enter this password.

-storetype storetype

> Specify the type of keystroke that the keytool should operate on. This defaults to the keystroke type in the *java.security* file, which defaults to JKS, the keystore type provided by the Sun security provider.

-v

> Verbose—print some information about the operations keytool is performing.

Adding a Certificate Entry

In order to add a certificate entry to the database, you use this command:

-import

> Import a certificate into the database. This command either creates a new certificate entry or imports a certificate for an existing key entry. This command supports the following options:

-alias alias
-keypass keypass
-keystore keystore
-storepass storepass
-storetype storetype
-v
-file inputFile

> The file containing the certificate that is being imported. The certificate must be in RFC 1421 format. The default is to read the data from System.in.

-noprompt

> Do not prompt the user about whether or not the certificate should be accepted.

-trustcacerts

> Use the *cacerts* file to obtain trusted certificates from certificate autorities that have signed the certificate that is being imported.

When you import a certificate, the information contained in that certificate is printed out; this information includes the distinguished names of the issuer and the principal, and the fingerprint of the certificate. Well-known certificate authorities will publish their fingerprints (on the Web, in trade papers, and elsewhere). It is very important for you to verify the displayed fingerprint with the published fingerprint in order to verify that the certificate does indeed belong to the principal named in the certificate.

Let's say that I have a certificate for the ACME certificate authority in the file *amce.cer*. I can import it with this command:

```
piccolo% keytool -import -alias acme -file acme.cer
Enter keystore password:  ******
Owner: CN=ACME, OU=ACME CA Services, O=ACME Inc., L=New York, S=NY,
C=US
Issuer: CN=ACME, OU=ACME CA Services, O=ACME Inc., L=New York, S=NY,
C=US
Serial Number: 34cbd057
Valid from: Sun Jan 25 18:52:55 EST 1998 until: Sat Apr 25 19:52:55 EDT
1998
Certificate Fingerprints:
    MD5:  51:4E:52:2C:1B:14:38:52:DB:30:5D:46:A9:46:FF:BB
    SHA1: 9F:B2:18:4A:63:8B:F8:EB:A6:A0:56:DB:C7:1B:B3:CC:F5:4B:BA:72
Trust this certificate? [no]: yes
```

After typing in the command, keytool prints the given names, serial number, and fingerprints, and asks for verification before it actually enters the certificate into the keystore. After receiving a yes answer, the entry is made.

Adding a Key Entry

To add a key entry to the database (that is, an entry containing a private key), use this command:

-genkey

> Generate a key pair and add that entry to the keystore. This command supports these options:

> > *-alias alias*
> > *-dname DN*
> > *-keypass keypass*
> > *-keystore keystore*
> > *-storepass storepass*
> > *-storetype storetype*

> > *-keyalg AlgorithmName*

> > > Use the given algorithm to generate the key pair. For the default Sun security provider, the name must be DSA, which is also the default value for this option. Despite the presence of this option, you cannot really specify another algorithm name, nor, for that matter, can you use a non-Sun DSA provider. Internally, keytool expects the key generator to produce keys that belong to a specific class in the sun package.

> > *-keysize keysize*

> > > Use the given keysize to initialize the key pair generator. The default value for this option is 1024. Since the key is a DSA key, the value must be between 512 and 1024 and be a multiple of 64.

> > *-sigalg signatureAlgorithm*

> > > Specify the signature algorithm that will be used to create the self-signed certificate; this defaults to SHA-1/DSA, which is supported by the Sun security provider. Like the key algorithm, this option is not particularly useful at present, since you cannot use your own security provider classes to implement the signature.

> > *-validity nDays*

> > > Specify the number of days for which the self-signed certificate should be valid. The default value for this option is 90 days.

The key entry that is created in this manner has the generated private key. In addition, the public key is placed into a self-signed certificate; that is, a certificate that identitifies the holder of the public key (using the distinguished name argument) and is signed by the holder of the key itself. This is a valid certificate in all senses, although other sites will probably not accept the certificate since it is not signed by a known certificate authority (CA). But the self-signed certificate can be used to obtain a certificate from a CA.

In order to use this self-signed certificate to obtain a certificate from a CA, you must first generate a certificate signing request (CSR). The CSR contains the distinguished name and public key for a particular alias and is signed using the private key of the alias; the CA can then verify that signature and issue a certificate verifying the public key. CSRs are generated with this option:

-certreq

> Generate a certificate signing request. This command supports the following options:

> *-alias alias*
> *-keypass keypass*
> *-keystore keystore*
> *-storepass storepass*
> *-storetype storetype*
>
> *-v*
>
> *-sigalg signatureAlgorithm*
>> Use the given algorithm to sign the CSR. This option is not presently useful, as the internal design of keytool only supports SHA-1/DSA signatures created by the Sun security provider.
>
> *-file outputFile*
>> Store the CSR in the given file. The format of the CSR is defined in PKCS#10. The default is to write the CSR to System.out.

Once you have the CSR in a file, you must send it to the CA of your choice. Different CAs have different procedures for doing this, but all of them will send you back a certificate they have signed that verifies the public key you have sent to them. There are a few different formats in which the CA will send back a certificate; the only format that is presently supported by keytool is RFC 1421 (so you should use a CA that supports this format, of course). You must also use a CA for whom you have a certificate entry (but the CA will often send you its self-signed certificate anyway).

Once you've received the file containing the new certificate, you can import it into the keystore using the -import command we discussed previously.

Here's an example of how all these commands can be used to create an entry with a private key and a certified public key. First, we must create the entry:

```
piccolo% keytool -genkey -alias sdo
Enter keystore password:  ******
What is your first and last name?
  [Unknown]:  Scott Oaks
What is the name of your organizational unit?
  [Unknown]:  SMCC
```

```
What is the name of your organization?
   [Unknown]:  Sun Microsystems
What is the name of your City or Locality?
   [Unknown]:  New York
What is the name of your State or Province?
   [Unknown]:  NY
What is the two-letter country code for this unit?
   [Unknown]:  US
Is <CN=Scott Oaks, OU=SMCC, O=Sun Microsystems, L=New York, S=NY, C=US>
correct?
   [no]:  yes


Enter key password for <sdo>
        (RETURN if same as keystore password):  ******
```

At this point, we now have an entry for sdo in the keystore. That entry has a self-signed certificate; note that we had the tool prompt us for all the entries that comprise the DN rather than attempting to type it all in on the command line. The next step is to generate the CSR:

```
piccolo% keytool -certreq -alias sdo -file sdoCSR.cer
Enter keystore password:  ******
```

The file *sdoCSR.cer* contains the CSR which must now be sent to a CA. Note that we must send the CSR to an authority for whom we already have a certificate entry—that is, for whom we already have a public key. Otherwise, when the response to the CSR comes, we will be unable to verify the signature of the CA that issued the new certificate.

When the response does come, we must save it to a file. If we save it to the file *sdo.cer*, we can import it with this command:

```
piccolo% keytool -import -file sdo.cer -alias sdo
Enter keystore password:  ******
```

Assuming that the certificate is valid, this imports the new certificate into the keystore. The certificate is invalid if the public key for sdo does not match the previously defined public key in the database, or if the certificate was issued by an authority for whom we do not possess a public key, or if the certificate signature is invalid (which would be the case if data in the certificate had been modified in transit).

The state of the sdo entry in the keystore has changed during this example:

- After the first command, the sdo entry has a single certificate; that certificate is issued by sdo.

- After the import command, the sdo entry has two certificates in its certificate chain: the first certificate is issued by Acme and has a principal of sdo; the second certificate is Acme's self-signed certificate (a copy of the one that was imported when the Acme certificate entry was created).

In programmatic terms, the getCertificateChain() method of the KeyStore class will return an array of one and two elements, respectively, for these cases.

We've mentioned in this section that in order to import a certificate like this, the self-signed certificate of the certificate authority must already be in the keystore. However, there's a bootstrapping issue involved in this: how do you get the initial certificates for the certificate authorities into a keystore?

The JDK comes with a set of five pre-installed certificates: four from VeriSign, which issues certificates at different levels, and one from RSA Data, Inc. These certificates are in the *cacerts* file in the *${JAVAHOME}/lib/security* directory. While those certificates are not present in your *.keystore* file, you can still import certificates into your *.keystore* file by using the *-trustcacerts* option: in that case, as long as the certificate you're importing has been signed by one of the authorities in the *cacerts* file, the import operation will succeed.

Hence, if we'd sent our CSR request in the above example to VeriSign and the returned certificate from VeriSign was stored in the *sdo.cer* file, we could import it with this comand:

```
piccolo% keytool -import -file sdo.cer -alias sdo -trustcacerts
```

If you want to use the certificates of the certificate authorities programatically, you may do so by creating a keystore of type JKS, and loading that keystore from the *cacerts* file.

Modifying Keystore Entries

There is no practical way to modify a certificate entry in the keystore. You may delete an existing entry and add a new one if required.

There is one command that can modify the data within a key entry:

-selfcert
> Change the certificate chain associated with the target key entry. Any previous certificates (including ones that may have been imported from a valid certificate authority) are deleted and replaced with a new self-signed certificate; this certificate can be used to generate a new CSR. The public and private keys associated with the alias are unchanged, but you may specify a new value for the DN on the command line. Hence, one use for this command is to change the DN for a particular entry.

This command supports the following options:

-alias alias
-dname DN
-keypass keypass
-keystore keystore
-storepass storepass
-storetype storetype
-sigalg algorithmName
> Use the given algorithm to generate the signature in the self-signed certificate; as in other cases, this option only supports the DSA algorithm no matter what algorithms may be supported by your security provider.

-validity nDays
> The number of days for which the self-signed certificate is valid. The default is 90 days.

The *-keyclone* command is often used with this command, which can create a copy of the original entry before the DN is changed:

-keyclone
> Clone the target entry. The cloned entry will have the same private key and certificate chain as the original entry. This command supports the following options:

-alias alias
-keypass keypass
-keystore keystore
-storepass storepass
-storetype storetype
-v
-dest newAlias
> The new alias name of the cloned entry. If this is not specified, you will be prompted for it.

-new newPassword
> The new password for the cloned entry. If this is not specified, you will be prompted for it.

To change the password associated with a particular key entry, use this command:

-keypasswd
> Change the password for the given key entry. This command supports the following options:

-alias alias
-keystore keystore
-storepass storePassword
-storetype storetype
-keypass originalPassword
-new newPassword

> Specify the new password for the entry. If this option is not supplied, you will be prompted for the new password.

Deleting Keystore Entries

There is a single command to delete either a key entry or a certificate entry:

-delete

> Delete the entry of the specified alias. If a certificate entry for a certificate authority is deleted, there is no effect upon key entries that have been validated by the authority. This command supports the following options:

-alias alias
-keystore keystore
-storepass storepass
-storetype storetype
-v

Examining Keystore Data

If you want to examine one or more entries in the keystore, you may use the following commands:

-list

> List (to System.out) one or more entries in the keystore. If an alias option is given to this command, only that alias will be listed; otherwise, all entries in the keystore are listed. This command supports the following options:

-alias alias
-keystore keystore
-storepass storepass
-storetype storetype
-v
-rfc

> When displaying certificates, display them in RFC 1421 standard. This option is incompatible with the *-v* option.

-export

Export the certificate for the given alias to a given file. The certificate is exported in RFC 1421 format. If the target alias is a certificate entry, that certificate is exported. Otherwise, the first certificate in the target key entry's certificate chain will be exported. This command supports the following options:

-alias alias
-keystore keystore
-storepass storepass
-storetype storetype
-v
-file outputFile

The file in which to store the certificate. The default is to write the certificate to System.out.

-printcert

Print out a certificate. The input to this command must be a certificate in RFC 1421 format; this command will display that certificate in readable form so that you may verify its fingerprint. Unlike all other commands, this command does not use the keystore itself, and it requires no keystore passwords to operate. It supports the following options:

-v
-file certificateFile

The file containing the RFC 1421 format certificate. The default is to read the certificate from System.in.

Importing a 1.1-Based Identity Database

The keystore in 1.2 is incompatible with the identity database in 1.1, but the keytool is capable of converting between the two. To convert a 1.1 identity database to a 1.2 keystore, use this command:

-identitydb

Convert a 1.1 identity database. This command has the following options

-v
-keystore keystore
-keypass keypass
-storepass storepass
-stereotype stereotype
-file db_file

The file name of the 1.1 identity database. The default for this is *identitydb.obj* in the user's home directory.

With this command, each trusted entry in the identity database will be created as a key entry in the keystore. All other entries in the identity database will be ignored.

Miscellaneous Commands

There are two remaining commands. The first allows you to change the global password of the keystore:

-storepasswd
> Change the global password of the keystore. This command supports the following options:
>
> *-keystore keystore*
> *-storepass storepass*
> *-storetype storetype*
> *-v*
> *-new newPassword*
>> The new global password for the keystore. If you do not specify this value, you will be prompted for it.

Finally, you can get a summary of all commands with this command:

-help
> Print out a summary of the usage of keytool.

The jarsigner Tool

The next tool we'll look at is the jarsigner tool; this tool creates signed JAR files. The jarsigner tool uses the information in a keystore to look up information about a particular entity and uses that information either to sign or to verify a JAR file. As we discussed in the section on keytool, the keystore that jarsigner uses is subject to the KeyStore class that has been installed into the virtual machine; if you have your own keystore implementation, jarsigner will be able to use it. Similarly, if you use the standard keystore implementation, but hold the keys in a file other than the default *.keystore* file, jarsigner will allow you to use that other file as well.

A signed JAR file is identical to a standard JAR file except that a signed JAR file contains two additional entries:

* *SIGNER.SF*—A file containing an SHA message digest for each class file in the archive. The digest is calculated from the three lines in the manifest for the class file. The base of this name (SIGNER) varies; it is typically based upon the alias of the keystore entry used to sign the archive.

- *SIGNER.DSA*—A file containing the digital signature of the .SF file. The base of this name matches the first part of the .SF file; the extension is the algorithm used to generate the signature. This file also contains the certificate of the entity that signed the archive.

The algorithm used to generate the signature depends upon the type of the key found in the keystore: if the key is a X509 (DSA) key, a DSA signature will be generated. If the key is an RSA key, an RSA signature will be generated (assuming you have installed a security provider capable of producing such signatures). If you have a keystore that contains other types of keys, jarsigner will be unable to use them to sign the JAR file.

These entries are held in the META-INF directory of the JAR file.

Creating a Signed JAR File

The simplest command to sign a JAR file is:

```
piccolo% jarsigner xyz.jar sdo
```

This command takes the existing JAR file *xyz.jar* and signs it using the private key of the given alias (sdo). The private key is obtained by searching for the given alias from the default keystore (which will be the *.keystore* file in the user.home directory unless a command-line argument is given). The signature files in this example will be named *SDO.SF* and *SDO.DSA* and will be added to the existing JAR file.

A JAR file can be signed by any number of entities simply by executing this command multiple times with different aliases. Each act of signing the JAR file creates a new set of *.SF* and *.DSA* files in the archive.

There are a number of options that can be used in conjunction with this command:

-keystore keystore
  Specify the filename that the KeyStore class should use as the keystore.

-storepass storepass
  Specify the global password that should be used to open the keystore. If this value is not provided, you will be prompted for it (which, as always, is the more secure way to enter a password).

-keypass password
  Specify the password for the key entry of the given alias. If this value is not provided, you will be prompted for it.

-sigfile file
  Specify the base name to be used for the *.SF* and *.DSA* files. The default for this value is the alias specified on the command line translated to all uppercase letters (e.g., *SDO* in the example above). If the alias name has more than

eight letters, only the first eight letters are used. The file argument in this option can only contain uppercase letters, the digits 0–9, and an underscore; it must contain eight or fewer letters.

-signedjar file

Write the signed JAR file to the named file instead of adding the signature entries to the existing JAR file.

-verbose

Print out information as jarsigner progresses.

Verifying a JAR File

In the process of verifying a JAR file, jarsigner will use the public key of the certificate embedded in the JAR file to verify that the signature is valid. The simplest command to verify a JAR file is:

```
piccolo% jarsigner -verify xyz.jar
jar verified.
```

If the signature in the JAR file is not valid, jarsigner will produce this output:

```
jar is unsigned. (signatures missing or not parsable)
```

Verification accepts the following options:

-sigfile file

Use the given base name to look up the *.SF* and *.DSA* files. This option is useful when the JAR file has been signed by multiple entities.

-verbose

Provide verbose output for the verification, indicating for each file if it was signed and whether or not the signer of the file has been found in the keystore. Sample output from this command might appear like this:

```
piccolo% jarsigner -verify -verbose xyz.jar

          402 Mon Jan 26 19:25:52 EST 1998 META-INF/SDO.SF
         1395 Mon Jan 26 19:25:52 EST 1998 META-INF/SDO.DSA
    smk   596 Sat Jan 24 22:18:22 EST 1998 XYZKey.class
    smk   814 Sat Jan 24 22:17:46 EST 1998 XYZKeyPairGenerator.class
    smk  1155 Sat Jan 24 21:56:40 EST 1998 XYZProvider.class
    smk   900 Sat Jan 24 22:11:22 EST 1998 XYZSignature.class

  s = signature was verified
  m = entry is listed in manifest
  k = at least one certificate was found in keystore

jar verified.
```

Note the legend for each file that is printed by this command. We know if the file was signed, whether or not it was listed in the JAR file's manifest, and whether or not the signer of the file was found in the keystore.

In the vast majority of cases, the information for each file will be the same: JAR files are usually signed all at once by the same person. However, there's nothing to prevent someone from adding a new class to a signed JAR file (in which case the class would appear as unsigned), or for a JAR file to contain multiple signers (some of whom may have signed some of the classes, while others may have signed only a few of the classes).

In order to determine whether the certificate was found in the keystore, jarsigner opens the default instance of the KeyStore class and loads it. Note that no password is required for this operation. As we mentioned in Chapter 11, reading the public information out of the keystore does not require a password (at least in the Sun implementation of the KeyStore class).

-ids

In conjunction with the -verbose option, print out the distinguished name and alias of the certificate (if any) that is found with each class. With this option, the output for a particular class looks like this:

```
smk     900 Sat Jan 24 22:11:22 EST 1998 XYZSignature.class
    CN=Scott Oaks, OU=SMCC, O=Sun Microsystems, L=NY, S=NY, C=US (sdo)
```

In this case, the class was signed by the given distinguished name; the name of the alias associated with the certificate is shown in parentheses (sdo).

This option has no effect unless the -verbose option is specified.

-keystore keystore

Use the given file as the name of the keystore to load. The default for this option is to use the .keystore file in the directory specified by the user.home property. This name is only used for the -verbose option to look up the certificates of the signer.

The policytool

The last security-related tool that comes with the Java platform is policytool. This tool allows you to manage entries in a java.policy file. Unlike the other tools we've discussed, policytool is a graphical tool. As such, it has no command-line options or arguments.

When you first start policytool, you see a blank window with two pull-down menus: File and Edit. Initially, there are no policy entries loaded into this tool; if you want to work on an existing policy file, the first thing you must do is choose the Open command from the File menu. Otherwise, you can add new entries and create a new file containing those entries. Whichever method you choose, keep in mind that policytool is designed to operate on a single policy file.

When you've completed editing the entries for a policy file, you can save your changes. Under the File menu, you can use the Save or Save As command to overwrite the file you loaded or to save your changes to a new file.

Managing Policy Codebases

The initial screen for this tool displays the name of the currently loaded policy file (which is blank if no file has been loaded); the name of the keystore referenced within this file; buttons to add, edit, or remove policy entries; and a list of the current set of policy entries. In this context, a policy entry is the URL from which classes will be loaded; that is, a codebase or a code source. Hence, a single policy entry may contain many individual permissions. In Figure A-1 we've loaded the default *java.policy* file, which has one policy entry: an entry that grants permissions to all codebases.

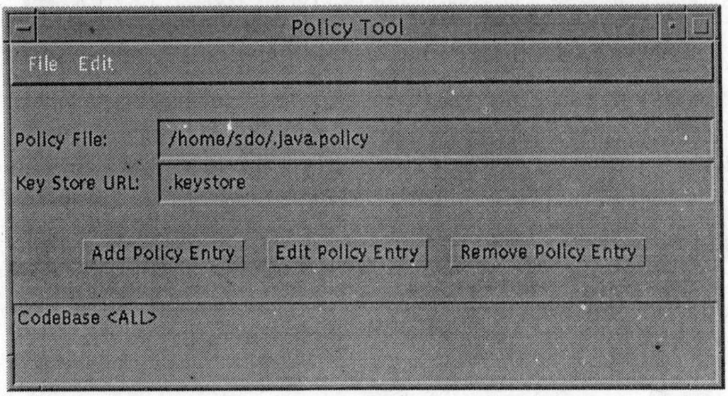

Figure A-1. policytool loaded with one policy entry

Note that the keystore entry for this file is *.keystore*. You can change that value through an option under the Edit menu.

You can add new codebases to this file by selecting the Add Policy Entry button; when you add a policy entry, you are allowed to specify a URL and a signer (both of which are optional). The entry for the signer should be an alias in the keystore; if you enter a signer who is not in the keystore, you'll get a warning, but the operation will continue.

You may delete codebases by selecting one and pressing the Remove Policy Entry button. Selecting a codebase and pressing the Edit Policy Entry button allows you to edit the specific set of permissions for a codebase.

Managing Permissions

When you press the Edit Policy Entry button, you get a window similar to that shown in Figure A-2. This window lists all permissions that are associated with the given codebase, and provides the opportunity to add or remove individual permissions.

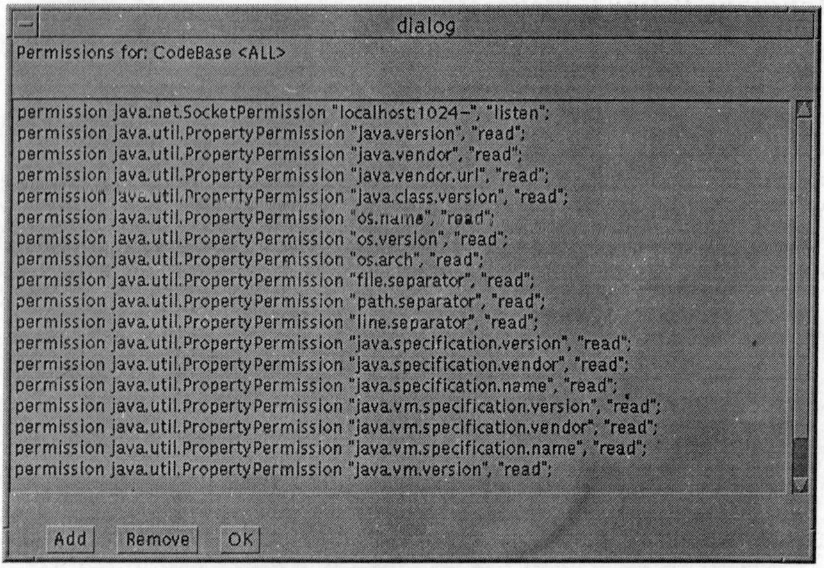

Figure A-2. A set of permissions for a codebase

Managing Certificate Entries

Policytool also allows you to perform some rudimentary operations on the default keystore (again, using whatever KeyStore class implementation has been installed into your Java platform). Under the Edit menu, there are options to add and remove public key aliases. These public key aliases are certificate entries in the keystore. In order to add an alias, you must specify a name for the alias and the name of a file containing a certificate (in RFC 1421 format) to import for that alias; you may remove an alias simply by name.

Files to Administer by Hand

There are two security-related files in the Java platform that must be modified by hand (rather than by a tool). We've talked about these files throughout the book, but for reference, we'll discuss the files and the information they hold.

The java.security File

The *java.security* file must be in the *$JAVAHOME/lib/security* directory. This file is consulted for the following information:

A list of security providers

You may have any number of entries in this file that specify a security provider that should be installed into the virtual machine. By default, there is one security provider specified by this entry:

```
security.provider.1=sun.security.provider.Sun
```

You may specify additional security providers by listing their full class name in this file. Make sure that all security providers are numbered consecutively starting with 1; additional providers can be added before the Sun provider as long as the number assigned to the Sun provider is adjusted accordingly (or the Sun provider could be removed altogether). Remember that this list of providers is consulted when the virtual machine first starts, but that programs with sufficient permissions may add and delete providers from this list.

A KeyStore type

You must have and entry in this file that lists the default type of keystore that an application should use. By default, that type is listed as:

```
keystore.type=jks
```

If you change the type listed in this entry, the new type will be used whenever anyone requests the default keystore implementation.

A Policy class implementation

You must have an entry in this file that lists the class that should be used to provide the implementation of the Policy class. By default, that class is listed as:

```
policy.provider=sun.security.provider.PolicyFile
```

If you change the class listed in this entry, the new class will be instantiated when the policy object is required (i.e., when the permissions for a given codebase are first used). There can be only one policy entry in this file.

The names of the default policy files

When the default implementation of the Policy class reads in permissions, it will read them from the URLs listed as this set of properties:

```
policy.url.1=file:${java.home}/lib/security/java.policy
policy.url.2=file:${user.home}/.java.policy
```

You may specify any number of files in this manner, but the list must start at 1 and be numbered consecutively. The set of permissions will be the aggregate of all permissions found in these URLs.

Remember that these URLs contain only global permissions. You may also specify on the command line a file containing policies with the -Djava.security.policy argument. If the name following the -Djava.security.policy argument begins with an equals sign, the URLs listed in the *java.security* file are ignored:

```
-Djava.security.policy=/globals/java.policy
```

adds the policies in the */globals/java.policy* file to the set of policies in force, but:

```
-Djava.security.policy==/globals/java.policy
```

sets the policy only to the entries contained in the */globals/java.policy* file. The -Djava.security.policy argument must be with the -Djava.security.manager; if you want to use only the files listed in the *java.security* file, specify -Djava.security.manager without -Djava.security.policy.

Other implementations of the Policy class may or may not use these properties.

Whether or not property substitution is allowed
The ability to make property substitutions for entries in the *java.security* file or in the *java.policy* file depends on this entry:

```
policy.expandProperties=true
```

Whether or not the -Djava.security.policy argument can be used
The ability to use the -Djava.security.policy argument depends on this entry:

```
policy.allowSystemProperty=true
```

The java.policy File

In many cases, you'll use policytool to modify the entries in a *java.policy* file (or create a new one). However, if you need to add custom permissions to this file that aren't supported by policytool, you must edit it by hand.

The format of the *java.policy* file is as follows:

```
keystore "<keystore_url>";

grant [signedBy "<signer1[, signer2]>"] [codeBase "<URL>"] {
    permission <classname> ["<name>"] [, "<actions>"]
                    [, signedBy "<signer1[, signer2]>"];
    ...
};
...
```

Items in square brackets are optional. Items in angled brackets are replaced by specific information, e.g., a signer must be a valid alias in the keystore. Within a grant block, there may be any number of permissions, and within a file, there may be any number of grant blocks.

For example, here are some typical entries in the *java.policy* file:

```
grant {
    permission java.util.PropertyPermission "java.version", "read";
}


grant signedBy "sdo", codeBase "http://piccolo/" {
    permission java.io.FilePermission "${/}tmp${/}-", "read, write,
    delete";
    permission XYZPayrollPermission "*", "read, write";
}


grant codeBase "http://www.sun.com" {
    permission java.io.FilePermission "${/}tmp${/}-", "read";
    permission java.io.FilePermission "${/}tmp${/}-",
            "read, write, delete", signedBy "sdo";
}
```

In the first block, permission is given to code that comes from any location to access the java.version property. The second block grants permissions (including a custom XYZ payroll permission) to any code that is loaded from the site *piccolo* and that is signed by sdo. The third block grants permission to any code that is loaded from *www.sun.com* to read files in the */tmp* directory (or any of its subdirectories); if that code is signed by sdo, it is allowed to read, write, and delete such files.

B

Identity-Based Key Management

In Java 1.1, the primary tool that was used for key management was javakey, which is based heavily on the Identity and IdentityScope classes. The keytool utility that comes with 1.2* is a better way to implement key management, and the KeyStore class on which keytool is based is definitely more flexible than the classes on which javakey is based. In addition, the javakey database uses some classes and interfaces that have been deprecated in 1.2—primarily the java.security.Certificate interface.

Nonetheless, for developers who are still using 1.1, a key management system based upon the Identity and IdentityScope classes is the only possible solution. In this appendix, we'll show how these classes can be used for key management. All of the techniques we'll discuss in this appendix have a complementary technique in key management with the KeyStore class. In addition, the Identity and IdentityScope classes have been deprecated in 1.2, so you should really move to the keystore implementation as soon as possible.

Identities

You probably noticed in Chapter 10 that none of the key classes had any notion of whom the key belonged to. Keys are really just an arbitrary-appearing series of bytes. The set of classes we'll examine now deal with the notion of identity: the entity to which a key belongs. An identity can represent an individual or a corporation (or anything else that can possess a public or a private key).

---

* 1.2 is now Java 2.

The Identity Class

First we'll look at the primary class used to encapsulate an entity that has a public key, the Identity class (java.security.Identity):

public abstract class Identity implements Principal, Serializable ☆
Implement an identity—an entity that has a public key. In 1.1, this class is abstract.

An identity object holds only a public key; private keys are held in a different type of object (the signer object, which we'll look at a little later). Hence, identity objects represent the entities in the world who have sent you their public keys in order for you to verify their identity.

An identity contains five pieces of information:

* A name—the name of the identity; this satisfies the Principal interface that the identity implements.

* A public key.

* An optional information string describing the identity.

* An optional identity scope. Identities can be aggregated into a collection, which is called an identity scope.

* A list of certificates that vouch for the identity.

Note that the default implementation of an identity object carries with it no notion of trustworthiness. You're free to add that feature to your own identity class.

Using the identity class

If you want to use an identity object, you have the following methods at your disposal:

public final String getName() ☆
Return the name of the identity.

public final IdentityScope getScope() ☆
Return the identity scope to which the identity belongs.

public PublicKey getPublicKey() ☆
Return the public key associated with the identity.

public void setPublicKey(PublicKey key) throws KeyManagementException ☆
Set the public key associated with the identity to the given public key. This replaces any previous public key as well as any previous certificates associated with this identity. If the public key is already associated with another identity in the identity scope to which this identity belongs, a KeyManagementExcep-

tion is thrown. The implementation of this method in the base class does not actually check the identity scope to see if the key already exists in another identity; it's up to the concrete subclass to provide this functionality.

public String getInfo() ☆

Return the information string associated with the identity.

public void setInfo(String info) ☆

Set the information string in the identity, replacing any existing information string.

public void addCertificate(java.security.Certificate certificate) ☆

Add the given certificate to the list of certificates in the identity. If the identity has a public key and that public key does not match the public key in the certificate, a KeyManagementException is thrown. If the identity does not have a public key, the public key in the certificate becomes the public key for the identity. Like the setPublicKey() method, this should generate a KeyManagementException if this conflicts with another key in the identity scope, but the implementation in the base class doesn't automatically provide that.

public void removeCertificate(java.security.Certificate certificate) ☆

Remove the given certificate from the list of certificates in the identity. If the given certificate isn't in the identity's list of certificates, no exception is thrown.

public java.security.Certificate[] certificates() ☆

Return a copy of the array of certificates held in the identity. The array itself is a copy of what is held by the object, but the certificate objects themselves are not.

public final boolean equals(Object id) ☆

Test if the given identity is equal to the current object. Identities are considered equal if they are in the same scope and have the same name. Otherwise, they are considered equal if the identityEquals() method returns true. By default, identities in different scopes are considered equal by the identityEquals() method if they have the same name and the same public key.

There are two ways to obtain an identity object—via the getIdentity() method of the IdentityScope class or by implementing and constructing an instance of your own subclass of the Identity class.

Implementing an Identity class

An application that wants to work with identities will typically provide its own identity class. A typical implementation of the Identity class is trivial:

```
public class XYZIdentity extends Identity {
    public XYZIdentity(String name)throws KeyManagementException {
```

```
        super(name);
    }
}
```

Because all of the methods in the Identity class are fully implemented, our class need only construct itself. Here are the constructors in the Identity class that we have the option of calling:

protected Identity() ☆
Construct an unnamed identity. This constructor is not designed to be used directly; it is provided for use by object serialization only.

public Identity(String name) ☆
Construct an identity object that does not belong to an identity scope.

public Identity(String name, IdentityScope scope) throws KeyManagementException ☆
Construct an identity object that belongs to the given scope. A KeyManagementException is thrown if the given name already exists in the identity scope.

We've chosen in this example only to implement the second of these constructors.

Other than the constructor, we are not required to implement any methods in our class. If you are implementing an identity within an identity scope, there are methods that you'll need to override in order to get the expected semantics.

Our identity class has one other option available to it, and that is the ability to determine when two identities will compare as equal (via the equals() method). The equals() method itself is final, and it will claim that two identities are equal if they exist in the same scope and have the same name. If either of those tests fails, however, the equals() method relies on the following method to check for equality:

protected boolean identityEquals(Identity id)
Test for equality between the given identity and this identity. The default behavior for this method is to return true if the identities have the same name and the same key.

If your identity class has other information, you may want to override this method to take that other information into account.

The Identity class and the security manager

The identity class uses the checkSecurityAccess() method of the security manager to prevent many of its operations from being performed by untrusted classes. Table B-1 lists the methods of the Identity class that make this check and the argument they pass to the checkSecurityAccess() method.

Table B-1. Methods in the Identity Class that Call the Security Manager

Method	Argument
setPublicKey()	set.public.key
setInfo()	set.info
addCertificate()	add.certificate
removeCertificate()	remove.certificate
toString()	print

The argument to the checkSecurityAccess() method is constructed from four pieces of information: the name of the class that is providing the implementation of the identity class, the string listed in the table above, the name of the particular identity in question (that is, the string returned by the getName() method), and the name of the class that implements the identity scope to which the identity belongs (if any).

In common implementations of the security manager, this string is ignored and trusted classes are typically able to work with identities, while untrusted classes are not.

Signers

An identity has a public key, which can be used to verify the digital signature of something signed by the identity. In order to create a digital signature, we need a private key. An identity that carries with it a private key is modeled by the Signer class (java.security.Signer):

public abstract class Signer extends Identity ☆

A class to model an entity that has both a public key and a private key. Since this is a subclass of the Identity class, the public key comes from the implementation of that class, and a signer class needs only to be concerned with the private key.

The Signer class is fully implemented even though it is declared as abstract; an implementation of the Signer class need not implement any methods.

Using the Signer class

A signer is used just like an identity, with these additional methods:

public PrivateKey getPrivateKey() ☆

Return the private key of the signer.

public final void setKeyPair(KeyPair pair) ☆

Set both the public and private key of the signer. Since public and private keys must match in order to be used, this class requires that in order to set the private key, the public key must be set at the same time. If only one key is present in the key pair, an InvalidParameterException is thrown. The act of setting the public key might generate a KeyManagementException (a subclass of KeyException, which this method throws).

Except for these two operations, a signer is identical to an identity.

Implementing a signer

Signers are trivial to implement, given that none of their methods are abstract. Hence, it is simply a matter of calling the appropriate constructor:

```
public class XYZSigner extends Signer {
    public XYZSigner(String name) throws KeyManagementException {
        super(name);
    }
}
```

Note an unfortunate problem here: if you've added additional logic to your identity subclass, your signer subclass cannot use that logic. Your own signer subclass must extend Java's Signer class, not your own identity subclass.

Signers and the security manager

In addition to the security checks that will be made as part of the methods of the Identity class, the signer class calls the checkSecurityAccess() method of the security manager in the following cases with the strings in Table B-2.

Table B-2. Methods of the Signer Class That Call the Security Manager

Method	Parameter
getPrivateKey()	get.private.key
setKeyPair()	set.private.keypair

As with the Identity class, the actual string passed to the security manager is preceded with the name of the class, and the name of the identity is appended to the class along with the name of the identity's scope.

Identity Scopes

The database that an identity is held in is an identity scope. There can be multiple identity scopes in a Java program, though typically there is only a system identity scope. By default, the system identity scope for all Java programs is read from a file; this file is the database that javakey operates on. But the architecture of an identity scope can be more complex than a single scope.

As Figure B-1 shows, multiple identity scopes can be nested, or they can be disjoint. This is because an identity scope may itself be scoped—that is, just like an identity can belong to a particular scope, an identity scope can belong to another scope.

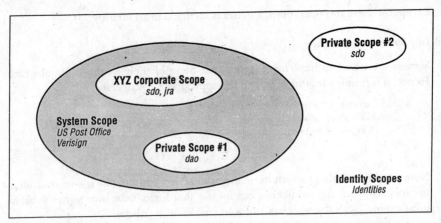

Figure B-1. Identity scopes

This architecture is not as useful as it might seem, since the identity scope class does not give any particular semantics to the notion of a nested identity scope. If you search the system scope in the figure for sdo's identity, you may or may not find it, depending on how the system identity scope is implemented. That's because there's no requirement that an identity scope recursively search its enclosed scopes for any information. And the default identity scope does not do such a recursive search.

This is not to prevent you from writing identity scope classes that use such semantics—indeed, writing such a scope is the goal of this appendix.

The idea of an identity scope, of course, is to hold one or more unique identities. However, possible implementations of an IdentityScope class (java.security.IdentityScope) are conceivably more complicated than that because of the definition of this class:

public abstract class IdentityScope extends Identity ☆
>   Implementations of this class are responsible for storing a set of identities and
>   for performing certain operations on those identities.

Hence, an identity scope is also an identity. That means that an identity scope might have a name and a public key, which gives you the ability to model an identity database in very different ways. Conceivably, you might want an identity scope for an organization that contains all the identities of individuals within that organization. Rather than having a separate identity for the organization itself, the organization's identity can be subsumed by the identity scope. Since the organization itself also needs a name and a public key, this type of model might offer some flexibility over the alternative: a model that just has a list of identities, some of which are individuals and one of which is the organization.

However, we'll ignore that possibility for now, and just explore the identity scope class with a view to its simplest use: as a holder of one or more identities.

Using the IdentityScope Class

The IdentityScope class is an abstract class, and there are no classes in the core JDK that extend the IdentityScope class. Like other classes in the security package, instances of it may be retrieved by a static method (albeit with a different name than we've been led to expect):

public static IdentityScope getSystemScope() ☆
Return the default identity scope provided by the virtual machine. For javakey, this is the identity scope held in the *identitydb.obj* file in the user's home directory (or an alternate file specified in the *java.security* property file).

Once you have retrieved the system's default scope (or any other identity scope), you can operate on it with the following methods:

public abstract int size() ☆
Return the number of identities that are held in this scope. By default, this does not include the number of nested identities in other scopes that are held in this scope.

public abstract Identity getIdentity(String name) ☆
Return the identity object associated with the corresponding name.

public abstract Identity getIdentity(Principal principal) ☆
Using the principal's name, return the identity object associated with the corresponding principal.

public abstract Identity getIdentity(PublicKey key) ☆
Return the identity object associated with the corresponding public key.

public abstract void addIdentity(Identity identity) ☆
Add the given identity to this identity scope. A KeyManagementException is thrown if the identity has the same name or public key as another identity in this scope.

public abstract void removeIdentity(Identity identity) ☆
Remove the given identity from this identity scope. A KeyManagementException is thrown if the identity is not present in this scope.

public abstract Enumeration identities() ☆
>   Return an enumeration of all the identities in this scope.

For the most part, using these methods is straightforward. For example, to list all the identities in the default identity database, we need only find the system identity scope and enumerate it:

```
public class Test {
    public static void main(String args[]) {
        try {
            IdentityScope is = IdentityScope.getSystemScope();
            System.out.println(is);
            Enumeration e = is.identities();
            while (e.hasMoreElements()) {
                Identity id = (Identity) e.nextElement();
                System.out.println(id);
            }
        } catch (Exception ex) {}
    }
}
```

There is one exception to this idea of simplicity, however. An identity scope is typically persistent—the javakey database is in a local persistent file, and you could write your own scope that was saved in a file, a database, or some other storage. However, you'll notice that there are no methods in the IdentityScope class that allow you to save the database for a particular scope. Hence, we could add a new identity to the system identity scope like this:

```
IdentityScope is = IdentityScope.getSystemScope();
Identity me = somehowCreateIdentity("sdo");
try {
    is.addIdentity(me);
} catch (KeyManagementException kme) {}
```

That adds an sdo identity to the system identity scope for the current execution of the virtual machine, but unless we can somehow save that scope to the *identitydb.obj* file, the sdo identity will be lost when we exit the virtual machine. Unfortunately, there are no public methods to save the identity scope.

As an aside, we'll note that the *identitydb.obj* file just happens to be the serialized version of an IdentityScope object—to save the database, we need only open an ObjectOutputStream and write the is instance variable to that output stream.

There's another point here that we must mention: the JDK's notion of the system identity scope expects to hold identity objects that are instances of a particular class that exists only in the sun package. This means that we can't actually write a fully correct somehowCreateIdentity() method—we can create identities, but they will not be of the exact class that the system identity scope expects. This can affect some of the operations of the javakey database, since some of those operations are dependent on properties of the Sun implementation of an identity that are not in the generic idea of an identity. When we write our own identity-based database at the end of this appendix, that will no longer be a problem (but we won't be able to use the javakey utility on that database, either).

Writing an Identity Scope

We'll now implement our own identity scope, which will be one of the classes that we'll use at the end of this appendix to put together an identity-based key management database. We'll write a generic identity scope that implements the notion that its identities are held in a file:

```java
public class XYZFileScope extends IdentityScope {
    private Hashtable ids;
    private static String fname;

    public XYZFileScope(String fname) throws KeyManagementException {
        super("XYZFileScope");
        this.fname = fname;
        try {
            FileInputStream fis = new FileInputStream(fname);
            ObjectInputStream ois = new ObjectInputStream(fis);
            ids = (Hashtable) ois.readObject();
        } catch (FileNotFoundException fnfe) {
            ids = new Hashtable();
        } catch (Exception e) {
            throw new KeyManagementException(
                    "Can't load identity database " + fname);
        }
    }

    public int size() {
        return ids.size();
    }

    public Identity getIdentity(String name) {
        Identity id;
        id = (Identity) ids.get(name);
        return id;
    }

    public Identity getIdentity(PublicKey key) {
        if (key == null)
            return null;
        Identity id;
        for (Enumeration e = ids.elements(); e.hasMoreElements(); ) {
            id = (Identity) e.nextElement();
```

```
        PublicKey k = id.getPublicKey();
        if (k != null && k.equals(key))
            return id;
    }
    return null;
}

public void addIdentity(Identity identity)
                    throws KeyManagementException {
    String name = identity.getName();
    if (getIdentity(name) != null)
        throw new KeyManagementException(
                    name + " already in identity scope");

    PublicKey k = identity.getPublicKey();
    if (getIdentity(k) != null)
        throw new KeyManagementException(
                    name + " already in identity scope");
    ids.put(name, identity);
}

public void removeIdentity(Identity identity)
                        throws KeyManagementException {
    String name = identity.getName();
    if (ids.get(name) == null)
        throw new KeyManagementException(
                    name + " isn't in the identity scope");
    ids.remove(name);
}

public Enumeration identities() {
    return ids.elements();
}

public void save() {
    try {
        FileOutputStream fos = new FileOutputStream(fname);
        ObjectOutputStream oos = new ObjectOutputStream(fos);
        oos.writeObject(ids);
    } catch (Exception e) {
        System.out.println(e);
        throw new RuntimeException("Can't save id database");
    }
}
}
```

Let's delve into the implementation of this class. First, there are two instance variables. The ids variable will hold the identities themselves; we've decided to hold the identities in a hashtable so that we can easily search them based on a key. That key will be their name, which makes locating identities in this scope by name very easy (but notice that locating them by public key is harder). The second variable, fname, is the name of the file that will hold the persistent copy of this identity scope.

There are three constructors in the IdentityScope class that are available to us:

protected IdentityScope() ☆
> Construct an unnamed identity scope. This constructor is not designed to be used by programmers; it is provided only so that an identity scope may be subject to object serialization.

public IdentityScope(String name) ☆
public IdentityScope(String name, IdentityScope scope) ☆
> Construct an identity scope with the given name. If an identity scope is specified, the new identity scope will be scoped within the specified scope; otherwise, the new identity scope will have no scope associated with it (like Private Scope #2 in figure Figure B-1). A KeyManagementException will be thrown if an identity or identity scope with the desired name already exists in the given scope.

In our case, we've chosen only to provide our identity scope with a name. After calling the appropriate superclass constructor, our class opens up the stored version of the identity database and reads it in. Like the default javakey implementation, we've chosen the simple expedient of object serialization to a persistent file to provide our storage. If the file isn't found, we create an empty identity scope.

We've provided a simple save() method that serializes the private database out to the same file that we read it in from; this method has a package protection so that it will only be accessible by the code we develop. The remaining methods in our class are all methods we are required to implement, because they are methods that are abstract in our superclass. Because we're storing identities in a hashtable, their implementations are usually simple:

- The size() method can simply return the size of the hashtable.

- The getIdentity(name) method can simply use the name as the lookup key into the hashtable.

- The getIdentity(key) method is the most complex method, although only slightly: it merely needs to enumerate the identities and test each one individually to see if the keys match.

- The addIdentity() method can search to make sure that the name and public key of the new identity are unique and then simply store the identity into the hashtable with the name as its key.

- The removeIdentity() method can just tell the hashtable to remove the identity with the appropriate key.

- The identities() method can just return the hashtable enumeration.

There is one remaining protected method of the IdentityScope class:

protected static void setSystemScope(IdentityScope scope)
  Set the system identity scope to be the given scope.

We haven't used this method in this example, but it is one that we'll rely on later when we extend this example. This method replaces the system identity database. Replacing the system database makes things easier for developers. When developers need to operate on identities, they expect to access those identities through the system database. Now that our class is the system database, we can return identities whether they exist in the user's private key database or in the shared public key database.

IdentityScope and the Security Manager

Like the Identity class, the IdentityScope class uses the checkSecurityAccess() method of the security manager to protect many of its operations from being performed by untrusted classes. This method is called by the setSystemScope() method (with an argument of "set.system.scope"); no other methods of the IdentityScope class call this method by default.

However, in the default identity scope implemented in the sun package, in the following situations, these methods call the checkSecurityAccess() method with the given string:

- When the getIdentity() method would return a signer—that is, an identity that has a private key ("get.signer")

- When the addIdentity() and removeIdentity() methods are called ("add.identity" and "remove.identity", respectively)

- When the database is written to a file via object serialization ("serialize.identity.database")

When we implemented the abstract methods of our IdentityScope class, we probably should have made the decision to let the security manager override the ability of an untrusted (or other) class to perform these operations. Hence, a better implementation of the getIdentity() method would be:

```
public Identity getIdentity(String name) {
    Identity id;
    id = (Identity) ids.get(name);
    if (id instanceof Signer) {
        SecurityManager sec = System.getSecurityManager();
```

```
        if (sec != null)
            sec.checkSecurityAccess("get.signer");
    }
    return id;
}
```

Key Management in an Identity Scope

We're now going to put together the identity scope with the information about the identity class to produce another key management system. One of the primary limitations of the default identity scope is that it's based upon a single file. If you're in a corporation, you may want to have an identity scope that encompasses the public keys of every employee in the corporation—but you can't afford to put the private keys of the employees in that database. Every employee needs read access to the database to obtain his or her own key; there's no practical way with a single identity scope to prevent these users from reading each other's private keys.

Hence, in this example, we're going to develop an identity scope that provides for the architecture shown in Figure B-2.

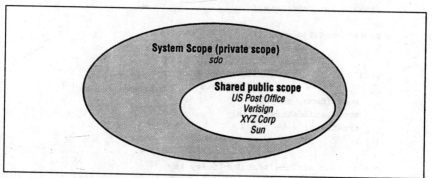

Figure B-2. A key management architecture

There are two simple goals to this example:

- There should be a central database (identity scope) managed by the system administrators of the XYZ Corporation. This database will hold the public keys of all identities that are used in the system, along with a security level that is assigned to each identity.

- Each user should have a private database that holds the user's private key. The user's private key will be certified by the XYZ Corporation itself, so this private database will need to have the public key of the XYZ Corporation. We'll make this scope the system scope so that it can encapsulate the knowledge that there are two scopes in use; to a program, it will appear as only a single scope.

This architecture allows a program to access the user's private key, but not anyone else's private key; it also allows the corporation to set security policies for classes that are signed by particular entities.

There's a certain schizophrenic approach that a system administrator must take in order to use a system like the one we're describing here. Many of the operations that are provided by javakey cannot be duplicated by a standard Java program. Hence, we must always rely on javakey to perform certain operations (like importing a 1.1-based certificate), and then we need to convert from the javakey database to our own database.

We must implement three classes for this example: an identity class, a signer class, and a shared identity scope class (which will be based upon the XYZFileScope class that we showed above).

Implementing an Identity Class

First, let's look at an implementation of the identity class:

```
public class XYZIdentity extends Identity {
    private int trustLevel;

    protected XYZIdentity() {
    }

    public XYZIdentity(String name, IdentityScope scope)
                        throws KeyManagementException {
        super(name, scope);
        scope.addIdentity(this);
        trustLevel = 0;
    }

    public void setPublicKey(PublicKey key)
                        throws KeyManagementException {
        IdentityScope is = getScope();
        Identity i = is.getIdentity(key);
        if (i != null && !equals(i))
            throw new KeyManagementException("Duplicate public key");
        super.setPublicKey(key);
    }

    public void addCertificate(Certificate cert)
                            throws KeyManagementException {
        Identity i = getScope().getIdentity(cert.getPublicKey());
        if (i != null && !equals(i))
            throw new KeyManagementException("Duplicate public key");
        super.addCertificate(cert);
    }
```

```
        public int getTrust() {
            return trustLevel;
        }

        void setTrust(int x) {
            if (x < 0 || x > 10)
                throw new IllegalArgumentException("Invalid trust level");
            trustLevel = x;
        }

        public String toString() {
            return super.toString() + " trust level: " + trustLevel;
        }
    }
```

We've chosen in this class to ensure that an identity always belongs to a scope and so we only provided one constructor. There's a somewhat confusing point here, however. Constructing an identity as part of a scope does not automatically add that identity to the scope. That logic is required either in the constructor (as we've done), or the design of the class will require that the developer using the class explicitly assigns the identity to the scope later. The former case is probably more useful; make sure to assign your identities inside their constructors.

Other than the constructor, we're not required to implement any other methods in our identity class. However, we've chosen to override the setPublicKey() and addCertificate() methods so that those methods throw an exception when an identity is to be assigned a public key that already exists in the identity scope. You'll recall that when we first introduced the Identity class, we mentioned that this logic was not present. Adding that logic is a simple matter of checking to see if the public key in question is already in the identity scope.

Finally, we've introduced a variable in our identity to determine the level of trust that we place in this identity. This is similar to the binary option that javakey gives us as to whether an identity is trusted or not; in our version, we allow the identity to have a level of trust. A trust level of 3 might indicate that the identity is fully trusted and hence should have access to all files; a level of 2 might indicate that the identity should be allowed access only to files in the user's temporary directory; a level of 1 might indicate that the identity should never be allowed to access a local file. The point is, the notion of trust associated with an identity is completely up to the programmer to decide—you're free to assign whatever semantics you like for this (or any other value), or to dispense with such an idea altogether. The idea behind this variable is that the security manager might use it (or other such information) to determine an appropriate security policy.

Implementing a Signer Class

Implementing the Signer class that we require follows virtually the same process:

```
public class XYZSigner extends Signer {
    private int trustLevel;

    public XYZSigner(String name, IdentityScope scope)
                                    throws KeyManagementException {
        super(name, scope);
        scope.addIdentity(this);
    }

    public void setPublicKey(PublicKey key)
                                    throws KeyManagementException {
        IdentityScope scope = getScope();
        if (scope != null) {
            Identity i = getScope().getIdentity(key);
            if (i != null && !equals(i))
                throw new KeyManagementException(
                                        "Duplicate public key");
        }
        super.setPublicKey(key);
    }

    public void addCertificate(Certificate cert)
                                    throws KeyManagementException {
        IdentityScope scope = getScope();
        if (scope != null) {
            Identity i = getScope().getIdentity(cert.getPublicKey());
            if (i != null && !equals(i))
                throw new KeyManagementException(
                                        "Duplicate public key");
        }
        super.addCertificate(cert);
    }

    public int getTrust() {
        return trustLevel;
    }

    void setTrust(int x) {
        if (x < 0 || x > 10)
            throw new IllegalArgumentException("Invalid trust level");
        trustLevel = x;
    }

    public String toString() {
        return super.toString() + " trust level: " + trustLevel;
    }
}
```

We do not need to provide an overridden method for the setKeyPair() method of the Signer class to ensure that a duplicate private key is not inserted into the identity scope. Since we can only insert a private key with a public key, and since there is a one-to-one correspondence between such keys, we know that if the public keys are unique, the private keys are unique as well.

A Shared System Identity Scope

In the architecture we're examining, there are two identity scopes:

- The private scope. This scope will hold one and only one instance of XYZ-Signer. This signer will represent the user who owns that particular database.

- The public scope. This scope will hold several instances of XYZIdentity, but no signers—since it is to be shared, we don't want it to contain any private keys.

Each of these scopes will be an instance of the XYZFileScope that we showed earlier. To combine them, we'll create another identity scope that holds a reference to both scopes:

```
public class XYZIdentityScope extends IdentityScope {
    private transient IdentityScope publicScope;
    private transient IdentityScope privateScope;

    public XYZIdentityScope() throws KeyManagementException {
        super("XYZIdentityScope");
        privateScope = new XYZFileScope("/floppy/floppy0/private");
        publicScope = new XYZFileScope("/auto/shared/sharedScope");
        setSystemScope(this);
    }

    public int size() {
        return publicScope.size() + privateScope.size();
    }

    public Identity getIdentity(String name) {
        Identity id;
        id = privateScope.getIdentity(name);
        if (id == null)
            id = publicScope.getIdentity(name);
        return id;
    }

    public Identity getIdentity(PublicKey key) {
        Identity id;
        id = privateScope.getIdentity(key);
        if (id == null)
            id = publicScope.getIdentity(key);
```

```java
        return id;
    }

    public void addIdentity(Identity identity)
                            throws KeyManagementException {
        throw new KeyManagementException(
                "This scope does not support adding identities");
    }

    public void removeIdentity(Identity identity)
                            throws KeyManagementException {
        throw new KeyManagementException(
                "This scope does not support removing identities");
    }

    class XYZIdentityScopeEnumerator implements Enumeration {
        private boolean donePrivate = false;
        Enumeration pubEnum = null, privEnum = null;

        XYZIdentityScopeEnumerator() {
            pubEnum = publicScope.identities();
            privEnum = privateScope.identities();
            if (!privEnum.hasMoreElements())
                donePrivate = true;
        }

        public boolean hasMoreElements() {
            return pubEnum.hasMoreElements() ||
                    privEnum.hasMoreElements();
        }

        public Object nextElement() {
            Object o = null;
            if (!donePrivate) {
                o = privEnum.nextElement();
                if (!privEnum.hasMoreElements())
                    donePrivate = true;
            }
            else o = pubEnum.nextElement();
            if (o == null)
                throw new NoSuchElementException(
                        "XYZIdentityScopeEnumerator");
            return o;
        }
    }

    public Enumeration identities() {
        return new XYZIdentityScopeEnumerator();
    }
}
}
```

The idea behind this class is that it is going to hold identities containing private keys, and that those private keys should be held somewhere safe. For this example, we're assuming that the private identity scope database will be stored on a floppy disk somewhere—that way, a user can move the identity scope around with her, and the private key won't be left on a disk where some malicious person might attempt to retrieve it.

This class is completely tailored to a Solaris machine, since we've hardwired the name of the private file to a file on the default floppy drive of a Solaris machine, and we've hardwired the name of the public file to a file that can be automounted on the user's machine. On other machines, the name of the floppy drive will vary, and a complete implementation of this class would really require that filename to be a property. The property can be set to the appropriate value for the hardware on which the Java virtual machine is running. The public database probably shouldn't even be a file; it should be held on a remote machine somewhere and accessed via RMI or another technique. We'll leave those enhancements as an exercise for the reader.

Now that we have the two scopes we're interested in, completing the implementation is a simple matter of:

- Setting this identity scope to be the system identity scope. This allows the developer to use the standard methods we've already seen to extract information from this scope.

- Overriding the getIdentity() and identities() methods so that they operate on both included identity scopes. Remember that often identity scopes are disjoint; in this case, however, it makes sense for there to be a single interface to the two identity scopes.

- Overriding the addIdentity() and removeIdentity() methods to prevent them from changing the underlying identity databases. We'll see how to manipulate the individual database in the next section.

Creating Identities

The XYZ Corporation is concerned about two sorts of identities: identities from corporations and individuals outside the corporation, and identities of employees. The latter must all have private keys in order for the employees to be able to sign documents and will be instances of the XYZSigner class; the former need only public keys and will be instances of the XYZIdentity class.

In order to create these identities, we're going to rely on the facilities provided by javakey to do the bulk of the work for us, then we're going to read the generic entity out of the javakey database and turn it into an XYZ-based entity. This allows us to import or create certificates for these identities, which is something that only javakey can do in Java 1.1.

When a new employee comes to the XYZ Corporation, we must generate a private identity database for that employee on a floppy that can be given to the employee. As a first step, however, we must create the employee in a standard javakey database so that the employee can be given a certificate to accompany her identity. Once we've got the employee into the javakey database, here's the code we use to convert the javakey entry into the XYZIdentityScope we just examined:

```
public class NewEmployee {
    public static void main(String args[]) {
        try {
            IdentityScope is = IdentityScope.getSystemScope();
            Signer origSigner = (Signer) is.getIdentity(args[0]);

            System.out.println(
                "Please insert the floppy for " + args[0]);
            System.out.print("Press enter when ready: ");
            System.in.read();
            XYZFileScope privateScope =
                    new XYZFileScope("/floppy/floppy0/private");
            XYZSigner newSigner = new XYZSigner(args[0], privateScope);
            KeyPair kp = new KeyPair(origSigner.getPublicKey(),
                                origSigner.getPrivateKey());
            newSigner.setKeyPair(kp);
            newSigner.setInfo(origSigner.getInfo());
            Certificate certs[] = origSigner.certificates();
            for (int i = 0; i < certs.length; i++)
                newSigner.addCertificate(certs[i]);
            newSigner.setTrust(Integer.parseInt(args[1]));
            privateScope.save();

            XYZFileScope sharedScope =
                    new XYZFileScope("/auto/shared/sharedScope");
            XYZIdentity newId = new XYZIdentity(args[0], sharedScope);
            newId.setPublicKey(origSigner.getPublicKey());
            newId.setInfo(origSigner.getInfo());
            certs = origSigner.certificates();
            for (int i = 0; i < certs.length; i++)
                newId.addCertificate(certs[i]);
            newId.setTrust(Integer.parseInt(args[1]));
            sharedScope.save();
        } catch (Exception e) {
            System.out.println(e);
        }
    }
}
```

This program is then run with the name of the employee as an argument. When the program is run, two things happen:

1. The correct private key database is created and written to the floppy. The private key database has the signing identity of the new employee loaded into it.

2. The shared public database is opened, and the identity of the new employee is added to it.

In both cases, it was necessary to read the existing data out of the entity read from the javakey database and convert that data into an XYZ-based class. We could have used the existing object (a subclass of the Identity or Signer class), but that would not have allowed us to associate a level of trust with these entities in our database. After the program has run, both databases have the desired entity, with the desired set of keys.

When the system administrator for the XYZ Corporation receives a public key (and a certificate) for an entity that is not going to be a signer within the XYZ Corporation, a similar procedure would need to be followed to enter the certificate into the javakey database, and then extract out the new identity and update only the shared identity scope. Code to do that would be very similar to the code shown above.

Summary

In this appendix, we've shown an example of an identity-based key management system. Such a system is the only choice for key management for developers in Java 1.1.

The identity-based key management system does have one advantage: it allows the retrieval of identity objects from the database, while the keystore-based system only allows for retrieval of keys and certificates. This means that an identity-based system can embed within it other information about an entity (including, for example, a level of trust associated with that individual); this other information is available to users of the database in a straightforward way.

C

Security Resources

Books are very useful for learning some things, and hopefully you've gotten some benefit from the one you're holding in your hand. However, for some types of information, the Internet remains the better choice. In this appendix, we'll list and discuss various network resources that relate to Java and security.

One reason why this information is better found on the Internet is because it is subject to rapid change. The APIs we've discussed may remain fairly stable (despite the big changes in many of them between 1.1 and 1.2*), but the information to be found in these resources is more dynamic.

Security Bugs

Early in my computer science career, I handed in an exam that ended up receiving a lower grade than I had expected.† As part of the exam, I was asked to write an algorithm, prove that it was correct, and then provide an implementation of the algorithm.

While my algorithm and its accompanying proof were completely correct, my implementation received a failing grade. This was a rather dispiriting result: I had come up with a solution and proved that the solution was correct. But the "real" solution—the implementation—was still flawed.

Such is the potential problem with implementing a security model. A lot of design and analysis has gone into Java's default security model, and hopefully you'll put your own effort into making your own applications secure. But no matter how

---

* 1.2 is now Java 2.

† Okay, that was not an unusual event for me...

sound the design of a security model, in the end it is the implementation that matters.

In this section, we'll discuss some past bugs in Java's security implementation and list some common resources for finding out about and fixing present bugs.

Few issues in the Java world receive more attention than security bugs; report of a new bug is guaranteed to produce a flurry of activity. As a result, readers of the trade press often have the idea that Java is riddled with security bugs, or that it isn't secure to begin with. This is not the case. While some important bugs in Java's security implementation have been reported, the impact of these bugs has (at least until now) been minimal.

Bugs that are reported against Java's security model fall into one of five categories:

1. Reports that are not bugs, but that arise from a lack of understanding of Java's security model

   There are two types of very common bugs in this category: applets that perform annoying tasks, and applets that seem to break out of the sandbox. The former category includes applets that take lots of CPU time or otherwise consume many resources. As we mentioned at the outset of this book, such attacks are annoying but are not security attacks.

   The latter category often involves bugs that hinge upon someone having installed a local class file (or worse, a local native library); as we know by now, these local class files are treated as trusted classes. When one of these local classes is able to read (or remove) files on your disk, contact a machine on your local network, or engage in some other potentially malicious behavior, word goes out that Java is not secure, or at best has bugs in its security model.

   The lesson to learn from these reports is this: no computer security model is a substitute for vigilant practices by the end user. If your policy is never to run shareware programs downloaded from the Internet, then your policy should be never to install local classes on your system. And while newer versions of browsers, along with the ability in 1.2 to run applications in a secure environment, help to mitigate the potential danger of installing a local class file, such features will never obviate the need for users and system administrators to understand and work with the security model. There may be real bugs in the Java implementation—but don't assume that all reports you hear about the sandbox being broken fall into that category.

2. Bugs that are misclassified; that is, actual bugs that are reported as being security bugs when they are not

   As we've seen, security is pervasive in the Java platform—the bytecode verifier, the class loader, the security manager, and the compiler all have aspects of security to them. Hence, bugs in these areas are often considered security bugs even when they are not. For example, a bug in the bytecode verifier is usually assumed to be a security bug, even if it is not; if the verifier doesn't accept a particular construct that it should accept, for example, no security concerns arise.

3. Web-related bugs that are not Java-specific

Often, security problems on the Internet are associated with Java without any direct cause. In particular, bugs related to JavaScript™ and to ActiveX often fall into this category.

When the first reports of ActiveX security bugs were circulated, there was a lot of discussion about "active content"; the assertion in many quarters was that the security problems that plagued ActiveX were inherent in any active content system. This assertion attempted to place Java in the same light as ActiveX since both were active content systems. The reality is that Java and ActiveX have very different security models.

Similarly, bugs about JavaScript are often confused with bugs about Java, in part because of the name. It is probably well known by this point, but it doesn't hurt to reiterate: JavaScript and Java are completely different technologies produced by separate companies (Netscape and Sun, respectively). The two technologies are complementary in many ways, but they are fundamentally different from a security perspective.

Finally, Java is not immune to security problems that plague the Web in general. Data that is sent between sites among Java applets and servers can be snooped just like data that is sent via HTTP can be snooped (unless the Java traffic is using SSL or another encryption technique). A hacker that sets up a site to impersonate *XYZ.com* will be able to serve Java applets just as it is able to serve HTML.

4. Bugs in third-party trusted classes

When you install third-party classes, it is possible that one of them may breach the security model that you think is in place: it may provide a mechanism for an untrusted class to open a file, for example, based upon the permissions normally given to the third-party class.

Complicating this factor is the manner in which these classes are often installed: they are often put into a directory and the user's CLASSPATH is globally set to include those classes. Now untrusted classes will be able to access the third-party classes.

5. Bugs in the Java implementation

There have been several well-publicized bugs that do involve Java's security implementation; as with any large computer system, there are bound to be others.

This last point should not minimized—there have been and will be bugs in the Java security implementation. But the potential for bugs and their potential impact must be weighed against the potential benefits of using Java. I know of one corporation where Java is not allowed to be used for any internal project. This site is not worried about employees doing malicious things to other employees, and they filter out Java class files at their corporate firewall, but developers at this company are still not permitted to use Java for any internal project due to security concerns.

When I asked about this policy, I was told that this corporation had "zero-tolerance" for security problems, and the mere risk of a Java security bug was enough for them to forbid the use of Java. Of course, this site that had zero-tolerance for security problems had a floppy disk drive on every one of their desktop computers, and users routinely took files to and from the office via floppy disks. The potential for a virus being spread by floppy disk drive (which is very real) was outweighed for them by the benefit of their users doing work at home. Meanwhile, the thought that Java would somehow spontaneously corrupt their isolated network was, for them, enough to outweigh any of the potential benefits they saw to using Java within their extremely distributed, heterogeneous network. Assessing the security of a platform always involves assessing the potential risks and the potential rewards, though apparently that is sometimes hard to do.

Java Security Bugs

One of the ways to assess the potential impact of Java security bugs is to understand the bugs that have occurred to date and their relative impact. The fact that all these bugs have been fairly minor and quickly fixed is of some comfort. That is not to say that a future bug won't be more devastating or harder to fix; the point here is really to shed light on the bugs that have been found.

The bugs we'll discuss in this section all have another property: attacks based on these bugs were very hard to construct. In fact, attacks based on these bugs never made it out onto the Internet or other networks; the bugs were all reported by various researchers, and often even the researchers had difficulty in constructing an attack against them.

Here's a chronology of security bugs that have been found in Java through November 1998. There was an additional bug reported in July 1998 regarding the class loader, but this applied only to Netscape's implementation, not to the standard JDK.

DNS spoofing

In February 1996, the first Java security bug was posted. It involved a DNS spoofing scenario in which an applet could make a connection to a third-party host other than the one from which it was loaded. Such an attack required access by the attacker to a DNS server that was used by the user and knowledge of the IP address of the third-party machine. DNS spoofing is a general problem (i.e., this bug falls into category 3 in our above list), but Java was fixed in 1.0.1 to circumvent this scenario.

Class loader implementation bug

In March 1996, a bug was found that allowed an applet to load a class referenced by an absolute pathname. This bug was fixed in 1.0.1.

Verifier implementation bug

In March 1996, a bug was discovered that took advantage of an implementation error in the bytecode verifier. An attack via this bug needed to be very sophisticated, but it did allow the applet to perform any operation (delete a file, write a file, etc.) on the user's machine. This bug was fixed in 1.0.2.

URL name resolution attack

In April 1996, a bug related to an obscure network configuration was reported. This bug required that the user's machine ·be running in a DNS domain that it was not registered to and that the attacker's machine be running in that same DNS domain. This bug was fixed in 1.0.2.

Class loader bug

In May 1996, a bug in the class loader was discovered that allowed two applets loaded in different class loaders to exploit a way of casting between different classes with the same distinct name. This bug was fixed in 1.1.

Verifier implementation bug

In March 1997, Sun discovered a bug in the implementation of the verifier. Exploiting this bug would have required knowledge of the bug itself as well as writing Java bytecodes by hand. This bug was fixed in 1.1.1.

Class signing bug

A bug in the getSigners() method of the Class class was discovered in April 1997. This bug allowed code signed by one entity to be treated as if were signed by a different entity (possibly with more access to the user's machine). This bug was fixed in 1.1.2.

Verifier implementation bug

A bug that could allow the VM to crash in the bytecode verifier was discovered in May 1997; this bug was fixed in 1.1.2.

Illegal type casting

A bug related to illegal type casting was reported in June 1996. This bug allowed an applet to undermine the typing system of Java. This bug was fixed in 1.1.3.

Tracking Security Bugs

The nature of tracking security bugs makes it impossible to track them through a book such as this; we're sure that the above list is already out of date. Hence, the better way to track security issues with Java's implementation is to check periodically the following resources on the Web.

An important point to realize about these sites and the bugs we've just listed is that much of the research on security implementation bugs occurs outside of Sun. Sun's approach to Java security is to achieve security by openness—that is, the more people who can examine the platform for implementation bugs, the better that implementation will become. This is one reason why the JDK source code is freely available for noncommercial purposes.

http://java.sun.com/sfaq/chronology.html

This page lists the known bugs in the security implementation (the above list was culled from this page). New bugs and their fixes are reported here first.

http://www.cert.org/

The CERT organization tracks security-related bugs for all types of computer systems, including Java implementations. Java-related security bugs are often published as CERT advisories.

http://www.cs.princeton.edu/sip/

Many of the bugs in Java's security implementation have been discovered as a result of work done at Princeton's Security Internet Programming (SIP) group. This page summarizes their work, including several of the bugs that were listed above.

.Work at SIP is funded by many companies, including Sun itself.

news://comp.security.announce

This newsgroup tracks security-related announcements about all systems, including Java.

http://kimera.cs.washington.edu/

This research group is also responsible for finding some of the bugs that were listed above.

http://www.alw.nih.gov/Security/security-advisories.html

This site has links to several services that publish advisories when Java (and other) security-related bugs are discovered.

Third-Party Security Providers

There is an increasing number of third-party security providers for both the standard Java Cryptography Architecture and for the Java Cryptography Extension. A partial list of these security providers follows. Note that most of them are based outside the United States. As we discussed in Chapter 13, this frees some restrictions and places other restrictions upon their use: the non-U.S. implementations of the JCE are freed from the export restrictions of the U.S. government (but may still be subject to other export and import restrictions). However, these packages may be subject to patent restrictions—especially within the United States if they include RSA or RC4 forms of cryptography (even if the package originated outside the United States), and within the U.S. and Europe if they include IDEA encryption.

The following list is not exclusive: new providers will certainly have been written in the time this book has been published, and the algorithms provided by each entry in the list are subject to change. In addition to the listed engines, these packages will all provide the necessary key classes and engines to support the algorithms in the package.

- Baltimore Technologies (*http://www.baltimore.ie/jcrypto.htm*)

  The J/Crypto product of Baltimore Technologies in Ireland furnishes a security provider for the standard JCA that includes implementations of the following engines:

  Message digests: MD5 and SHA
  Digital signatures: DSA and RSA/SHA

  In addition, J/Crypto provides a JCE-compatible replacement that includes the following engines:

  Cipher: DES, DESede, RSA, RC4, PBE
  Key agreement: Diffie-Hellman

- IAIK-JCE (*http://kopernikus.iaik.tu-graz.ac.at/JavaSecurity/index.htm*)

  This package from the Institute for Applied Information Processing and Communications in Austria (IAIK) comes with a security provider that performs the following:

  Digital signatures: RSA/MD5 and RSA/SHA
  Message digests: MD5 and SHA
  Certificate and CRL classes: X509

  While IAIK must be purchased for commercial use, it is free for noncommercial use.

  IAIK also provides a JCE-compatible replacement that includes the following engines:

  Cipher: DES, DESede, IDEA, RC2, RC4

- JCP Computer Services LTD (*http://www.jcp.co.uk/products/index.html*)

  The JCP Crypto product of JCP Computer Services LTD in the United Kingdom furnishes a security provider that includes implementations of the following engines:

  Message digests: MD5 and SHA
  Digital signatures: RSA/MD5 and RSA/SHA

  JCP Crypto also comes with a JCE replacement that includes implementations of the following:

  Cipher: DES, DESede, IDEA, RSA, RC4

- Systemics LTD (*http://www.systemics.com/software/cryptix-java/*)

  The Cryptix package from Systemics LTD in the United Kingdom furnishes a security provider that includes implementations of the following engines:

  Message digest: Haval, MD2, MD4, MD5, RIPE-MD128, RIPE-MD160, SHA
  Digital signature: RSA with MD2, MD4, MD5 and SHA, El Gamal

  In addition, Cryptix supplies a replacement for the JCE that includes the following:

  Cipher: Blowfish, CAST 5, DES, DESede, IDEA, Loki, RC2, RC4, Safer, Speed, Square, El Gamal

  Cryptix is freely available.

- RSA Data Security, Inc. (*http://www.rsa.com/rsa/products/jsafe/*)

  The JSafe product from RSA Data Security in the United States furnishes a security provider that implements the following:

  Message digest: MD5, SHA
  Digital signature: RSA/MD5, RSA/SHA

  In addition, JSafe has a JCE-security provider that implements the following:

  Cipher: DES, DESede, RC2, RC4, RC5
  Key agreement: Diffie-Hellman

  Since RSA is the holder of the patents for these algorithms in the United States, they are able to sell licenses for this technology within the U.S. Note that unlike the other items listed in this section, the JCE security provider is just that; it requires the official JCE from Sun. The remaining JCE packages come with their own JCE implementation.

Security References

Finally, here is a number of white papers and other references that are of general interest:

http://java.sun.com/security/
This is the main index site for all security-related features of the JDK. In particular, this page has links to security white papers, API and tool documentation, security specifications, and more. This site also has links to many of the other sites we've listed here.

http://java.sun.com/sfaq/
This is the Frequently Asked Questions page for Java security. This page primarily addresses what applets can and cannot do.

http://java.sun.com/products/jdk1.2/docs/guide/security/security-spec.html
This document is the specification for the 1.2 Java security architecture; it provided invaluable background for this book. When you download the JDK 1.2 documentation, this document can be found at *$JAVA-HOME/docs/guide/security/spec/security-spec.html*.

http://www.users.zetnet.co.uk/hopwood/papers/compsec97.html
This document gives an interesting perspective on the topic of authentication, and in particular whether Java's techniques for authentication are secure.

http://www.doc.gov/
The Department of Commerce of the U.S. government. The Commerce Department governs and publishes the export restrictions of encryption and can grant exceptions for exporting encryption technology.

http://www.crypto.com/
The Export Policy Resource page contains a number of links and other references to sites concerned with the U.S. government encryption policies.

Bruce Schneier. Applied Cryptography. *John Wiley & Sons, New York, NY. 1996*
Okay, it is not a web site, but this book is another invaluable reference for details of all the cryptographic topics of this book (Mr. Schneier's web site, for the library-impaired, is *http://www.counterpane.com/*).

Jonathan Knudsen. Java Cryptography. *O'Reilly & Associates, Sebastopol, CA. 1998*
For a discussion of implementing cryptographic algorithms in Java with a series of excellent examples, check out this book.

D

Quick Reference

This appendix contains a quick-reference guide to the classes that we have discussed in this book. The primary focus is on classes that are in the java.security package and its sub-packages, as well as the javax.crypto extension package. Accordingly, the classes listed in this appendix are organized by their primary package. Of course, there are a number of security-related classes—such as the various permission classes—that do not belong to one of these packages; these are listed in the "Miscellaneous Packages" section at the end of this appendix. Information in this appendix is based only on Java 1.2.*

Package java.security

Class java.security.AccessControlContext

An access control context allows the access controller to substitute a different context (that is, a different set of protection domains) than the context provided by the stack of the current thread. This class might be used by a server thread to determine if a particular calling thread should be allowed to perform particular operations.

Class Definition

```
public final class java.security.AccessControlContext
    extends java.lang.Object {
```

---

* 1.2 is now Java 2.

```
        // Constructors
        public AccessControlContext(ProtectionDomain[]);

        // Instance Methods
        public void checkPermission(Permission);
        public boolean equals(Object);
        public int hashCode();
    }
```

See also: AccessController

Class java.security.AccessController

The access controller is responsible for determining whether or not the current thread can execute a given operation. This decision occurs in the checkPermission() method and is based upon all the protection domains that are on the stack of the calling thread and the set of permissions that have been granted to those protection domains. The access controller is heavily used by the security manager to enforce a specific security policy, and it may be used by arbitrary code to enforce an application-specific security policy as well.

Class Definition

```
    public final class java.security.AccessController
        extends java.lang.Object {

        // Class Methods
        public static native Object doPrivileged(PrivilegedAction);
        public static native Object doPrivileged(PrivilegedAction,
                                    AccessControlContext);
        public static native Object
                            doPrivileged(PrivilegedExceptionAction);
        public static native Object doPrivileged(PrivilegedExceptionAction,
                                    AccessControlContext);
        public static void checkPermission(Permission);
        public static AccessControlContext getContext();
    }
```

See Also: Permission, ProtectionDomain, Policy

Class java.security.AlgorithmParameterGenerator

This engine class is used to generate algorithm-specific parameters, which may then be turned into algorithm parameters specifications to be used to initialize other engine classes. In normal usage, those engines can be initialized directly via the same init() methods that exist in this class; hence, this class is little used.

Class Definition

```
public class java.security.AlgorithmParameterGenerator {

    // Constructors
    protected AlgorithmParameterGenerator(
                    AlgorithmParameterGeneratorSpi, Provider, String);

    // Class Methods
    public static final AlgorithmParameterGenerator
                                getInstance(String);
    public static final AlgorithmParameterGenerator
                                getInstance(String, String);

    // Instance Methods
    public final String getAlgorithm();
    public final Provider getProvider();
    public final void init(int);
    public final void init(int, SecureRandom);
    public final void init(AlgorithmParameterSpec);
    public final void init(AlgorithmParameterSpec, SecureRandom);
    public final AlgorithmParameters generateParameters();
}
```

See also: AlgorithmParameters

Class
java.security.AlgorithmParameterGeneratorSpi

This class is the Security Provider Interface for the algorithm parameter generator. If you want to implement your own algorithm parameter generator, you subclass this class and register your implementation with an appropriate security provider.

Class Definition

```
public abstract class java.security.AlgorithmParameterGeneratorSpi {

    // Instance Methods
    protected abstract void engineInit(int, SecureRandom);
    protected abstract void engineInit(
                        AlgorithmParameterSpec, SecureRandom);
    protected abstract AlgorithmParameters engineGenerateParameters();
}
```

See also: AlgorithmParameterGenerator

Class java.security.AlgorithmParameters

This engine class is used to generate algorithm-specific parameter specifications, which may then be used to initialize other engine classes. In normal usage, those engines can be initialized directly via the same init() methods that exist in this class; hence, this class is little used.

Class Definition

```
public class java.security.AlgorithmParameters {

    // Class Methods
    public static final AlgorithmParameters getInstance(String);
    public static final AlgorithmParameters getInstance(
                                    String, String);

    // Constructors
    protected AlgorithmParameters(AlgorithmParametersSpi,
                             Provider, String);

    // Instance Methods
    public final String getAlgorithm();
    public final Provider getProvider();
    public final void init(AlgorithmParameterSpec);
    public final void init(byte[]);
    public final void init(byte[], String);
    public final AlgorithmParameterSpec getParameterSpec(Class);
    public final byte[] getEncoded();
    public final byte[] getEncoded(String);
    public final String toString();

}
```

See also: KeyPairGenerator

Class java.security.AlgorithmParametersSpi

This is the Security Provider Interface for algorithm parameters. If you want to implement your own algorithm parameters, you do so by subclassing this class and registering your implementation with an appropriate security provider.

Class Definition

```
public abstract class java.security.AlgorithmParametersSpi
        extends java.lang.Object {

    // Constructors
    public AlgorithmParametersSpi();

    // Protected Instance Methods
```

```
         protected abstract byte[] engineGetEncoded();
         protected abstract byte[] engineGetEncoded(String);
         protected abstract AlgorithmParameterSpec
                            engineGetParameterSpec(Class);
         protected abstract void engineInit(AlgorithmParameterSpec);
         protected abstract void engineInit(byte[]);
         protected abstract void engineInit(byte[], String);
         protected abstract String engineToString();
     }
```

See also: AlgorithmParameters

Class java.security.AllPermission

This class represents permissions to perform any operation. This permission is typically granted to extension classes, which (like the core API) need to be able to perform any operation. Although it is a permission class, instances of this class have no name and no actions. The implies() method of this class always returns true.

Class Definition

```
    public final class java.security.AllPermission
         extends java.security.Permission {

         // Constructors
         public AllPermission();
         public AllPermission(String, String);

         // Instance Methods
         public boolean equals(Object);
         public String getActions();
         public int hashCode();
         public boolean implies(Permission);
         public PermissionCollection newPermissionCollection();
     }
```

See also: Permission

Class java.security.BasicPermission

A basic permission represents a binary permission—that is, a permission that you either have or do not have. Hence, the action string in a basic permission is unused. A basic permission follows the same naming convention as java properties: a series of period-separated words, like "exitVM" or "xyz.payrollPermission".

The BasicPermission class is capable of wildcard matching if the last word in the permission is an asterisk. This class serves as the superclass for a number of default permission classes.

Class Definition

```
public abstract class java.security.BasicPermission
    extends java.security.Permission
    implements java.io.Serializable {

    // Constructors
    public BasicPermission(String);
    public BasicPermission(String, String);

    // Instance Methods
    public boolean equals(Object);
    public String getActions();
    public int hashCode();
    public boolean implies(Permission);
    public PermissionCollection newPermissionCollection();
}
```

See also: Permission, PermissionCollection

Class java.security.CodeSource

A code source encapsulates the location from which a particular class was loaded and the public keys (if any) that were used to sign the class. This information is used by a secure class loader to define a protection domain associated with the class; typically, the class loader is the only object that uses a code source.

Class Definition

```
public class java.security.CodeSource
    extends java.lang.Object
    implements java.io.Serializable {

    // Constructors
    public CodeSource(URL, Certificate[]);

    // Instance Methods
    public boolean equals(Object);
    public final Certificate[] getCertificates();
    public boolean implies();
    public final URL getLocation();
    public int hashCode();
    public String toString();
}
```

See also: SecureClassLoader, ProtectionDomain

Class java.security.DigestInputStream

A digest input stream is an input filter stream that is associated with a message digest object. As data is read from the input stream, it is automatically passed to its associated message digest object; once all the data has been read, the message digest object will return the hash of the input data. You must have an existing input stream and an initialized message digest object to construct this class; once the data has passed through the stream, call the methods of the message digest object explicitly to obtain the hash.

Class Definition

```
public class java.security.DigestInputStream
    extends java.io.FilterInputStream {

    // Variables
    protected MessageDigest digest;

    // Constructors
    public DigestInputStream(InputStream, MessageDigest);

    // Instance Methods
    public MessageDigest getMessageDigest();
    public void on(boolean);
    public int read();
    public int read(byte[], int, int);
    public void setMessageDigest(MessageDigest);
    public String toString();
}
```

See also: DigestOutputStream, MessageDigest

Class java.security.DigestOutputStream

A digest output stream is a filter output stream that is associated with a message digest object. When data is written to the output stream, it is also passed to the message digest object so that when the data has all been written to the output stream, the hash of that data may be obtained from the digest object. You must have an existing output stream and an initialized message digest object to use this class.

Class Definition

```
public classs java.security.DigestOutputStream
    extends java.io.FilterOutputStream {
```

```
        // Variables
        protected MessageDigest digest;

        // Constructors
        public DigestOutputStream(OutputStream, MessageDigest);

        // Instance Methods
        public MessageDigest getMessageDigest();
        public void on(boolean);
        public void setMessageDigest(MessageDigest);
        public String toString();
        public void write(int);
        public void write(byte[], int, int);
}
```

See also: DigestInputStream, MessageDigest

Interface java.security.Guard

An object of a class that implements the Guard interface may be used to protect access to a resource. In typical usage, a guard is an object of the Permission class, so that access to the guarded resource is granted if and only if the current thread has been granted the given permission. This interface is used by the GuardedObject class to guard access to another object.

Interface Definition

```
        public abstract interface java.security.Guard {

            // Instance Methods
            public abstract void checkGuard(Object);
        }
```

See also: GuardedObject, Permission

Class java.security.GuardedObject

A guarded object is a container for another object. The contained object is guarded using an object that implements the Guard interface; in typical usage, that would be an instance of a Permission object. The guarded object stores a serialized version of the object it contains; the contained object will be deserialized and returned by the getObject() method only if the guard object allows access.

Class Definition

```
        public class java.security.GuardedObject
            extends java.lang.Object
```

```
        implements java.io.Serializable {

        // Constructors
        public GuardedObject(Serializable, Guard);

        // Instance Methods
        public Object getObject();
    }
```

See also: Guard

Class java.security.Identity

An identity encapsulates public knowledge about an entity (that is, a person or a corporation—or anything that could hold a public key). Identities have names and may hold a public key, along with a certificate chain to validate the public key. An identity may belong to an identity scope, but this feature is optional and is not typically used. This class is deprecated in 1.2.

Class Definition

```
    public abstract class java.security.Identity
        extends java.lang.Object
        implements java.security.Principal, java.io.Serializable {

        // Constructors
        protected Identity();
        public Identity(String);
        public Identity(String, IdentityScope);

        // Instance Methods
        public void addCertificate(Certificate);
        public final boolean equals(Object);
        public Certificate[] certificates();
        public String getInfo();
        public final String getName();
        public PublicKey getPublicKey();
        public final IdentityScope getScope();
        public int hashCode();
        public void removeCertificate(Certificate);
        public void setInfo(String);
        public void setPublicKey(PublicKey);
        public String toString();
        public String toString(boolean);

        // Protected Instance Methods
        protected boolean identityEquals(Identity);
    }
```

See also: Certificate, IdentityScope, Principal, PublicKey

Class java.security.IdentityScope

An identity scope is a collection of identities; an identity may belong to a single
identity scope. The notion is that scope is recursive: an identity scope may itself
belong to another identity scope (or it may be unscoped). This class is deprecated
in Java 1.2.

Class Definition

```
public abstract class java.security.IdentityScope
    extends java.security.Identity {

    // Constructors
    protected IdentityScope();
    public IdentityScope(String);
    public IdentityScope(String, IdentityScope);

    // Class Methods
    public static IdentityScope getSystemScope();
    protected static void setSystemScope(IdentityScope);

    // Instance Methods
    public abstract void addIdentity(Identity);
    public abstract Identity getIdentity(String);
    public Identity getIdentity(Principal);
    public abstract Identity getIdentity(PublicKey);
    public abstract Enumeration identities();
    public abstract void removeIdentity(Identity);
    public abstract int size();
    public String toString();
}
```

See also: Identity

Interface java.security.Key

A key is essentially a series of bytes that are used by a cryptographic algorithm.
Depending on the type of the key, the key may be used only for particular operations and only for particular algorithms, and it may have certain mathematical
properties (including a mathematical relationship to other keys). The series of
bytes that comprise a key is the encoded format of the key.

Interface Definition

```
public abstract interface java.security.Key
    implements java.io.Serializable {
```

```
// Instance Methods
public abstract String getAlgorithm();
public abstract byte[] getEncoded();
public abstract String getFormat();
}
```

See also: PrivateKey, PublicKey, SecretKey

Class java.security.keyFactory

A key factory is an engine class that is capable of translating between public or private key objects and their external format (and vice versa). Hence, key factories may be used to import or export keys, as well as to translate keys of one class (e.g., com.acme.DSAPublicKey) to another class (e.g., com.xyz.DSAPublicKeyImpl) as long as those classes share the same base class. Key factories operate in terms of key specifications; these specifications are the various external formats in which a key may be transmitted. Keys are imported via the generatePublic() and generatePrivate() methods, they are exported via the getKeySpec() method, and they are translated via the translateKey() method.

Class Definition

```
public class java.security.KeyFactory
    extends java.lang.Object {

    // Constructors
    protected KeyFactory(KeyFactorySpi, Provider, String);

    // Class Methods
    public static final KeyFactory getInstance(String);
    public static final KeyFactory getInstance(String, String);

    // Instance Methods
    public final PrivateKey generatePrivate(KeySpec);
    public final PublicKey generatePublic(KeySpec);
    public final String getAlgorithm();
    public final KeySpec getKeySpec(Key, Class);
    public final Provider getProvider();
    public final Key translateKey(Key);
}
```

See also: KeyFactorySpi, KeySpec

Class java.security.KeyFactorySpi

This is the Service Provider Interface for a key factory; if you want to implement your own key factory, you do so by extending this class and registering your implementation with an appropriate security provider. Instances of this class are expected to know how to create key objects from external key specifications and vice versa.

Class Definition

```
public abstract class java.security.KeyFactorySpi
    extends java.lang.Object {

    // Constructors
    public KeyFactorySpi();

    // Protected Instance Methods
    protected abstract PrivateKey engineGeneratePrivate(KeySpec);
    protected abstract PublicKey engineGeneratePublic(KeySpec);
    protected abstract KeySpec engineGetKeySpec(Key, Class);
    protected abstract Key engineTranslateKey(Key);
}
```

See also: KeyFactory, KeySpec

Class java.security.KeyPair   •

Public and private keys are mathematically related to each other and hence are generated together; this class provides an encapsulation of both the keys as a convenience to key generation.

Class Definition

```
public final class java.security.KeyPair
    extends java.lang.Object {

    // Constructors
    public KeyPair(PublicKey, PrivateKey);

    // Instance Methods
    public PrivateKey getPrivate();
    public PublicKey getPublic();
}
```

See also: KeyPairGenerator, PrivateKey, PublicKey

Class KeyPairGenerator

This is an engine class that is capable of generating a public key and its related private key. Instances of this class will generate key pairs that are appropriate for a particular algorithm (DSA, RSA, etc.). A key pair generator may be initialized to return keys of a particular strength (which is usually the number of bits in the key), or it may be initialized in an algorithmic-specific way; the former case is the one implemented by most key generators. An instance of this class may be used to generate any number of key pairs.

Class Definition

```
public abstract class java.security.KeyPairGenerator
    extends java.security.KeyPairGeneratorSpi {

    // Constructors
    protected KeyPairGenerator(String);

    // Class Methods
    public static KeyPairGenerator getInstance(String);
    public static KeyPairGenerator getInstance(String, String);

    // Instance Methods
    public final KeyPair genKeyPair();
    public String getAlgorithm();
    public final Provider getProvider();
    public void initialize(int);
    public void initialize(int, SecureRandom)
    public void initialize(AlgorithmParameterSpec, SecureRandom);
    public void initialize(AlgorithmParameterSpec);
}
```

See also: AlgorithmParameterSpec, KeyPair

Class KeyPairGeneratorSpi

This is the Service Provider Interface class for the key pair generation engine; if you want to implement your own key pair generator, you must extend this class and register your implementation with an appropriate security provider. Instances of this class must be prepared to generate key pairs of a particular strength (or length); they may optionally accept an algorithmic-specific set of initialization values.

Class Definition

```
public abstract class java.security.KeyPairGeneratorSpi
    extends java.lang.Object {
```

```
// Constructors
public KeyPairGeneratorSpi();

// Instance Methods
public abstract KeyPair generateKeyPair();
public abstract void initialize(int, SecureRandom);
public void initialize(AlgorithmParameterSpec, SecureRandom);
}
```

See also: AlgorithmParameterSpec, KeyPairGenerator, SecureRandom

Class java.security.KeyStore

This class is responsible for maintaining a set of keys and their related owners. In the default implementation, this class maintains the *.keystore* file held in the user's home directory, but you may provide an alternate implementation of this class that holds keys anywhere: in a database, on a remote filesystem, on a Java smart card, or any and all of the above. The class that is used to provide the default keystore implementation is specified by the keystore property in the *$JDKHOME/lib/java.security* file. The keystore may optionally require a passphrase for access to the entire keystore (via the load() method); this passphrase is often used only for sanity checking and is often not specified at all. On the other hand, private keys in the keystore should be protected (e.g., encrypted) by using a different passphrase for each private key.

Note that although the keystore associates entities with keys, it does not rely upon the Identity class itself.

Class Definition

```
public abstract class java.security.KeyStore
    extends java.lang.Object {

    // Constructors
    protected KeyStore(KeyStoreSpi, Provider, String);

    // Class Methods
    public static final String getDefaultType();
    public static KeyStore getInstance(String);
    public static KeyStore getInstance(String, String);

    // Instance Methods
    public final Enumeration aliases();
    public final boolean containsAlias(String);
    public final void deleteEntry(String);
    public final Certificate getCertificate(String);
```

```
    public final String getCertificateAlias(Certificate);
    public final Certificate[] getCertificateChain(String);
    public final Date getCreationDate(String);
    public final Key getKey(String, char[]);
    public final Provider getProvider();
    public final String getType();
    public final boolean isCertificateEntry(String);
    public final boolean isKeyEntry(String);
    public final void load(InputStream, char[]);
    public final void setCertificateEntry(String, Certificate);
    public final void setKeyEntry(String, Key, char[], Certificate[]);
    public final void setKeyEntry(String, byte[], Certificate[]);
    public final int size();
    public final void store(OutputStream, char[]);
}
```

See also: Certificate, PublicKey

Class java.security.MessageDigest

The message digest class is an engine class that can produce a one-way hash value for any arbitrary input. Message digests have two properties: they produce a unique hash for each set of input data (subject to the number of bits that are output), and the original input data is indiscernible from the hash output. The hash value is variously called a digital fingerprint or a digest. Message digests are components of digital signatures, but they are useful in their own right to verify that a set of data has not been corrupted. Once a digest object is created, data may be fed to it via the update() methods; the hash itself is returned via the digest() method.

Class Definition

```
    public abstract class java.security.MessageDigest
        extends java.security.MessageDigestSpi {

        // Constructors
        protected MessageDigest(String);

        // Class Methods
        public static MessageDigest getInstance(String);
        public static MessageDigest getInstance(String, String);
        public static boolean isEqual(byte[], byte[]);

        // Instance Methods
        public Object clone();
        public byte[] digest();
        public byte[] digest(byte[]);
```

```
        public int digest(byte[], int, int);
        public final String getAlgorithm();
        public final int getDigestLength();
        public final Provider getProvider();
        public void reset();
        public String toString();
        public void update(byte);
        public void update(byte[]);
        public void update(byte[], int, int);
}
```

Class java.security.MessageDigestSpi

This is the Service Provider Interface for the message digest engine; if you want to implement your own message digest class, you do so by extending this class and registering your implementation with an appropriate security provider. Since the MessageDigest class itself extends this class, you may also extend the MessageDigest class directly. Implementations of this class are expected to accumulate a hash value over data that is fed to it as a series of arbitrary bytes.

Class Definition

```
        public abstract class java.security.MessageDigestSpi
            extends java.lang.Object {

            // Constructors
            public MessageDigestSpi();

            // Instance Methods
            public Object clone();

            // Protected Instance Methods
            protected abstract byte[] engineDigest();
            protected int engineDigest(byte[], int, int);
            protected int engineGetDigestLength();
            protected abstract void engineReset();
            protected abstract void engineUpdate(byte);
            protected abstract void engineUpdate(byte[], int, int);
}
```

See also: MessageDigest

Class java.security.Permission

This class forms the base class for all types of permissions that are used by the access controller. A permission object encapsulates a particular operation (e.g., reading the file */tmp/foo).* It does not, however, grant permission for that operation; rather, the permission object is constructed and passed to the access controller to see if that operation is one which the current security policy has defined as a permissible operation.

Permissions have names (e.g., the name of the file, or the name of the operation) and may optionally have actions (the semantics of which are dependent upon the type of permission). It is up to the `implies()` method to determine if one permission grants another; this allows you to specify wildcard-type permissions that imply specific permissions (e.g., the permission named "*" may imply the permission named "myfile").

Class Definition

```
public abstract class java.security.Permission
    extends java.lang.Object
    implements java.security.Guard, java.io.Serializable {

    // Constructors
    public Permission(String);

    // Instance Methods
    public void checkGuard(Object);
    public abstract boolean equals(Object);
    public abstract String getActions();
    public final String getName();
    public abstract int hashCode();
    public abstract boolean isReadOnly();
    public void setReadOnly();
    public PermissionCollection newPermissionCollection();
    public String toString();
}
```

See also: AccessController, BasicPermission, PermissionCollection, Policy

---

Class java.security.PermissionCollection

As you might infer, a permission collection is a collection of permission objects. In theory, a permission collection can be a set of arbitrary, unrelated permission objects; however, that usage is best avoided and left to the Permissions class. Hence, a permission collection should be thought of as a collection of one type of permission: a set of file permissions, a set of socket permissions, etc. A permission collection is responsible for determining if an individual permission (passed as a parameter to the `implies()` method) is contained in the set of permissions in the object; presumably, it will do that more efficiently than by calling the implies() method on each permission in the collection. If you implement a new permission class that has wildcard semantics for its names, then you must implement a corresponding permission collection to aggregate instances of that class (if you don't need wildcard matching, the default implementation of the Permission class will provide an appropriate collection).

Class Definition

```
public abstract class java.security.PermissionCollection
    extends java.lang.Object
    implements java.io.Serializable {

    // Constructors
    public PermissionCollection();

    // Instance Methods
    public abstract void add(Permission);
    public abstract Enumeration elements();
    public abstract boolean implies(Permission);
    public boolean isReadOnly();
    public void setReadOnly();
    public String toString();
}
```

See also: Permission, Permissions

Class java.security.Permissions

This class is an aggregate of permission collections. Hence, it is an appropriate collection object for a group of unrelated permission, which is its typical use: the Policy class uses instances of this class to represent all the permissions associated with a particular protection domain.

Class Definition

```
public final class java.security.Permissions
    extends java.security.PermissionCollection
    implements java.io.Serializable {

    // Constructors
    public Permissions();

    // Instance Methods
    public void add(Permission);
    public Enumeration elements();
    public boolean implies(Permission);
}
```

See also: Permission, PermissionCollection, Policy

Class java.security.Policy

The Policy class encapsulates all the specific permissions that the virtual machine knows about. This set of permissions is by default read from a series of URLs specified by policy.url properties in the *$JDKHOME/lib/security/java.security* file, although applications may specify their own policy objects by using the setPolicy() method of this class. Alternately, a different default implementation of the policy class may be specified by changing the policy.provider property in the *java.security* file.

Class Definition

```
    public abstract class java.security.Policy
        extends java.lang.Object {

    // Constructors
    public Policy();

    // Class Methods
    public static Policy getPolicy();
    public static void setPolicy(Policy);

    // Instance Methods
    public abstract PermissionCollection getPermissions(CodeSource);
    public abstract void refresh();
    }
```

See also: Permission, Permissions

Interface java.security.Principal

A principal is anything that has a name, such as an identity. The name in this case is often an X.500 distinguished name, but that is not a requirement.

Interface Definition

```
    public abstract interface java.security.Principal {

    // Instance Methods
    public abstract boolean equals(Object);
    public abstract String getName();
    public abstract int hashCode();
    public abstract String toString();
    }
```

See also: Identity

Interface java.security.PrivateKey

A private key is a key with certain mathematical properties that allows it to perform inverse cryptographic operations with its matching public key. Classes implement this interface only for type identification.

Interface definition

```
public abstract interface java.security.PrivateKey
    implements java.security.Key {
}
```

See also: Key, PublicKey

Class java.security.ProtectionDomain

A protection domain encapsulates the location from which a class was loaded and the keys used to sign the class (that is, a CodeSource object) and the set of permissions that should be granted to that class. These protection domains are consulted by the access controller to determine if a particular operation should succeed; if the operation is in the set of permissions in each protection domain on the stack, then the operation will succeed. This class is typically only used within a class loader.

Class Definition

```
public class java.security.ProtectionDomain
    extends java.lang.Object {

    // Constructors
    public ProtectionDomain(CodeSource, PermissionCollection);

    // Instance Methods
    public final CodeSource getCodeSource();
    public final PermissionCollection getPermissions();
    public boolean implies(Permission);
    public String toString();
}
```

See also: AccessController, CodeSource, Permissions

Class java.security.Provider

An instance of the Provider class is responsible for mapping particular implementations to desired algorithm/engine pairs; instances of this class are consulted (indirectly) by the getInstance() methods of the engine classes to find a class that implements the desired operation. Instances of this class must be registered either with the Security class or by listing them in the *$JDKHOME/lib/security/java.security* file as a security.provider property.

Class Definition

```
public abstract class java.security.Provider
    extends java.util.Properties {

    // Constructors
    protected Provider(String, double, String);

    // Instance Methods
    public synchronized void clear();
    public Set entrySet();
    public String getInfo();
    public String getName();
    public double getVersion();
    public Set keySet();
    public synchronized void load(InputStream);
    public synchronized Object put(Object, Object);
    public synchronized void putAll(Map);
    public synchronized Object remove(Object);
    public String toString();
    public Collection values();
}
```

See also: Security

Interface java.security.PublicKey

A public key is a key with certain mathematical properties that allows it to perform inverse cryptographic operations with its matching private key. Classes implement this interface only for type identification.

Interface Definition

```
public abstract interface java.security.PublicKey
    implements java.security.Key {
}
```

See also: Key, PrivateKey

Class java.security.SecureClassLoader

A secure class loader is a class loader that is able to associate code sources (and hence protection domains) with the classes that it loads (classes loaded by a tradi-

tional class loader have a default, null protection domain). All new class loaders
are expected to extend this class.

Class Definition

```
public class java.security.SecureClassLoader
    extends java.lang.ClassLoader {

    // Constructors
    protected SecureClassLoader();
    protected SecureClassLoader(ClassLoader);

    // Protected Instance Methods
    protected final Class defineClass(String, byte[], int, int,
                            CodeSource);
    protected PermissionCollection getPermissions(CodeSource);
}
```

See also: ClassLoader, CodeSource, ProtectionDomain

Class java.security.SecureRandom

This class generates random numbers. Unlike the standard random-number
generator, numbers generated by this class are cryptographically secure—that is,
they are less subject to pattern guessing and other attacks that can be made upon a
traditional random-number generator.

Class Definition

```
public class java.security.SecureRandom
    extends java.util.Random {

    // Constructors
    public SecureRandom();
    public SecureRandom(byte[]);

    // Class Methods
    public static byte[] getSeed(int);

    // Instance Methods
    public synchronized void nextBytes(byte[]);
    public void setSeed(long);
    public synchronized void setSeed(byte[]);

    // Protected Instance Methods
    protected final int next(int);
}
```

Class java.security.Security

This class manages the list of providers that have been installed into the virtual machine; this list of providers is consulted to find an appropriate class to provide the implementation of a particular operation when the getInstance() method of an engine class is called. The list of providers initially comes from the *$JDKHOME/lib/security/java.security* file, and applications may use methods of this class to add and remove providers from that list.

Class Definition

```
public final class java.security.Security
    extends java.lang.Object {

    // Class Methods
    public static int addProvider(Provider);
    public static String getAlgorithmProperty(String, String);
    public static String getProperty(String);
    public static Provider getProvider(String);
    public static Provider[] getProviders();
    public static int insertProviderAt(Provider, int);
    public static void removeProvider(String);
    public static void setProperty(String, String);
}
```

See also: Provider

Class java.security.SecurityPermission

This class represents permissions to interact with the methods of the java.security package. This permission is a basic permission; it does not support actions. Security permissions are checked by the Identity, Signer, and Provider classes.

Class Definition

```
public final class java.security.SecurityPermission
    extends java.security.BasicPermission {

    // Constructors
    public SecurityPermission(String);
    public SecurityPermission(String, String);
}
```

See also: BasicPermission

Class java.security.Signature

This engine class provides the ability to create or verify digital signatures by employing different algorithms that have been registered with the Security class. As with all engine classes, instances of this class are obtained via the getInstance() method. The signature object must be initialized with the appropriate private key (to sign) or public key (to verify), then data must be fed to the object via the update() methods, and then the signature can be obtained (via the sign() method) or verified (via the verify() method). Signature objects may support algorithm-specific parameters, though this is not a common implementation.

Class Definition

```
public abstract class java.security.Signature
    extends java.security.SignatureSpi {

    // Constants
    protected static final int SIGN;
    protected static final int UNINITIALIZED;
    protected static final int VERIFY;

    // Variables
    protected int state;

    // Constructors
    protected Signature(String);

    // Class Methods
    public static Signature getInstance(String);
    public static Signature getInstance(String, String);

    // Instance Methods
    public Object clone();
    public final String getAlgorithm();
    public final Object getParameter(String);
    public final Provider getProvider();
    public final void initSign(PrivateKey);
    public final void initSign(PrivateKey, SecureRandom);
    public final void initVerify(PublicKey);
    public final void setParameter(String, Object);
    public final void setParameter(AlgorithmParameterSpec);
    public final byte[] sign();
    public final int sign(byte[], int, int);
    public String toString();
    public final void update(byte);
    public final void update(byte[]);
    public final void update(byte[], int, int);
    public final boolean verify(byte[]);
}
```

See also: Provider

Class java.security.SignatureSpi

This is the Security Provider Interface for the signature engine. If you want to implement your own signature engine, you must extend this class and register your implementation with an appropriate security provider. Since the Signature class already extends this class, your implementation may extend the Signature class directly. Implementations of this class must be prepared both to sign and to verify data that is passed to the engineUpdate() method. Initialization of the engine may optionally support a set of algorithm-specific parameters.

Class Definition

```
public abstract class java.security.SignatureSpi
    extends java.lang.Object {

    // Variables
    protected SecureRandom appRandom;

    // Constructors
    public SignatureSpi();

    // Instance Methods
    public Object clone();

    // Protected Instance Methods
    protected abstract Object engineGetParameter(String);
    protected abstract void engineInitSign(PrivateKey);
    protected void engineInitSign(PrivateKey, SecureRandom);
    protected abstract void engineInitVerify(PublicKey);
    protected abstract void engineSetParameter(String, Object);
    protected void engineSetParameter(AlgorithmParameterSpec);
    protected abstract byte[] engineSign();
    protected final int engineSign(byte[], int, int);
    protected abstract void engineUpdate(byte);
    protected abstract void engineUpdate(byte[], int, int);
    protected abstract boolean engineVerify(byte[]);
}
```

See also: Provider, Signature

Class java.security.SignedObject

A signed object is a container class for another (target) object; the signed object contains a serialized version of the target along with a digital signature of the data contained in the target object. You must provide a serializable object and a private key to create a signed object, after which you can remove the embedded object and verify the signature of the signed object by providing the appropriate public key.

Class Definition

```
public final class java.security.SignedObject
    extends java.lang.Object
    implements java.io.Serializable {

    // Constructors
    public SignedObject(Serializable, PrivateKey, Signature);

    // Instance Methods
    public String getAlgorithm();
    public Object getObject();
    public byte[] getSignature();
    public boolean verify(PublicKey, Signature);
}
```

See also: Signature

Class java.security.Signer

A signer abstracts the notion of a principal (that is, an individual or a corporation) that has a private key and a corresponding public key. Signers may optionally belong to an identity scope. This class is deprecated in1.2.

Class Definition

```
public abstract class java.security.Signer
    extends java.security.Identity {

    // Constructors
    protected Signer();
    public Signer(String);
    public Signer(String, IdentityScope);

    // Instance Methods
    public PrivateKey getPrivateKey();
    public final void setKeyPair(KeyPair);
    public String toString();
}
```

See also: Identity, Principal

Class java.security.UnresolvedPermission

An unresolved permission is one for which the implementing class has not been loaded. If you define a custom permission, the Policy class will represent that custom permission as an unresolved permission until it is time for the Policy class to actually load the class; if the class cannot be found, then it will remain an unresolved permission. By default, the implies() method of this class always returns false.

Class Definition

```
public final class UnresolvedPermission extends Permission
    implements java.io.Serializable {

    // Constructors
    public UnresolvedPermission(String, String, String, Certificate[]);

    // Instance methods
    public boolean equals(Object);
    public int hashCode();
    public boolean implies(Permission);
}
```

See also: Permission

Package java.security.cert

Class java.security.cert.Certificate

This class represents any type of cryptographic certificate. A certificate contains a public key (see getPublicKey()) and other associated information. The certificate contains an internal signature that protects its integrity. You can verify the integrity of the certificate by calling one of the verify() methods with the public key of the certificate's issuer. (Note: don't confuse this class with the java.security.Certificate interface, which is deprecated.)

Class Definition

```
public abstract class java.security.cert.Certificate
    extends java.lang.Object {

    // Constructors
    public Certificate();
```

```
// Instance Methods
public boolean equals(Object);
public abstract byte[] getEncoded();
public abstract PublicKey getPublicKey();
public int hashCode();
public abstract String toString();
public abstract void verify(PublicKey);
public abstract void verify(PublicKey, String);
}
```

See also: PublicKey, X509Certificate

Class java.security.cert.CertificateFactory

A certificate factory is used to import certificates or certificate revocation lists from a file or other input stream.

Class Definition

```
public java.security.cert.CertificateFactory
        extends java.lang.Object{

    //Constructors
    protected CertificateFactory(CertificateFactorySpi, Provider,
                            String);
    //Class Methods
    public static final CertificateFactory getInstance(String);
    public static final CertificateFactory getInstance(String,
                            String);
    //Instance Methods
    public final CRL generateCRL(InputStream);
    public final Collection generateCRLs(InputStream);
    public final Certificate generateCertificate(InputStream);
    public final Collection generateCertificates(InputStream);
    public final Provider getProvider();
    public final String getType();
    }
```

See also: X509Certificate, X509CRLEntry

Class java.security.cert.X509Certificate

This class represents certificates as defined in the X.509 standard. Such certificates associate a public key with a subject, which is usually a person or organization. You can find out the certificate's subject by calling getSubjectDN(), while you can retrieve the subject's public key using getPublicKey(). The certificate's issuer is the person or organization that generated and signed the certificate (see getIssuerDN()). If you have a certificate file in the format described by RFC 1421, you can create an X509Certificate from that data by using one of the getInstance() methods.

Class Definition

```
public abstract class java.security.cert.X509Certificate
    extends java.security.cert.Certificate
    implements java.security.cert.X509Extension {

    // Constructors
    public X509Certificate();

    // Instance Methods
    public abstract void checkValidity();
    public abstract void checkValidity(Date);
    public abstract int getBasicConstraints();
    public abstract Set getCriticalExtensionOIDs();
    public abstract byte[] getExtensionValue(String);
    public abstract Principal getIssuerDN();
    public abstract boolean[] getIssuerUniqueID();
    public abstract boolean[] getKeyUsage();
    public abstract Set getNonCriticalExtensionOIDs();
    public abstract Date getNotAfter();
    public abstract Date getNotBefore();
    public abstract BigInteger getSerialNumber();
    public abstract String getSigAlgName();
    public abstract String getSigAlgOID();
    public abstract byte[] getSigAlgParams();
    public abstract byte[] getSignature();
    public abstract Principal getSubjectDN();
    public abstract boolean[] getSubjectUniqueID();
    public abstract byte[] getTBSCertificate();
    public abstract int getVersion();
}
```

See also: Principal, PublicKey, X509Extension

Class java.security.cert.X509CRL

A Certificate Revocation List (CRL) is a list of certificates whose keys are no longer valid. This class represents CRLs as defined in the X.509 standard. If you have a CRL file that you would like to examine, you can construct an X509CRL object from the file using one of the getInstance() methods. A CRL, just like a certificate, has an internal signature that protects its integrity. To verify the integrity of the CRL itself, call one of the verify() methods with the issuer's public key. To find out if a particular certificate is revoked, call the isRevoked() method with the certificate's serial number.

Class Definition

```
public abstract class java.security.cert.X509CRL
    extends java.lang.Object
    implements java.security.cert.X509Extension {

    // Constructors
    public X509CRL();

    // Instance Methods
    public boolean equals(Object);
    public abstract Set getCriticalExtensionOIDs();
    public abstract byte[] getEncoded();
    public abstract byte[] getExtensionValue(String);
    public abstract Principal getIssuerDN();
    public abstract Date getNextUpdate();
    public abstract Set getNonCriticalExtensionOIDs();
    public abstract X509CRLEntry getRevokedCertificate(BigInteger);
    public abstract Set getRevokedCertificates();
    public abstract String getSigAlgName();
    public abstract String getSigAlgOID();
    public abstract byte[] getSigAlgParams();
    public abstract byte[] getSignature();
    public abstract byte[] getTBSCertList();
    public abstract Date getThisUpdate();
    public abstract int getVersion();
    public abstract boolean hasUnsupportedCriticalExtension();
    public int hashCode();
    public abstract boolean isRevoked(BigInteger);
    public abstract String toString();
    public abstract void verify(PublicKey);
    public abstract void verify(PublicKey, String);
}
```

See also: Certificate, PublicKey, X509CRLEntry, X509Extension

Class java.security.cert.X509CRLEntry

A revoked certificate represents a certificate whose contained key is no longer safe to use. Instances of this class are returned by X509CRL's getRevokedCertificate() method. You can examine the certificate's revocation date and X.509 extensions.

Class Definition

```
public abstract class java.security.cert.X509CRLEntry
    extends java.lang.Object
    implements java.security.cert.X509Extension {

    // Constructors
    public RevokedCertificate();

    // Instance Methods
    public abstract Set getCriticalExtensionOIDs();
    public abstract byte[] getExtensionValue(String);
    public abstract Set getNonCriticalExtensionOIDs();
    public abstract Date getRevocationDate();
    public abstract BigInteger getSerialNumber();
    public abstract boolean hasExtensions();
    public abstract boolean hasUnsupportedCriticalExtension();
    public abstract String toString();
}
```

See also: Certificate, X509CRL, X509Extension

Interface java.security.cert.X509Extension

The X509Extension interface represents the certificate extensions defined by the X.509v3 standard. Extensions are additional bits of information contained in a certificate. Each extension is designated as critical or non-critical. An application that handles a certificate should either correctly interpret the critical extensions or produce some kind of error if they cannot be recognized.

Class Definition

```
public abstract interface java.security.cert.X509Extension {

    // Instance Methods
    public abstract Set getCriticalExtensionOIDs();
    public abstract boolean hasUnsupportedCriticalExtension();
    public abstract byte[] getExtensionValue(String);
    public abstract Set getNonCriticalExtensionOIDs();
}
```

See also: X509CRLEntry, X509Certificate, X509CRL

Package java.security.interfaces

Interface java.security.interfaces.DSAKey

This interface represents public and private keys that are suitable for use in DSA signature algorithms. This interface allows you to retrieve DSA-specific information from a suitable DSA key.

Interface Definition

```
public interface java.security.interfaces.DSAKey {

    // Instance Methods
    public DSAParams getParams();
}
```

See also: PrivateKey, PublicKey

Interface java.security.interfaces.DSAKeyPairGenerator

This interface represents key generators that can be used to generate pairs of DSA keys. Key pair generators that implement this interface can be initialized with information specific to DSA key generation.

Interface Definition

```
public interface java.security.interfaces.DSAKeyPairGenerator {

    // Instance Methods
    public void initialize(DSAParams, SecureRandom);
    public void initialize(int, boolean, SecureRandom);
}
```

See also: KeyPairGenerator

Interface java.security.interfaces.DSAParams

Classes that implement this interface allow you to obtain the three variables that are common to both DSA public and private keys.

Interface Definition

```
public interface java.security.interfaces.DSAParams {

    // Instance Methods
    public BigInteger getP();
```

```
        public BigInteger getQ();
        public BigInteger getG();
    }
```

See also: DSAPrivateKey, DSAPublicKey

Interface java.security.interfaces.DSAPrivateKey

Classes that implement this interface allow you to retrieve the private key parameter used to calculate a DSA private key.

Interface Definition

```
    public interface java.security.interfaces.DSAPrivateKey {

        // Instance Methods
        public BigInteger getX();
    }
```

See also: DSAParams, DSAPublicKey

Interface java.security.interfaces.DSAPublicKey

Classes that implement this interface allow you to retrieve the public key parameter used to calculate a DSA public key.

Interface Definition

```
    public interface java.security.interfaces.DSAPublicKey {

        // Instance Methods
        public BigInteger getY();
    }
```

See also: DSAParams, DSAPrivateKey

Interface java.security.interfaces.RSAPrivateKey

RSAPrivateKey represents a private key, suitable for use with RSA cryptographic operations. Use of this class requires a third-party security provider.

Interface Definition

```
    public abstract interface java.security.interfaces.RSAPrivateKey
        implements java.security.PrivateKey {
```

```
    // Instance Methods
    public abstract BigInteger getModulus();
    public abstract BigInteger getPrivateExponent();
}
```

See also: PrivateKey, RSAPublicKey

Interface java.security.interfaces.RSAPublicKey

This class represents an RSA public key, suitable for use with an RSA cryptographic algorithm. You must have a third-party security provider to use this class.

Interface Definition

```
public abstract interface java.security.interfaces.RSAPublicKey
    implements java.security.PublicKey {

    // Instance Methods
    public abstract BigInteger getModulus();
    public abstract BigInteger getPublicExponent();
}
```

See also: PublicKey, RSAPrivateKey

Package java.security.spec

Interface java.security.spec.AlgorithmParameterSpec

Algorithm parameter specifications are used to import and export keys via a key factory. This interface is used strictly for type identification; the specifics of the parameters are left to the implementing class.

Interface Definition

```
public interface java.security.spec.AlgorithmParameterSpec {
}
```

See also: DSAParameterSpec, KeyFactory

Class java.security.spec.DSAParameterSpec

This class provides the basis for DSA key generation via parameters; it encapsulates the three parameters that are common to DSA algorithms.

Class Definition

```
public class java.security.spec.DSAParameterSpec
    extends java.lang.Object
    implements java.security.spec.AlgorithmParameterSpec,
               java.security.interfaces.DSAParams {

    // Constructors
    public DSAParameterSpec(BigInteger, BigInteger, BigInteger);

    // Instance Methods
    public BigInteger getG();
    public BigInteger getP();
    public BigInteger getQ();
}
```

See also: AlgorithmParameterSpec, DSAParams, DSAPrivateKeySpec, DSAPublicKeySpec

---

Class java.security.spec.DSAPrivateKeySpec

This class provides the ability to calculate a DSA private key based upon the four parameters that comprise the key.

Class Definition

```
public class java.security.spec.DSAPrivateKeySpec
    extends java.lang.Object
    implements java.security.spec.KeySpec {

    // Constructors
    public DSAPrivateKeySpec(BigInteger, BigInteger,
                             BigInteger, BigInteger);

    // Instance Methods
    public BigInteger getG();
    public BigInteger getP();
    public BigInteger getQ();
    public BigInteger getX();
}
```

See also: DSAPublicKeySpec, KeyFactory

Class java.security.spec.DSAPublicKeySpec

This class provides the ability to calculate a DSA public key based upon the four parameters that comprise the key.

Class Definition

```
public class java.security.spec.DSAPublicKeySpec
    extends java.lang.Object
    implements java.security.spec.KeySpec {

    // Constructors
    public DSAPublicKeySpec(BigInteger, BigInteger,
                                BigInteger, BigInteger);

    // Instance Methods
    public BigInteger getG();
    public BigInteger getP();
    public BigInteger getQ();
    public BigInteger getY();
}
```

See also: DSAPrivateKeySpec, KeyFactory

Class java.security.spec.EncodedKeySpec

This class is used to translate between keys and their external encoded format. The encoded format is always simply a series of bytes, but the format of the encoding of the key information into those bytes may vary depending upon the algorithm used to generate the key.

Class Definition

```
public abstract class java.security.spec.EncodedKeySpec
    extends java.lang.Object
    implements java.security.spec.KeySpec {

    // Constructors
    public EncodedKeySpec();

    // Instance Methods
    public abstract byte[] getEncoded();
    public abstract String getFormat();
}
```

See also: KeyFactory, KeySpec, PKCS8EncodedKeySpec, X509EncodedKeySpec

Interface java.security.spec.KeySpec

A key specification is used to import and export keys via a key factory. This may be done either based upon the algorithm parameters used to generate the key or via an encoded series of bytes that represent the key. Classes that deal with the latter case implement this interface, which is used strictly for type identification.

Interface Definition

```
public abstract interface java.security.spec.KeySpec {
}
```

See also: AlgorithmParameterSpec, EncodedKeySpec, KeyFactory

Class java.security.spec.PKCS8EncodedKeySpec

This class represents the PKCS#8 encoding of a private key; the key is encoded in DER format. This is the class that is typically used when dealing with DSA private keys in a key factory.

Class Definition

```
public class java.security.spec.PKCS8EncodedKeySpec
    extends java.security.spec.EncodedKeySpec {

    // Constructors
    public PKCS8EncodedKeySpec(byte[]);

    // Instance Methods
    public byte[] getEncoded();
    public final String getFormat();
}
```

See also: EncodedKeySpec, X509EncodedKeySpec

Class java.security.spec.RSAPrivateKeySpec

This class represents a key specification for an RSA private key; this specification uses a modulus and a private exponent. Instances of this class may be used with an appropriate key factory to generate private keys. Use of this class requires a third-party security provider.

Class Definition

```
public java.security.spec.RSAPrivateKeySpec
    extends java.lang.Object
```

```
    implements java.security.spec.KeySpec {

    // Constructors
    public RSAPrivateKeySpec(BigInteger, BigInteger);

    // Instance Methods
    public BigInteger getModulus();
    public BigInteger getPrivateExponent();
}
```

See also: KeyFactory, KeySpec, PrivateKey

Class java.security.spec.RSAPublicKeySpec

This class represents a key specification for an RSA public key. Instances of this class may be used with an appropriate key factory to generate public keys. Use of this class requires a third-party security provider.

Class Definition

```
    public java.security.spec.RSAPublicKeySpec
        extends java.lang.Object
        implements java.security.spec.KeySpec {

    // Constructors
    public RSAPublicKeySpec(BigInteger, BigInteger);

    // Instance Methods
    public BigInteger getModulus();
    public BigInteger getPublicExponent();
}
```

See also: KeyFactory, KeySpec, PublicKey

Class java.security.spec.X509EncodedKeySpec

This class represents the X509 encoding of a public key. It may also be used for private keys, although the PKCS#8 encoding is typically used for those keys.

Class Definition

```
    public class java.security.spec.X509EncodedKeySpec
        extends java.security.spec.EncodedKeySpec {

    // Constructors
    public X509EncodedKeySpec(byte[]);
```

```
        // Instance Methods
        public byte[] getEncoded();
        public final String getFormat();
    }
```

See also: EncodedKeySpec, PKCS8EncodedKeySpec

Package javax.crypto

Class javax.crypto.Cipher

This engine class represents a cryptographic cipher, either symmetric or asymmetric. To get a cipher for a particular algorithm, call one of the getInstance() methods, specifying an algorithm name, a cipher mode, and a padding scheme. The cipher should be initialized for encryption or decryption using an init() method and an appropriate key (and, optionally, a set of algorithm-specific parameters, though these are typically unused). Then you can perform the encryption or decryption, using the update() and doFinal() methods.

Class Definition

```
    public class javax.crypto.Cipher
        extends java.lang.Object {

        // Constants
        public static final int DECRYPT_MODE;
        public static final int ENCRYPT_MODE;

        // Constructors
        protected Cipher(CipherSpi, Provider, String);

        // Class Methods
        public static final Cipher getInstance(String);
        public static final Cipher getInstance(String, String);

        // Instance Methods
        public final byte[] doFinal();
        public final byte[] doFinal(byte[]);
        public final int doFinal(byte[], int);
        public final byte[] doFinal(byte[], int, int);
        public final int doFinal(byte[], int, int, byte[]);
        public final int doFinal(byte[], int, int, byte[], int);
        public final int getBlockSize();
        public final byte[] getIV();
```

```
        public final int getOutputSize(int);
        public final AlgorithmParameters getParameters();
        public final Provider getProvider();
        public final void init(int, Key);
        public final void init(int, Key, SecureRandom);
        public final void init(int, Key, AlgorithmParameterSpec);
        public final void init(int, Key, AlgorithmParameterSpec,
                        SecureRandom);
        public final void init(int, Key, AlgorithmParameters);
        public final void init(int, Key, AlgorithmParameters,
                        SecureRandom);
        public final byte[] update(byte[]);
        public final byte[] update(byte[], int, int);
        public final int update(byte[], int, int, byte[]);
        public final int update(byte[], int, int, byte[], int);
}
```

See also: AlgorithmParameterSpec, CipherSpi, Key, Provider, SecureRandom

---

Class javax.crypto.CipherInputStream

A cipher input stream is a filter stream that passes its data through a cipher. You can construct a cipher input stream by specifying an underlying stream and supplying an initialized cipher. For best results, use a byte-oriented cipher mode with this stream.

Class Definition

```
    public class javax.crypto.CipherInputStream
        extends java.io.FilterInputStream {

        // Constructors
        protected CipherInputStream(InputStream);
        public CipherInputStream(InputStream, Cipher);

        // Instance Methods
        public int available();
        public void close();
        public boolean markSupported();
        public int read();
        public int read(byte[]);
        public int read(byte[], int, int);
        public long skip(long);
    }
```

See also: Cipher

Class javax.crypto.CipherOutputStream

This class is a filter output stream that passes all its data through a cipher. You can construct a cipher output stream by specifying an underlying output stream and an initialized cipher. For best results, use a byte-oriented mode for the cipher.

Class Definition

```
public class javax.crypto.CipherOutputStream
    extends java.io.FilterOutputStream {

    // Constructors
    protected CipherOutputStream(OutputStream);
    public CipherOutputStream(OutputStream, Cipher);

    // Instance Methods
    public void close();
    public void flush();
    public void write(int);
    public void write(byte[]);
    public void write(byte[], int, int);
}
```

See also: Cipher

Class javax.crypto.CipherSpi

This class is the Security Provider Interface of the Cipher class. To implement a particular cipher algorithm, create a subclass of this class and register the class with an appropriate security provider. Like all SPI classes, the methods that begin with engine are called by their corresponding method (without engine) from the Cipher class.

Class Definition

```
public abstract class javax.crypto.CipherSpi
    extends java.lang.Object {

    // Constructors
    public CipherSpi();

    // Protected Instance Methods
    protected abstract byte[] engineDoFinal(byte[], int, int);
    protected abstract int engineDoFinal(byte[], int, int,
                                         byte[], int);
    protected abstract int engineGetBlockSize();
    protected abstract byte[] engineGetIV();
    protected abstract int engineGetOutputSize(int);
```

```
        protected abstract void engineInit(int, Key, SecureRandom);
        protected abstract void engineInit(int, Key,
                        AlgorithmParameterSpec, SecureRandom);
        protected abstract void engineInit(int, Key, AlgorithmParameters,
                        SecureRandom);
        protected abstract void engineSetMode(String);
        protected abstract void engineSetPadding(String);
        protected abstract byte[] engineUpdate(byte[], int, int);
        protected abstract int engineUpdate(byte[], int, int, byte[], int);
}
```

See also: AlgorithmParameterSpec, Cipher, Key, SecureRandom

Class javax.crypto.KeyAgreement

This engine class represents a key agreement protocol, which is an arrangement by which two parties can agree on a secret value. You can obtain an instance of this class by calling the getInstance() method. After initializing the object (see init()), you can step through the phases of the key agreement protocol using the doPhase() method. Once the phases are complete, the secret value (that is, the key) is returned from the generateSecret() method.

Class Definition

```
    public class javax.crypto.KeyAgreement
        extends java.lang.Object {

        // Constructors
        protected KeyAgreement(KeyAgreementSpi, Provider, String);

        // Class Methods
        public static final KeyAgreement getInstance(String);
        public static final KeyAgreement getInstance(String, String);

        // Instance Methods
        public final Key doPhase(Key, boolean);
        public final byte[] generateSecret();
        public final int generateSecret(byte[], int);
        public final String getAlgorithm();
        public final Provider getProvider();
        public final void init(Key);
        public final void init(Key, SecureRandom);
        public final void init(Key, AlgorithmParameterSpec);
        public final void init(Key, AlgorithmParameterSpec, SecureRandom);
    }
```

See also: AlgorithmParameterSpec, Key, KeyAgreementSpi, Provider,
SecureRandom

Class javax.crypto.KeyAgreementSpi

This is the Security Provider Interface class for the KeyAgreement class. If you want to implement a key agreement algorithm, create a subclass of this class and register it with an appropriate security provider.

Class Definition

```
public abstract class javax.crypto.KeyAgreementSpi
    extends java.lang.Object {

    // Constructors
    public KeyAgreementSpi();

    // Protected Instance Methods
    protected abstract Key engineDoPhase(Key, boolean);
    protected abstract byte[] engineGenerateSecret();
    protected abstract int engineGenerateSecret(byte[], int);
    protected abstract void engineInit(Key, SecureRandom);
    protected abstract void engineInit(Key, AlgorithmParameterSpec,
                                       SecureRandom);
}
```

See also: AlgorithmParameterSpec, Key, KeyAgreement, SecureRandom

---

Class javax.crypto.KeyGenerator

A key generator creates secret keys for use with symmetric ciphers. Key generators are obtained by calling the getInstance() method; they must then be initialized with an init() method. The key itself is then returned from the generateSecret() method.

Class Definition

```
public class javax.crypto.KeyGenerator
    extends java.lang.Object {

    // Constructors
    protected KeyGenerator(KeyGeneratorSpi, Provider, String);

    // Class Methods
    public static final KeyGenerator getInstance(String);
    public static final KeyGenerator getInstance(String, String);

    // Instance Methods
    public final SecretKey generateKey();
    public final String getAlgorithm();
    public final Provider getProvider();
```

```
       public final void init(int);
       public final void init(int, SecureRandom);
       public final void init(SecureRandom);
       public final void init(AlgorithmParameterSpec);
       public final void init(AlgorithmParameterSpec, SecureRandom);
}
```

See also: AlgorithmParameterSpec, KeyGeneratorSpi, Provider, SecretKey,
SecureRandom

Class javax.crypto.KeyGeneratorSpi

This is the Security Provider Interface for the KeyGenerator class. To create an
implementation of a key generation algorithm, make a subclass of this class and
register the implementation with an appropriate security provider.

Class Definition

```
       public abstract class javax.crypto.KeyGeneratorSpi
           extends java.lang.Object {

           // Constructors
           public KeyGeneratorSpi();

           // Protected Instance Methods
           protected abstract SecretKey engineGenerateKey();
           protected abstract void engineInit(int, SecureRandom);
           protected abstract void engineInit(SecureRandom);
           protected abstract void engineInit(AlgorithmParameterSpec,
                                         SecureRandom);
}
```

See also: AlgorithmParameterSpec, KeyGenerator, SecretKey, SecureRandom

---

Class javax.crypto.NullCipher

As its name implies, null cipher is a cipher that does nothing. You can use it to test
cryptographic programs. Since a null cipher performs no transformations, its
ciphertext will be exactly the same as its plaintext.

Class Definition

```
       public class javax.crypto.NullCipher
           extends javax.crypto.Cipher {
```

```
        // Constructors
        public NullCipher();
    }
```

See also: Cipher

Class *javax.crypto.SealedObject*

A sealed object is a container for another object. The contained object is serialized and then encrypted using a cipher. You can construct a sealed object using any serializable object and a cipher that is initialized for encryption. To decrypt the contained object, call the getObject() method with a cipher that is initialized for decryption.

Class Definition

```
        public class javax.crypto.SealedObject
            extends java.lang.Object
            implements java.io.Serializable {

            // Constructors
            public SealedObject(Serializable, Cipher);

            // Instance Methods
            public final Object getObject(Cipher);
            public final Object getObject(Key);
            public final Object getObject(Key, String);
        }
```

See also: PublicKey, PrivateKey

Interface *javax.crypto.SecretKey*

A secret key represents a key that is used with a symmetric cipher. This interface is used strictly for type identification.

Interface Definition

```
        public abstract interface javax.crypto.SecretKey
            implements java.security.Key {
        }
```

See also: Key

Class javax.crypto.SecretKeyFactory

A secret key factory is used to convert between secret key data formats; like a key factory, this is typically used to import a key based on its external format or to export a key to its encoded format or algorithm parameters. Instances of this class are obtained by calling the getInstance() method. Keys may be exported by using the translateKey() method; they are imported by using the generate Secret() method.

Class Definition

```
public class javax.crypto.SecretKeyFactory
    extends java.lang.Object {

    // Constructors
    protected SecretKeyFactory(SecretKeyFactorySpi, Provider);

    // Class Methods
    public static final SecretKeyFactory getInstance(String);
    public static final SecretKeyFactory getInstance(String, String);

    // Instance Methods
    public final SecretKey generateSecret(KeySpec);
    public final KeySpec getKeySpec(SecretKey, Class);
    public final Provider getProvider();
    public final SecretKey translateKey(SecretKey);
}
```

See also: KeySpec, Provider, SecretKey, SecretKeyFactorySpi

Class javax.crypto.SecretKeyFactorySpi

This class is the Security Provider Interface for the SecretKeyFactory class. To create a secret key factory, make a subclass of this class and register your implementation with an appropriate provider.

Class Definition

```
public abstract class javax.crypto.SecretKeyFactorySpi
    extends java.lang.Object {

    // Constructors
    public SecretKeyFactorySpi();

    // Protected Instance Methods
    protected abstract SecretKey engineGenerateSecret(KeySpec);
```

```
    protected abstract KeySpec engineGetKeySpec(SecretKey, Class);
    protected abstract SecretKey engineTranslateKey(SecretKey);
}
```

See also: KeySpec, Provider, SecretKey, SecretKeyFactory

Package javax.crypto.interfaces

Interface javax.crypto.interfaces.DHKey

This interface represents a public or private key used the Diffie-Hellman key agreement implementation.

Interface Definition

```
public abstract interface javax.crypto.interfaces.DHKey {

    // Instance Methods
    public abstract DHParameterSpec getParams();
}
```

See also: DHPrivateKey, DHPublicKey

Interface javax.crypto.interfaces.DHPrivateKey

This interface represents a private key in a Diffie-Hellman key agreement protocol.

Interface Definition

```
public abstract interface javax.crypto.interfaces.DHPrivateKey
    implements javax.crypto.interfaces.DHKey, java.security.PrivateKey {

    // Instance Methods
    public abstract BigInteger getX();
}
```

See also: DHKey, DHPublicKey, PrivateKey

Interface javax.crypto.interfaces.DHPublicKey

This interface represents a public key in a Diffie-Hellman key agreement protocol.

Interface Definition

```
public abstract interface javax.crypto.interfaces.DHPublicKey
    implements javax.crypto.interfaces.DHKey, java.security.PublicKey {

    // Instance Methods
    public abstract BigInteger getY();
}
```

See also: DHKey, DHPrivateKey, PublicKey

Package javax.crypto.spec

Class javax.crypto.spec.DESKeySpec

This class represents a key specification for DES keys; this specification may be used with a secret key factory to import and export DES keys.

Class Definition

```
public class javax.crypto.spec.DESKeySpec
    extends java.lang.Object
    implements java.security.spec.KeySpec {

    //Constants
    public static final int DES_KEY_LEN;

    // Constructors
    public DESKeySpec(byte[]);
    public DESKeySpec(byte[], int);

    // Class Methods
    public static boolean isParityAdjusted(byte[], int);
    public static boolean isWeak(byte[], int);

    // Instance Methods
    public byte[] getKey();
}
```

See also: SecretKeyFactory

Class javax.crypto.spec.DESedeKeySpec

This class represents a DESede key specification. It can be used with a secret key factory to import and export DESede keys.

Class Definition

```
public class javax.crypto.spec.DESedeKeySpec
    extends java.lang.Object
    implements java.security.spec.KeySpec {

    //Constants
    public static final int DES_EDE_KEY_LEN;

    // Constructors
    public DESedeKeySpec(byte[]);
    public DESedeKeySpec(byte[], int);

    // Class Methods
    public static boolean isParityAdjusted(byte[], int);

    // Instance Methods
    public byte[] getKey();
}
```

See also: `SecretKeyFactory`

Class javax.crypto.spec.DHGenParameterSpec

Instances of this class may be used to supply the algorithm-specific initialization method for generating Diffie-Hellman keys.

Class Definition

```
public class javax.crypto.spec.DHGenParameterSpec
    extends java.lang.Object
    implements java.security.spec.AlgorithmParameterSpec {

    // Constructors
    public DHGenParameterSpec(int, int);

    // Instance Methods
    public int getExponentSize();
    public int getPrimeSize();
}
```

See also: `AlgorithmParameterGenerator, AlgorithmParameterSpec`

Class javax.crypto.spec.DHParameterSpec

This class encapsulates the public parameters used in the Diffie-Hellman key agreement protocol. Instances of this class can be passed to the algorithm-specific initialization methods of a key pair generator.

Class Definition

```
public class javax.crypto.spec.DHParameterSpec
    extends java.lang.Object
    implements java.security.spec.AlgorithmParameterSpec {

    // Constructors
    public DHParameterSpec(BigInteger, BigInteger);
    public DHParameterSpec(BigInteger, BigInteger, int);

    // Instance Methods
    public BigInteger getG();
    public int getL();
    public BigInteger getP();
}
```

See also: AlgorithmParameterSpec, KeyPairGenerator

Class javax.crypto.spec.DHPrivateKeySpec

This class represents a key specification for Diffie-Hellman private keys. It can be used with a key factory to import and export Diffie-Hellman keys.

Class Definition

```
public class javax.crypto.spec.DHPrivateKeySpec
    extends java.lang.Object
    implements java.security.spec.KeySpec {

    // Constructors
    public DHPrivateKeySpec(BigInteger, BigInteger, BigInteger);
    public DHPrivateKeySpec(BigInteger, BigInteger, BigInteger, int);

    // Instance Methods
    public BigInteger getG();
    public int getL();
    public BigInteger getP();
    public BigInteger getX();
}
```

See also: DHParameterSpec, DHPublicKeySpec, KeySpec

Class javax.crypto.spec.DHPublicKeySpec

This class represents a key specification for Diffie-Hellman public keys. It can be used with a key factory to import and export Diffie-Hellman keys.

Class Definition

```
public class javax.crypto.spec.DHPublicKeySpec
    extends java.lang.Object
    implements java.security.spec.KeySpec {

    // Constructors
    public DHPublicKeySpec(BigInteger, BigInteger, BigInteger);
    public DHPublicKeySpec(BigInteger, BigInteger, BigInteger, int);

    // Instance Methods
    public BigInteger getG();
    public int getL();
    public BigInteger getP();
    public BigInteger getY();
}
```

See also: DHParameterSpec, DHPrivateKeySpec, KeySpec

Class javax.crypto.spec.IvParameterSpec

This class represents an IV (initialization vector) for a cipher that uses a feedback mode. Ciphers in CBC, PCBC, CFB, and OFB modes need to be initialized with an IV.

Class Definition

```
public javax.crypto.spec.IvParameterSpec
    extends java.lang.Object
    implements java.security.spec.AlgorithmParameterSpec {

    // Constructors
    public IvParameterSpec(byte[]);
    public IvParameterSpec(byte[], int, int);

    // Instance Methods
    public byte[] getIV();
}
```

See also: AlgorithmParameterSpec, Cipher

Class javax.crypto.spec.PBEKeySpec

This class represents a key specification for a key that is used with passphrase encryption.

Class Definition

```
public class javax.crypto.spec.PBEKeySpec
    extends java.lang.Object
    implements java.security.spec.KeySpec {

    // Constructors
    public PBEKeySpec(String);

    // Instance Methods
    public final String getPassword();
}
```

See also: PBEParameterSpec, SecretKey, SecretKeyFactory

Class javax.crypto.spec.PBEParameterSpec

This class encapsulates the salt and iteration count that are used in passphrase-based encryption.

Class Definition

```
public class javax.crypto.spec.PBEParameterSpec
    extends java.lang.Object
    implements java.security.spec.AlgorithmParameterSpec {

    // Constructors
    public PBEParameterSpec(byte[], int);

    // Instance Methods
    public int getIterationCount();
    public byte[] getSalt();
}
```

See also: AlgorithmParameterSpec, Cipher, PBEKeySpec

Miscellaneous Packages

This section lists security-related classes that appear in miscellaneous packages: permission classes, class loaders, and security managers.

Class java.awt.AWTPermission

This class represents permission to perform windowing operations, like opening a top-level window or examining the event queue. This is a basic permission, so it has no actions.

Class Definition

```
public final class java.awt.AWTPermission
    extends java.security.BasicPermission {

    // Constructors
    public AWTPermission(String);
    public AWTPermission(String, String);
}
```

See also: BasicPermission, Permission

Class java.io.FilePermission

This class represents permission to read, write, delete, or execute files. The name encapsulated in this permission is the name of the file; the string "<<ALL_FILES>>" represents all files, while an asterisk represents all files in a directory and a hyphen represents all files that descend from a directory. The actions for this permission are read, write, execute, and delete.

Class Definition

```
public final class java.io.FilePermission
    extends java.security.Permission
    implements java.io.Serializable {

    // Constructors
    public FilePermission(String, String);

    // Instance Methods
    public boolean equals(Object);
    public String getActions();
    public int hashCode();
    public boolean implies(Permission);
    public PermissionCollection newPermissionCollection();
}
```

See also: Permission

Class java.io.SerializablePermission

This class represents permission to perform specific operations during object serialization—specifically, whether or not object substitution may occur during serialization. As all basic permissions, there are no actions associated with this class, which has one valid name: enableSubstitution.

Class Definition

```
public final class java.io.SerializablePermission
    extends java.security.BasicPermission {

    // Constructors
    public SerializablePermission(String);
    public SerializablePermission(String, String);
}
```

See also: BasicPermission, Permission

Class java.lang.ClassLoader

This class is the basis for loading a class dynamically in Java. For historical reasons, it appears in this package, but it is recommended that all new class loaders subclass the SecureClassLoader class in the java.security package instead of using this class. Loading a class explicitly may be done with the loadClass() method of this class (though classes are usually simply loaded as needed).

Class Definition

```
public abstract class java.lang.ClassLoader
    extends java.lang.Object {

    // Constructors
    protected ClassLoader();
    protected ClassLoader(ClassLoader);

    // Class Methods
    public static ClassLoader getSystemClassLoader();
    public static URL getSystemResource(String);
    public static InputStream getSystemResourceAsStream(String);
    public static Enumeration getSystemResources(String);

    // Instance Methods
    public ClassLoader getParent();
    public URL getResource(String);
    public InputStream getResourceAsStream(String);
    public final Enumeration getResources(String);
    public Class loadClass(String);
```

```
        // Protected Instance Methods
        protected final Class defineClass(String, byte[], int, int);
        protected final Class defineClass(byte[], int, int);
        protected final Class defineClass(String, byte[], int, int,
                         ProtectionDomain);
        protected Package definePackage(String, String, String, String,
                         String, String, String, URL);
        protected Class findClass(String);
        protected String findLibrary(String);
        protected final Class findLoadedClass(String);
        protected Class findLocalClass(String);
        protected final Class findSystemClass(String);
        protected Package getPackage(String);
        protected Package[] getPackages();
        protected synchronized Class loadClass(String, boolean);
        protected final void resolveClass(Class);
        protected final void setSigners(Class, Object[]);
}
```

See also: SecureClassLoader, URLClassLoader

Class java.lang.RuntimePermission

This class represents permission to perform certain runtime operations, such as executing other programs. Like all basic permissions, runtime permissions have no actions.

Class Definition

```
        public final class java.lang.RuntimePermission
               extends java.security.BasicPermission {

               // Constructors
               public RuntimePermission(String);
               public RuntimePermission(String, String);
}
```

See also: BasicPermission, Permission

Class java.lang.SecurityManager

This class forms the primary interface to the security model of the virtual machine; it is recommended for backwards compatibility that access to that model occur through this class rather than by calling the access controller directly. However, most of the methods of this class simply call the access controller.

Class Definition

```
public class java.lang.SecurityManager
    extends java.lang.Object {

    // Variables
    protected boolean inCheck;

    // Constructors
    public SecurityManager();

    // Instance Methods
    public void checkAccept(String, int);
    public void checkAccess(Thread);
    public void checkAccess(ThreadGroup);
    public void checkAwtEventQueueAccess();
    public void checkConnect(String, int);
    public void checkConnect(String, int, Object);
    public void checkCreateClassLoader();
    public void checkDelete(String);
    public void checkExec(String);
    public void checkExit(int);
    public void checkLink(String);
    public void checkListen(int);
    public void checkMemberAccess(Class, int);
    public void checkMulticast(InetAddress);
    public void checkMulticast(InetAddress, byte);
    public void checkPackageAccess(String);
    public void checkPackageDefinition(String);
    public void checkPermission(Permission);
    public void checkPermission(Permission, Object);
    public void checkPrintJobAccess();
    public void checkPropertiesAccess();
    public void checkPropertyAccess(String);
    public void checkRead(FileDescriptor);
    public void checkRead(String);
    public void checkRead(String, Object);
    public void checkSecurityAccess(String);
    public void checkSetFactory();
    public void checkSystemClipboardAccess();
    public boolean checkTopLevelWindow(Object);
    public void checkWrite(FileDescriptor);
    public void checkWrite(String);
    public boolean getInCheck();
    public Object getSecurityContext();
    public ThreadGroup getThreadGroup();

    // Protected Instance Methods
    protected native int classDepth(String);
    protected native int classLoaderDepth();
```

```
        protected native ClassLoader currentClassLoader();
        protected Class currentLoadedClass();
        protected native Class[] getClassContext();
        protected boolean inClass(String);
        protected boolean inClassLoader();
}
```

See also: AccessController

Class java.lang.reflect.ReflectPermission

This class represents the ability to obtain information via object reflections; specifically, whether private and protected variables and methods may be accessed through object reflection. As all basic permissions, this permission carries no actions; it has a single name: access.

Class Definition

```
public final class java.lang.reflect.ReflectPermission
    extends java.security.BasicPermission {

    // Constructors
    public ReflectPermission(String);
    public ReflectPermission(String, String);
}
```

See also: BasicPermission, Permission

Class java.net.NetPermission

This class represents the ability to work with multicast sockets and the ability to use the authenticator classes. As all basic permissions, this class carries no actions.

Class Definition

```
public final class java.net.NetPermission
    extends java.security.BasicPermission {

    // Constructors
    public NetPermission(String);
    public NetPermission(String, String);
}
```

See also: BasicPermission, Permission

Class java.net.SocketPermission

This class represents the ability to work with certain sockets. The name of this permission is constructed from the hostname or IP address of the machine on the other end of the socket and the port number; either portion of the name is subject to wildcard matching. Valid actions for this class include connect, accept, and listen.

Class Definition

```
public final class java.net.SocketPermission
    extends java.security.Permission
    implements java.io.Serializable {

    // Constructors
    public SocketPermission(String, String);

    // Instance Methods
    public boolean equals(Object);
    public String getActions();
    public int hashCode();
    public boolean implies(Permission);
    public PermissionCollection newPermissionCollection();
}
```

See also: Permission

Class java.net.URLClassLoader

This class provides a concrete class loader that may be used to load classes from one or more URLs (either http-based or file-based URLs). Since it is a secure class loader, classes loaded from a URL class loader will be fully integrated into the access controller's security model.

Class Definition

```
public class java.net.URLClassLoader
    extends java.security.SecureClassLoader {

    // Constructors
    public URLClassLoader(URL[], ClassLoader);
    public URLClassLoader(URL[]);
    public URLCLassLoader(URL[], ClassLoader, URLStreamHandlerFactory);

    // Class Methods
    public static URLClassLoader newInstance(URL[]);
    public static URLClassLoader newInstance(URL[], ClassLoader);
```

```
        // Instance Methods
        public URL findResource(String);
        public Enumeration findResources(String);
        public URL[] getURLs();

        // Protected Instance Methods
        protected void addURL(URL);
        protected Package definePackage(String, Manifest, URL);
        protected Class findClass(String);
        protected PermissionCollection getPermissions(CodeSource);
    }
```

See also: ClassLoader, SecureClassLoader

Class java.rmi.RMISecurityManager

The RMI security manager provides a security manager that is suitable for many RMI servers. It provides the ability for RMI applications to make socket-based connections to each other, and otherwise follows the default security manager implementation.

Class Definition

```
    public class java.rmi.RMISecurityManager
        extends java.lang.SecurityManager {

        // Constructors
        public RMISecurityManager();

        // Instance Methods
    }
```

See also: SecurityManager

Class java.rmi.server.RMIClassLoader

While not a traditional class loader, this class allows classes to be loaded via the same mechanics as a class loader: the loadClass() method may be called to load a class explicitly, and this class will also be used to load all subsequent classes required by the target class. This class loader will only load classes from the URL specified by the java.rmi.server.codebase property. The internal class loader used by this class is a secure class loader, so the security model of the access controller will be used by classes loaded in this manner.

Class Definition

```
public class java.rmi.server.RMIClassLoader
    extends java.lang.Object {

    // Class Methods
    public static Object getSecurityContext(ClassLoader);
    public static Class loadClass(String);
    public static Class loadClass(String, String);
    public static Class loadClass(URL, String);
}
```

See also: ClassLoader, SecureClassLoader

Class java.util.PropertyPermission

This class represents the ability to read or write properties. The name of a property permission is the name of the property itself; the action for a property permission is either set or get.

Class Definition

```
public final class java.util.PropertyPermission
    extends java.security.BasicPermission {

    // Constructors
    public PropertyPermission(String, String);

    // Instance Methods
    public boolean equals(Object);
    public String getActions();
    public int hashCode();
    public boolean implies(Permission);
    public PermissionCollection newPermissionCollection();
}
```

See also: Permission

Index

About the Author

Scott Oaks is a Java Technologist at Sun Microsystems, where he has worked since 1987. While at Sun, he has specialized in many disparate technologies, from the SunOS kernel to network programming and RPCs to the X Window System to threading. Since early 1995, he has primarily focused on Java and bringing Java technology to end users; he writes a monthly column on Java solutions for *The Java Report*. Around the Internet, Scott is best known as the author of olvwm, the OPEN LOOK window manager.

Scott holds a Bachelor of Science in mathematics and computer science from the University of Denver and a Master of Science in computer science from Brown University. Prior to joining Sun, he worked in the research division of Bear, Stearns.

In his other life, Scott enjoys music (he plays flute and piccolo with community groups in New York), cooking, theatre, and traveling with his husband James.

Colophon

Our look is the result of reader comments, our own experimentation, and feedback from distribution channels. Distinctive covers complement our distinctive approach to technical topics, breathing personality and life into potentially dry subjects.

Hanna Dyer designed the cover of *Java Security*, based on a series design by Edie Freedman. The image of a bird's nest was photographed by Kevin Thomas and manipulated in Adobe Photoshop by Michael Snow. The cover layout was produced with Quark XPress 3.3 using the Bodoni Black font from URW Software and Bodoni BT Bold Italic from Bitstream. The inside layout was designed by Nancy Priest. Text was prepared by Mike Sierra in FrameMaker 5.0. The heading font is Bodoni BT; the text font is New Baskerville. The illustrations that appear in the book were created in Macromedia Freehand 7.0 by Robert Romano.

Whenever possible, our books use RepKover™, a durable and flexible lay-flat binding. If the page count exceeds RepKover's limit, perfect binding is used.

Price-List / Order Form

QTY	ISBN	Title	Author	Price

Published Titles

QTY	ISBN	Title	Author	Price
___	8173661006	Access Database Design and Programming 2/e, *448 Pages*	Roman	250.00*
___	8173662525	Apache Pocket Reference, *112 Pages*	Ford	75.00*
___	8173661782	ASP in a Nutshell 2/e, *496 Pages*	Weissinger	300.00*
___	8173662347	AutoCAD 2000 In a Nutshell, *592 Pages*	Kent	325.00*
___	8173661014	Building Internet Firewalls 2/e, *900 Pages*	Zwicky	475.00*
___	8173661391	Building Linux Clusters (BOOK/CD-ROM), *360 Pages*	Spector	350.00*
___	817366045X	CGI Programming with Perl 2/e, *476 Pages*	Gundavaram	300.00*
___	8173660638	Creating Effective JavaHelp, *196 Pages*	Lewis	125.00*
___	8173662363	Database Nation: The Death of Privacy in the 21st Century, *336 Pages*	Garfinkel	235.00*
___	8173662894	Database Programming with JDBC and Java 2/e, *348 Pages*	Reese	175.00*
___	8173663203	Designing Active Server Pages, *368 Pages*	Mitchell	175.00*
___	8173660468	Developing ASP Components, *500 Pages*	Powers	275.00
___	8173660476	Developing Visual Basic Add-ins, *192 Pages*	Roman	135.00
___	8173660484	Director in a Nutshell, *648 Pages*	Epstein	285.00
___	8173660492	DNS and BIND 3/e, *504 Pages*	Albitz	275.00
___	8173660506	DNS on Windows NT, *352 Pages*	Albitz	195.00
___	8173660263	Dynamic HTML: The Definitive Reference, *1,096 Pages*	Goodman	510.00
___	8173662703	Enterprise JavaBeans, 2/e, *496 Pages*	Monson-Haefel	245.00*
___	8173660247	Essential System Administration 2/e, *788 Pages*	Frisch	310.00
___	8173660255	Essential Windows NT System Administration, *488 Pages*	Frisch	220.00
___	8173662495	Ethernet: The Definitive Guide, *528 Pages*	Spurgeon	300.00*
___	8173662754	Excel 2000 In a Nutshell, *560 Pages*	Simon	300.00*
___	8173661715	HTML & XHTML: The Definitive Guide 4/e, *678 Pages*	Musciano	350.00*
___	8173662479	HTML Pocket Reference, *100 Pages*	Niederst	65.00
___	8173661057	Internet Core Protocols: The Definitive Guide (BOOK/CD), *476 Pages*	Hall	375.00*
___	8173660158	Internet in a Nutshell, *456 Pages*	Quercia	215.00
___	8173660522	Java 2D Graphics, *376 Pages*	Knudsen	195.00
___	8173661480	Java and XML, *504 Pages*	McLaughlin	300.00*
___	8173660530	Java Enterprise in a Nutshell, *624 Pages*	Farley	275.00
___	8173662843	Java Examples in a Nutshell 2/e, *592 Pages*	Flanagan	225.00*
___	8173660557	Java Foundation Classes in a Nutshell, *752 Pages*	Flanagan	305.00
___	8173661065	Java in a Nutshell 3/e, *672 Pages*	Flanagan	325.00
___	8173662312	Java Network Programming 2/e, *768 Pages*	Harold	350.00*
___	8173662819	Java Performance Tuning, *448 Pages*	Shirazi	225.00*
___	8173661081	Java Security, *474 Pages*	Oaks	285.00
___	8173660565	Java Servlet Programming, *528 Pages*	Hunter	275.00
___	817366109X	Java Swing, *1,252 Pages*	Eckstein	550.00
___	8173660573	Java Threads, 2/e, *336 Pages*	Oaks	180.00
___	8173661103	JavaScript Application Cookbook, *512 Pages*	Bradenbaugh	275.00
___	8173661111	JavaScript Pocket Reference, *96 Pages*	Flanagan	65.00
___	8173660581	JavaScript: The Definitive Guide, 3/e, *800 Pages*	Flanagan	385.00
___	8173662509	Jini in a Nutshell, *420 Pages*	Oaks	225.00
___	817366059X	Learning DCOM, *400 Pages*	Thai	220.00
___	8173662320	Learning Java (BOOK/CD-ROM), *732 Pages*	Niemeyer	475.00*
___	817366112X	Learning Perl 2/e, *302 Pages*	Schwartz	185.00

QTY	ISBN	Title	Author	Price
___	8173660603	Learning Perl/Tk, *380 Pages*	Walsh	225.00
___	8173661138	Learning Red Hat Linux (BOOK/CD-ROM), *400 Pages*	McCarty	350.00*
___	8173660611	Learning the vi Editor 6/e, *352 Pages*	Lamb	205.00
___	8173663173	Learning WML & WMLScript, *204 Pages*	Frost	125.00*
___	817366062X	lex & yacc 2/e, *392 Pages*	Levine	205.00
___	8173660646	Linux Device Drivers, *424 Pages*	Rubini	210.00
___	8173660654	Linux in a Nutshell, 2/e, *624 Pages*	Siever	275.00
___	8173660271	Managing IP Networks with Cisco Routers, *352 Pages*	Ballew	200.00
___	8173661162	Mastering Algorithms with C (BOOK/DISK), *568 Pages*	Loudon	375.00*
___	8173660182	MCSE: The Electives in a Nutshell, *376 Pages*	Moncur	200.00
___	8173660921	Microsoft Exchange Server in a Nutshell, *400 Pages*	Tulloch	200.00
___	8173662517	MP3: The Definitive Guide, *408 Pages*	Hacker	225.00*
___	8173660662	MySQL & mSQL, *504 Pages*	Yarger	275.00
___	8173661170	Oracle Built-in Packages (BOOK/DISK), *956 Pages*	Feuerstein	475.00
___	8173660670	Oracle Database Administration: The Essential Reference, *552 Pages*	Kreines	275.00
___	8173660689	Oracle Distributed Systems (BOOK/DISK), *552 Pages*	Dye	325.00
___	8173661405	Oracle Essentials: Oracle8 and Oracle8i, *360 Pages*	Greenwald	235.00*
___	8173661189	Oracle PL/SQL Built-ins Pocket Reference, *78 Pages*	Feuerstein	60.00*
___	8173660697	Oracle PL/SQL Language Pocket Reference, *80 Pages*	Feuerstein	50.00
___	8173660700	Oracle PL/SQL Programming 2/e (BOOK/DISK), *1,032 Pages*	Feuerstein	400.00
___	8173662401	Oracle PL/SQL Programming: A Developer's Workbook, *576 Pages*	Feuerstein	300.00*
___	8173661197	Oracle PL/SQL Programming: Guide to Oracle8i (B/D), *264 Pages*	Feuerstein	235.00*
___	8173661200	Oracle SAP Administration, *208 Pages*	Burleson	150.00*
___	8173660298	Oracle Scripts (BOOK/CD-ROM), *208 Pages*	Lomansky	220.00
___	8173660719	Oracle Security, *448 Pages*	Theriault	220.00
___	8173661588	Oracle SQL*Plus Pocket Reference, *100 Pages*	Gennick	70.00*
___	8173660727	Oracle SQL*Plus: The Definitive Guide, *512 Pages*	Gennick	240.00*
___	8173661219	Oracle Web Applications: PL/SQL Developer's Intro, *264 Pages*	Odewahn	175.00*
___	817366028X	Oracle8 Design Tips, *136 Pages*	Ensor	120.00
___	817366241X	Oracle8i Internal Services for Waits, Latches, Locks and Memory, *140 Pages*	Adams	100.00*
___	8173661227	Perl 5 Pocket Reference, 2nd Edition, *100 Pages*	Vromans	70.00
___	8173661235	Perl Cookbook, *794 Pages*	Christiansen	375.00
___	8173660735	Perl in a Nutshell, *688 Pages*	Siever	345.00
___	8173661243	Perl/Tk Pocket Reference, *104 Pages*	Lidie	65.00
___	817366269X	PHP Pocket Reference, *124 Pages*	Lerdorf	70.00*
___	8173661251	PNG: The Definitive Guide, *344 Pages*	Roelofs	250.00*
___	8173660301	Practical C Programming 3/e, *456 Pages*	Oualline	215.00
___	817366031X	Practical C++ Programming, *584 Pages*	Oualline	260.00
___	817366126X	Practical Internet Groupware, *520 Pages*	Udell	320.00*
___	8173660751	Practical UNIX & Internet Security, 2/e, *1,008 Pages*	Garfinkel	400.00
___	817366076X	Programming Embedded Systems in C and C++, *200 Pages*	Barr	145.00*
___	8173661278	Programming Internet Email, *384 Pages*	Wood	275.00*
___	8173662657	Programming Perl 3/e, *1108 Pages*	Wall	550.00*
___	8173662371	Programming the Perl DBI, *372 Pages*	Descartes	200.00*
___	8173660190	QuarkXPress in a Nutshell, *552 Pages*	O'Quinn	240.00
___	8173661286	Running Linux, 3ed, *752 Pages*	Welsh	500.00*
___	8173662487	sed & awk Pocket Reference, *60 Pages*	Robbins	55.00*
___	8173660786	sed & awk, 2/e, *440 Pages*	Dougherty	235.00

QTY	ISBN	Title	Author	Price
___	8173661294	sendmail Desktop Reference, *74 Pages*	Costales	60.00
___	8173660794	sendmail, 2/e, *1,056 Pages*	Costales	475.00
___	817366093X	Tcl/Tk in a Nutshell, *480 Pages*	Raines	240.00
___	8173662606	Tcl/Tk Pocket Reference, *100 Pages*	Raines	65.00
___	8173660336	TCP/IP Network Administration 2/e, *632 Pages*	Hunt	275.00
___	8173661308	The Whole Internet: The Next Generation, *576 Pages*	Conner/Krol	425.00*
___	8173660816	Transact-SQL Programming (BOOK/CD-ROM), *856 Pages*	Kline	495.00
___	8173660352	UML in a Nutshell, *336 Pages*	Alhir	210.00
___	8173661316	UNIX Backup and Recovery (BOOK/CD-ROM), *734 Pages*	Preston	450.00*
___	8173661324	UNIX in a Nutshell: System V, 3/e, *616 Pages*	Robbins	325.00*
___	8173660344	UNIX Power Tools 2/e (BOOK/CD-ROM), *1,120 Pages*	Peek	630.00
___	8173660948	Using & Managing PPP, *464 Pages*	Sun	240.00*
___	8173661332	Using Samba (BOOK/CD-ROM), *424 Pages*	Kelly	340.00*
___	8173660832	VB & VBA in a Nutshell: The Language, *656 Pages*	Lomax	285.00
___	8173662576	VBScript in a Nutshell, *520 Pages*	Lomax	250.00*
___	8173662622	vi Editor Pocket Reference, *76 Pages*	Robbins	60.00
___	8173661340	Virtual Private Networks, 2nd Edition, *228 Pages*	Scott	150.00*
___	8173660964	Visual Basic Controls in a Nutshell, *512 Pages*	Dictor	310.00*
___	8173660956	Web Design in a Nutshell, *592 Pages*	Niederst	275.00*
___	8173661359	Webmaster in a Nutshell, 2ed, *540 Pages*	Spainhour	325.00*
___	8173661367	Win32 API Programming with Visual Basic (BOOK/CD-ROM), *534 Pages*	Roman	375.00*
___	8173660972	Win32 Multithreaded Programming (BOOK/CD-ROM), *728 Pages*	Cohen	430.00
___	8173662630	Windows 2000 Active Directory, *624 Pages*	Lowe-Norris	325.00*
___	8173660220	Windows 95 in a Nutshell, *552 Pages*	O'Reilly	250.00
___	8173660239	Windows NT in a Nutshell, *368 Pages*	Pearce	200.00
___	8173660883	Windows NT TCP/IP Network Administration, *512 Pages*	Hunt	250.00
___	8173660891	Writing Excel Macros, *560 Pages*	Roman	275.00*
___	8173660778	Writing Word Macros, *416 Pages*	Roman	275.00*
___	8173661375	XML Pocket Reference, *100 Pages*	Eckstein	65.00*
___	8173660360	Year 2000 in a Nutshell, *320 Pages*	Shakespeare	200.00

Forthcoming Titles

November 2000

QTY	ISBN	Title	Author	Price
___	8173662886	Building Oracle XML Applications, 824 Pages (BOOK/CD-ROM)	Muench	400.00*
___	8173662584	Cascading Style Sheets: The Definitive Guide, *476 Pages*	Meyer	300.00*
___	8173662266	CDO and MAPI Programming with Visual Basic, *388 Pages*	Grundgeiger	175.00*
___	8173660212	HTTP Pocket Reference, *90 Pages*	Wong	70.00*
___	8173662797	Linux in a Nutshell 3/e, *824 Pages*	Siever	300.00*
___	8173662541	Linux Network Administrator's Guide, 2ed, *512 Pages*	Kirch	375.00*
___	8173662746	Managing IMAP, *412 Pages*	Mullet	200.00*
___	8173662800	Managing the Windows 2000 Registry, *564 Pages*	Robicheaux	225.00*
___	8173662193	MCSD in a Nutshell: The Visual Basic Exams, *640 Pages*	Foxall	250.00*
___	8173662916	Oracle SQL: The Essential Reference, *424 Pages*	Kreines	200.00*
___	8173662752	PC Hardware in a Nutshell, *532 Pages*	Thompson	225.00*
___	8173661847	Perl for System Administration, *452 Pages*	Blank-Edelman	200.00*
___	8173662339	Understanding the Linux Kernel, *628 Pages*	Bovet	375.00*
___	817366255X	Visual Basic Shell Programming, *354 Pages*	Hamilton	225.00*
___	8173663122	Windows Me: The Missing Manual, *434 Pages*	Ivens	250.00*

QTY	ISBN	Title	Author	Price
___	8173662770	Word 2000 in a Nutshell, *516 Pages*	Glenn	225.00*

December 2000

QTY	ISBN	Title	Author	Price
___	8173661154	Evil Geniuses in a Nutshell, *126 Pages*	Illiad	100.00*
___	8173662711	Java Internationalization, *356 Pages*	Deitsch	175.00*
___	8173663211	Java Message Service, *300 Pages*	Monson-Haefel	150.00*
___	817366286X	JavaServer Pages, *452 Pages*	Bergsten	200.00*
___	8173662568	Lotus Domino in a Nutshell, *376 Pages*	Neilson	175.00*
___	8173663246	Oracle Net8 Configuration and Troubleshooting (Book/CD), *300 Pages*	Mahapatra	275.00*
___	8173663262	Securing Windows NT/2000 Servers for the Internet, *200 Pages*	Norberg	125.00*
___	8173663270	SQL in a Nutshell, *300 Pages*	Kline	150.00*
___	8173662924	SSH, The Secure Shell: The Definitive Guide, *228 Pages*	Barrett	150.00*
___	8173662827	Windows 2000 Pro: The Missing Manual, *456 Pages*	Crawford	225.00*

January 2001

QTY	ISBN	Title	Author	Price
___	817366319X	C# Pocket Reference, *100 Pages*	Merrill	70.00*
___	8173662355	DAO Object Model: The Definitive Reference, *412 Pages*	Feddema	175.00*
___	8173660905	Java Native Methods, *304 Pages*	Descartes	150.00*
___	8173663149	Learning XML, *352 Pages*	Ray	175.00*
___	8173660743	Windows 2000 Quick Fixes, *400 Pages*	Boyce	175.00*
___	8173663289	XML in a Nutshell, *400 Pages*	Means	175.00*

February 2001

QTY	ISBN	Title	Author	Price
___	8173662878	Developing ASP Components 2/e, *600 Pages*	Powers	250.00*
___	8173662851	Java Servlet Programming 2/e, *600 Pages*	Hunter	275.00*
___	8173661677	Learning Web Design: A Complete Guide to HTML, Graphics, and the Web Environment, *300 Pages*	Niederst	150.00*
___	8173663238	Malicious Mobile Code, *300 Pages*	Grimes	150.00*
___	8173662398	MCSE in a Nutshell: The Windows 2000 Exams, *504 Pages*	Moncur	225.00*
___	817366188X	Programming ColdFusion, *504 Pages*	Brooks-Bilson	220.00*
___	8173662045	Programming Web Applications with SOAP, *354 Pages*	Snell	175.00*
___	817366207X	Programming Web Applications with XML-RPC, *354 Pages*	St. Laurent	175.00*
___	8173662789	Windows 2000 Administration in a Nutshell, *1000 Pages*	Tulloch	350.00*

March 2001

QTY	ISBN	Title	Author	Price
___	8173660875	ADO: The Definitive Guide, *456 Pages*	Roff	200.00*
___	8173662614	The Cathedral & The Bazaar, *288 Pages*	Raymond	150.00*

April 2001

QTY	ISBN	Title	Author	Price
___	8173661146	Cisco IOS in a Nutshell, *504 Pages*	Boney	225.00*
___	8173661049	Internet Application Protocols: The Definitive Guide (BOOK/CD), *704 Pages*	Hall	475.00*
___	8173661073	Perl 5 Pocket Reference, 3ed, *100 Pages*	Vromans	70.00*

June 2001

QTY	ISBN	Title	Author	Price
___	8173663165	Linux Security, *700 Pages*	Wreski	350.00*
___	8173663130	Networking Red Hat Linux, *704 Pages*	McCarty	400.00*

- **Dates and Prices of Forthcoming titles are tentative and subject to change without notice.**
- **All Prices are in Indian Rupees.**
- **New Titles are marked with *.**